Communications in Computer and Information Science 635

Commenced Publication in 2007
Founding and Former Series Editors:
Alfredo Cuzzocrea, Dominik Ślęzak, and Xiaokang Yang

More information about this series at http://www.springer.com/series/7899

Alberto Cañas · Priit Reiska
Joseph Novak (Eds.)

Innovating with Concept Mapping

7th International Conference on Concept Mapping, CMC 2016
Tallinn, Estonia, September 5–9, 2016
Proceedings

 Springer

Editors
Alberto Cañas
Institute for Human and Machine Cognition
Pensacola, FL
USA

Joseph Novak
Institute for Human and Machine Cognition
Pensacola, FL
USA

Priit Reiska
Tallinn University
Tallinn
Estonia

ISSN 1865-0929 ISSN 1865-0937 (electronic)
Communications in Computer and Information Science
ISBN 978-3-319-45500-6 ISBN 978-3-319-45501-3 (eBook)
DOI 10.1007/978-3-319-45501-3

Library of Congress Control Number: 2016948786

This Springer imprint is published by Springer Nature
The registered company is Springer International Publishing AG Switzerland

Preface

Welcome to CMC 2016, the Seventh International Conference on Concept Mapping, and to Tallinn, Estonia.

We returned to Estonia for the seventh conference in the series as a more mature, experienced community. As participation has expanded and now includes more papers from the Middle East and Asia, we have welcomed into our community participants from countries that had not previously taken part in the conference.

CMC 2016 was smaller than previous conferences. The financial situation in many parts of the world prevented a number of authors from attending personally. We opened virtual participation so that they could present their work, and many in the Cmappers community took advantage of this option. But just as with concept maps, smaller is sometimes better. We had the opportunity to get to know each other better, and having part of the conference on a cruise ship to Stockholm helped consolidate our community, both academically and socially.

This Springer volume consists of a small set of selected full papers from CMC 2016. The remaining full papers, posters, and innovative experiences, including all papers in Spanish and Portuguese, were published as regular conference proceedings books.

Once again we had a strong program that covered a variety of topics resulting from the Program Committee's tough time selecting the papers to be presented orally, virtually, or as posters from a large number of high-quality submissions. We again thank the members of the Program Committee for their effort and hard work. And of course, the conference could not have taken place if it were not for all the authors that are willing to share their work with the concept mapping community.

Outstanding invited speakers complemented the high quality of papers: Joseph D. Novak, who joined us via videoconference, and Joel J. Mintzes, Jari M. Lavonen, Brian Moon, and Tobias Ley shared their insight, knowledge, and experience in their talks.

The Local Organization Committee performed a wonderful job, not only with the organization of the conference, but also by making sure we felt at home in Tallinn and on the cruise ship and that we had a great time through the superb social program.

Finally, we thank the sponsors whose support was crucial in making the conference a reality.

July 2016

Alberto J. Cañas
Priit Reiska

Organization

Program Committee Chairs

Priit Reiska   Tallinn University, Estonia
Alberto J. Cañas   Institute for Human and Machine Cognition, USA

Program Committee Honorary Chair

Joseph Novak   Cornell University and Institute for Human
     and Machine Cognition, USA

Program Committee

Manuel F. Aguilar Tamayo   Universidad Autónoma del Estado de Morelos, México
Mauri Åhlberg   University of Helsinki, Finland
Alla Anohina-Naumeca   Riga Technical University, Latvia
Carlos Araya-Rivera   Universidad de Costa Rica, Costa Rica
Liberato Cardellini   Università Politecnica delle Marche, Italy
Mary Jo Carnot   Chadron State College, USA
Rodrigo Carvajal   Moffitt Cancer Center & Research Institute, USA
Carmen M. Collado   Independent Consultant, USA
Paulo Correia   Universidade de São Paulo, Brazil
Davidson Cury   Universidade Federal do Espírito Santo, Brazil
Barbara J. Daley   University of Wisconsin – Milwaukee, USA
Natalia Derbentseva   Defence Research and Development Canada, Canada
Italo Dutra   Universidade Federal do Rio Grande do Sul, Brazil
Lea Fagundes   Universidade Federal do Rio Grande do Sul, Brazil
Gunnar Friege   Leibniz Universität Hannover, Germany
Louis Fourie   Cape Peninsula University of Technology,
     South Africa
Gloria Gómez   University of Southern Denmark, Denmark
Maria Grigoriadou   University of Athens, Greece
Janis Grundspenkis   Riga Technical University, Latvia
Jin-Xing (Gordon) Hao   Beihang University, China
Imbi Henno   Tallinn University, Estonia
Sumitra Himangshu   Middle Georgia State University, USA
     Pennybacker
Ian Kinchin   University of Surrey, UK
Ismo T. Koponen   University of Helsinki, Finland
Ely Kozminsky   Ben-Gurion University, Israel
Mart Laanpere   Tallinn University, Estonia

Evelyse dos Santos Lemos	Instituto Oswaldo Cruz, Fiocruz, Brazil
Guadalupe Martínez Borrequero	Universidad de Extremadura, Spain
Norma Miller	Universidad Tecnológica de Panamá, Panama
Heather Monroe-Ossi	University of North Florida, USA
Brian Moon	Perigean Technologies LLC, USA
Marcos A. Moreira	Universidade Federal do Rio Grande do Sul, Brazil
Leda Muñoz	Fundación Omar Dengo, Costa Rica
Maija Nousiainen	Helsinki University, Finland
Kyparisia Papanikolaou	School of Pedagogical and Technological Education, Greece
Kai Pata	Tallinn University, Estonia
Ángel Luis Pérez	Universidad de Extremadura, Spain
Miia Rannikmäe	University of Tartu, Estonia
Zoja Raud	Tallinn University of Technology, Estonia
Thomas Reichherzer	University of West Florida, USA
Ma. Luz Rodriguez	Centro de Educación a Distancia – Tenerife, Spain
Nancy Romance	Florida Atlantic University, USA
Jesús Salinas	Universitat de les Illes Balears, Spain
Jaime Sánchez	Universidad de Chile, Chile
Patrícia B. Schäfer	B&S Educação e Tecnologia, Brazil
Beat Schwendimann	École Polytechnique Fédérale de Lausanne (EPFL), Switzerland
Martin Sillaots	Tallinn University, Estonia
Maija Strautmane	Riga Technical University, Latvia
María Isabel Suero	Universidad de Extremadura, Spain
Svetlana Kostromina	Saint Petersburg State University, Russia
Kairit Tammets	Tallinn University, Estonia
Alfredo Tifi	Istituto Tecnico Industriale Statale "Eustachio Divini", Italy
Giuseppe Valitutti	Università di Urbino, Italy
Terje Väljataga	Tallinn University, Estonia
Jacqueline Vanhear	Ministry for Education and Employment, Malta
Valery Vodovozov	Tallinn University of Technology, Estonia
Sephanie Wehry	University of North Florida, USA
Jinshan Wu	Beijing Normal University, China
Guoqing Zhao	Beijing Normal University, China

Organization Committee Chairs

Priit Reiska	Tallinn University, Estonia
Alberto J. Cañas	Institute for Human and Machine Cognition, USA

Estonia
Positively surprising

European Union
European Social Fund

Investing
in your future

Sponsors

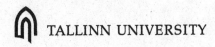

TALLINN UNIVERSITY

Contents

Cmaps with Errors: Why not? Comparing Two Cmap-Based Assessment Tasks to Evaluate Conceptual Understanding

Paulo Correia[✉], Gisele Cabral, and Joana Aguiar

Universidade de São Paulo, São Paulo, Brazil
prmc@usp.br

Abstract. Student-generated concept maps (Cmaps) have been the preferred choice to design assessment tasks, which are time-consuming in real classroom settings. We have proposed the use of Cmap with errors (elaborated by teachers) to develop assessment tasks, as a way to address the logistical practicality obstacles usually found in classrooms. This paper compared two different tasks, finding the errors and judging the selected propositions in Cmap with errors, exploring two topics with different levels of difficulty. Our results confirmed Cmap with errors as a straightforward approach to include concept mapping into the classroom routine to foster the pedagogic resonance (the bridge between teacher knowledge and student learning), which is critical for motivating students to learn meaningfully. Moreover, Cmaps with errors are also amenable for on-line learning platforms. Future works of our research group will develop an automated process for evaluation and feedback using the task formats presented in this paper.

Keywords: Assessment · Concept maps · Distance learning · Feedback · Pedagogic resonance

1 Introduction

Learning involves much more than the ability to recall information, facts, and names. It requires engagement in a personal process of sense making between novel information and prior knowledge. Meaningful learning occurs when students are able to apply the acquired knowledge in different contexts even after a long period [1, 2]. Assessment plays a key role in promoting meaningful learning rather than rote learning throughout the duration of any course. Precise and frequent feedback is critical to foster pedagogic resonance, i.e., the bridge between teacher knowledge and student learning [3, 4].

Concept maps (Cmaps) can make the students' knowledge structures visible, and they have been explored as assessment tool for more than 20 years [e.g., 5–10]. Ruiz-Primo and Shavelson published a remarkable paper to describe assessment tools using Cmaps [11], highlighting the following parameters:

- Task that invites students to provide evidence of their knowledge structure in a domain;
- Format for the students' response;
- Scoring system by which the students' knowledge can be evaluated.

© Springer International Publishing Switzerland 2016
A. Cañas et al. (Eds.): CMC 2016, CCIS 635, pp. 1–15, 2016.
DOI: 10.1007/978-3-319-45501-3_1

These three components can vary according to the situation to which they are applied. Who is the mapper (students or teacher) is a question rarely explored by researchers and educators. In real classroom settings, the most prevalent assessment tasks consider the students as mappers who need to represent their conceptual knowledge about the content under study. The teacher, who is usually responsible for making comments and giving scores, assesses students' knowledge representation (Cmap). McClure, Sonak, and Suen discussed some critical issues that may hinder the use of Cmaps in real classrooms [12]. We have proposed the use of Cmap with errors (elaborated by teachers) to develop assessment tasks [13, 14], as a way to address the logistical practicality obstacles usually found in real classrooms. Table 1 highlights how Cmap with errors can be used as a straightforward approach to disseminate concept mapping into teachers' routine.

The aim of this paper is to compare two assessment tasks based on Cmap with errors (find the errors and judge the selected propositions) exploring two topics with different levels of difficulty.

Table 1. Comparison of logistical practicality related to assessment tasks using Cmaps when students and teachers act as mappers.

Practicality aspect	Students elaborate their Cmaps	Teacher elaborates Cmap with errors
Time needed to train users to understand concept mapping	High	Low
	Cmap would reflect the students' cognitive structure only if they master the technique	Teacher has to be trained to make good Cmaps while students need only to know to read a Cmap
Time to accomplish the task	High	Low
	Preparing good Cmaps requires time to organize the concepts, make clear and correct propositions, and select those who properly answer the focus question	Teacher can previously prepare a Cmap and add some conceptual errors. Students only need to read and check the correctness of propositions to accomplish the task
Time needed to evaluate students' knowledge	High	Low
	Each student-generated Cmap has to be read and evaluated by the teacher through a comparative process (there is no predefined template to guide this process)	The conceptual errors added by the teacher produces a predefined template for the right answers (making faster and easier the evaluation of the students' responses)

2   Method

2.1   Context and Participants

One-hundred and ten undergraduate students enrolled in the "Natural Science Course" offered at the University of São Paulo (Brazil) participated in this study. The data collection occurred during the 15th class, when a formal assessment was scheduled to check students' conceptual understanding of Creationism/Evolutionism (CrEv) and Molecular Biology (MoBi). The classroom activities developed through 11–15th classes were:

- Class 11: Content discussion
  - Creationism and evolutionism: two different ways to explain the complexity of life.
  - Concept of intelligent design.
  - Principles of Natural Selection Theory.
  - Earth's age and scientific evidences that support evolution.
- Class 12: Content discussion
  - Review of concepts regarding molecular biology, such as DNA translation, human genome and mutations.
  - Advances in molecular biology related to cloning and stem cells.
- Class 13: Content discussion
  - Ethical issues on scientific researches related to health issues.
- Class 14: Content discussion
  - Concept of bioethics and the implications of molecular biology advances on contemporary society.
- Class 15: Test
  - Formal assessment using questionnaire (conceptual understanding test) and Cmap with errors (find the errors and judge the selected propositions).

2.2   Experimental Design and Procedures

A 2 X 2 (Assessment task format X Topic evaluated) quasi-experimental design was conducted in this study (Table 2).

Table 2. Experimental conditions used to combine assessment task formats (Find/Judge) and topics (CrEv/MoBi).

Group	N	Task format		Topic	
		Find the errors	Judge the selected propositions	Creationism/evolutionism	Molecular biology
I	25	XXX		XXX	
II	29		XXX	XXX	
III	30		XXX		XXX
IV	26	XXX			XXX

The assessment tasks based on Cmap with errors included finding the errors in the Cmap (Find group) or judging the conceptual correctness of selected propositions (Judge group). The topics evaluated were Creationism/Evolutionism (CrEv group) or Molecular Biology (MoBi group). The students were randomly assigned into four possible experimental conditions (I-IV).

The data collection procedure involved 10 min to answer the questionnaire and up to 20 min to accomplish the Cmap-based assessment task. Each student marked the time spent (in minutes) during the Cmap activity. Lastly, the teacher made some comments about the conceptual errors added to the Cmaps.

2.3   Materials

Assessment Tasks Using Cmap with Errors. The teacher prepared two Cmaps about the topics to be evaluated. The Cmap about Creationism/Evolutionism (CrEv, Fig. 1a) presents 19 concepts and 24 propositions to address the focus question, "How can the complexity of life be explained?". Modifications were made to include 8 conceptual errors at propositions 2, 8, 11, 15, 16, 21, 23, and 24 (in red, Fig. 1a).

The Cmap about molecular biology (MoBi, Fig. 1b) presents 26 concepts and 32 propositions to address the focus question, "How can the molecular biology affect human life?". Modifications were made to include 9 conceptual errors at propositions 5, 10, 13, 18, 23, 25, 26, 29, and 31 (in red, Fig. 1b).

Both Cmaps were used to check students' conceptual understanding, considering that only students who grasped the topics identified the conceptual errors. Two Cmap-based assessment tasks were proposed to find the errors and judge the selected propositions. Table 3 details these assessment tasks according to the components proposed by Ruiz-Primo and Shavelson [11].

Questionnaire. Students' conceptual understanding was also evaluated using 20 statements about the topics. Ten of them were about Creationism/Evolutionism (CrEv) and ten were about Molecular Biology (MoBi). The students had to judge each statement, agreeing or disagreeing with them. For each correct judgment, the student gained 1 point. Some examples of correct and incorrect affirmations are presented below:

- Creationism/Evolutionism
  - Evidences play a key role in the development of scientific knowledge (Correct).
  - The appearance of life on Earth occurred approximately 10,000 years ago (Incorrect).
- Molecular Biology
  - Pluripotent cells are useful for producing tissue in a laboratory (Correct).
  - The chromosomes are within genes (Incorrect).

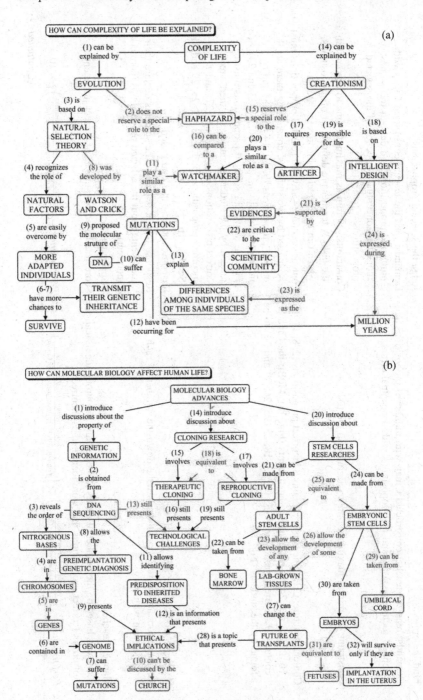

Fig. 1. Cmaps with errors (highlighted in red) prepared by the teacher as assessment tool to evaluate students' conceptual understanding about (a) Creationism/Evolutionism (CrEv) and (b) Molecular Biology (MoBi). Students received black and white Cmaps. (Color figure online)

Table 3. Assessment tasks characterization used in this study, considering the three components proposed by Ruiz-Primo and Shavelson [11].

	Find the errors	Judge the selected propositions
Task	Demands: read the teacher-constructed Cmap with numbered propositions and defined focus question. Find the propositions with conceptual errors	Demands: read the teacher-constructed Cmap with numbered propositions and defined focus question. Judge the conceptual correction of the selected propositions
	Constraint: 20 min as maximum time to accomplish the task	Constraints: 20 min as maximum time to accomplish the task. A teacher pre-defined set of propositions, which can be correct or incorrect
	Content structure: CrEv: the Cmap contains 8 incorrect propositions (2, 8, 11, 15, 16, 21, 23 and 24) to be found by the students (Fig. 1a). MoBi: the Cmap contains 9 incorrect propositions (5, 10, 13, 18, 23, 25, 26, 29 and 31) to be found by the students (Fig. 1b)	Content structure: CrEv: 10 selected propositions must be judged by the students, considering there are 4 correct propositions (9, 10, 14 and 18) and 6 incorrect propositions (2, 11, 16, 21, 23 and 24). See Fig. 1a. MoBi: 11 selected propositions must be judged by the students, considering there are 4 correct propositions (4, 12, 19 and 27) and 8 incorrect propositions (5, 13, 18, 23, 25, 29 and 31). See Fig. 1b
Response	Response mode: paper and pencil	Response mode: paper and pencil
	Response format features: The students write down the number of each proposition with error	Response format features: The students declare their judgments about the selected propositions (correct or incorrect)
	Mapper: teacher	Mapper: teacher
Score system	Score was based on the number of errors identified and the wrong identifications of errors (correct propositions that were identified as incorrect)	Score was based on number of correct judgments
	$Performance = \left[\left(\frac{Number\ of\ errors\ identified}{Total\ of\ errors\ in\ the\ Cmap} \right) - \left(\frac{Number\ of\ wrong\ identifications}{Total\ of\ correct\ propositions\ in\ the\ Cmap} \right) \right] \times 10$	$Performance = \left[\left(\frac{Number\ of\ correct\ judgments}{Total\ of\ propositions\ to\ be\ judge} \right) \right] \times 10$

(Continued)

Table 3. (Continued)

	Find the errors	Judge the selected propositions
Scoring example	Consider a Cmap with 20 propositions. Five of them present errors and 15 of them are correct. If the student identified 4 errors, the first ratio is given by 4/5 (0.800). If the student misjudges two correct propositions, saying that they are wrong, s/he presented two false identifications among 15 correct propositions. The second ratio is given by 2/15 (0.133). The student's performance (P) can be calculated as follows: $P = (0.800 - 0.133) \times 10 \rightarrow P = 6.67$ (considering a 0–10 point scale)	Consider a set of seven propositions to be judged by the student (some of them are correct and some are incorrect). If the student correctly judges four of these propositions, the ratio is given by 4/7 (0.571). The student's performance (P) can be calculated as follows: $P = 0.571 \times 10 \rightarrow P = 5.71$ (considering a 0–10 point scale)

2.4   Data Analysis

Means and standard deviations were calculated for each experimental conditions, considering students' performance on the questionnaire (0–10 point scale), performance on task involving finding errors or judging propositions calculated according scoring system described in Table 3 (0–10 point scale), and time to accomplish the Cmap-based task in minutes (up to 20 min). The data were analysed using a two-way Analysis of Variance (ANOVA) in order to compare different tasks (Find X Judge) within the same topic, and different topics (CrEv X MoBi) within the same task. All statistical analyses were conducted using SPSS 22.0 (IBM, USA), and .05 level of significance was used throughout this research.

3   Results and Discussion

Table 4 summarizes the results and Fig. 2 highlights the interaction between the independent variables.

Table 4. Means (M) and standard deviations (SD) for questionnaire performance, time to accomplish the Cmap assessment task (in minutes), and performance to find the error or judge the propositions for each experimental group.

Groups	N	Questionnaire performance		Time in task		Task performance	
		M	SD	M	SD	M	SD
I (Find/CrEv)	25	7.70	.84	13.78	4.89	4.88	2.40
II (Judge/CrEv)	29	7.45	.80	12.11	4.81	5.69	1.77
III (Find/MoBi)	26	6.83	1.32	13.08	3.79	3.83	1.76
IV (Judge/MoBi)	30	6.54	1.49	12.80	4.50	6.08	1.43

3.1   Students' Performance on the Questionnaire

The results showed a significant main effect of type of topic $F(1,106) = 16.33$, $p = .0001$, suggesting that students' overall performance on CrEv was significantly higher compared to their performance on MoBi test. The effect of type of format tasks (Find or Judge) was non-significant, $F(1,106) = 1.16$, $p > .05$. There is evidence that regardless the format tasks, the students have more knowledge of CrEv compared to MoBi (Fig. 2a).

Creationism and evolutionism topics are introduced in high school; thus, students' prior knowledge supported the discussions proposed during the course. Students could revise and refine their understanding of creationism and evolutionism meaningfully because they had a conceptual starting point. In contrast, molecular biology and its ethical implications are rarely presented in high school; therefore, students needed to process the course content using little or no prior knowledge about this topic. Bioethics was a fresh new theme for many of them, and they did not have enough time to assimilate this part of the content as well as the discussion involving creationism and evolutionism. The performance on the questionnaire confirmed that these topics presented different challenges to the students, indicating that molecular biology was more difficult to grasp compared to creationism and evolutionism.

3.2 Time to Accomplish the Task

Even though the direction of means indicated that the Judge group accomplished the task faster compared to the Find group for both topics (Fig. 2b), the main effect for assessment task was non-significant, $F(1,96) = 1.16$. The results also demonstrated no main effect of topics within the same task, $F(1,96) = .01$. The finding further confirmed

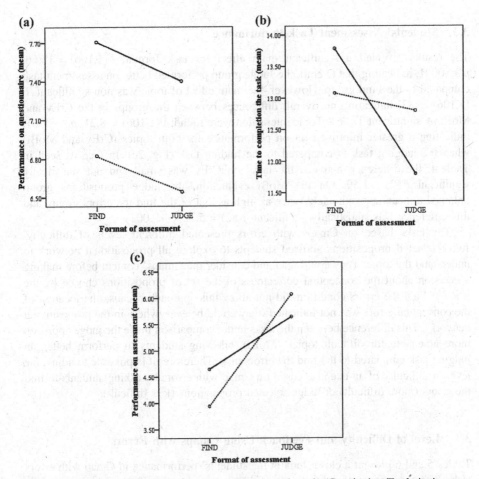

Fig. 2. Independent variables interaction: Topic evaluated (Creationism/Evolutionism or Molecular Biology) X Format of assessment (Find errors or Judge the selected propositions) for (a) performance on questionnaire, (b) time to completion the task, (c) performance on assessment. Solid line: Creationism/Evolutionism; dashed line: Molecular Biology.

no Task X Topic interaction, $F(1,96) = .057$, indicating that regardless of the topic, both assessment tasks are equally time consuming (approximately 13 min).

It's worthy to note that the average time used by the students to accomplish the Cmap-based tasks was less than 70 % of the maximum time available. These tasks were embedded in a formal assessment of the course, and 20 min were enough to ask students to carefully read and analyze one Cmap (CrEv or MoBi, Fig. 1). The time allotted to this task was lower compared to the usual time required of students to make their own Cmaps (we estimate students need at least 60 min to create and revise a Cmap). The practicability of the Cmap with errors is suitable for the operational conditions of real classrooms. Moreover, Cmaps made by the teacher can present both easy and difficult parts of the content, while students can avoid unclear conceptual relationships in their own Cmaps.

3.3 Students' Assessment Task Performance

The results revealed a significant main effect for task format, $F(1,106) = 18.66$, $p < .0001$, indicating that overall, the Judge group performed better on assessment task compared to the Find group. However, the main effect of topic was non-significant, $F(1,106) = .83$, indicating no overall differences between the groups in the CrEv and MoBi. A significant Task X Topic interaction were found, $F(1,106) = 8.21$, $p < .0001$, indicating a greater improvement on performance for both topics (CrEv and MoBi) when the judging task is compared to the finding task (Fig. 2c). In fact, as seen in Table 4, the difference between the tasks on CrEv was small and not statistically significant $t(52) = 1.59$. On the MoBi evaluation, the judge propositions group obtained a mean approximately twice as high as that of the find the errors group, and this difference was statistically significant, $t(52) = 5.22$, $p < .001$.

The tasks based on Cmaps with errors presented different levels of difficulty. Judge-selected propositions allowed students to explore all propositional network to understand the topic. They could read and consider the Cmaps' content before making a decision about the conceptual correctness of the set of propositions chosen by the teacher. Find the errors condition did not allow this approach because the location of the conceptual errors was not indicated (they could be everywhere in the propositional network). This difference between the tasks under comparison made the judge approach more amenable for difficult topics (MoBi), allowing students to perform better on judging task compared to the find the errors task. Therefore, it is possible to adjust the level of difficulty of an exercise based on Cmap with errors by asking students to find the errors (more difficult) or judge selected propositions (less difficult).

3.4 Level of Difficulty and Feedback Using Cmaps with Errors

Tables 5 and 6 present a closer look at the students' performance in Cmap with errors tasks. The percentages of right answers (RA) were used to classify the propositions into the following difficulty levels:

Table 5. Percentage of right answers, level of difficulty, and feedback for propositions from the Creationism/Evolutionism Cmap.

Proposition	% of right answers		Level of difficulty	Feedback for wrong answers			
	Find group	Judge group		11	12	13	14
2. Evolution - don't destine a special role to the → haphazard	44	45	Moderate	X			
8. Natural Selection Theory - was developed by → Watson and Crick	84	-	Very easy	X	X		
9. Watson and Crick - proposed the molecular structure for → DNA[a]	-	83	Very easy		X		
10. DNA - can suffer → mutations[a]	-	97	Very easy		X		
11. Mutations - play a similar role as a → watchmaker	68	69	Easy	X	X		
14. Complexity of life - can be explained by → creationism[a]	-	28	Difficult	X			
15. Creationism - has a special role to the → haphazard	52	-	Moderate	X			
16. Haphazard - can be compared to a → watchmaker[b]	52	66	Moderate/easy	X			
18. Creationism - is based on → intelligent design[a]	-	76	Easy	X			
21. Intelligent design - is supported by → evidences[b]	80	59	Very easy/moderate	X			
23. Intelligent design - is expressed at the → differences among individuals of the same species	20	38	Difficult	X			
24. Intelligent design - is expressed during → million years	28	28	Difficult	X			

[a]Correct propositions used only for the Judge group. [b]Level of difficult was influenced by task format.

- Very easy: RA ≥ 80 %
- Easy: 60 % ≤ RA < 80 %
- Moderate: 40 % ≤ RA < 60 %
- Difficult: 20 % ≤ RA < 40 %
- Very difficult: RA < 20 %.

Both Cmaps presented subtle (Natural Selection Theory - was developed by → Watson and Crick)/unsubtle (Embryonic stem cells - can be taken from → umbilical cord) errors (Find group) and easy (DNA - can suffer → mutation, right)/difficult (Complexity of life - can be explained by → creationism, right) propositions to be judge (Judge group). The implementation of a broad range of level of difficulty is

Table 6. Percentage of right answers, level of difficulty, and feedback for propositions from the Molecular Biology Cmap.

Proposition	% of right answers		Level of difficulty	Feedback for wrong answers			
	Find group	Judge group		11	12	13	14
4. Nitrogenous bases - are in → chromosomes[a]	-	81	Very easy		X		
5. Chromosomes - are in → genes[b]	17	46	Difficult/moderate		X		
10. Ethical implications - can't be discussed by the → Church	80	-	Very easy			X	X
12. Predisposition to inherited diseases - is an information that presents → ethical implications[a]	-	69	Easy			X	X
13. DNA sequencing - still presents → technological challenges[b]	23	46	Difficult/moderate		X		
18. Reproductive cloning - is equivalent to → therapeutic cloning[b]	53	73	Moderate/easy			X	X
19. Reproductive cloning - still presents → technological challenges[a]	-	88	Very easy			X	
23. Adult stem cells - allow the development of any → lab-grown tissues	70	65	Easy			X	
25. Embryonic stem cells - are equivalent to → adult stem cells	60	65	Easy			X	
26. Embryonic stem cells - allow the development of some → lab-grown tissues	40	-	Moderate			X	
27. Lab-grown tissues - can change the → future of transplants[a]	-	92	Very easy			X	X
29. Embryonic stem cells - can be taken from → umbilical cord[b]	20	12	Difficult/Very difficult			X	
31. Embryos - are equivalent to → fetuses	80	85	Very easy			X	X

[a]Correct propositions used only for the Judge group. [b]Level of difficult was influenced by task format.

straightforward and the teacher can adjust the propositions in few minutes to create a more easy/difficult test.

The reported percentages can also be valuable to identify learning obstacles that the students face. Learning obstacles are close to the moderate, difficult, and very difficult propositions. Table 5 highlights "intelligent design" as a troublesome concept because of the following propositions:

- Creationism - is based on → intelligent design (P18) was easy.
- Intelligent design - is supported by → evidences (P21) was very easy/moderate.

- Intelligent design - is expressed at the → differences among individuals of the same species (P23) was difficult.
- Intelligent design - is expressed during → million years (P24) was difficult.

This information helps the teacher to provide a fast and precise feedback according to the answers presented by each student. The content related to the "intelligent design" concept was discussed during the class 11 (Table 5), and specific parts of the study materials (videos and text) used in that class can be indicated to the students for a new period of study to overcome this learning obstacle.

A similar rationale for feedback can be obtained from Table 6. The understanding of "embryonic stem cells" can be evaluated from the following set of propositions:

- Embryonic stem cells - are equivalent to → adult stem cells (P25) was easy.
- Embryonic stem cells - allow the development of some → lab-grown tissues (P26) was moderate.
- Embryonic stem cells - can be taken from → umbilical cord (P29) was difficult/very difficult.

The content related to the "embryonic stem cells" concept was presented during the class 13 (Table 6), and specific parts of the study materials (videos and text) used in that class can be indicated to the students to foster conceptual remediation. The one-size-fits-all feedback can be easily replaced by this customized approach when Cmaps with errors are used as assessment tool.

4   Conclusion

Cmap with errors are useful to prepare Cmap-based assessment tasks. They present logistical practicality and fit nicely into the stringent conditions imposed by real classrooms, without compromising the reliability or validity of the assessment task. We summarize 5 reasons to consider including Cmap with errors into the classroom routine to foster the pedagogic resonance (the bridge between teacher knowledge and student learning) throughout the entire course.

- The time needed to administer Cmap with error tasks is shorter (20 min) compared to the time needed for students to elaborate their own Cmaps (at least 60 min).
- Teacher-elaborated Cmap makes possible to include difficult conceptual relationships, which students would avoid if they were asked to elaborate their own Cmaps (they tend to avoid the content they do not master).
- The teacher can choose between 2 different task formats (find the errors or judge the selected propositions) using the same Cmap with errors.
- The teacher can easily adjust the task difficulty level by changing and/or adding propositions with conceptual errors.
- The time needed to correct a set of Cmaps with errors and to provide precise feedback to the students fits into the schedule of real classrooms.

14   P. Correia et al.

Finally, Cmaps with errors are also amenable for on-line learning platforms. Figure 3 highlights the possibility to develop an automated process for feedback and evaluation using the task formats presented in this paper. The expected right answers (template) allow the creation of a rubric and a set of comments to be delivered according to the students' answers. This automated approach has been limited to structural features of Cmaps until now. Cmaps with errors expand automation to content features of Cmaps. Future works of our research group will explore the use of Cmap with errors as an assessment tool for online learning purposes.

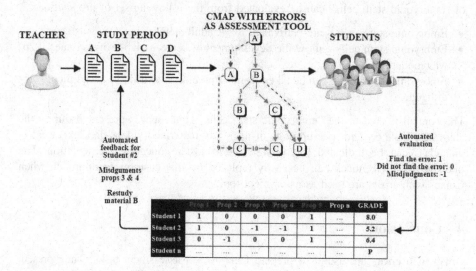

Fig. 3. Cmap with errors as assessment tool can be easily adapted to an automated process of evaluation and feedback. Teaching materials (A-D) used during the study period guide the assessment task design. They code the error addition, the automated correction, and the feedback to be presented to each student. Green and red propositions refer to right and wrong statements, respectively. (Color figure online)

Acknowledgements. We thank FAPESP (Grant # 2012/22693-5, São Paulo Research Foundation) for funding our research group. J. G. A. thanks CAPES (Coordination for the Improvement of Higher Education Personnel) for her scholarship.

References

1. Ausubel, D.P.: The Acquisition and Retention of Knowledge: A Cognitive View. Kluwer Academic Publishers, Dordrecht (2000)
2. Novak, J.D.: Learning, Creating, and Using Knowledge: Concept Maps as Facilitative Tools in Schools and Corporations, 2nd edn. Routledge, London (2010)
3. Kinchin, I.M., Lygo-Baker, S., Hay, D.B.: Universities as centres of non-learning. Stud. High. Educ. **33**(1), 89–103 (2008)

4. Trigwell, K., Shale, S.: Student learning and the scholarship of university teaching. Stud. High. Educ. **29**(4), 523–536 (2004)
5. Hay, D., Kinchin, I.M., Lygo-Baker, S.: Making learning visible: the role of concept mapping in higher education. Stud. High. Educ. **33**(3), 295–311 (2008)
6. Hung, P.H., Hwang, G.J., Su, I.H., Lin, I.H.: A concept-map integrated dynamic assessment system for improving ecology observation competencies in mobile learning activities. Turk. Online J. Educ. Technol. **11**(1), 10–19 (2012)
7. Kinchin, I.M.: Concept mapping in biology. J. Biol. Educ. **34**(2), 61–68 (2000)
8. Pendley, B.D., Bretz, R.L., Novak, J.D.: Concept maps as a tool to assess learning in chemistry. J. Chem. Educ. **71**(1), 9–15 (1994)
9. Soika, K., Reiska, P.: Using concept mapping for assessment in science education. J. Baltic Sci. Educ. **13**(5), 662–673 (2014)
10. Stoddart, T., Abrams, R., Gasper, E., Canaday, D.: Concept maps as assessment in science inquiry learning - a report of methodology. Int. J. Sci. Educ. **22**(12), 1221–1246 (2000)
11. Ruiz-Primo, M.A., Shavelson, R.J.: Problems and issues in the use of concept maps in science assessment. J. Res. Sci. Teach. **33**(6), 569–600 (1996)
12. McClure, J.R., Sonak, B., Suen, H.K.: Concept map assessment of classroom learning: reliability, validity, and logistical practicality. J. Res. Sci. Teach. **36**(4), 475–492 (1999)
13. Aguiar, J.G., Correia, P.R.M.: Is a concept mapping with errors useful for evaluating learning outcomes? A study on declarative knowledge and reading strategies using eye-tracking. Paper presented at the 6th International Conference on Concept Mapping (2014)
14. Aguiar, J.G., Correia, P.R.M.: Assessment task based on concept map with errors to foster pedagogic resonance in higher education. Paper presented at the 16th Biennial EARLI (European Association for Research on Learning and Instruction) Conference (2015)

Comparing Expert and Novice Concept Map Construction Through a Talk-Aloud Protocol

Beat A. Schwendimann[✉]

École Polytechnique Fédérale de Lausanne (EPFL),
Lausanne, Switzerland
beat.schwendimann@gmail.com

Abstract. Concept map analysis usually focuses only on the final product. This case study used a talk aloud protocol to study the concept map construction processes of novices and experts. Three biology experts and three novices (9th/10th grade high school students) constructed a concept map from a given list of concepts. Findings suggest that final concept maps of high performing students cannot be distinguished from expert-generated maps. However, analysis of oral elaborations during the construction process revealed that experts often used the same link labels as novices but associated more complex knowledge with the label. Some final propositions would be considered incorrect without an oral explanation. Findings suggest extending concept map evaluation by complementing the final product with an analysis of intermediate stages and accompanying elaborations. Additionally, this study highlights that each expert created a different map and that there is no single best expert map.

Keywords: Concept map construction · Case study · Expert-novice comparison · Talk-aloud protocol · Science education · Biology education

1 Introduction

Concept maps can reveal learners' knowledge organization by showing connections, clusters of concepts, hierarchical levels, and cross-links between concepts from different levels [1]. Connections between concepts can be seen as an indicator for more integrated knowledge [2, 3]. Concept maps can be a helpful metacognitive tool to visualize the interaction between prior and new conceptual understanding of learners.

However, concept map analysis often uses only the final product without taking the construction process into account. The ability to construct a concept map illustrates two important properties of understanding: Representation and organization of concepts [4]. As a representation, concept maps include not all but selected aspects of the represented world. Experts and novices differ in how they structure and connect concepts [5, 6] and in their abilities to distinguish salient surface features from structurally important features of a representation [7]. Experts can better decide how a certain external representation allows them to illustrate, communicate, and analyze a certain principle and create new forms of representations, if required. Developing expertise in a domain includes learning how to detect important elements and organize information.

© Springer International Publishing Switzerland 2016
A. Cañas et al. (Eds.): CMC 2016, CCIS 635, pp. 16–28, 2016.
DOI: 10.1007/978-3-319-45501-3_2

This case study investigates how experts and novices differ in their concept map construction using a talk-aloud protocol to distinguish two modes of reasoning, *constraint-based* and *model-based* reasoning [8]. *Constraint-based* reasoning refers to the cognitive process of finding values for a set of variables that will satisfy a given set of constraints. When utilizing this kind of reasoning, learners focus primarily on the constraints, one at a time. The second mode is *model-based reasoning*. Using this holistic approach, learners try to address all or most constraints at the same time to create a global model of the whole scenario.

This study aims to answer the research questions:

1. How do novices and experts differ in their concept map construction processes?
2. How do novices of different academic performance levels differ in their concept map construction?
3. How does verbal reasoning (talk aloud) align with concept map construction?

2 Methods

2.1 Procedure

Prior to the concept mapping task, each participant was interviewed about their familiarity with concept mapping in general, their self-assessment of their evolution biology knowledge, and their experience with concept mapping software. Each participant received initial training in basic concept mapping techniques and the software 'Inspiration' by a researcher. The training phase included the presentation of a sample concept map and a step-by-step concept map construction protocol. The participants were instructed to (1) group related concepts, (2) link concepts with arrows, (3) label each link, (4) add cross-links, and (5) revise the whole map.

All participants were instructed to talk aloud to describe their actions and reasoning while constructing their concept map. The think-aloud technique has been found to reveal thought processes in a variety of tasks [9], for example concept map construction [10], multiple-choice test taking [11], performance assessment [12], and problem solving [13]. Ericsson suggests that verbalization is a direct encoding of heeded thoughts that reflects their structure [9]. Verbalizing one's inner dialogue does not need translation and does not require a significant amount of additional processing; therefore, talking aloud does not slow down task performance – as long as connections between concepts can be recalled from memory. When connections between concepts need to be newly generated, it leads to measurably slower verbalization. Because of their greater existing content knowledge, experts might need to generate fewer new propositions (connections between concepts) when constructing concept maps in their area of expertise than novices. Experts might therefore show more fluent and faster construction of concept maps.

Each participant was instructed to construct a concept map from a given list of eighteen concepts (see Table 1). These concepts were identified as core elements in the US national educational standards for cell biology, genetics, and evolution. Concepts from all three different areas (DNA, cell, and evolution) were chosen and provided in a randomly arranged list (without the grouping shown in Table 1). The forced-choice design constrained participants to use only the provided concepts but allowed them to generate their own links and labels. The important concept 'mutation' was deliberately omitted from the list to investigate if participants would introduce the concept on their own as a link label. [14] highlighted the importance of iteratively revising concept maps. Therefore, participants received no time limit and were allowed to revise their concept map until satisfied with the final product.

Table 1. List of given concepts (organized by areas)

DNA	Chromosomes, chromatids, crossing over, random segregation of chromosomes
Cell	Cell division, random fusion of gametes, clones, diploid, haploid, mitosis, meiosis, body cells, sex cells (gametes), sperm cells, egg cells (ovum)
Evolution	Evolution, genetic variability, natural selection

Data Sources. Three different kinds of data were collected:

- Concept maps can be drawn by hand or by using specialized computer software. Royer's comparison between these two methods indicated significantly more complex concept maps when generated using concept mapping software [15]. This study used the concept mapping tool 'Inspiration' [16].
- Screen recording software [17] was used to capture the concept map construction process. To describe the concept map construction process, two screenshots of intermediate stages and the final product were captured.
- Voice recorders captured the talk aloud utterances of the participants during the concept map construction process.

2.2   Participants

This case study included three adult domain experts (two postdoctoral biology researchers and one experienced biology teacher) and three 9th and 10th grade students from a public high school. Following purposive sampling, the experts were selected to represent two different forms of expertise (research and teaching) while the students represented the range of general academic performance levels (high, middle, and low). The students received extra credit from their teacher for their voluntary participation. All three high school students attended the same biology class. Prior to participating in the study, each student completed a week-long session on cell biology and genetics that included all concepts provided for the concept mapping activity. All three students were familiar with concept mapping techniques but none of the students used the software 'Inspiration' before.

3   Results

The result section describes the concept map construction and critique tasks by the three experts and the three novices.

3.1   Experts

Biology Expert A. Expert A was a postdoctoral fellow in biophysical sciences at a major U.S. research university. A had no prior experience with concept mapping or the 'Inspiration' software, but frequently used flow charts in professional presentations. Expert A quickly understood the principles of concept mapping and the handling of the Inspiration software after the training session.

Concept map construction task: Expert A began the concept map by dividing the provided concepts into two groups: cell division/meiosis/mitosis/clones and body cells/sex cells/sperm cells/crossing over/random fusion of gametes (see Table 2, stage 2). Expert A placed the most comprehensive concept 'evolution' on top, 'cell division' at the bottom and then grouped related terms around them. In a second arrangement phase, A divided the concepts into the groups 'meiosis' and 'mitosis'. Only after arranging and clustering all concepts, A began linking them. Expert A said "I am thinking hierarchically, but the connectors are not going to be very hierarchical because sometimes a concept is the subject and sometimes an object", while pointing at a horizontal chain of concepts (see stage 3). At the end of the systematic construction activity, which took only 15 min, expert A started adding cross-links. This lead to the final concept map (see stage 4), which partially followed the 'circle of life'-model: Random fusion of gametes → fertilized ovum → mitosis → meiosis → new gametes. Expert A did not create a connection between egg cells and sex cells because of A's interpretation of egg cells as being already fertilized. Expert A also did not connect meiosis with genetic variability, arguing that the central concept 'mutation' was missing in the list of given concepts and that without mutation meiosis will not enhance genetic variability.

Biology Expert B. Expert B was a postdoctoctoral fellow in neurogenetics at a major U.S. research university and had no prior experience with concept mapping or 'Inspiration'. Expert B understood the principles of concept mapping quickly after the initial training phase.

Concept map construction task: B began the concept map by clustering the related concepts 'sex cells', 'sperm cells', and 'egg cells'. From this starting point, B developed a temporal chain to illustrate meiotic and mitotic cell division. Like both other experts, B noticed the absence of the concept 'mutation' in the provided list of concepts. Expert B explained that without mutation there would be no alleles and therefore no variability in meiosis. B stated that a reduction of evolution to the Darwinian view of natural selection and survival of the fittest leads to an inaccurate oversimplification. B suggested that 'genetic drift' should be added to the list of concepts. B created an interesting connection between body cells/mitosis/meiosis, by arguing that body cells can undergo either one of these two cell division processes. While working on the

Table 2. Concept map development of expert A.

| Stage 1 | Stage 2 |
| Stage 3 | Stage 4 |

concept map, B tried to construct the concept map from the viewpoint of a high school student, as B perceived the given concepts as a constraint that forced making "over-simplifications and large logical stretches". B made several connections, especially to evolutionary concepts, which implied several sub-steps (which B explained verbally). These sub-steps were only explained orally and could therefore not be detected in the final concept map. After finishing the first phase of connections, B began adding cross-links. Expert B did not connect the concepts 'cell division' with 'meiosis' and 'mitosis'. B's final map did not show a hierarchical structure but consisted mostly of temporal chains. B invested 27 min on the concept map.

Biology Expert C. Expert C was an experienced biology teacher at a U.S. public high school. C has not used concept maps as a personal tool but taught concept mapping techniques to students.

Concept map construction task: C started by grouping the concepts into 'meiosis' and 'mitosis' under the top-level concept 'cell division'. Expert C placed chromosomes and chromatids between the two groups, as they belonged to both. The evolutionary concepts 'evolution' and 'natural selection' were singled out until the end of the activity. C then arranged and connected concepts in each group either according to structure (e.g. cell type, haploid) or function (e.g. crossing over, genetic variability). In a second phase, C rearranged the concepts to follow closely the 'life-cycle model' found in biology textbooks (similar to expert A): meiosis → fusion of gametes → body cells → mitosis. C identified this approach as a deliberate strategy. Throughout the construction phase, 'chromosomes' remained the connecting element in the center. Finally, C added multiple cross-links and connected the evolution group with the cell division group, through the concept 'genetic variability'. Like the other two experts, C noticed the absence of the concept 'mutation' and worked around this constraint by referring to mutation in the link label between chromosomes and genetic variability. Concluding, C stated that this activity has been 'really hard' and that it provided a better appreciation for tasks assigned to students. Expert C spent 33 min until satisfied with the final concept map. C created the concept map with the most cross-links of all six participants.

3.2 Novices

Novice D. Student D was high performing 9th grade student. D showed complex and coherent understanding of the topic, despite being in a lower grade than the other two novice participants. D was the most articulate of all three novices and engaged in checking, revising, and investing the most amount of time the concept map (45 min) of all six participants.

Concept map construction task: Like expert C, novice D first grouped all concepts into two groups ('meiosis' and 'mitosis') and placed the concept 'chromosomes' in-between them. D then arranged and linked the concepts in each groups according to procedural criteria (see Table 3, stage 3). D correctly linked 'evolution' to the meiosis cluster, but did not create connections between the related concepts 'genetic variability', 'random segregation', and 'random fusion of gametes'. D created a proposition that genetic variability leads to natural selection, which would have to be considered incorrect at first. However, after prompting, D provided a comprehensive oral description of the relations between meiosis, genetic variability, natural selection, and evolution. Finally, D added several cross-links and checked each proposition again (see Table 3, stage 4). D revised the validity of every proposition again each time after adding another concept. D's approach was thorough and systematic.

Novice E. Student E was a 10th grade student classified as an average student.

Concept map construction task: Novice E first divided all concepts into two groups ('mitosis' and 'meiosis'). Like expert C, E placed 'chromosomes' between the two cell division subgroups. E singled out 'evolution' and 'natural selection' and did not connect them until the end of the activity (also similar to expert C). E was not sure about the meaning of the concepts 'haploid' and 'diploid', but nevertheless used them correctly. E did not use the concepts 'chromatids' and 'crossing over' as E could not recall their meaning (These two concepts remained unconnected). Like all three experts, E noticed the absence of the important concept 'mutation'. E worked systematic and fast, finishing the concept map in only 12 min. This supports the assumption that E had an existing understanding of the connections between the given concepts and did not have to newly generate them.

Table 3. Concept map development of student D.

Stage 1	Stage 2
Stage 3	Stage 4

Novice F. Student F was a 10th grade student described as a low performing student by the teacher. F was unfamiliar with a majority of the provided concepts and needed more support by the experimenter than the other five participants.

Concept map construction task: F started by creating three different groups: cell division/meiosis/mitosis, evolution/natural selection, and sex cells/sperm cells/egg cells. F expressed confusion regarding the meaning of the concepts 'mitosis' and 'meiosis' and could not remember the meaning of 'haploid' and 'diploid'. F began to connect concepts in a rather hesitant and unsystematic way. F's three initial groups evolved first into pairs (see Table 4, stage 2), which were then prolonged into three independent chains. Each chain represented a temporal flow (Table 4, stage 3). F's labels were mostly very short, for example *and*, *or*, or *then*. F did not create an overarching order in the map. Even after prompting by the researcher, F failed to identify any cross-links between the three separate chains (see Table 4, stage 4). F spent 25 min on constructing the map and expressed satisfaction after all links were "somehow connected". The map, as well as F's knowledge of the domain, seemed to be very fragmented and incomplete.

Table 4. Concept map development of student F.

Stage 1	**Stage 2**
Stage 3	**Stage 4**

4 Discussion

This section discusses observations made during each stage of the concept map construction process, proceeding from initial layouts and revisions to the final product.

During the initial construction process, the three experts and novices D and E (high performing participants) fluidly generated their concept maps, which suggests that they had previously existing knowledge of propositions. All high performing participants demonstrated their ability to move between the two modes of reasoning by switching back and forth between the big picture view of model-based reasoning ('gestalt' effect) to arrange and re-arrange their concepts into clusters and the more detailed view of constraint-based reasoning when creating individual propositions. Experts and knowledgeable students demonstrated their awareness of given constraints by noting that the provided concepts allowed only a limited representation of their actual understanding. However, they found ways to work around this limitation, for example by introducing the omitted concept 'mutation' in a link label. It is noteworthy that all three experts, but only one of the students, mentioned that the important concept 'mutation' was missing. Identifying central concepts (or noticing their absence) can be seen as an indicator of expertise.

In contrast, the academically weakest student F progressed slowly and struggled creating connections, which suggests that F's knowledge of biology concepts was not well integrated and that connections had to be newly constructed. F showed the greatest difficulties and created a fragmented, mostly linear concept map. F accepted the given constraints without questioning and used a constraint-based approach by adding one concept at a time. F seemed more focused on task completion than using concept maps to creatively express one's understanding. These observations suggest that concepts map construction can allow for both constraint-based reasoning and model-based reasoning, depending on the level of expertise of the participant. More knowledgeable participants were able to move fluidly back and forth between constraint-based and model-based modes of reasoning.

During the revision process, the high performing participants commended that they hesitated at times adding more links to avoid "making a mess". This suggests that aesthetic reasoning (in addition to constraint-based and model-based reasoning) can also influence concept map construction.

Initial groupings and hierarchies disappeared during the further development of the concept map. These intermediate stages are not accessible in the final concept map. During concept map construction and revision, some initially correct propositions were changed to invalid propositions, and vice versa.

Interestingly, the final concept maps constructed by the participants differed much less from each other than anticipated. The construction processes and final concept map of high performing students did not noticeably differ from expert-generated maps. Teacher-expert C created the most complex map, followed by novices D and E. Experts and novices did not significantly differ regarding their ability to create clusters and hierarchies. Maps of knowledgeable students showed as many cross-links and network complexities as maps created by experts.

Comparing talk aloud utterances to the developing concept maps provided valuable insights. Several times, oral explanations clarified concept map propositions that would otherwise have to be considered invalid (for example, expert A created the proposition "mitosis contributes to evolution" but then argued that without mitosis there would be no higher organisms and their evolution, as their bodies developed through mitotic cell division). Such an additional elaboration may reveal more extensive conceptual knowledge than the condensed and constrained form of the concept map propositions reflect. Expert participants provided more detailed oral explanations than novice participants. Experts' link labels were often shorthand for several intermediate steps (which they explained orally). Further analysis of talk aloud utterances also revealed several noticeable differences between the experts. The research-experts expressed greater difficulties generating their concept maps than the teacher-expert or the students. Several factors could contribute to this observation: The research-experts had only limited prior experience in generating concepts maps. The two research experts experienced it as a challenge to express their complex and sophisticated understanding in the constrained format of a concept map. In contrast, teacher-expert C showed fewer difficulties representing conceptual understanding in the shorthand form of concept maps because concept maps are frequently found in biology textbooks.

Overall, this case study suggests that concept maps can reveal differences in knowledge of experts and (low performing) novices. High performing participants (experts and novices) demonstrated their ability to fluidly move back and forth between a big picture view (model-based reasoning) and a more detailed view when creating individual links (constraint-based reasoning). Concept map construction processes and the final products indicated few differences between high performing novices and experts. Nevertheless, experts expressed their deeper understanding orally, because they could not adequately express their extensive knowledge due to task and aesthetic constraints of concept maps. The shorthand form used to describe relations between concepts allows keeping an aesthetic big-picture view but limits capturing explanatory depth. Experts and novices often used the same link labels to describe a relation between concepts, but oral elaboration revealed that experts often compressed more knowledge into a link label (called higher "epistemic density" by [18] and used the same linking words to represent different meanings [19]. Accompanying explanations are needed to further explain understanding represented by a proposition.

5   Implications and Limitations

As a case study with a small sample size, analysis can offer only limited insights. However, several suggestions can be offered.

Concept maps are used as assessment tools to track changes in students' understanding, for example in standardized large-scale assessments in the U.S. National Assessment of Educational Progress (NAEP) [20]. Usually, only the final concept maps are evaluated. Results from this study highlight the possible divergence between the concept map construction process and the finished product. During the construction process, most participants created meaningful clusters of related concepts and/or followed a temporal flow. However, these clusters or temporal flows were often no longer identifiable in the final product. A teacher or researcher who evaluates only the final product will often lack this additional information. Final concept maps elicit only a limited snapshot of a learner's integrated knowledge. Participants' oral explanations of their thought processes often diverged or expanded the reasoning leading to certain propositions. Some link labels might even have to be considered incorrect without the accompanying oral explanation. One way to triangulate this hidden understanding could be looking at written assessments (e.g. essays) or oral explanations that cover the same concepts. In such longer explanations, learners can express their understanding in more detail and provide supporting evidence.

This study used a concept map form that represents a compromise between open and heavily constrained formats by providing a list of concepts but leaving link generation to the participant. Open-ended concept maps, where students can choose their own concepts and links, might reflect students' knowledge structures more accurately, but they are more difficult to compare, require more time, and could be more challenging especially for weaker students [21]. On the other hand, more constrained forms of concept maps can lead to ceiling effects [10, 22]. Due to the constraints of the concept mapping task (for example, provided list of concepts; only one relation between two concepts, short link labels), a high performing student's map can be difficult to distinguish from an expert's map. Many participants generated only short link labels (maybe due to aesthetical graphical restrictions (limited space between two nodes) that did not represent the same understanding as their oral elaborations. Accompanying explanations (oral or written) could provide valuable insights into the meaning of propositions and the reasoning process during construction.

Experts were very selective about which propositions to include. Experts' selection processes could serve as scaffolds for novices to support their critical reflection and informed decision-making on which connections are relevant to include in their maps.

Expert-generated concept maps are often used as references for evaluation. Using expert-generated maps benchmark maps might falsely suggest that there is only one correct answer [23]. Findings from this study suggest that there is no single expert reference map. Each expert in this study generated a valid map but constructed different propositions and structures. Expert maps can differ from one another [24], even when using a limited number of provided concepts. This also raises the question of who is considered an "expert". There are many different kinds of experts, for example researchers, practitioners, proficient amateurs, and science teachers [25]. More research is needed to address the "expert problem" by providing better descriptions of what constitutes an "expert" and distinguishing different types and levels of experts.

As a compromise, an expert reference map could be created as an aggregate of several expert-generated maps [10]. However, even an aggregated expert map represents only one of many possible valid solutions and should only be used with caution for a direct comparison with novice-generated maps. Multiple concept map analysis strategies can be used to complement each other and triangulate changes in learners' understanding [26]. Concept map generation and analysis should reflect the constructivist perspective that knowledge can and should be constructed and represented in many different ways.

Acknowledgements. The research for this paper was supported by the National Science Foundation grant DRL-0334199 ("The Educational Accelerator: Technology Enhanced Learning in Science"). I thank my advisor Prof. Marcia C. Linn for her mentorship during the research for this paper and Prof. Pierre Dillenbourg for his support leading to the publication of this paper.

References

1. Shavelson, R.J., Ruiz-Primo, M.A., Wiley, E.W.: Windows into the mind. High. Educ. **49** (4), 413–430 (2005)
2. Bransford, J., Brown, A.L., Crocking, R.R.: How People Learn: Brain, Mind, Experience, and School, Expanded edn. National Academy Press, Washington, D.C. (2000)
3. Novak, J.D., Gowin, D.B.: Learning How to Learn. Cambridge University Press, Cambridge (1984)
4. Halford, G.S.: Children's Understanding: The Development of Mental Models. Lawrence Erlbaum Associates, Australia Hillsdale (1993)
5. Chi, M.T.H., Feltovich, P., Glaser, R.: Categorization and representation of physics problems by experts and novices. Cogn. Sci. **5**, 121–151 (1981)
6. Mintzes, J.J., Wandersee, J.H., Novak, J.D.: Meaningful learning in science: the human constructivist perspective. In: Handbook of Academic Learning: Construction of Knowledge. The Educational Psychology Series, pp. 405–447. Department of Biological Science, U North Carolina, Wilmington. Academic Press, US San Diego (1977)
7. Leinhardt, G., Zaslavsky, O., Stein, M.K.: Functions, graphs, and graphing: tasks, learning, and teaching. Rev. Educ. Res. **60**(1), 1–63 (1990). Special Issue: Toward a Unified Approach to Learning as a Multisource Phenomenon
8. Parnafes, O., diSessa, A.A.: Relations between types of reasoning and computational representations. Int. J. Comput. Math. Learn. **9**(3), 251–280 (2004)
9. Ericsson, K.A., Simon, H.A.: Protocol Analysis: Verbal Reports as Data. MIT Press, Cambridge (1985)
10. Ruiz-Primo, M.A., Schultz, S.E., Li, M., Shavelson, R.J.: Comparison of the reliability and validity of scores from two concept-mapping techniques. J. Res. Sci. Teach. **38**(2), 260–278 (2001)
11. Levine, R.: Cognitive Lab Report (Report Prepared for the National Assessment Governing Board). American Institutes for Research, Palo Alto (1998)
12. Ayala, C.C., Yin, Y., Shavelson, R.J., Vanides, J.: Investigating the cognitive validity of science performance assessment with think alouds: technical aspects. In: American Educational Researcher Association, New Orleans, LA (2002)
13. Baxter, G.P., Glaser, R.: Investigating the cognitive complexity of science assessments. Educ. Measur.: Issues Pract. **17**(3), 37–45 (1998)
14. Schwendimann, B.A., Linn, M.C.: Comparing two forms of concept map critique activities to facilitate knowledge integration processes in evolution education. J. Res. Sci. Teach. **53**, 70–94 (2015)
15. Royer, R., Royer, J.: Comparing hand drawn and computer generated concept mapping. J. Comput. Math. Sci. Teach. **23**(1), 67–81 (2004)
16. Inspiration (2016)
17. Wisdom Soft: AutoScreenRecorder 2.0. [Computer Software] (2016)
18. Maton, K., Doran, Y.J.: Semantic Density: A Translation Device for Revealing Complexity of Knowledge Practices in Discourse, Part 1 - Wording, Onomázein, August 2016 (in press)
19. Ariew, A.: Ernst Mayr's 'Ultimate/Proximate' distinction reconsidered and reconstructed. Biol. Philos. **18**(4), 553–565 (2003)
20. Ruiz-Primo, M.A., Iverson, H., Yin, Y.: Towards the use of concept maps in large-scale assessments: exploring the efficiency of two scoring methods. In: NARST Conference (2009)

21. Cañas, A.J., Novak, J.D., Reiska, P.: Freedom vs. restriction of content and structure during concept mapping–possibilities and limitations for construction and assessment. In: Proceedings of 5th International Conference on Concept Mapping, pp. 247–257 (2012)
22. Yin, Y., Vanides, J., Ruiz-Primo, M.A., Ayala, C.C., Shavelson, R.J.: Comparison of two concept-mapping techniques: implications for scoring, interpretation, and use. J. Res. Sci. Teach. **42**(2), 166–184 (2005)
23. Kinchin, I.M.: Concept mapping in biology. J. Biol. Educ. **34**(2), 61–68 (2000)
24. Acton, W.H., Johnson, P.J., Goldsmith, T.E.: Structural knowledge assessment - comparison of referent structures. J. Educ. Psychol. **86**(2), 303–311 (1994)
25. Hmelo-Silver, C.E., Marathe, S., Liu, L.: Fish swim, rocks sit, and lungs breathe: expert–novice understanding of complex systems. J. Learn. Sci. **16**(3), 307–331 (2007)
26. Schwendimann, B.A.: Making sense of knowledge integration maps. In: Ifenthaler, D., Hanewald, R. (eds.) Digital Knowledge Maps in Education: Technology Enhanced Support for Teachers and Learners. Springer, New York (2014)

Concept Mapping in High School: An Experience on Teaching Geography to Measure Deep, Surface and Non-learning Outcomes

Leandro Fabrício Campelo[1](✉) and Stela C. Bertholo Piconez[2]

[1] Federal Institute of São Paulo (IFSP), Suzano, Brazil
campelo@ifsp.edu.br
[2] University of Sao Paulo (USP), Sao Paulo, Brazil
spiconez@usp.br

Abstract. This study investigates to what extent conceptual maps can foster meaningful learning in high school students. Forty students of the discipline of Geography took part in the study. The students made a map during the second stage of research, and these maps were compared to other semi-structured ones made in the fourth stage. For the analysis of these maps we use the Hay's (2007) methodology to measure deep, surface and non-learning. Nowadays students take tests with the objective of memorizing content, the rote learning continues to prevail in high school, using concepts maps in elementary and high school can change the future of our students. The results show that students need more time to practice concept maps, we observed progress in the development of concept maps, but no student achieved deep learning.

Keywords: Concept maps · Geography · Meaningful learning · High school

1 Introduction

This paper is about a hope of change coming to education and learning. The world has changed so much in the last few years that the roles of learning and education in day-to-day life have also changed. The education of students in the world today is very traditional. We need to think about how to improve it, how we can help children to get better educated. The problem is that there is so much for students to do and the system of education is so poorly organized. All over the world it is very similar, in Brazil, in Asia or the United States, no matter what country, everyone is in the same battle against the failures in education [1].

Nowadays students graduating from high school, technical colleges, and universities are sorely lacking some basic skills and a large number of applied skills: critical thinking, problem solving, teamwork and collaboration, just to name a few. The competitiveness and wealth of corporations and countries is completely dependent on having a well-educated workforce – as a report from 2006 called it, "Learning is Earning" improving

© Springer International Publishing Switzerland 2016
A. Cañas et al. (Eds.): CMC 2016, CCIS 635, pp. 29–39, 2016.
DOI: 10.1007/978-3-319-45501-3_3

a country's literacy rate by a small amount can have positive economic impacts. Education also increases the worker's potential income – an additional year of schooling can enhance a person's lifetime salary by 10 percent or more [2].

We are seeing the rise of a new kind of labor force, the new generation comes with a different philosophy of work, is able to accept new technologies, is creative and is socially connected. So why is education falling short from preparing students for 21st century jobs? This is not an easy question to answer [3]. We believe that conceptual maps applied to elementary and high school can contribute to a change in education. Concept mapping is a meta-learning strategy based on Ausubel's theory of meaningful learning [4–6]. However, we need to present to all teachers that concept maps should be used in all levels of education. A complete major survey of the high school science teachers in the state of Louisiana showed that 50 % of them were aware of the instructional technique of concept mapping [7]. We need to help more teachers become familiar with this vital technique.

A new mix of skills is required in the 21st century labor force. Jobs that require manual routines and thinking skills are giving way to jobs that involve higher levels of knowledge and applied skills, like expert thinking and complex communicating. The new challenges posed by the post-industrial society are consequences of scientific-technological development and globalization [8]. In the same direction Novak says, with the acceleration of globalization, companies need to be more competitive, and what has been shown in recent decades is that there is significant growth in corporate interest in educating students. In the future new partnerships will be formed between businesses and educational institutions, "the first few decades of the twenty-first century are likely to be revolutionary in many respects and most importantly in how we learn better to educate people for whatever the needs may be" [9].

Figure 1 lists examples of jobs requiring routines, manual skills and those with high demand for complex communication and thinking skills. The rising demand for a highly skilled workforce also means that there will be a growing income gap between less educated, relatively unskilled workers and highly educated workers. Routine tasks are increasingly being automated, and the routine jobs, still done by people, are barely paying a suitable wage for someone to live comfortably.

The great challenge is getting students to learn in a meaningful way, so their expertise can be used in the future. Too often we may fail in the challenge of providing meaningful learning and students resort to rote learning, even though we know that learning in such a way will soon be forgotten. Such fragile learning may allow us to go through school exams, but it contributes little or nothing to future learning [10].

This article is based on the study of Hay entitled 'Using concept maps to measure deep, surface and non-learning outcomes', which reports the use of conceptual maps to reveal patterns of student's learning (or non-learning) [11]. The idea is to use a similar methodology to Hay, with high school geography students. The focus question that we try to answer in this paper is: "Do concept maps help students learn the content of 'Seasons' in Geography?

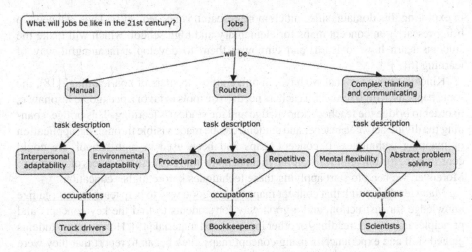

Fig. 1. Adapted from Fadel and Trilling, 2009, p.9.

2   Concept Mapping in Elementary and High School

An analysis to the Proceedings of the 6th Conference on Concept Mapping (CMC) held in the city of Santos (Brazil) in 2014, showed that, out of the 67 full papers, two tendencies were noted: first, the predominance of research in the science area, but this is not new to those who study concept maps; and second, there is more research available at higher levels of education. Elementary and high schools are poorly researched – just four full papers (7.5 %) were found in the review.

Among those four papers presented during the CMC in 2014, we found interesting ideas about the use of concept maps in elementary and high schools. The first paper presented their findings about making short films with high school students as a strategy for promoting meaningful learning in chemistry. Students made concept maps before and after the short film, the production of short films helped to foster meaningful chemistry learning [12].

Another idea about the use of maps was in the second paper, as the researcher writes his paper explaining the way teachers, cooperating among themselves used maps to create a knowledge portfolio which has contributed to changes in the school and fostered the efforts against students dropping out of school early [13]. The third paper, which is supported by digital technology, used *Wiki* and concept maps to validate learning projects as a methodology that gives opportunity to students to learn from their interest and possibilities, favoring reflection and knowledge construction. It also validates CmapTools [14] as a highly effective resource in the teacher's intervention and monitoring of student's learning [15]. The fourth paper showed that the use of concept maps in elementary school can improve student's grades in physics. These full papers showed innovative ideas about using concept maps for all levels of education [16].

Wandersee comments about the potential of such graphic meta-cognitive tools, to help science teachers and science educators improve science instruction, and invite all researchers interested in the graphic representation of scientific knowledge "to join us in exploring this domain, since much more research is needed" [17]. Thus, we need to bring research on concept maps for elementary and high school, which will make the students learn how to learn, and empower them to develop a meaningful way of learning [6].

Kinchin showed us that we have, in universities, 'centers of non-learning' [18], the same happens in high schools. Teachers need to use tools to favor a pedagogic resonance, in order to bridge the teacher's knowledge and the student's learning. This bridge, spanning the divide between teacher and student, can be made visible through the application of mapping techniques. If concept maps had been used in high school, we could contribute to the universities, helping them become more effective 'centers of learning'. Moreover, we need to start applying these techniques before higher education.

Many teachers think that concept maps were a good way to help teachers to organize knowledge for instruction, and a good way for students to find the key concepts and principles in lectures, readings or other instructional material [19]. However, as students gained skill and experience in using concept maps, they began to report that they were 'learning how to learn' [9].

3 Methodology

This research was done by students (between 14 and 18 years −86 % of the students are aged between 14 and 15 years old) from a public high school in Brazil in the geography discipline. The work was done with a group of 40 students, and the concept maps produced individually by the students during the second and the fourth stages are shown in detail. The first stage was to make a concept map on a blackboard with the students (the theme was chosen by them) at this time they had no knowledge of concept maps techniques, the result can be seen in Fig. 2. The concept map was made without a focus question. The idea was just to observe if students already knew the techniques. Just three students commented that they had already seen something like a concept map.

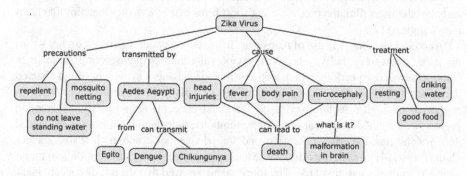

Fig. 2. Concept map made by the students on the blackboard (it was done in CmapTools by the authors).

During the second stage, students had 30 min of lessons on the basics of concept maps. They had a week to prepare a concept map with the theme 'Seasons', a subject already studied by the students. It was observed that students didn't use CmapTools, they made the concept maps on paper. After a week, 40 students handed their individual maps on the theme 'Seasons'. In the third stage, the students received feedback for their concept map about the 'Seasons' and another 30-min lecture about the techniques of concept maps. In this stage the students were gathered in eight groups of five members. And collaboratively, they discussed the feedback from their concept maps and then they created a map in response to the following focus question: What is the influence of the earth's rotation around the sun on the different seasons? In this article the part that involves collaborative learning was not worked on (third stage - Fig. 3), it will be included in future research.

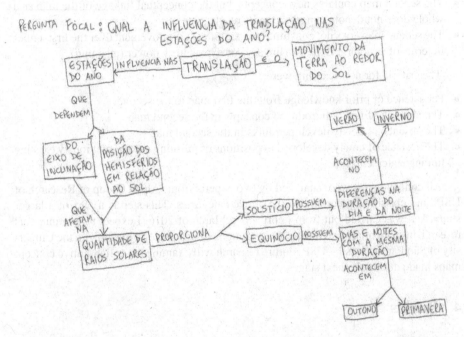

Fig. 3. Concept map made collaboratively with the participation of five students (in Portuguese).

During the fourth stage, all students received feedback about the collaborative concept map, using the Likert Scale. Next, students individually had 50 min to analyze the feedback and make a semi-structured map [20] with eight concepts (The Earth's orbit being an obligatory concept). The maps were made on paper. The theme was about the 'Seasons', but the students should choose their focus question.

We will use the same criteria as Hay's to distinguish deep, surface and non-learning [11]. The following criteria were used to identify deep learning:

- The second map shows both newly learnt concepts (that were not included in the first) and the student's original conceptions.

- The second map shows that the new knowledge has to be linked to the prior knowledge in ways that are meaningful (i.e. that the linking statements are valid and explanatory and provide evidence of meaning in the mind of the map's author).
- The overall knowledge structure of the second map identifies a significant improvement on the first (i.e. shows better organization, higher linkage and richer exposition of meaning).

The criteria for surface learning were:

- The second map shows significant numbers of newly introduced concepts (ones that were not evident in the first), but these are not integrated with prior knowledge by linkage to concepts that are persistent from the first to the second map.
- The second map contains new concepts, but the conceptual linkage of the map as a whole does not denote expansion in its results.
- The second map does not constitute any significant improvement over the first, either in terms of structural richness (linkage) or explanatory power (meaning).

The criteria for non-learning were:

- Persistence of prior knowledge from the first map to the second.
- The absence of newly introduced concepts in the second map.
- The absence of newly developed links in the second map.
- The absence of newly developed expositions of meaning among previously existing linking statements

All concept maps were analyzed by two experts from 'Alpha Group of Research of USP' and classified according to the above categories. This step is a part of a larger study, and was carried out from February to March of 2016. I expect to continue this research in sequential steps during the development of a doctoral thesis from the University of São Paulo, Brasil – USP. Future research will examine the collaborative concept maps made during the next stages.

4   Results

A total of 80 concept maps were analyzed, 40 from the second stage and 40 from the fourth stage. Here only four concept maps are shown in detail, and the names under which these maps are presented are pseudonyms. These were chosen from the total number of 80 maps to represent two categories – surface and non-learning.

4.1   Deep Learning

None of the concept maps has achieved the criteria to be classified as deep learning.

4.2   Surface Learning

The maps made by a student identified as Fabiano provide evidence of surface learning. His first map (Fig. 4) is closer to what Kinchin calls *spokes* (where all subordinate concepts link directly to the key idea) indicating a beginner [22]. We can see a concept mistake in '365 days and 6 h – cause – rotation'. Some terms of connection seemed inconsistent because they were created without the verb 'rotation – day' and 'solstice – winter'.

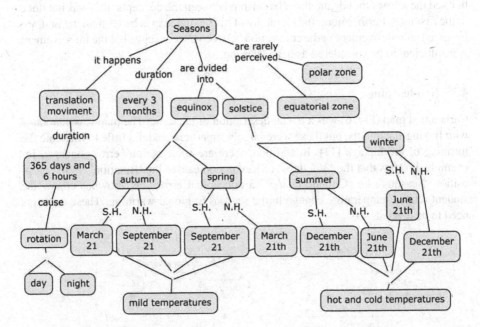

Fig. 4. Fabiano's first map. Focus question: explain the reasons for the seasons?

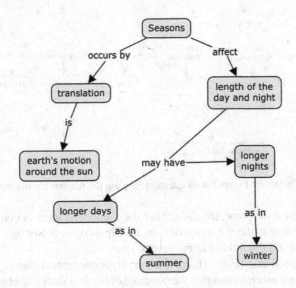

Fig. 5. Fabiano's second map semi-structured. Focus question: what the seasons affect?

In his second map (Fig. 5), Fabiano used three concepts from his first map, 'seasons', 'winter' and 'summer'. Otherwise he rejected his previous knowledge and replaced it with new content. This is clearly evidence of surface (or rote) learning [11]. We could not notice that he integrated new information to his prior knowledge. In his second map, he used the arrows to indicate the relationship between the concepts; this was not done in the first map. Furthermore, the hierarchy of his second map is better than the first, we observed an improvement in the connection between the concepts, but the improvement is insufficient to be considered as deep learning.

4.3 Non-learning

Carla's first map (Fig. 6) was a trivial description of the topic. The map was annotated with linking statements, but these were largely superficial and did little to illustrate the meaning of the linkage [11]. In addition, there are some serious error concepts, for example, it states that the '365 days' of Revolution causes the 'Rotation'. In the proposition 'Seasons' are 'Climate change' a conceptual error was shown. Perhaps the student related temperature change in the seasons to global warming. These concepts need to be revised.

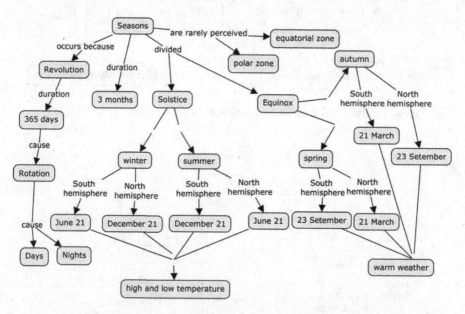

Fig. 6. Carla's first map. Focus question: explain the reasons for the seasons?

On her map, at some point, she did not use the connection term. A concept has been connected to another without explanation, as in 'Equinox — > Spring'. She repeated the same concept and the linking terms several times.

In Carla's second map (Fig. 7) there was very little conceptual change from the first map, it is important to remember that the structure of her first map was changed because the latter is semi-structured. Although Carla does not repeat the same concepts, her changes have not shown changes in her knowledge about the subject 'seasons'. Some new concepts were introduced: 'tilt of the Earth' and 'Revolution movement' but it's not related to any other knowledge in the framework.

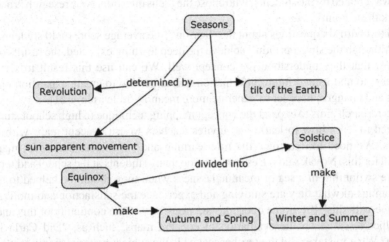

Fig. 7. Carla's second map semi-structured. Focus question: explain the reasons for the seasons?

The rest of the map shows no change, it only compressed the concepts for the new framework. The absence of newly developed expositions of meaning among previously existing linking statements was noted.

The second map was not an advance of the first, the conceptual richness of the map was not improved. Overall Carla's conception of the topic was reinforced but not changed in any meaningful way.

5 Some Implications for Future Research

This data presentation provides evidence for the meaningful distinction of surface and non-learning. It suggests that concept maps can be used to measure and typify the quality of learning [11]. Unfortunately, there were no deep learning maps in our research, however this does not mean that the students didn't learn anything.

Why was there no map made by the students evidencing deep learning? Does this mean that they did not have meaningful learning (deep learning)? These questions are important because they have an influence on the results of the paper.

This work is a small part of a larger research that is underway, the students need more time to make good maps. Due to time constraints, the students were only able to spend 3 h on this project. Taking into consideration that this was their first time to attempt this new concept, it is clear that the students need more than 10 h of training. This will be given to them in the next stage of research where the students will work their concept maps with the CmapTools software and not just representations on paper.

Despite using Hay's ideas, the methodology included an open concept map in stage two, and afterwards, a semi-structured map. Perhaps this has undermined the creativity of the students who were not used to concept maps. Thus, for the first map made by the students the focus question was created by the professor but in the other semi-structured map it was created by the students, who chose the focus question. New research is needed to check these points.

In a test with six questions about the 'Seasons' the average score of 40 students was 78 %. Although the students didn't achieve the deep learning expected, the results of the test show that they understood the concept well. We can use this result to serve as subsumers to understand future information and to be able to create expansion opportunities and changes, in order to generate more meaningful learning [21].

This research aims to expand the concept mapping technique to high school students who need to learn how to learn, and invites teachers to use concept maps with their students. We need to overcome the rote learning and expansion of concept maps is essential for this. Novak said the essential, "Too many students at the school and tertiary level are swimming in a sea of meaninglessness when they should be helped to grasp the meanings of what they are studying and experience the satisfaction and motivation that come with this" [9]. Some questions are necessary to the continuity of this and for the further research on the evaluation of concept maps, such as, "Did Carla learn nothing? What mistakes did the teacher make? Is the subject material significant?"

Acknowledgements.   This research project was supported by the Federal Institute of Education, Science and Technology of São Paulo (IFSP) and Alpha Group of Research of University of Sao Paulo (USP).

References

1. Prensky, M.: Teacher should help students to be autodidact. J Estado de São Paulo (2013). http://marcprensky.com/interviews. Accessed 03 April 2016
2. Fadel, C., Trilling, B.: 21st Century Skills - Learning for Life in Our Times. Jossey-Bass, San Francisco (2009) '
3. Tapscott, D., Williams, A.D.: Wikinomics: How Mass Collaboration Changes Everything. Penguin Group, New York (2006)
4. Ausubel, D.P., Novak, J.D., Hanesian, H.: Educational Psychology: A Cognitive View, 2nd edn. Holt, Rinehart and Winston, New York (1978)
5. Novak, J.D.: A Theory of Education. Cornell University Press, Ithaca, NY (1977)
6. Novak, J.D., Gowin, D.B.: Learning How to Learn. Cambridge University Press, New York (1984)
7. McCoy, M.H., Wandersee, J.H., Good, R.G.: A Science Education Awareness Map of the State of Louisiana (1990). https://csedweek.org
8. Correia, P.R.M., Infante-Malachias, M.E.: Expanded collaborative learning and concept mapping: a road to empowering students in classrooms. In: Lupion Torres, P., Cássia Veiga Marriot, R. (eds.) Handbook of Research on Collaborative Learning using Concept Mapping, pp. 283–300. IGI Global, Hershey (2010)
9. Novak, J.D.: Learning, Creating and Using Knowledge: Concept Maps as Facilitative Tools in Schools and Corporations. Routledge, New York (2010)

10. Edmondson, K.M., Novak, J.D.: The interplay of scientific epistemological views, learning strategies, and attitudes of college students. J. Res. Sci. Teach. **32**(6), 547–559 (1993)
11. Hay, D.B.: Using concept maps to measure deep, Surfasse and non-learning outcomes. Stud. High. Educ. **32**(1), 39–57 (2007)
12. Aquino, K.A.S, Cavalcante, P.S.: Concept maps as a strategy to assess chemistry learning in short film productions by high school students. In: Proceedings of the Sixth International Conference on Concept Mapping. vol. 1, Part 1, p. 179. http://cmc.ihmc.us/cmc/CMCProcee dings.html. Accessed 03 Mar 2016
13. Genito, L: Cooperative teaching, concept maps and creation of knowledge portfolio for school success. In: Proceedings of the Sixth International Conference on Concept Mapping, vol. 1, Part 1, p. 195 (2014). http://cmc.ihmc.us/cmc/CMCProceedings.html. Accessed 03 Mar 2016
14. Cañas, A.J., Hill, G., Carff, R., Suri, N., Lott, J., Gómez, G., Eskridge, T., Arroyo, M., Carvajal, R.: CmapTools: A knowledge modeling and sharing environment. In: Cañas, A.J., Hill, G., Carff, R., Suri, N., Lott, J., Gómez, G., Eskridge, T., Arroyo, M., Carvajal, R. (eds.) Concept Maps: Theory, Methodology, Technology, Proceedings of the First International Conference on Concept Mapping, Pamplona, Spain, Editorial Universidad Pública de Navarra (2004)
15. Lacerda, R.P., Fagundes, L.C., Lima, J.V.: Intervenção em Mapas Conceituais: uma Experiência na Educação Básica. In: Proceedings of the Sixth International Conference on Concept Mapping, vol. 1, Part 2, p. 283 (2014). http://cmc.ihmc.us/cmc/CMCProceedings.html. Accessed 03 Mar 2016
16. Silveira, F.P.B., Mendonça, C.A.S.: O Mapa Conceitual como Recurso Didático e Facilitador da Aprendizagem Significativa de Conceitos Científicos do Tema Propriedade da Matéria: um Estudo com Alunos do Ensino Fundamental. In: Proceedings of the Sixth International Conference on Concept Mapping, vol. 1, Part. 2, p. 379 (2014). http://cmc.ihmc.us/cmc/ CMCProceedings.html. Accessed 03 Mar 2016
17. Wandersee, J.H.: Concept mapping and the cartography of cognition. J. Res. Sci. Teach. **27**(10), 923–936 (1990)
18. Kinchin, I.M., Lygo-Baker, S., Hay, D.B.: Universities as centres of non-learning. Stud. High. Educ. **33**(1), 89–103 (2008)
19. Novak, J.D.: Clarify with Concept Maps. The Science Teacher **58**(7), 45–49 (1991)
20. Correia, P.R.M., Aguiar, J.G.: Como Fazer bons Mapas Conceituais? Estabelecendo Parâmetros de Referências e Propondo Atividades de Treinamento. Revista Brasileira de pesquisa em Educação em Ciências, vol. 13, no. 2 (2013)
21. Ausubel, D.P.: The Acquisition and Retention of Knowledge: A Cognitive View. Kluwer, Dordrecht (2000)
22. Kinchin, I.M., Hay, D.B., Adams, A.: How a qualitative approach to concept map analysis can be used to aid learning by illustrating patterns of conceptual development. Educ. Res. **42**(1), 43–57 (2000)

Critiquing as an Alternative to Generating Concept Maps to Support Knowledge Integration Processes

Beat A. Schwendimann[✉]

École Polytechnique Fédérale de Lausanne (EPFL), Lausanne, Switzerland
beat.schwendimann@gmail.com

Abstract. As constructing concept maps from scratch can be time consuming, this study explores critiquing given concept maps with deliberate errors as an alternative. A form of concept map that distinguishes between different levels, called Knowledge Integration Map (KIM), was used as an assessment and embedded learning tool. The technology-enhanced biology unit was implemented in four high school science classes (n = 93). Student dyads in each class were randomly assigned to the KIM *generation* (n = 41) or *critique* (n = 52) task. Dyads in the *generation* group created their own connections from a given list of concepts, while dyads in the *critique* group received a concept map that included commonly found errors. KIMs in both groups consisted of the same concepts. Findings indicate that generating or critiquing KIMs can facilitate the construction of cross-level connections. Furthermore, results suggest that critiquing concept maps might be a more time-efficient alternative to generating concept maps from scratch.

Keywords: Concept map · Assessment · Concept map generation · Concept map critique · Collaboration · Comparison study · Knowledge integration map · Science education · Biology education

1 Introduction

The theory of evolution is a unifying theory of modern biology, and notoriously difficult for students to understand (for example [1, 2]). To form a coherent understanding of biology, students need to connect micro-level (genotype) concepts to macro-level (phenotype) concepts. The distinction between genotype and phenotype level concepts is fundamental to understanding heredity and the development of organisms [3]. Genotype level concepts describe the genetic material and its changes over time, for example genes and mutations. Phenotype level concepts describe the phenotype of an organism and its interactions with the environment, for example natural selection and fitness. An integrated understanding of evolution requires simultaneous thinking in and linking genotype and phenotype levels. However, research suggests that students have difficulty reasoning across different levels [4, 5].

Previous studies suggested that a combination of generating and critiquing concept maps can support integrating evolution concepts within and across levels, but also that the combination of activities can be time-consuming [6]. As time in science classrooms

© Springer International Publishing Switzerland 2016
A. Cañas et al. (Eds.): CMC 2016, CCIS 635, pp. 40–53, 2016.
DOI: 10.1007/978-3-319-45501-3_4

is limited and valuable, this study aims to identify and develop a more efficient concept mapping activity by distinguishing the time requirements and learning effects from either collaboratively generating or critiquing concept maps that integrate phenotype and genotype level concepts. Both co-generation and co-critique of concept maps is expected to facilitate learning gains but they might differ in their time requirements.

1.1 Theoretical Framework

This study uses knowledge integration (KI) [7] as its operational framework to build and evaluate an evolution unit that focuses on the connection between genotype and phenotype concepts. The KI pattern supports students to make their existing non-normative concepts and the connections between them explicit, critically sort them out by comparing them against scientific evidence, and apply scientific concepts more frequently in multiple contexts. Students who connect concepts across different levels might be better at identifying important evolution concepts as well as distinguishing normative from non-normative concepts. To support integrating concepts related to evolution, this study contrasts generating to critiquing concept maps.

Generating Concept Maps. This study uses generative concept mapping activities to elicit students' existing concepts, add normative concepts, connect concepts within and across levels, and help students distinguish and sort out concepts. Generating artifacts, such as concept maps, can promote conceptual learning [8]. The "generation effect" [9] has been well-documented in a variety of different settings. For example, Chi [10] found that generating explanations of a text or diagram, whether for oneself or for others, can be more effective for learning than receiving explanations. Using concept maps throughout a unit as an embedded learning tool may allow learners to collect and connect concepts from different contexts. However, research suggests that generating concept maps from scratch can often be time-consuming and cognitively demanding [6].

Critiquing Concept Maps. Critique is an essential step in the knowledge integration process of distinguishing alternative concepts. This study explores if critiquing existing concepts maps that include common non-normative propositions can provide more efficient scaffolding to learning about evolution concepts than generating concept maps from scratch. Asking students to critique and revise has been found to support the development of more coherent criteria [11]. Critiquing is the process of creating a set of criteria, applying criteria to compare one's own or others' alternative concepts against each other, reflecting on how those concepts apply to different concepts, and selecting supported concepts based on evidence [12]. To develop critical thinking, learners need to elicit connections between existing and new concepts and develop their own criteria to distinguish alternative concepts [7]. The social process of reaching agreement is critical in shaping one's concepts [13]. Students need authentic opportunities to develop criteria to distinguish valid alternative concepts based on evidence and scrutinize the reliability of sources [14]. However, students have often few opportunities to critique [12]. Critiquing one's own work can be challenging, for novices as well experts [15]. As an alternative, learners could critique work generated by peers [16]. However, critiquing peers may be socially difficult as students tend to give overly generous or overly critical feedback [17] and students receive artefacts of varying quality. Therefore, this study investigates using another option: Critiquing a concept map that combines non-normative propositions commonly found in student-generated work. Using such a combined map for a critique activity provides all students with the same artefact and could reduce discrimination issues inherent in peer critique (as it cannot be attributed to a specific peer).

2 Method

2.1 Participants

A week-long technology-enhanced unit on evolution, delivered through the WISE platform [18], was implemented by a science teacher in four classes in a high school with an ethnically and socio-economically diverse student population of 9th and 10th grade students (n = 93). The high school had an enrolment of around 2000 students and was located in the urban fringe of a large city. The participating teacher was an experienced master teacher with nine years of teaching experience. The teacher implemented the unit as an introduction to the subsequent topic of evolution after completing several weeks of introduction to genetics. The teacher randomly grouped students into dyads. Students worked collaboratively in dyads by sharing a computer throughout the project.

   Student dyads in each class were randomly assigned to the concept map *generation* (n = 41) or *critique* (n = 52) task. Student dyads in the *generation* group created their own connections from a given list of concepts. Generating their own connections allows students to elicit their existing and missing connections and organize concepts in context to each other. Student dyads in the *critique* group received a concept map that included errors in connections and concept placements commonly found in student-generated concept maps and the literature. The concept maps of the *generation* and *critique* groups consisted of the same concepts. Students were instructed to generate their own criteria to review the presented concept map and negotiate with their partner how to critique and revise the map.

2.2 Knowledge Integration Maps (KIM)

To distinguish different levels (genotype and phenotype) of concepts, the unit used knowledge integration maps (KIM). KIMs are a non-hierarchical form of concept map that divides the drawing space into subject-specific areas (see Fig. 1) [19]. KIMs used in this study divide the drawing space into the evolution-specific levels 'genotype' and 'phenotype'. KIMs were designed to provide a balance between constraints (usage of given list of concepts) and openness that allows expressing a variety of concepts (student-generated connections and placement of concepts). Learners received a list of concepts that needed to be categorized and placed in the corresponding areas.

KIMs can elicit connections within and across levels. Cross-level connections are especially desirable as they represent connections between concepts on different levels.

When KIMs are collaboratively constructed, they become shared social artifacts that can make existing and missing connections explicit and spur discussion among students and teachers. As each connection between two concepts can consist of only one link, students need to negotiate which connection to make. This constraint requires student dyads to negotiate and make decisions about which connection to revise or add, which creates an authentic need for effective criteria and supporting evidence to distinguish among concepts in students' repertoires [20]. For KIM activities, the java-based concept-mapping tool Cmap [21] has been used (Table 1).

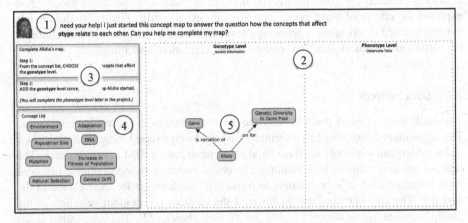

Fig. 1. Embedded KIM worksheet (*generation* group): (1) focus question, (2) evolution-specific areas (genotype and phenotype), (3) instructions, (4) given list of concepts, (5) starter map

Table 1. KIM tasks

KIM task	Training (individual and in dyads)	Pretest (individual)	Embedded KIM 1: Genotype level (in dyads)	Embedded KIM 2: Phenotype level (in dyads)	Posttest (individual)
Generation group	KIM generation and critique activity	Genotype & Phenotype KIM generation and critique activity	KIM generation map 1	KIM generation map 2	Genotype & Phenotype KIM generation and critique activity
Critique group	KIM generation and critique activity	Genotype & Phenotype KIM generation and critique activity	KIM critique map 1	KIM critique map 2	Genotype & Phenotype KIM generation and critique activity

2.3   Procedure

The teacher introduced all students to the concept mapping method and the Cmap software. Students individually received identical pretests and posttests delivered through the WISE environment. The WISE unit consisted of five consecutive activities. The first three activities focused on changes in the genotype caused by mutations. The third activity presented an overview of the connections between mutations and genetic variability in the gene pool. Student dyads either generated or critiqued a genotype-level KIM (see Fig. 1) using the provided six concepts DNA, gene, allele, genetic drift, genetic diversity, and mutation. The second section focused on phenotype level concepts. The fourth activity presented two guided inquiry activities to explore the connections between mutations, natural selection, and genetic diversity. The fifth activity introduced the concept 'genetic drift' as an additional selection process and explored the effects of small population sizes on genetic drift. Finally, student dyads either generated or critiqued a phenotype-level KIM, using the provided five concepts population size, natural selection, environment, adaptation, and fitness.

2.4   Data Sources

This study used a pretest-posttest design to measure changes in knowledge integration. The assessment consisted of five identical two-tired items (combining multiple choice and a subsequent explanation), three short essay items, and a KIM generation task. The first tier presents students with multiple choices of common misconceptions, followed by the second tier that asks students to provide an explanation for their choice in the first tier. The two-tier item design lowered the chances for random selection in the multiple-choice tier as students had to justify their choice [22]. The pre/posttest items underwent systematic revisions after pilot testing with biology teachers, students, and assessment experts. Liu et al. [23] reported the validity and reliability of knowledge integration test construction and analysis. The KIM generation task provided students with the combined list of concepts from the embedded KIM 1 and 2 (11 concepts: natural selection, adaptation, DNA, mutation, genetic drift, genetic diversity, population size, gene, fitness, gene, allele, and environment). Students were instructed to place the concepts in the corresponding area (genotype or phenotype) and generate connections (within and across levels).

2.5   Analysis

The two-tired items were scored using a five-level knowledge integration rubric (see Table 2) [24]. Higher knowledge integration scores indicate more complex normative links among different concepts relevant to the genetic basis of evolution. Paired t-tests, chi-square tests and effect sizes were calculated. Multiple regression analysis and ANOVA was used to investigate whether the two groups (*generation* and *critique*) differed from each other in learning gains and KIM usage.

Table 2. Knowledge integration rubric: sample item: "What changes occur gradually over time in groups of finches that live in different environments?"

	KI score	Sample answers
No answer (blank)	0	None
Offtask	1	I don't know
Irrelevant/Incorrect	2	Finches develop new beaks to adapt to a new environment
Partial	3	Finches inherit traits from their parents
Basic	4	Finches have differently shaped beaks that give them different chances to survive natural selection
Complex	5	Natural selection causes those finches with helpful mutations to their beaks to be more genetically fit and adapt to the environment better. Therefore, the finches with the beaks adapted to their environment are more likely to reproduce and the trait gradually becomes dominant in the group

This study used a multi-tiered KIM analysis method [19], including presences or absence of connections, quality of connections, network density, and spatial placement of concepts. The main goal of the KIM analysis was to identify students' non-normative concepts about evolution and track changes throughout the sequence of concept maps.

KIM Generation Analysis

- Propositional level: A five-level knowledge integration rubric for KIM propositions [19] was used to determine changes in link quality. The propositional analysis focused on overall and essential connections. Essential connections were identified from a benchmark KIM generated by a group of experts.
- Network level: An analysis method that focuses only on isolated propositions does not account for the network character of a whole map. To capture this information, network analysis methods were used to identify changes in the prominence (incoming and outgoing connections) of expert-selected indicator concepts: 'Mutation' for the genotype-level and 'natural selection' for the phenotype level. Multiplied with the KI score for each connection, a 'weighted prominence score' for each of the two indicator concepts was calculated (see Figs. 4 and 5). A better integration of genotype and phenotype concepts would be expected to lead to a more frequent use of the normative concept 'mutation'.

To describe semantic changes in the relationships between concepts, qualitative variables are needed. This study used the structure-behavior-function (SBF) framework to create the super-categories of the taxonomy. The SBF framework was originally developed by Goel [25, 26] to describe complex systems in computer science, and then applied to complex biological systems by Hmelo-Silver and colleagues [2, 27]. The taxonomy is both theory-driven and informed by empirical data from previous studies [6, 19]. The taxonomy distinguishes between structure (what is the structure/static relation?); behavior (what is the dynamic relation between concepts?); and function (what are the functional relations between concepts?) (see Table 3). The sub-categories (for example part-whole, deterministic, probabilistic, quantified, procedural-temporal) for the taxonomy emerged from KIM analysis and were reported in [19].

Table 3. Categories of different KIM link labels

Super-category	Sub-category	Code	Examples
Unrelated	No connection	0	
	No label (just line)	1	
	Unrelated label	2	
Structure [What is the structure (in relation to other parts)?]	Part-whole [Hierarchical)]	3	Is a/are a; is a member of; consists of; contains; is part of; made of; composed of; includes; is example of
	Similarity/Comparison/Contrast	4	Contrasts to; is like; is different than
	Spatial proximity	5	Is adjacent to; is next to; takes place in
	Attribute/Property/Characteristic (Quality (permanent) or State (temporary)	6	Can be in state
			Is form of
Behavior [What action does it do? How does it work/influence others?	Causal-deterministic (A always influences B)	7	Contributes to; produces; creates; causes; influences; leads to; effects; depends on; adapts to; changes; makes; results in; forces; codes for; determines
	Causal-probability (modality)	8	Leads to with high/low probability; often/rarely leads to; might/could lead to; sometimes leads to
	Causal-quantified	9	Increases/Decreases
	Mechanistic	10	Explains domain-specific mechanism/Adds specific details or intermediary steps
	Procedural-temporal (A happens before B)	11	Next/follows; goes to; undergoes; develops into; based on; transfers to; happens before/during/after; occurs when; forms from

(Continued)

Table 3. (*Continued*)

Super-category	Sub-category	Code	Examples
Function [Why is it needed?]	Functional	12	Is needed; is required; in order to; is made for
	Teleological	13	Intends to; wants to

3   Results

Pretest-posttest results: Findings indicate that students overall made significant learning gains from pretest to posttest. Paired $t(93) = 6.08$, $p < 0.0001$ (two-tailed)]; effect size (Cohen's d) = 0.63 (SD pretest = 2.24, SD posttest = 2.41). Results indicate a shift towards higher knowledge integration scores (KI score 3 or higher).

Students in both KIM task groups (*critique* and *generation*) used significantly fewer non-normative concepts in the posttest than in the pretest ($t(96) = -2.67$, $p < 0.01$). For example, in the pretest, a student chose three non-normative options in the multiple-choice item and focused only on phenotype level concepts in the explanation. In the posttest, the same student chose only the normative option and provided an explanation that used the normative genotype level concept 'mutation'.

Students can improve their KIM performance not only quantitatively (the number of links and knowledge integration score of KIM connections) but also qualitatively change the types of relationships (see Fig. 2). Using the structure-behavior-function (SBF) framework to categorize different types of relations, students most frequently generated links in the 'behavior' category (to describe dynamic relations).

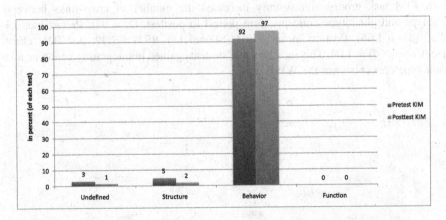

Fig. 2. Changes in KIM relation super-categories from pretest to posttest.

A more detailed analysis of the relation types in each super-category revealed that students generated fewer causal-deterministic (−7 %) and more causal-probabilistic (+4 %) (for example 'could lead to') and quantified (+11 %) (for example 'increases') KIM relations in the posttest (see Fig. 3). The increase in causal probabilistic relationships can be seen as shift towards more statistical thinking on the gene pool level. The increase of quantified relations could indicate a shift towards thinking more in dynamic relationships that reflects the functional interdependency of evolution concepts [28].

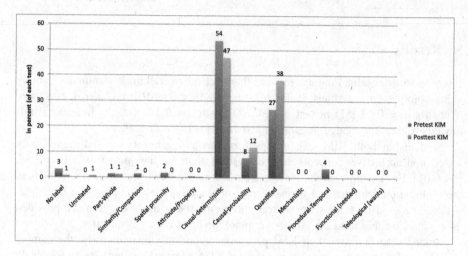

Fig. 3. Changes in KIM relationship sub-categories from pretest to posttest.

Multiple regression analysis indicates that both groups gained significantly in their average KIM knowledge integration scores, $R2 = 2.013$, $F(2, 88) = 11.09$, $p = 0.000$. Both KIM task groups significantly increased the number of cross-links between genotype and phenotype concepts from pretest to posttest, $(N = 94)$: Pretest mean = 2.52 (SD = 1.66), Posttest mean = 1.03 (SD = 1.15). $t(93) = 7.49$, $p < .001$; effect size (Cohen's d) = 1.04. This indicates that students gained in integrating genotype and phenotype concepts after the WISE unit.

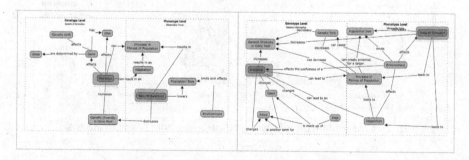

Fig. 4. Example of a student's pretest and posttest KIM (critique group). The posttest KIM shows a higher number of cross-connections and more connections to/from the indicator concepts 'mutation' and 'natural selection'.

In accordance with gains in prominence of the KIM indicator concepts 'mutation' and 'natural selection', multiple regression analysis suggests that students overall used normative evolution concepts more often than non-normative concepts in the posttest than in the pretest ($R2 = 0.18$, $F(1,94) = 20.18$, $p < .001$ (see Fig. 4).

Findings from network analysis suggest that students in both groups created significantly more links to and from the two indicator concepts in the posttest: 'Mutation' ($t(93) = 5.39$, $p = 0.00$) and 'natural selection' ($t(93) = 5.83$, $p = 0.00$) (see Fig. 4). These observations indicate that the two normative indicator concepts gained in explanatory strength in students' repertoire of evolution concepts. The KIM variables 'weighted prominence score' for the indicator concepts 'mutation' and 'natural selection' (see Fig. 5) are strongly correlated with the overall KIM KI score: 'Mutation' $r(94) = 0.75$, $p < 0.001$, and 'natural selection' $r(94) = 0.70$, $p < 0.001$.

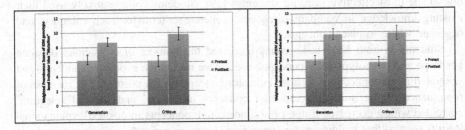

Fig. 5. Weighted prominence scores of the KIM indicator concepts 'mutation' (left) and 'natural selection' (right).

Regarding time, students in both KIM task groups spent about the same average amount of time on the pretest KIM (14 min) and posttest KIM (13 min) (see Table 4). Both groups showed equal KIM posttest performance. However, the *critique* group needed significantly less time for the embedded KIM activities, $p < 0.05$ ($t(27) = 2.72$, $p = 0.01$). These results indicate that KIM critique tasks were more time efficient than the KIM generation tasks while leading to the same posttest gains.

Table 4. Time spent on KIM tasks.

In minutes	Generation group mean	Critique group mean	Total mean (median)
KIM 1 (Genotype)	11.94	6.55	9.03 (8)
KIM 2 (Phenotype)	8.62	5.39	6.54 (4)
Pretest	14.95	13.39	14.12 (16)
Posttest	13.65	13.06	13.35 (12.5)

4 Discussion

Overall, findings suggest that the combination of collaborative KIM tasks and technology-enhanced inquiry tasks in the WISE unit improved students' integration of evolution concepts. Findings indicate that the collaborative technology-enhanced concept mapping form 'Knowledge Integration Map' facilitated students' generation of connections between and across genotype and phenotype levels. As anticipated, students in both KIM task groups showed equal improvement in the posttest tasks. Results from this study suggest that generating or critiquing KIMs can effectively support knowledge integration of evolution concepts. This could be explained by the relatively short duration of the two embedded KIM activities (only about twenty minutes out of a week-long unit), the similarities of the tasks (same given concepts, same drawing areas), and that both generation and critique activities can support knowledge integration [6]. Both KIM tasks were designed to support students' knowledge integration through adding, connecting, distinguishing, sorting out, and contrasting evolution concepts on different levels. Sorting concepts into domain-specific levels can provide scaffolds for students to think about why concepts belong into a specific category. This aligns with Marzano's findings that the identification of similarities and differences is one of the most effective learning strategies [29]. Students collaboratively used their existing knowledge to compare categories, generate criteria for each category, and negotiate where to place concepts.

Students in both KIM task groups increased the number of cross-links between genotype and phenotype level concepts, used more normative evolution concepts, and generated more connections to/from indicator concepts in the posttest. The increase of prominence of the normative indicator concepts 'mutation' and 'natural selection' coincided with a decreased usage of non-normative concepts in posttest explanations. Results suggest that building more connections between genotype and phenotype level concepts can reduce the usage of non-normative concepts when generating explanations of evolutionary change. Students not only generated more connections in the KIM posttest, but they generated more quantified relationships, which can be seen as an indicator for deeper understanding [28]. Working on KIMs collaboratively in pairs required students to negotiate and make their criteria explicit. The visual knowledge representation of KIMs can support collaborative work by enabling efficient information retrieval and exchange. Multiple embedded KIMs can allow students to self-monitor their learning progress by making existing and absent connections explicit.

Previous studies [6, 16] suggested that the combination of generating and critiquing KIMs can support students' integration of concepts related evolution. However, the combination of both tasks can be time-consuming. This study developed and investigated critiquing as a more time-effective KIM activity designs. Despite similar learning outcomes, the critique group required significantly less time to complete their two embedded KIM tasks. The critique group might have been faster because generating new links from scratch can be more challenging than revising existing connections, and it requires in-depth reflection of smaller selection of propositions. Critique-task KIMs can reduce the demanding decision-making process as students only revise connections they disagree with. On the other hand, students in the KIM generation group needed to make decisions for each proposition and placement. As time in the classroom is limited and precious, this study suggests that collaborative KIM critique tasks can be a beneficial and more time-efficient alternative to generating concept maps from scratch. Critiquing and sorting out of alternative concepts is a central process of knowledge integration and an important skill for autonomous, lifelong learning.

5   Implications

This study demonstrates that Knowledge Integration Map tasks embedded within a technology-enhanced evolution unit focused on knowledge integration have the potential to transform learning in biology classrooms where time is limited and precious. This study developed and explored critiquing KIMs as a time-effective form of collaborative concept mapping task that can foster knowledge integration of complex scientific knowledge, such as evolution. Additionally, critiquing KIMs can elicit criteria to distinguish non-normative concepts and provide students with a genuine opportunity to negotiate and apply critique. For Knowledge Integration Maps to provide maximum benefit to students, KIM activities should be integrated with a variety of other learning activities, such as scaffolded inquiry activities. Learning how to generate KIMs and how to revise KIMs takes time and practice. Ideally, KIMs would be introduced early in a student's academic career rather than later, so they can integrate it into their developing study strategies (for example see [30]). Critiquing KIMs that include common non-normative concepts can generate genuine opportunities for students to reflect on their own knowledge and apply critique. Critique activities can support criteria generation as student dyads have to negotiate which elements they want to revise. Critiquing KIMs can encourage knowledge integration by fostering self-monitoring of learning progress, identifying gaps in knowledge, and distinguishing non-normative concepts. A forced-choice design for KIM concepts but free choice for concept placement, connections, and labels was found to be an effective and balanced form of concept mapping.

To capture the wide variety of students' non-normative concepts, this study suggests using a combination of quantitative and qualitative KIM analysis methods in addition to traditional assessment methods [18]. KIMs can contain different forms of information: Presence or absence of connections, quality of connections, different types of link labels, different types of networks, and spatial placement of concepts. To account for these different aspects of KIMs, several different analysis strategies need to be applied to triangulate changes over time. Findings from this study are valuable for the design of effective collaborative learning environments to support more integrated understanding of biology.

Acknowledgements. The research for this paper was supported by the National Science Foundation grant DRL-0334199 ("The Educational Accelerator: Technology Enhanced Learning in Science"). I thank my advisor Prof. Marcia C. Linn for her mentorship during the research for this paper and Prof. Pierre Dillenbourg for his support leading to the publication of this paper.

References

1. Alters, B.J., Nelson, C.E.: Perspective: teaching evolution in higher education. Evolution **56** (10), 1891–1901 (2002)
2. Hmelo-Silver, C.E., Marathe, S., Liu, L.: Fish swim, rocks sit, and lungs breathe: expert–novice understanding of complex systems. J. Learn. Sci. **16**(3), 307–331 (2007)

3. Mayr, E.: Towards a New Philosophy of Biology: Observations of an Evolutionist, p. 564. Harvard University Press, Cambridge (1988)
4. Hmelo, C.E., Holton, D.L., Kolodner, J.L.: Designing to learn about complex systems. J. Learn. Sci. **9**(3), 247–298 (2000)
5. Penner, D.E.: Explaining systems: investigating middle school students' understanding of emergent phenomena. J. Res. Sci. Teach. **37**(8), 784–806 (2000)
6. Schwendimann, B.A., Linn, M.C.: Comparing two forms of concept map critique activities to facilitate knowledge integration processes in evolution education. J. Res. Sci. Teach. **4** (2015). doi:10.1002/tea.21244
7. Linn, M.C., Davis, E.A., Eylon, B.-S.: The scaffolded knowledge integration framework for instruction. In: Linn, M.C., Davis, E.A., Bell, P. (eds.) Internet Environments for Science Education, pp. 47–72. Lawrence Erlbaum Associates, Mahwah (2004)
8. van Amelsvoort, M., Andriessen, J., Kanselaar, G.: Using representational tools to support historical reasoning in computer-supported collaborative learning. Technol. Pedag. Educ. **14** (1), 25–41 (2005)
9. Osborne, R.J., Wittrock, M.C.: Learning science: a generative process. Sci. Educ. **67**(4), 489–508 (1983)
10. Chi, M.T.H.: Self-explaining: the dual processes of generating inference and repairing mental models. In: Advances in Instructional Psychology: Educational Design and Cognitive Science, vol. 5, pp. 161–238. Lawrence Erlbaum Associates Publishers, Mahwah (2000)
11. Lehrer, R., Schauble, L.: Modeling natural variation through distribution. Am. Educ. Res. J. **41**(3), 635–679 (2004)
12. Shen, J.: Nurturing students' critical knowledge using technology-enhanced scaffolding strategies in science education. J. Sci. Educ. Technol. **19**(1), 1–12 (2010). doi:10.1007/s10956-009-9183-1
13. Clark, D.B., Sampson, V.: Assessing dialogic argumentation in online environments to relate structure, grounds, and conceptual quality. J. Res. Sci. Teach. **45**(3), 293–321 (2008). doi:10.1002/tea.20216
14. Cuthbert, A., Slotta, J.: Fostering lifelong learning skills on the world wide web: critiquing, questioning and searching for evidence. Int. J. Sci. Educ. **27**(7), 821–844 (2004)
15. Guindon, R.: Designing the design process: exploiting opportunistic thoughts. Hum. Comput. Interact. **5**(2), 305–344 (1990)
16. Schwendimann, B.A.: Scaffolding an integrated understanding of biology through dynamic visualizations and critique-focused concept mapping. In: Annual Meeting of the American Education Research Association (AERA), San Diego, CA (2009)
17. Hoadley, C., Kirby, J.: Socially relevant representations in interfaces for learning. In: Kafai, Y.B., Sandoval, W.A., Enyedy, N., Nixon, A.S., Herrera, F. (eds.) Embracing Diversity in the Learning Sciences: Proceedings of the Sixth International Conference of the Learning Sciences, pp. 262–269. Lawrence Erlbaum Associates, Mahwah (2004)
18. Linn, M.C., Hsi, S.: Computers, Teachers, Peers: Science Learning Partners. Lawrence Erlbaum Associates, Mahwah (2000)
19. Schwendimann, B.A.: Making sense of knowledge integration maps. In: Ifenthaler, D., Hanewald, R. (eds.) Digital Knowledge Maps in Education: Technology Enhanced Support for Teachers and Learners, pp. 17–40. Springer, New York (2014). https://www.springer.com/education+%26+language/learning+%26+instruction/book/978-1-4614-3177-0
20. Berland, L.K., Reiser, B.J.: Making sense of argumentation and explanation. Sci. Educ. **93** (1), 26–55 (2009). doi:10.1002/sce.20286

21. Cañas, A.J., Hill, G., Carff, R., Suri, N., Lott, J., Gómez, G., Eskridge, T., Arroyo, M. Carvajal, R.: CmapTools: a knowledge modeling and sharing environment. In: Concept Maps: Theory, Methodology, Technology, Proceedings of the First International Conference on Concept Mapping, Pamplona, Spain, Editorial Universidad Pública de Navarra (2004)

22. Tsui, C., Treagust, D.: Evaluating secondary students' scientific reasoning in genetics using a two-tier diagnostic instrument. Int. J. Sci. Educ. **32**(8), 1073–1098 (2010). http://www.informaworld.com/10.1080/09500690902951429

23. Liu, O.L., Lee, H.S., Linn, M.C.: Multifaceted assessment of inquiry-based science learning. Educ. Assess. **15**(2), 69–86 (2010)

24. Linn, M.C., Lee, H.-S., Tinker, R., Husic, F., Chiu, J.L.: Teaching and assessing knowledge integration in science. Science **313**(5790), 1049–1050 (2006)

25. Goel, A., Chandrasekaran, B.: Functional representation of designs and redesign problem solving. In: Proceedings of the 11th International Joint Conference on Artificial Intelligence, vol. 2, pp. 1388–1394 (1989)

26. Goel, A.K., Rugaber, S., Vattam, S.: Structure, behavior, and function of complex systems: the structure, behavior, and function modeling language. Artif. Intell. Eng. Des. Anal. Manuf. **23**, 23 (2008)

27. Liu, L., Hmelo-Silver, C.E.: Promoting complex systems learning through the use of conceptual representations in hypermedia. J. Res. Sci. Teach. **46**, 1023–1040 (2009)

28. Derbentseva, N., Safayeni, F., Cañas, A.J.: Concept maps: experiments on dynamic thinking. J. Res. Sci. Teach. **44**(3), 448–465 (2007)

29. Marzano, R.J., Pickering, D., Pollock, J.E.: Classroom Instruction that Works: Research-Based Strategies for Increasing Student Achievement. ASCD, Alexandria (2001)

30. Santhanam, E., Leach, C., Dawson, C.: Concept mapping: how should it be introduced, and is there evidence for long term benefit? High. Educ. **35**(3), 317–328 (1998)

Design and Validation of a Teaching Sequence Based on Concept Maps to Achieve Meaningful Learning of Science Content in Primary Education

Guadalupe Martínez[(✉)], Milagros Mateos, and Francisco L. Naranjo

University of Extremadura, Badajoz, Spain
{mmarbor, mmateoslm, naranjo}@unex.es

Abstract. A comparative study was conducted between a traditional methodology for teaching scientific contents and an experimental methodology based on the construction of a didactic sequence using concept maps as a resource for teaching-learning. Four groups of students aged 9–10 were selected, two acting as Control Groups and two as Experimental Groups. The objective was to find out the differences between the selected educational methods, in terms of the learning that 4th grade students acquire. The results showed a higher degree of effectiveness on the teaching methods used in the EG against the methods used in the CG. Students in the CG did not remember on the long term the contents taught in a traditional way, which seems related to rote learning. By contrast, students using concept maps had a more meaningful learning. In conclusion, concept maps are an important resource for improving the acquisition of scientific knowledge in primary education.

Keywords: Concept maps · Primary education · Scientific content · Comparative study

1 Introduction

Currently, research in didactics of experimental sciences highlight the importance of awakening scientific vocations from early age. From an educational point of view, it is necessary to highlight the great social value of teaching science content to help students to deal with society and to achieve greater intellectual maturity. However, some researchers have analysed from different perspectives the difficulties in the learning process of science. For example, many students think that scientific knowledge is articulated in the form of equations and definitions that have to be memorized instead of understood [1]. Such factors constitute an obstacle to science learning and, to some extent, may be responsible for part of the existing school failure [2]. Another major problem arises in teaching and learning science at school: the negative attitude of students towards it [3]. Some authors [4] maintain that there is a great lack of interest in science and an attitudinal decline towards it, which makes students turn away from science as their age increases. Because of this, there is a current trend of research in the area of Didactic of Experimental Sciences, focused on emotions in teaching science [5].

© Springer International Publishing Switzerland 2016
A. Cañas et al. (Eds.): CMC 2016, CCIS 635, pp. 54–65, 2016.
DOI: 10.1007/978-3-319-45501-3_5

As shown in several studies [6–8], the students acknowledge that science is of great importance to society, yet most of them do not want to continue studying science in the post-compulsory stage. On the other hand, Gil [9] indicates that another major problem in science education is the gap between the teaching-learning situations and how scientific knowledge is constructed.

In schools, students are expected to learn science focusing on the successful transmission of conceptual content, giving low priority to the construction process of knowledge through the development of practical activities [10]. It is often forgotten that students should not only learn science, but they must also learn to do science [11]. In this sense, the experimental method provides students the opportunity to learn what is really science and how scientific knowledge develops [12].

In line with this background, it is noteworthy that, although there are different methodologies for science education, in many schools traditional instruction is still preferred. This traditional teaching is focused primarily on the acquisition of conceptual contents, which are then required to students in most cases by rote, without ensuring that there is adequate knowledge construction. Because of this, the school curriculum and most textbooks used in schools have been based on conceptual content. This aspect is one of the most serious shortcomings of science education [13, 14] since students have little room to think and structure clearly some knowledge, as they are required by rote without proper development of theoretical thinking. Authors like Furió and Guisasola [15] indicate that to learn scientific concepts it is necessary to apply methodologies that stay away from rote learning. According to Torres [16], the traditional way of teaching science is as a set of facts that the textbook contains and that the student is supposed to memorize to answer the questions required in the examination. For this reason, one of the problems of traditional teaching is that, given the importance that has been assigned to content, rote learning of knowledge has been encouraged. It is not checked whether the students are able to apply these contents, for example in situations in everyday life, or to relate the physical phenomena explained with what they observe in their environment. This can be worrying, because if learning is rote is very likely that students will eventually forget what has been taught by traditional methodology. Rote learning does not usually integrate new knowledge with existing knowledge, which yield two negative consequences: first, the knowledge learned by rote tends to be quickly forgotten, and secondly, the student's cognitive structure is not improved or modified to clarify misconceptions. Therefore, misconceptions will persist, and there will be little or no chance of the knowledge learned will be used in future learning or applied to problem solving [17].

Several studies indicate that for learning to be considered long-term learning has to be meaningful learning. Currently, the theory of meaningful learning [18] is considered as the most appropriate to acquire and maintain knowledge over time, being useful to improve student learning [19]. To Coll [20], meaningful learning is related to the process of constructing meaning. Because of this, one of the teaching methods of our research group is the use of teaching tools that promote meaningful and lasting learning in our students, such as concept maps. Concept maps [21] are one of the main cognitive learning tools that help build meanings of scientific concepts. As it is well known, a concept map represents schematically and hierarchically key concepts of a subject in order to organize the knowledge someone has of said subject and show the semantic relationships between the concepts involved. Concept maps are also useful to organize knowledge that we place in our long-term memory and, at the same time, they have the function of a mental scaffolding for assembling information isolated in our working memory [22].

Based on the contributions of Novak, some research has been conducted showing that concept maps are very effective tools to capture the knowledge of an expert by developing Knowledge Models based on concept maps [23–25]. There are several studies on the use of concept maps in all academic fields, both in primary and secondary school. Some authors have used the technique of concept maps with children in primary school [26]. Others emphasize the value of the concept mapping technique in the design of curriculum materials, planning and evaluation [27]. For these authors, concept maps represent a link between learning theory and teaching. Fraser and Edwards [28] analysed whether concept maps affected the academic performance of students in traditional class tests and they found that the construction of concept maps by students produced an improvement in these tests. In addition, they found out that students who improved their technique in creating concept maps experience significant progress in academia.

Some authors conducted a study on the teaching effectiveness of concept maps and knowledge models for learning physics concepts in engineering students [29]. Moreover, concept maps have been used to explain the reasoning of an expert teacher in solving problems of kinematics, showing their effectiveness in students of secondary education [30]. Some authors consider also important to highlight the utility teachers can give to concept maps [31]. For example, certain investigations use them as prior organizer of the contents of a topic, or as prior diagnosis of the degree of organization of the knowledge possessed by students before starting the process of teaching and learning of the selected topic. Thus, students become aware of what they previously know before the teaching of the new didactic unit. In the study by Fuatai [32], the training given to secondary school students in learning mathematics was analysed through concept maps. Using concept maps students also improved in solving problems of this area.

The usefulness of concept maps is so broad that some authors like Martínez, who conducted a study on the effectiveness of different environments simulations in teaching physics [33], used concept maps in their methodology to understand how students think. Overall, we can say that concept maps help students learn to learn [21] and help to make science conceptually transparent to both teachers and students [34]. Specifically, it can be said that concept maps help you see the conceptual and propositional nature of knowledge and its relation to human understanding. Even children learn easily to construct concept maps about readings of texts, word lists of important concepts, class discussions of experiments, field trips or other sources of experiences. In the present work, we will use concept maps as a teaching resource to develop a teaching sequence as a methodology we will compare with traditional teaching, in order to determine experimentally the educational value to achieve a significant and long-term science learning in primary education.

2 Methodology

2.1 Objectives and Hypothesis

In this work we have tried to check whether a methodology based on the traditional teaching is sufficient to achieve the acquisition of scientific knowledge at primary school, or if it is necessary to expand this method by applying other teaching strategies such as Knowledge Models developed with concept maps. The objectives in this research were:

- Objective 1: Design and validation of a teaching sequence based on the use of concept maps to improve the acquisition of scientific competence in the primary classroom.
- Objective 2: Comparison, in terms of the learning reached by students, of a traditional teaching methodology versus a methodology based on the delivery of content using a knowledge model.
- Objective 3: Check whether scientific concepts learned by primary students through different methodologies persists or is forgotten over time.

Based on the proposed objectives the following hypothesis have been formulated:

- Hypothesis 1 (H1): There are statistically significant differences in the mean learning achieved by students using traditional methodology versus an experimental methodology based on the development of a knowledge model with concept maps.
- Hypothesis 2 (H2): Traditional teaching facilitates rote learning of scientific concepts, which are easily forgotten over time.
- Hypothesis 3 (H3): Concept maps facilitate long-term, meaningful learning in primary students.

2.2 Experience Design

To achieve the objectives set in this research, a school has been chosen randomly, and through a convenience sampling a total of 78 students between 9 and 10 years old have been selected. The experience was carried out with an experimental design with pre-test, two post-tests, control group and experimental group. To make a comparative study between two teaching methods, the students were divided into 4 groups of sample size of 17 to 21 students each. Two of these groups were designated as experimental groups, and the remaining two were selected as control groups. The students and faculty who participated in the research were voluntaries. The independent variable was the teaching methodology used with each group: using concept maps (Experimental Group, EG) or not using them (Control Group, CG). The dependent variable was the average learning achieved by each group.

Work Methodology in the Control and Experimental Groups. The traditional methodology of work in the two control groups (CG1 and CG2) has been carried out by their teachers. The resources used in the classroom have been their textbooks and supplemental and reinforcement worksheets. However, in the two experimental groups

(EG1 and EG2) it has been used a teaching methodology based on the development of a knowledge model with concept maps. This model was made up of several interlinked concept maps made with the software CmapTools, with different interactive resources, images and videos annexed to support the propositions of the cmap. Both control groups and experimental groups used the same time for the delivery of the content selected. The curricular level of the students was taken into account when designing the educational intervention based on concept mapping in the classroom. In Fig. 1 is shown, as way of example, one of the concept maps developed for the experimental groups.

The topic chosen belongs to the block of "Matter" in the area of Knowledge of the Environment in the 4th grade of Primary Education. Students of this stage should be familiar with some of the concepts involved in this issue, such as the states of matter or some of its properties. This unit was chosen because it is a subject that appears in our daily lives. We intended to foster the acquisition of concepts so that they are maintained over time, as we wanted to make a meaningful and long term learning. For this reason, it was decided to work with concept maps in the experimental groups. In principle, it does not seem an overly complex and difficult subject to develop in the classroom. We found, however, that many students were unaware of the concept, or found it difficult to explain other related concepts, as the changes in matter.

Evaluation Instruments. We used three assessment tools that were fulfilled by all the students involved in this study, from control and experimental groups.

- **Pre-test:** It was designed with 9 questions in order to detect which was the initial knowledge possessed by the students about the selected topic. The test was carried out the beginning of the course, before the beginning of the delivery of content. The results of this survey were used as starting point for the development of the teaching materials to be used in the study of the topic chosen.
- **Post-test I:** It was designed to test the effectiveness of the teaching methodology used in each group. It consisted of 10 questions related to the subject taught in both groups. It was done by students as a final evaluation test in order to determine the degree of acquisition of the contents explained in terms of the methodology used in the classroom.
- **Post- test II:** It consisted of 9 questions regarding the same contents as the previous questionnaires. It was completed by the students of all groups 7 months after Post-test I. The objective was to verify if the students remembered the contents explained and if they had achieved a meaningful learning.

3   Results

The results obtained by all students in the Pre-test done at the beginning of the course revealed an initial lack of knowledge regarding the subject of matter. Overall, it should be noted that approximately 90 % of students did not know what to answer in the Pre-test. They did not know the concepts and they had misconceptions about them.

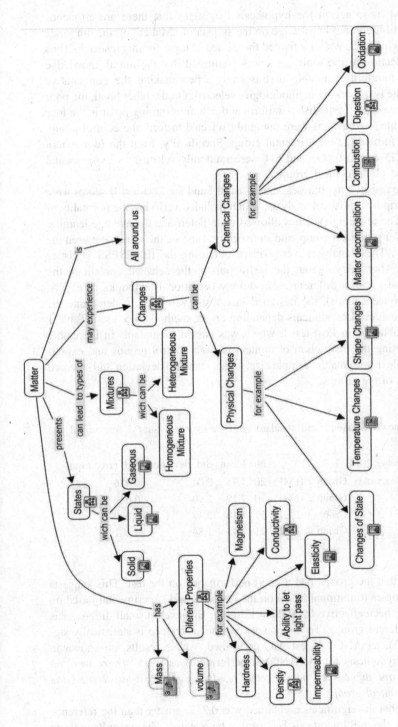

Fig. 1. Example of one of the concept maps that make up the knowledge model developed for the experimental groups

These results allow us to accept the hypothesis that states that there are erroneous preconceptions and little initial knowledge on the subject of "Matter" on the 4th grade primary students, which was what motivated the choice of topic for this research. Thus was settled the selection of the topic, as it was confirmed that the initial knowledge would not be an interfering variable in this study when making the comparative analysis between the two working methodologies selected. On the other hand, the poor Pre-test results allowed us to establish a uniform and common starting point in the four working groups. Thus, two groups were randomly selected to form the control group, and the other two formed the experimental group. Specifically, from the four school groups (G1, G2, G3 and G4), G1 and G4 were randomly selected as experimental groups, and G2 and G3 as control groups.

Next, to test the research hypotheses, the Post-test I and the Post-test II scores were subjected to a descriptive statistical analysis, which included verifying the normality of their distribution. The resulting statistics allowed us to determine the average learning attained by the students of each group, and statistically compare the results between the two methodologies. These analyses were carried out using the IBM SPSS Statistics program package. After carrying out the instruction of the selected content in the different groups, each with a different methodology (traditional textbooks or experimental based on concept maps), the designed Post-test I was used to determine the degree of learning achieved by students depending on the methodology used. Table 1 shows the results obtained in Post-test I, which was passed to students in December 2014, after completing the instruction of content in both control groups and experimental groups. Table 1 presents the sample size, mean, standard deviation and standard error mean in each of the groups.

Table 1. Mean, standard deviation and standard error mean in Post-test I for control and experimental groups.

Post-test I (December 2014)		N	Mean	Std. deviation	Std. error mean
4th grade (9–10 years old)	Group 1 (EG1)	20	7.75	2.04	0.456
	Group 2 (CG1)	20	7.19	2.90	0.649
	Group 3 (CG2)	17	6.18	2.47	0.599
	Group 4 (EG2)	21	7.45	1.84	0.401

Table 1 shows that the groups had a good performance on the test. This suggests that both methodologies (traditional based on the textbook and experimental based on concept maps) have been effective for student learning. However, a small difference is shown between different groups. To check whether this difference is statistically significant (Sig < 0.05), an ANOVA test was performed, whose results are shown in Table 2. The null hypothesis for the ANOVA performed was $H1_0$: *"There were no statistically significant differences between the results of the Post-test I from the experimental and control groups"*.

Table 2 shows that the significance obtained was 0.217, greater than the reference value of 0.05. Thus, the null hypothesis $H1_0$ cannot be rejected. These results indicate

Table 2. ANOVA test in Post-test I

	Sum of squares	d.f.	Mean square	F	Sig.
Between groups	24.951	3	8.317	1.519	0.217
Within groups	405.074	74	5.474		
Total	430.026	77			

that students in all groups, both control and experimental, have a priori learned similarly the scientific content instructed in the classroom, fulfilling the Objectives 1 and 2 proposed in this paper.

To achieve Objective 3, however, we need to test hypotheses H1, H2 and H3. To do so, at the end of the school year the students of all groups were asked to complete Post-test II, designed as a final evaluation of the course, to verify if the concepts learned persisted over time. Table 3 shows the results obtained in Post-test II, passed in June 2015. The sample size, mean, standard deviation and standard error mean for the control and experimental groups is presented.

Table 3. Mean, standard deviation and standard error mean in Post-test II for control and experimental groups.

Post-test II (June 2015)	N	Mean	Std. deviation	Std. error mean
Group 1 (EG1)	20	6.39	1.93	0.43
Group 2 (CG1)	20	2.55	1.60	0.35
Group 3 (CG2)	17	2.51	2.29	0.55
Group 4 (EG2)	21	6.03	2.44	0.53

Table 3 shows that there is a clear difference between the scores of the control groups against the experimental groups, which scored higher. The students that were part of the control groups receive very low average scores (2.55 and 2.51 points out of 10). Both scores are very similar, with no significant differences between them. However, students in the experimental groups obtained in this second Post-test much higher average scores than students in the control groups (6.39 and 6.03 points out of 10, with no significant differences between them).

To check whether this difference is statistically significant (Sig. < 0.05), an ANOVA test was performed, with the null hypothesis $H2_0$: *"There were no statistically significant differences in the results obtained in Post-test II between experimental and control groups"*. The results are shown in Table 4. The significance obtained was much less than 0.05, so $H2_0$ can be rejected, and the H1 hypothesis of this research can be accepted: *"There are statistically significant differences in the mean learning achieved by students using traditional methodology versus an experimental methodology based on the development of a knowledge model with concept maps"*.

Figure 2 shows the average scores obtained by the different groups in Post-test I and Post-test II.

Table 4. ANOVA test in Post-test II

	Sum of squares	d.f.	Mean square	F	Sig.
Between groups	264.276	3	88.092	20.129	0.000
Within groups	323.854	74	4.376		
Total	588.130	77			

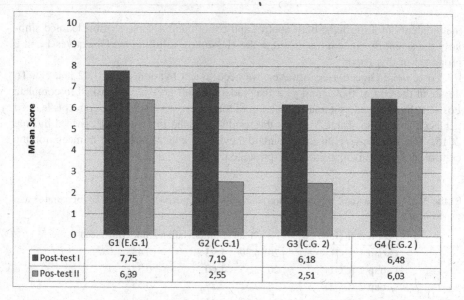

	G1 (E.G.1)	G2 (C.G.1)	G3 (C.G. 2)	G4 (E.G.2)
■ Post-test I	7,75	7,19	6,18	6,48
▦ Pos-test II	6,39	2,55	2,51	6,03

Fig. 2. Comparison of the mean scores of the experimental groups (G1 and G4) and the control groups (G2 and G3) in Post-test I and II

The comparison of the results between Post-test I and Post-test II in different groups allow us to accept the other hypotheses of this research, H2 *("Traditional teaching facilitates rote learning of scientific concepts, which are easily forgotten over time")* and H3 *("Concept maps facilitate long-term, meaningful learning in primary students")*. These results make clear that the contents instructed during the traditional methodology are forgotten over time, but this does not happen in the groups who worked with concept maps. Therefore, we consider it necessary to think about the way the delivery of content is carried out in many schools, with the aim of trying to promote the use of innovative methodologies that are useful to retain over time the content explained, promoting a meaningful learning in students.

4   Conclusions

The above results indicate that students in the experimental groups, who worked with a knowledge model based on concept maps, have assimilated knowledge in a satisfactory manner, with a lasting learning over time. However, students in the control groups have forgotten over time the contents learned with the traditional methodology. This means that the learning of content through the traditional methodology has been short-term and probably rote. We believe that these results are evidence of the educational validity of concept maps when carrying out science teaching/learning interventions at the stage of primary education. These results are consistent with the previous works indicated at the beginning of this paper. We believe it is necessary to supplement those teaching methodologies that are only limited to simply providing content using always the same materials, without being reinforced with other activities or other methodological resources. We could say that one of the reasons that lead to forgot the theoretical contents of science is how teachers teach them. Students tend to forget, so it is necessary that the models of teaching and learning science at early ages focus additionally on aspects related to motivation and interest in the field. This could be achieved by complementing these traditional methodologies with innovative and appealing activities for students such as, for example, knowledge models made with concept maps and virtual resources. Thus, an authentic learning can be achieved, that is, a long-term learning not easily forgotten. The teacher didactic strategy must be connected with the previous ideas of students and the information must be presented in a consistent and structured way, firmly building concepts, interconnecting them with each other in the form of knowledge models. This work is therefore a small step that strengthens the educational value of concept maps to achieve meaningful learning of scientific concepts, to achieve the acquisition of scientific literacy from early age.

Acknowledgements. The authors are grateful for the funding received for this research to the Regional Government of Extremadura and the European Regional Development Fund (Grant GR15009), and to the Ministry of Economy and Competitiveness of Spain (Project EDU2012-34140).

References

1. Campanario, J.M., Moya, A.: How to teach science? Main trends and proposals. Ens. Cienc. **17**(2), 179–192 (1999). (in Spanish)
2. Linder, C.: A challenge to conceptual change. Sci. Educ. **77**, 293–300 (1993)
3. Fensham, P.J.: Beyond knowledge: other scientific qualities as outcomes for school science education. In: Janiuk, R.M., Samonek-Miciuk, E. (eds.) Science and Technology Education for a Diverse World - Dilemmas, Needs and Partnerships. Maria Curie-Skłodowska University Press, Lublin (2004)
4. Vázquez, A., Manassero, M.A.: The decline in attitudes toward science of boys and girls in compulsory education. Cienc. Educ. **17**(2), 249–268 (2011). (in Spanish)
5. Mellado, V., Borrachero, A.B., Brígido, M., Melo, L.V., Dávila, M.A., Cañada, F., Conde, M.C., Costillo, E., Cubero, J., Esteban, R., Martínez, G., Ruíz, C., Sánchez, J., Garritz, A., Mellado, L., Vázquez, B., Jiménez, R., Bermejo, M.L.: Emotions in the teaching of science. Ens. Cienc. **32**, 11–36 (2014). (in Spanish)
6. Jenkins, E.W.: The student voice and school science education. St. Sci. Educ. **42**, 49–88 (2006)
7. OECD: Evolution of student interest in science and technology studies. Policy report. OECD, Paris (2006)

8. Vázquez, A., Manassero, M.A.: The Relevance of Science Education. Universitat de les Illes Balears, Palma de Mallorca (2007). (in Spanish)
9. Gil, D.: Relations between school knowledge and scientific knowledge. Invest. Esc. **23**, 17–32 (1994). (in Spanish)
10. González-Dávila, M., López Ramos, C., Sánchez Robles, S., De Agüero Ormaza, A.G., Arlanzón Lázaro, V.: Didactic Approach to the Study of Nature. La Muralla, Madrid (1998). (in Spanish)
11. Hodson, D.: Towards a more critical approach on laboratory work. Ens. Cienc. **12**, 299–313 (1994). (in Spanish)
12. Diego-Rasilla, F.J.: Action research as a means to innovate in the experimental sciences. Pulso **30**, 103–118 (2007). (in Spanish)
13. Campanario, J.M.: Using citation classics to study the incidence of serendipity in scientific discovery. Scientometrics **37**, 3–24 (1996)
14. Lenox, R.S.: Education for the serendipitous discovery. J. Chem. Educ. **62**, 283–285 (1985)
15. Furió, C., Guisasola, J.: Alternative ideas and learning difficulties in electrostatics. Selection of questions developed for the detection and handling. Ens. Cienc. **17**(3), 441–452 (1999). (in Spanish)
16. Torres, M.I.: Traditional teaching of science vs new educational trends. Educare **14**(1), 131–142 (2010). (in Spanish)
17. Novak, J.D.: Meaningful learning: the essential factor for conceptual change in limited or inappropriate propositional hierarchies (LIPHs) leading to empowerment of learners. Sci. Educ. **86**(4), 548–571 (2002)
18. Ausubel, D.P.: Educational Psychology: A Cognitive View. Holt, Rinehart & Winston, New York (1968)
19. González, F.M., Novak, J.D.: Meaningful Learning. Techniques and Applications. Ediciones Pedagógicas, Madrid (1996). (in Spanish)
20. Coll, C.: School Learning and Knowledge Building. Paidós, Madrid (1990). (in Spanish)
21. Novak, J.D., Gowin, D.B.: Learning How to Learn. Cambridge University Press, New York (1984)
22. Lara, J., Lara, L.: Resources for meaningful learning. Ens. Cienc. **22**, 341–368 (2004). (in Spanish)
23. Cañas, A.J., Ford, K.M., Coffey, J., Reichherzer, T., Carff, R., Shamma, D., Breedy, M.: Tools to build and share knowledge models based on concept maps. Rev. Inform. Educ. **13** (2), 145–158 (2000). (in Spanish)
24. Nesbit, J.C., Olusola, O.: Learning with concept and knowledge maps: a meta-analysis. Rev. Educ. Res. **76**(3), 413–448 (2006)
25. Novak, J.D.: Learning, Creating, and Using Knowledge: Concept Maps as Facilitative Tools in Schools and Corporations. Lawrence Erlbaum Associates, Mahweh (1998)
26. Álvarez, M., Risco, V.: Concept maps and Vee diagrams: a visual representation of children's thinking. In: AERA Annual Meeting, Washington (1987)
27. Stewart, J., Van Kirk, J., Rowell, R.: Concept maps: a tool for use in biology teaching. Am. Biol. Teach. **41**(3), 171–175 (1979)
28. Fraser, K., Edwards, J.: The effects of training in concept mapping on student achievement in traditional classroom tests. Res. Sci. Educ. **15**, 158–165 (1985)
29. Martínez, G., Pérez, Á.L., Suero, M.I., Pardo, P.J.: The Effectiveness of concept maps in teaching physics concepts applied to engineering education: experimental comparison of the amount of learning achieved with and without concept maps. J. Sci. Educ. Technol. **22**(2), 204–214 (2013)

30. Martínez, G., Pérez, Á.L., Suero, M.I., Pardo, P.J., Naranjo, F.L.: Using concept maps to create reasoning models to teach thinking: an application for solving Kinematics problems. Knowl. Manage. E-Learn. **7**(1), 162–178 (2015)

31. Ontoria, A., Ballesteros, A., Cuevas, C., Giraldo, L., Martín, I., Molina, A., Rodríguez, A., Vélez, U.: Concept Maps. A Learning Technique. Narcea, Madrid (1995). (in Spanish)

32. Fuata'i, K.A.: Use of Vee Maps and Concept Maps in the Learning of Form Five Mathematics in Samoa College Western Samoa. Corriell University, Ithaca (1985)

33. Martínez, G., Naranjo, F.L., Pérez, A.L., Suero, M.I., Pardo, P.J.: Comparative study of the effectiveness of some learning environments: hyper-realistic virtual simulations, traditional schematic simulations and traditional laboratory. Phys Rev Spec Top-Phys Educ. Res. **7**(2), 1–12 (2011). Article ID: 020111

34. González, F.M.: Novakian concept maps as tools for researching in didactics of the experimental sciences. Ens. Cienc. **10**(2), 148–158 (1992). (in Spanish)

Eliciting, Representing, and Evaluating Adult Knowledge: A Model for Organizational Use of Concept Mapping and Concept Maps

Brian Moon[1(✉)], Charles Johnston[1], Sana Rizvi[1], and Carl Dister[2]

[1] Perigean Technologies LLC, Spotsylvania, VA, USA
{Brian,Chip,Sana}@perigeantechnologies.com
[2] ReliabilityFirst Corporation, Independence, OH, USA
Carl.Dister@rfirst.org

Abstract. After nearly two decades of knowledge preservation activity, relatively little work has explored the organizational use of Concept Maps elicited from experts. This paper describes an attempt to get back to the roots of Concept Mapping as a means of both representing and evaluating knowledge, in the context of professional work. It describes a pilot project in which the authors used Concept Mapping to elicit and represent knowledge from domain experts, then demonstrated the use of Concept Maps for assessing the mental models of other professionals. The authors introduce Sero! – a prototype Concept Map-based learning assessment platform, and a general model for the organizational use of Concept Mapping and Concept Maps.

1 Introduction

"Out of the necessity to find a better way to represent children's conceptual understanding emerged the idea of representing children's knowledge in the form of a concept map... One of the powerful uses of concept maps is not only as a learning tool but also as an evaluation tool" [1].

Since the emergence of Concept Mapping, applications of the technique and its artifacts have expanded far beyond representing "children's knowledge". Indeed, professional applications of Concept Mapping have extended the technique into realms that stretch the notion of knowledge representation [2]. A primary use with adults has been the elicitation and representation of adults' knowledge, particularly for the purpose of preservation in the face of an aging workforce [3]. After nearly two decades of knowledge preservation activity, relatively little work has explored the organizational use of Concept Maps elicited from experts. While some have suggested that such products could be used to accelerate the achievement of expertise [4] and organize knowledge for transfer [5], answering the question, "Now what do we use these?", remains a daunting challenge for professional Concept Mappers [6].

This paper describes an attempt to get back to the roots of Concept Mapping as a means of both representing *and* evaluating knowledge, in the context of professional

A. Cañas et al. (Eds.): CMC 2016, CCIS 635, pp. 66–82, 2016.
DOI: 10.1007/978-3-319-45501-3_6

work. We describe a pilot project in which we used Concept Mapping to elicit and represent knowledge from domain experts, then demonstrated the use of Concept Maps for assessing the mental models of other professionals. For the latter, we introduced Sero! – a prototype Concept Map-based learning assessment software platform. The project produced a model for a general approach for the organizational use of Concept Mapping and Concept Maps.

2 Project Motivation

Globally, human beings are facing serious challenges from demographic imbalances related to aging. In the United States, for example, the number of people age 65+ will more than double, increasing from 13 % of total population in 2010 to 21 % of total in 2050 [7]. Thus, experienced, proficient workers will populate the workforce as they near, then enter, retirement. Their eventual exit sets up the prospect of widespread knowledge loss. DeLong [8] has chronicled four big costs of this trend for organizations: reduced capacity to innovate, threatened ability to pursue growth strategies, increased incidence of errors, and increased number of efficiency losses—and how they can wreak havoc across a variety of industries. Particular segments of the economy will feel these costs more acutely, for example the utilities and power industries. The sheer size of the problem for the utility industry in the U.S.—i.e., as of 2008, 65 % of senior engineers were eligible for retirement within three years—means that some of the costs will be unavoidable.

ReliabilityFirst is one of the eight Federal Energy Regulatory Commission-approved Regional Entities responsible for ensuring the reliability of the North American Bulk-Power System (BPS). Early in the company's formation, a classic regulatory scheme was adopted, to enforce adherence to grid reliability and cybersecurity standards and requirements. As time progressed, the regulatory scheme evolved to focus on providing education and assistance to the power industry to move beyond simply compliance into reliability and security "beyond the standards." This evolution, coupled with the aging of the electric industry workforce, highlighted the need to mitigate the risk of losing internal expert knowledge. Therefore, ReliabilityFirst retained Perigean Technologies in 2015 for a pilot project demonstrating knowledge elicitation (KE), including Applied Concept Mapping, for the preservation of expert knowledge.

2.1 Knowledge Elicitation as a Means of Preservation

Knowledge elicitation (KE) is the process of scaffolding the expression of knowledge, wisdom and knowhow through in-depth interviews and observations about cognitive events, structures, or models [9]. As suggested by the Electric Power Research Institute, "there is no right or wrong knowledge elicitation method or set of methods. The choice depends on a range of considerations, some of which may not come into play until knowledge elicitation is under way" [10]. Applied Concept Mapping has been employed extensively throughout the U.S. utilities industry as a preferred knowledge elicitation method, primarily due to its flexibility and efficiency [11–13].

2.2 Assessment as a Means to Reintroduce Expertise

Learning assessment in adult workplaces is an understudied phenomenon [14]. Several reasons underlie the lack of attention, not the least of which is the organizational tension between learning and getting the job done [15]. It is not entirely clear how prevalent the formal assessment of learning is, though the use of cognitive assessments for the purposes of selection has been growing along with the rise of other psychological assessments of candidate recruits [16]. Such assessments are typically focused on generalized knowledge and capabilities, rather than specific knowledge domains.

From what is known, learning assessment is carried out in formal and informal ways, with the latter comprising methods such as providing on-the-spot feedback following task performances, which may not even be recognized as an assessment activity [15]. Where it is formalized, it is often employed for the purpose of granting some form of certification, reviewing performance, or enforcing accountability. The "view that the purpose of assessment is to support current learning and foster further learning has not tended to be the primary purpose of assessment in relation to industry training" [17]. Despite being a *sine qua non* to the development of expertise [18], "[a]ssessment is often treated as separate from learning when it should be considered a part of learning" [19].

Yet, the "demand for ongoing learning has implications for workplace assessment" [20]. These include: who creates and proctors the assessment; when and why it might be given; and how results might be used. In workplace settings, supervisors, mentors, and/or trainers may take on the role of assessor and may or may not be responsible for the creation of the assessment. Also, the traditional boundaries between formative and summative assessment are looser than in educational settings, which opens the door for pragmatic learning assessment approaches. "Sometimes summative forms of assessment can be used in formative ways—for example, written comments on tests or discussion of test results. The discussion occurs in order to further the learner's understanding of what (the test showed that) they do and do not know. Without that discussion, the learner simply receives a judgement with no explanations and is unlikely to learn further from that judgement on its own" [21].

The relative openness of adult workplace learning assessment environment offers an opportunity to use novel assessment practices as a means to reintroduce expert-derived Concept Maps created through knowledge elicitation back into the organization. Such a program can draw on the assessment approaches that have been used with children, and faces many of the same and some additional new challenges.

3 Sero! – Learning Assessment Platform Using Concept Maps

Since 2012, the authors from Perigean Technologies LLC have been developing a software platform to enable learning assessment using Concept Maps. The project has been built upon prior lessons learned in developing a Concept Mapping game (also called Sero!) [22] that stemmed from traditional motivations for game development – i.e., fun. The learning assessment version of Sero! grew out of motivations aligned more closely with traditional applications of Concept Mapping.

3.1 Motivations

Meaningful diagrams have for decades shown to be highly diagnostic of how learners organize and represent knowledge across the novice to expert spectrum [23, 24]. In an early example, Cooke and Schvaneveldt [25] demonstrated how similar meaningful diagrams (Pathfinder networks) revealed differences in memory structures and conceptual representations for naïve, novice, intermediate and advanced computer programmers. The U.S. Department of Education calls for Cmapping as one of the types of Interactive Computer Tasks that is "highly recommended" [26, 27] for inclusion in every National Assessment of Educational Progress (NAEP) Science Assessment at the 8th and 12th grade levels [28].

Adult Learner Assessment using Concept Maps. Compared to the volumes of research in K-12 and higher education environments, relatively little work has explored Concept Maps for use in adult workplace assessment, learning and training contexts. Stevens [29] used pre-drawn fill-in Cmaps for assessing adult learning in a 40-hour training course called Hazardous Waste Operations and Emergency Response, which was taught to personnel working with hazardous waste and offered in various sites across the U.S. The Cmapping method was shown to have higher reliability than the control (multiple-choice test), and both were positively and moderately correlated in post-test use. In the context of a Counter-Improvised Explosive Device (IED) training solution evaluation, Moon et al. [30] demonstrated that Cmaps provided an efficient means to model levels (novice, intermediate, and expert) of U.S. Marine Corps personnel's Counter-IED knowledge and skills. Knowledge and skill models were represented in Cmaps, which enabled both quantitative and qualitative analysis of the differences across groups. Once modeled as Cmaps, the same descriptions of expert knowledge were used to assess learning using Multiple-Choice Concept Maps. When presented to learners in a pre/post-intervention assessment context, clear learning performance differences were discovered.

More recently, Knollmann-Ritschel and Durning [31] explored the use of Cmap-based assessment for team-based learning in the context of military medical instruction. To assess understanding of content across a learning fundamentals module at the Uniformed Services University of the Health Sciences, the researchers replaced an individual assessment using multiple-choice questions with Cmaps, and combined the assessment with a group assessment and application exercise wherein teams created

Cmaps. Learner performance and feedback from faculty and learners support the use of Cmaps in team-based learning. They also demonstrated the benefit of Cmapping in knowledge acquisition, organization of prior and new knowledge, and synthesis of that knowledge across disciplines.

Assessment Approaches and Challenges. Strautmane [32] offered a comprehensive review of the variety of assessment tasks. One method involves starting a map from scratch, and asking the learner to generate and organize all of the content (i.e., concepts, links, linking phrases, arrowheads, propositions). This is a highly unconstrained task that is notoriously difficult to analyze. Additional constraints can be placed upon the task, and these constraints also simplify the process of analyzing the learner responses. Learners can be provided a skeleton map with some content provided and some content missing, and then required to fill-in and/or organize the content by creating linking lines. This approach is referred to as a generate-and-fill-in (GAFI), and it can be performed with or without any diagram organizing tasks – i.e., spatial organization, arrowhead additions. A skeleton map can also be provided, along with a set of content for the learner to use to fill-in the rest of the map. This approach is called select-and-fill-in (SAFI), and it also does not require organizing tasks. The SAFI task can be made more complex by presenting distractor content. A Multiple-Choice Cmap (MCCM) provides all of the content in the map but requires learners to select content from provided choices, which can include distractors that can be drawn from within the same Cmap or other sources [30, 33].

There are numerous challenges to implementing a Concept Map-based assessment system. Given the proliferation of techniques available, it is no surprise that assessors and learner understanding of Cmaps and their purpose can also hinder successful implementation, an issue that has been seen repeatedly in partial implementations [34–36]. Guidance for selecting which Cmap-based assessment technique(s) to use for which learning purpose is scarce in the literature. Ruiz-Primo offers some guidance to assessors: "in order to better determine the cognitive demands evoked by different mapping techniques, it is important to consider not only what is provided, but also the extent/amount of what is provided, the significance of what is provided, and what is required from the examinees" [37].

With regard to scoring, a wide range of rubrics and methods has been explored. They range from subjective measures (e.g., number and appropriate inclusion/exclusion of concepts and propositions, structure of the map) that are typically used with the more unconstrained tasks [38], to objective measures of correctness that are feasible with more constrained tasks. McClure and colleagues [35] compared holistic, relational and structural scoring methods without and with the use of a master map unveiling a high reliability for the latter. While challenges in scoring reliability were cited early in the research [39], it has been broadly demonstrated that methods that compare the learners' performance against a master/criterion/reference/expert map are the most valid and reliable method for scoring Cmap tests [40].

Technology Gap. The time and labor required to manually set-up an assessment, analyze the maps, or transcribe their content for analysis, can be considerable [41]. Above all else, *this is the challenge that has bedeviled broadscale deployment of Concept Map-based assessment.* Indeed, this challenge is only magnified in adult workplace learning environments. Several prototype software tools have demonstrated rudimentary, prototype capabilities to compare and assess Cmaps for the purposes of learning assessment [42]. Yet, as Strautmane has stated, *"there is still a need for a [Cmap]-based knowledge assessment system that could perform the assessment automatically with a little intervention by the [instructor]"* (emphasis added, [43]). Our aim with Sero! is to attempt to meet the challenges described above with a software tool that enables learning assessment using Concept Maps derived from domain experts.

3.2   Software Description

Sero! is a browser-based application hosted in the cloud that currently enables basic functionality for designing, distributing, and analyzing two Cmap-based assessment tasks (i.e., GAFI and MCCM). A notional view of the current Sero! architecture is shown in Fig. 1.

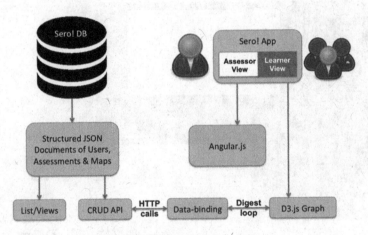

Fig. 1. Sero! notional architecture.

The Sero! research and development database (DB) utilizes a CouchDB cloud repository to store structured JSON documents that represent users, assessments, and Cmaps. The client-side browser application renders the app as a single HTML page using Angular.js and the D3.js rendering library to create force-directed graphs based on Cmap data. The DB creates aggregate views and indexes that provide metrics about assessment data to the application. CouchDB provides a RESTful API to add/edit/render documents and views.

In Sero! the two user types are Assessor and Learner; Assessors create assessments then proctor them to a class of Learners. Every user regardless of type will interact with

Cmaps in different stages of completion by, for example, manipulating the position of the nodes or changing the words inside the nodes to create different propositions. This functionality is the heart of the application, first used by the Assessor to create new assessments, then by the Learners to complete the assessments, and again by the Assessor to provide feedback on finished assessments. Manipulation of the graph in the graphical user interface (GUI) updates the local JSON representation of the Cmap. This document is loaded to CouchDB via web services when the assessment is first created by the Assessor and then updated when completed by a Learner.

To date, our internal software engineering efforts have focused primarily on architecture development and basic GUI. Sero! currently provides basic mechanisms for conducting two types of Cmap-based assessment. Figure 2 shows the Sero! GUI from the learner and assessor views. In the assessor view (left side of the figure), assessors can select which content will be assessed, assign an assessment type (GAFI or MCCM), and generate distractors (for the MCCM). In the learner view (right side of the figure), the concepts, linking phrases, and propositions in yellow are items that need to be addressed by the learner, either by filling in content (i.e., GAFI method) —which requires recall—or selecting from alternatives (i.e., MCCM)—which requires recognition.

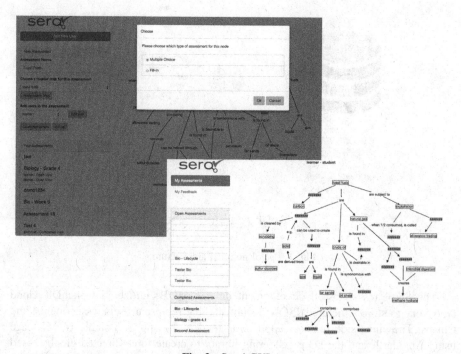

Fig. 2. Sero! GUI.

Having described Sero! and the motivations underlying its development, we now turn to our demonstration project, which attempted an end-to-end implementation of a model for the organizational use of Concept Mapping and Concept Maps.

4 Demonstration: Knowledge Elicitation Activity

The focus of the knowledge elicitation activities was to preserve any potential high level knowledge from the three chosen experts, and to assess the organizational use of knowledge elicitation and transfer methods.

4.1 Process

Our KE process followed a modified version of the recommended Cmapping technique. In the described technique, which is shown in Table 1:

Table 1. Comparing recommended and modified techniques for Concept Mapping knowledge elicitation

Recommended	Executed with SME?	Modified	Executed with SME?
Step 1: Select the Domain and Focus	Yes	Step 1: Select the Domain and Focus	Typically, though both may be provided prior to the KE
Step 2: Set up the "Parking Lot" and Arrange the Concepts	Yes	Step 2: Set up the "Parking Lot" and Arrange the Concepts – *while audio recording*	Yes
Step 3: Begin to Link the Concepts	Yes	Step 3: Link the Concepts, Refine the Concept Map, Look for New Relations and Cross-Links, and Further Refine the Concept Map, Build the Knowledge Model, if appropriate	No
Step 4: Refine the Concept Map	Yes	Step 4: SME review of Concept Map(s)	Possibly, or SME reviews alone
Step 5: Look for New Relations and Cross-Links, and Further Refine the Concept Map	Yes		
Step 6: Build the Knowledge Model	No		

one researcher acts as a facilitator and provides support in the form of suggestions and probe questions, while the other acts as the mapper and captures the participant's statements in the Concept Map, which is projected on a screen for all to see. The mapper needs to be proficient at quickly and accurately conducting the mapping work on the fly. This includes a facility for glancing to and from the computer monitor and the projector screen to follow the facilitator's guidance and the participant's statements [44].

In our demonstration, as in many KE sessions the lead author has executed, the roles of facilitator and mapper are executed by a single facilitator/mapper – i.e., elicitor. The most common reason for this modification is funding, as one knowledge elicitor is cheaper than two. Having a single elicitor introduces many challenges and advantages. The main challenge involves maintaining continuous engagement with the SME while also building the map. The main advantage is the removal of coordination activities between facilitator and mapper.

The main challenge is very difficult to reconcile and is aggravated by other factors. In the experience of the lead author, many SMEs prefer engaging directly with the facilitator/mapper, ignoring the projected, emerging Concept Map altogether. Concept Mapping is often new to them, and given that they are sharing their intimate knowledge, having a conversation may feel much more comfortable than building a diagram. In some cases, projecting the Concept Map for all to see is not feasible.

For these reasons, the lead author's technique for Concept Mapping KE *as a single facilitator/mapper* typically proceeds as shown in Table 1, which also contrasts the modifications of the recommended technique. Of course, with either technique, a great deal of experience with KE and Concept Mapping is required [45].

The main contrast is the collapsing of steps 3–6 into a single step 3, which is executed by the mapper *after* the KE session. The mapper uses the parking lot arranged concepts captured during the session, linking them together based on the recorded statements from the SME. The draft Concept Map(s) are then provided back to the SME for review, which can be done in a format most comfortable for the SME.

We have not conducted a formal comparison of the modified technique with the recommended technique. We suspect the modified technique would yield greater volume, as the amount of discussion possible without the burden of map-making during the KE session is likely greater. We also suspect that the modified technique offers some efficiency gains – i.e., measured by propositions per minute [46] – especially if the audio recording is played back at a faster rate than the original recording. Efficiency comparisons would also need to include the time necessary for iterative review. In our demonstration, we received different amounts of feedback from our SMEs. One provided only a few minor changes, while another suggested major restructuring.

4.2   Validation Check

For an additional validation check of the elicited knowledge, we compared the Concept Maps we created to a previously developed report — 2015 RF Regional Risk Assessment (RRA; [47]) — that focused on topics that were relevant to the knowledge we elicited. The validation was fruitful, and helped to cross-check the data-driven, quantitative RRA report with the qualitative results of the experts in the Concept Maps, helping to illuminate to potential areas to research in the 2016 assessment.

5   Demonstration: Concept Map Products

Our KE process yielded two Concept Maps per SME. One Concept Map described the specific domain – i.e., cybersecurity, generation, transmission – and the second described aspects of the SMEs' jobs and tasks – i.e., how they performed analysis and outreach. In hindsight, it is not surprising that as the SMEs described the outcomes of their work, they quickly got into the macrocognitive challenges involved in producing the outcomes [48]. While some of these aspects were described throughout the KE session, the mapper was able to organize the content into distinct Concept Maps after the sessions. Sample, sanitized Concept Maps are shown in the next sections. They were created using CmapTools [49] Figs. 3, 4 and 5.

5.1   Risk Maps

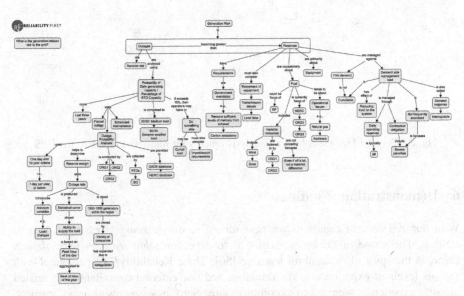

Fig. 3. Concept Map describing generation risks to the BPS

5.2   Job and Task Maps

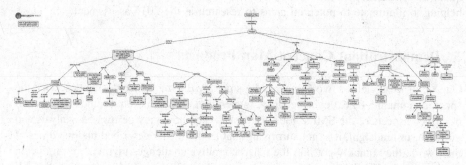

Fig. 4. Concept Map describing an analysis process for generation risk to the BPS

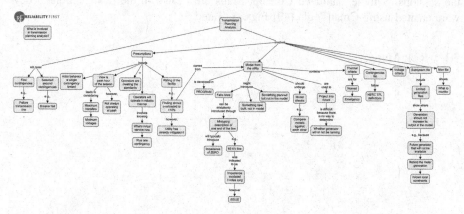

Fig. 5. Concept Map describing an analysis process for transmission risk to the BPS

6   Demonstration: Findings

With our KE content captured, we next turned to our learning assessment demonstration. The scope of the assessment was to *ascertain what learners may already know*, in the spirit of meaningful learning [50]. Three Reliability*First* personnel with various levels of experience in the domains, and one external consultant with related industry experience, were asked to complete three Sero! assessments as proxy learners.

6.1   Assessment Set up

The first step in setting up the assessments was bringing the CmapTools-created Concept Maps into Sero!. The mechanics for doing so were straightforward – export propositions as text, save as a.csv file, import into Sero!. The prototype version of Sero! used for the demonstration rendered the Concept Map, and allowed for basic spatial manipulation. We did not import the Concept Maps in total. While there are certainly view-ability constraints on rendering the Concept Maps given their sizes, there are likely also constraints on size with regard to assessment. We opted to use Concept Maps with approximately 25 to 35 elements (concepts and linking phrases), as these seemed manageable for any given assessment. This often required finding reasonable breaking points within the larger Concept Maps, which in some cases required repeating content across assessments.

The next step involved determining which sections of the Concept Maps were amenable to assessment. There were several considerations for making the determination. Sero! can currently enable GAFI and MCCM assessment items. For more elaborate concepts or linking phrases, it was not reasonable to expect a learner to generate matching content. But while elaborate concepts and linking phrases were appropriate for MCCM items, it was necessary to determine what sorts of distractor content was appropriate in order to make selection challenging. Here we drew on other content within the map where the item required several distractors. For MCCM items at the linking phrases, we also looked for linking phrases whose opposites or scales could be offered for selection – e.g., increases/decreases, every 4/30/60 s. We also considered the relative importance of concepts and linking phrases in the larger context of the Concept Map. Concepts and linking phrases that had multiple outgoing and/or incoming connectors were deemed high priority for assessment. Linking phrases that were central to demonstrating understanding of the domain were also deemed valuable for assessment. We frequently used fans [51] as a queue for GAFI items, as these exercise recall skills that can reasonably be thought to also assess conceptual organization.

6.2   Assessment Taking

Our participants were provided access to their three assessments via the Internet. Figure 6 shows the user interaction for a GAFI item (left side of the figure) and for a MCCM item (right side of the figure) for one of the transmission assessment Concept Maps.

6.3   Scoring

The prototype version of Sero! enabled scoring correct answers for the MCCM items, and a simple match for GAFI items. Results were accessible in the assessor role, but not available automatically to the learner role. We manually produced result sets for review by the participants by overlaying the assessment items (in yellow highlight) with the comparative results, green for correct/match and red for incorrect/mismatch, as shown in Fig. 7. In this example, three items did not match, and one did.

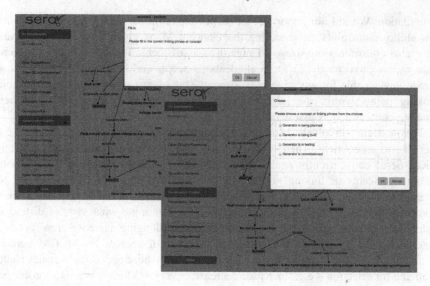

Fig. 6. Concept Map describing an analysis process for transmission risk to the BPS

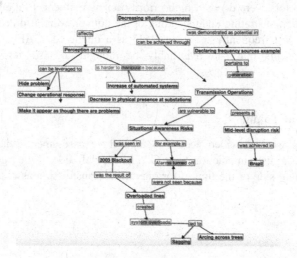

Fig. 7. Sero! results

6.4 Participant Feedback on Process

Our participants provided feedback on the process. All reported having enjoyed the process and being challenged by the assessment task. Regarding the individual assessment items, they found several points of disagreement, particularly with the GAFI items. Their objections were warranted, given the immaturity of the prototype Sero!'s basic matching algorithm.

Most importantly, all indicated that working through the Concept Maps revealed gaps in their mental models of the domains. Interestingly, because the assessment context was not controlled, they all reported executing information search strategies to seek answers for the assessment – strongly suggesting the capacity for Sero! assessments to prompt self-learning activities.

7 Future Directions

Our project will continue along two pathways. We will continue to conduct KE with at-risk Reliability*First* personnel. As of this writing, target topics and personnel are being selected.

We will also advance our development of Sero! through involvement in the U.S. Government's Advanced Distributed Learning (ADL) Initiative (www.adlnet.gov). ADL is developing a Training and Learning Architecture (TLA), a set of standardized Web service specifications and Open Source Software designed to create a rich environment for connected training and learning – i.e., an intelligent learning ecosystem. The authors from Perigean Technologies LLC will be advancing Sero!'s design and development to provide the TLA with a deep learning assessment capability to inform on learner progress and to prime learning content, toward enabling a personalized learning environment for adults. Advancements will include maturing Sero!'s GUI, comparison algorithms, mechanisms for cumulating and aggregating results, and integrating with the TLA.

8 Summary

This paper has demonstrated a general approach for organizational use of Concept Mapping and Concept Maps. Beginning with knowledge elicitation and continuing through learning assessment, our approach holds great opportunity to reduce the risks of organizational knowledge loss, and to create new opportunities for leveraging this knowledge for improved risk management and employee engagement. Achieving such benefits requires advances in techniques and software, which we have offered here.

Acknowledgements. Thanks to Reliability*First* for supporting this effort, and the Reliability*First* experts and their managers for making time available for our demonstration.

References

1. Novak, J.D., Cañas, A.J.: The Theory Underlying Concept Maps and How to Construct and Use Them. Institute for Human and Machine Cognition, Pensacola (2008)
2. Moon, B., Hoffman, R.R., Novak, J.D., Cañas, A.J. (eds.): Applied Concept Mapping: Capturing, Analyzing, and Organizing Knowledge. CRC Press, New York (2011)
3. Moon, B., Hoffman, R.R., Ziebell, D.: How did you do that. Electr. Perspect. **34**(1), 20–29 (2009)

4. Ziebell, D., Hoffman, R.R., Feltovich, P., Klein, G., Fiore, S., Moon, B.: Accelerating the Achievement of Mission-Critical Expertise: A Research Roadmap. EPRI, Palo Alto (2008)
5. Schafermeyer, R.G., Hoffman, R.R.: Using knowledge libraries to transfer expert knowledge. IEEE Intell. Syst. **31**(2), 89–93 (2016)
6. Moon, B.M., Baxter, H.C., Klein, G.: Expertise management: challenges for adopting naturalistic decision making as a knowledge management paradigm. McLean (2015)
7. Hayutin, A., Beals, M., Borges, E.: The Aging us Workforce: A Chartbook of Demographic Shifts, vol. 7. Stanford Center on Longevity, Stanford (2013). http://library.constantcontact.com/download/get/file/1102783429573-323/The+Aging+US+Workforce
8. DeLong, D.W.: Lost Knowledge: Confronting the Threat of an Aging Workforce. Oxford University Press, New York (2004)
9. Crandall, B., Klein, G.A., Hoffman, R.R.: Working Minds: A Practitioner's Guide to Cognitive Task Analysis. MIT Press, Cambridge (2006)
10. Electric Power Research Institute: Guidelines for Capturing Valuable Undocumented Knowledge from Energy Industry Personnel, Palo Alto (2002)
11. Kelley, M., Sass, M., Moon, B.: Maturity of a nuclear-related knowledge management solution. In: Annual Meeting of the American Nuclear Society (2013)
12. Moon, B., Kelley, M.: Lessons learned in knowledge elicitation with nuclear experts. In: 7th International Topical Meeting on Nuclear Plant Instrumentation, Control and Human Machine Interface Technologies, Las Vegas (2010)
13. Hoffman, R., Moon, B.: Knowledge capture for the utilities. In: 7th International Topical Meeting on Nuclear Plant Instrumentation, Control and Human Machine Interface Technologies (2010)
14. Vaughan, K.: Workplace Learning: A Literature Review. Competenz, Auckland (2008)
15. Vaughan, K., Cameron, M.: Assessment of Learning in the Workplace: A Background Paper. Industry Training Federation, Wellington (2009)
16. Weber, L.: Today's personality tests raise the bar for job seekers. Wall Str. J. (2015)
17. Bound, H., Lin, M.: Singapore Workforce Skills Qualifications (WSQ), Workplace Learning and Assessment (Stage I), p. 26. Institute of Adult Learning, Singapore (2010)
18. Hoffman, R.R., Ward, P., Feltovich, P.J., DiBello, L., Fiore, S.M., Andrews, D.H.: Accelerated Expertise: Training for High Proficiency in a Complex World. Psychology Press, New York (2013)
19. Bound, H., Lin, M.: Singapore Workforce Skills Qualifications (WSQ), Workplace Learning and Assessment (Stage I), p. 25. Institute of Adult Learning, Singapore (2010)
20. Vaughan, K., Cameron, M.: Assessment of Learning in the Workplace: A Background Paper, p. 5. Industry Training Federation, Wellington (2009)
21. Vaughan, K., Cameron, M.: Assessment of Learning in the Workplace: A Background Paper, p. 9. Industry Training Federation, New Zealand, Wellington (2009)
22. Moon, B., Johnston, C., Tuxbury, B., Hoffman, R.R., Guarino, S., Jarvis, R., Young, D., Romero, V.: Sero!: evaluating a concept mapping game for its potential to improve cognitive capabilities. In: Proceedings of the Sixth International Conference on Concept Mapping, Sao Paulo (2014)
23. Ruiz-Primo, M.A., Shavelson, R.R.: Problems and issues in the use of concept maps in science assessment. J. Res. Sci. Teach. **33**(6), 569–600 (1996). Wiley, Hoboken
24. Shavelson, R.J., Ruiz-Primo, M.A.: On the Psychometrics of Assessing Science Understanding. Assessing Science Understanding, pp. 303–341. Academic Press, Cambridge (2000)
25. Cooke, N.J., Schvaneveldt, R.W.: Effects of computer programming experience on network representations of abstract programming concepts. Int. J. Man-Mach. Stud. **29**(4), 407–427 (1988). Elsevier Ltd, Houston

26. WestEd, Council of Chief State Officers: Science Framework for the 2009/2011, p. 110. NAEP (2010)
27. WestEd, CCSO: Science Assessment and Item Specifications for the 2009, p. 171. NAEP (2007)
28. National Assessment Governing Board: Science Framework for the 2015 NAEP (2015)
29. Stevens, P.A.: Using concept maps for assessing adult learners in training situations. Ph.D. dissertation, Harvard, Cambridge
30. Moon, B., Ross, K., Phillips, J.: Cmap-based assessment for adult learners. In: Proceedings of the Fourth International Conference on Concept Mapping, Chile (2010)
31. Knollmann-Ritschel, B.E.C., Durning, S.J.: Using concept maps in a modified team-based learning exercise. Mil. Med. **180**(4 Suppl.), 64–70 (2015). The Society of the Federal Health Professionals, Bethesda
32. Strautmane, M.: Cmap-based knowledge assessment tasks and their scoring criteria: an overview. In: Proceedings of the Fifth International Conference on Concept Mapping, Valletta (2012)
33. Sas, J.C.: The Multiple-Choice Concept Map (MCCM): An Interactive Computer-Cased Assessment Method. Digital Scholarship@UNLV, Las Vegas (2010)
34. Ayala, C.C., Shavelson, R.J., Ruiz-Primo, M.A., Brandon, P.R., Yin, Y., Furtak, E.M., Young, D.B., Tomita, M.K.: From formal embedded assessments to reflective lessons: the development of formative assessment studies. Appl. Measur. Educ. **21**(4), 315–334 (2008)
35. McClure, J.R., Sonak, B., Suen, H.K.: Concept map assessment of classroom learning: reliability, validity, and logistical practicality. J. Res. Sci. Teach. **36**(4), 475–492 (1999)
36. Schau, C., Mattern, N., Weber, R.W.: Use of fill-in concept maps to assess middle school students' connected understanding of science. Chicago (1997)
37. Ruiz-Primo, M.A.: Examining concept maps as an assessment tool. In: Proceedings of the Fist International Conference on Concept Mapping, Universidad Pública de Navarra, Pamplona, pp. 555–563 (2004)
38. Besterfield-Sacre, M., Gerchak, J., Lyons, M.R., Shuman, L.J., Wolfe, J.: Scoring concept maps: an integrated rubric for assessing engineering education. J. Eng. Educ. **93**(2), 105–115 (2004). Pennsylvania
39. Ruiz-Primo, M.A., Schultz, S.E., Li, M., Shavelson, R.J.: Comparison of the reliability and validity of scores from two concept-mapping techniques. J. Res. Sci. Teach. **38**(2), 260–278 (2001). Wiley, Hoboken
40. Himangshu, S., Cassata-Widera, A.: Beyond individual classrooms: how valid are concept maps for large scale assessment? In: Proceedings of the 4th International Conference on Concept Mapping, Universidad de Chile, Viña del Mar (2010)
41. Cañas, A.J., Bunch, L., Novak, J.D., Reiska, P.: CmapAnalysis: an extensible concept map analysis tool. J. Educ. Teach. Train. **1**, 36–46 (2013). Universidad de Granada, Granada
42. Liu, J.: The assessment agent system: assessing comprehensive understanding based on concept maps. Ph.D. dissertation, Virginia Polytechnic Institute and State University, Blacksburg (2010)
43. Strautmane, M.: Cmap-based knowledge assessment tasks and their scoring criteria: an overview. In: Proceedings of the 5th International Conference on Concept Mapping, Valletta, Malta (2012)
44. Crandall, B., Klein, G.A., Hoffman, R.R.: Working Minds: A Practitioner's Guide to Cognitive Task Analysis, pp. 55–66. MIT Press, Cambridge (2006)
45. Moon, B., Hoffman, R.R., Eskridge, T., Coffey, J.: Skills in concept mapping. In: Moon, B., Hoffman, R.R., Novak, J.D., Cañas, A.J. (eds.) Applied Concept Mapping: Capturing, Analyzing, and Organizing Knowledge, New York, pp. 23–46 (2011)

46. Hoffman, R.R., Coffey, J.W., Carnot, M.J., Novak, J.D.: An empirical comparison of methods for eliciting and modeling expert knowledge. In: Proceedings of the Human Factors and Ergonomics Society Annual Meeting, vol. 46, no. 3, pp. 482–486. SAGE Publications (2002)
47. ReliabilityFirst: 2015 RF Regional Risk Assessment Report (2015)
48. Lintern, G., Moon, B., Klein, G.A., Hoffman, R.R.: Eliciting and representing the knowledge of the expert practitioner. In: Ericsson, K. et al. (eds.) Cambridge Handbook of Expertise and Expert Performance, 2nd edn., Cambridge (In press)
49. Cañas, A.J., Hill, G., Carff, R., Suri, N., Lott, J., Eskridge, T., Gómez, G., Arroyo, M., Carvajal, R.: CmapTools: a knowledge modeling and sharing environment. concept maps: theory, methodology, technology. In: Proceedings of the First International Conference on Concept Mapping, Pamplona, vol. 1 (2004)
50. Ausubel, D.P.: The Psychology of Meaningful Learning; An Introduction to School Learning, p. vi. Grune and Stratton, New York (1968)
51. Kinchin, I.M: The qualitative analysis of concept maps: some unforeseen consequences and emerging opportunities. In: Keynote Address at the Third International Conference on Concept Mapping, Tallinn (2008)

Enhancing the Value of Active Learning Programs for Students' Knowledge Acquisition by Using the Concept Mapping Method

Priit Reiska[1]([✉]), Aet Möllits[1], and Miia Rannikmäe[2]

[1] Tallinn University, Tallinn, Estonia
{priit.reiska,aet.mollits}@tlu.ee
[2] University of Tartu, Tallinn, Estonia
miia.rannikmae@ut.ee

Abstract. The use of active learning programs in combination with new learning and assessment methods like concept mapping could be lead to the more student oriented learning and teaching. The aim of the study is to evaluate active learning programs by using a Concept Mapping method and to make suggestion for further development of the programs. In the study 414 concept maps from 207 basic school students were collected before and after participation in on of the active learning programs (ALPs). The results showed that active learning programs helped the students to acquire new knowledge and reduce misconceptions. To increase the efficiency of the ALPs it is recommended to increase the duration and also compose one-class multi-day programs.

Keywords: Concept mapping · Active learning program · Assessment · Experiential learning

1 Introduction

The low motivation and unpopularity of learning the natural sciences is a problem in most countries. Despite the fact that the learning process is becoming more exploratory and investigative, there is still a need for methodological diversity to assess learning processes in science. Today's modern biology is composed of many sub-disciplines and therefore it is important to motivate students to learn concepts in real life content, instead of simply memorizing biology concept, definitions or propositional statements.

The use of active learning programs might be one way to overcome the unpopularity of learning of natural sciences. In combination with new learning and assessment methods like concept mapping the learning process could be organized in the way, which is more student oriented and therefore more relevant for them.

The learning outcomes of curricula provides for students' expanded view of scientific world, improved skills to solve everyday life problems and ability to cope with natural and social environment. To achieve these goals, the new assessment methods are needed, that evaluate changes in students' thinking and ability orientate between different (science) subject areas.

© Springer International Publishing Switzerland 2016
A. Cañas et al. (Eds.): CMC 2016, CCIS 635, pp. 83–97, 2016.
DOI: 10.1007/978-3-319-45501-3_7

The aim of the study is to evaluate Tallinn Zoo active learning programs by using a Concept Mapping method and to make suggestion for further development of the programs.

The study has the following research questions:

1. Do students learn during the active learning programs (ALPs) (increase of correct proposition in concept maps)?
2. Do students have less misconceptions after the ALPs (decrease of incorrect proposition)?
3. Are there learning differences between outcomes from different ALPs?

2 Theoretical Background

2.1 Active Learning Theory

Active learning has been seen as an alternative way of using traditional teaching methods throughout the centuries. For example, educational philosophers such as Rosseau, Dewey, Piaget and Kolb have emphasized the importance of learning through play, doing things practically and having sensory experiences to promote meaningful learning. The theory of constructivism, which emphasizes the fact that learners construct or build their own understanding, is a base for the definition of active learning.

According to Bonwell [1], active learning can be defined as anything that "involves students in doing things and thinking about the things they are doing."

Active learning is a process that keeps students mentally and physically active and involves gathering information, thinking and problem solving. That kind of learning engage activities that requires from students' to assess their own understanding and skills of using concepts or solving problems in a particular discipline. The knowledge acquisition in experiential learning comes through participating and contributing to the process [2].

There are general characteristics that can be associated with the use of active learning in the classroom [1]:

- students are participants not only listeners;
- less emphasis is placed on transmitting knowledge from teacher to student; there is a focus on developing students' skills;
- students need to use higher-order thinking skills (analysis, synthesis, evaluation);
- students are involved in activities (e.g., reading, discussing, writing);
- the emphasis is placed on students' exploration of their own attitudes and values.

There are variety of forms of active learning such as action learning, adventure learning, free choice learning, cooperative learning, and experiential learning. Experiential learning is a learning through experience and it requires an "active phase" of learning [3]. In learning from experiences the role of emotion and feelings has an important part of experiential learning [4]. One example of experiential learning is going to the zoo and learning through observation and interaction with the zoo environment [5].

According to Kolb [6], both personal and environmental experiences are important for gaining knowledge from experience. He puts forward four abilities that are needed to gain knowledge from their experiences:

- the student must be actively involved in the experience;
- the student must be able to reflect on the experience;
- the student must possess and use analytical skills to conceptualize the experience;
- the student must possess decision making and problem solving skills in order to use the new ideas gained from the experience.

Together with learner's experience, a skilled facilitator is also important. Jacobson and Ruddy [7] state that "a skilled facilitator, asking the right questions and guiding reflective conversation before, during, and after an experience, can help open a gateway for the learner to powerful new thinking and learning."

There are different active learning approaches that are used in student-centered learning e.g. (a) problem-based, or case-based learning; (b) cooperative/collaborative learning; (c) think-pair-share, or peer instruction; (d) inquiry-based learning; (e) discovery learning [8]. Active learning is often contrasted to the traditional lecture through which students passively receive information from the instructor. The elements of active learning are student activity and engagement in the learning process [9].

2.2   Concept Mapping as an Assessment Method

The concept mapping method was developed by Joseph Novak and his research team at Cornell University in 1972 [10]. It was based on David Ausubel's [11] cognitive learning theory, which states: (1) learning takes place only when new knowledge is associated with that already existing forming a logical system; (2) reorganization and integration of old knowledge with new information facilitates meaningful learning. A concept map is a graphical tool that represents meaningful relationships between concepts [12]. Concept maps include key concepts that are enclosed in circles and are connected using linking words or phrases (propositions) to other concepts explain the relationship between the interconnected concepts. Propositions are needed to make a meaningful statement [10].

The efficacy of the learning process is highly visible when students are able to create links between previous knowledge and that which is new [13]. To identify changes in students' thinking it is not enough to assess students by means of knowledge tests, usually used at school (multiple choice, true or false etc.). To find out how new knowledge is integrating into students' cognitive thinking, there is a need to use a versatile evaluation tool, for example concept mapping [14].

Concept mapping is useful for assessment, because it illustrates different aspects of student's knowledge which can be used as a measure of learning [15]. The concept mapping method can be used to evaluate the integration between new and existing knowledge and from this, an understanding of the topic. The concept mapping method is an effective tool for assessing an individual's knowledge structure and decision making [10].

Concept maps allow students' knowledge or an individual's achievement in a certain field to be assessed in different ways and the assessment from the mapping is directly related to the 'map' compiled using the building blocks - concept, propositions, and structure. For example, a tasks for students to 'fill-in-a-map' means students are provided with concepts, linking lines and linking words, whereas a 'construct-a-map' task allows students a free hand to use their own concepts and develop original propositions. This means that different methods of scoring maps within the same way of use concept mapping may be measuring different aspects within the knowledge domain [15].

There are a variety of concept mapping scoring methods that are described in the literature, but the most commonly used methods are traditional, holistic, and categorical [16–18]. Five concept map metrics that are often used to describe maps: the closeness index [19, 20] similarity [21]; and the triplet of metrics named correctness, comprehensiveness, and organization [18].

Traditional metrics [12, 17, 18] score maps in three different categories:

(a) knowledge breadth - The number of concepts included in the concept map is counted. No consideration is given to quality or correctness of concepts.
(b) knowledge depth - The number of hierarchies (defined by propositions that include the concept map topic) included in the concept map is counted. The highest level of hierarchy (number of concepts in the longest path down a hierarchy) is recorded.
(c) knowledge connectedness - the number of cross-links, which create propositions using concepts from different hierarchies, is counted. No consideration is generally given to quality or correctness of the cross-link.

The literature includes different measures for analyzing concept maps quantitatively, when the numerical values describe the concept maps [20]. In this way, many characteristics can be assessed [22] e.g. number of concepts, number of propositions, number of cross-links.

Reiska et al. [23] and Cañas et al. [24] describe the assessment of concept maps in three categories: "size", "quality" and "structure". The size of maps is described by number of concepts, number of propositions and number of linking words. The structure of the map is described by centrality of concepts, number of cross-links, density of the concept maps, inter- and intra cluster proposition count and branch point count. The structure characteristics (help to?) evaluate how the concepts are connected to each other. The quality of the maps is described by the number of correct proposition, the average rating of propositions and the relevance of concepts, or propositions. To assess the quality of the concept maps, an expert rating is necessary.

3   Methodology and Data Collection

3.1   Research Design

In the data collection phase, 414 concept maps from 207 basic school students were collected, from those who participated in Tallinn Zoo active learning programs (ALPs). In first phase, each student was asked to create a concept map about the topic of the ALP (see Fig. 1.). In the second phase, the students participated in one active learning program. In the third phase, after the ALP, the students complimented their earlier concept maps.

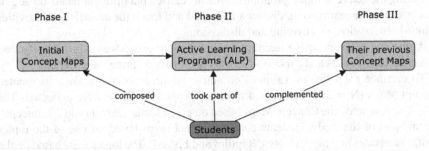

Fig. 1. Research design

The following schema (Fig. 2.) describes the process of data collection, analysis and interpretation.

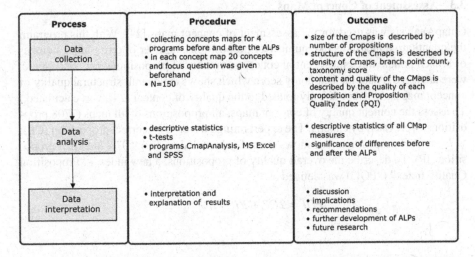

Fig. 2. Process of data collection, analysis and interpretation

3.2 Used Active Learning Programs (ALP)

Four different Active Learning Programs (ALPs), each about 1.5 h were used: "Soil, Vertebrates and Invertebrates, Reptiles and Fishes". In each program, students were divided into small groups (4-6 students) and asked to solve different exercises related to the topics. In each group, different roles were given for the students (e.g. in the program on "Soil," roles were "note-taker," "digger," "collector" and "holder").

An instructor (a teacher) led the activities, but the degree of guidance varied according to the task e.g., if students had to dissect a fish, then students were clearly instructed how to do this by the teacher, but when students sought to discover what was inside the soil there was no interaction by the teacher.

During the active learning programs, students carried out different hands-on activities e.g. dig out an earthworm, dissect a fish, feed and touch the animals. All activities included observation, discovering and discussion.

At the end of every active learning program, every group was asked to reflect by presenting their results and explain what they had learned during the program.

To enhance the value of Tallinn Zoo active learning programs, students created Concept Maps (N = 207, before and after the programs. These were collected. The students constructed the Concept Maps based on given focus question and 20 concepts. For this part of the study, students created concept maps based on one of the topics "Soil, Vertebrates and Invertebrates, Reptiles and Fishes". The topics were based on the basic school biology curriculum. To make sure the reliability and validity of the concept mapping task, students were introduced to the basics of concept mapping before creating the initial concept maps.

3.3   Assessment of Concept Maps

CmapAnalysis was used for the assessment of concept maps [24]. With this program, the quantitative measures like number of propositions, number of cross-links, number of branch points, three most central concepts, number of propositions per concept etc. were analyzed. Also, the taxonomy score which shows the overall structural quality of concept maps and is not directly related to the quality of content [24], was calculated.. To assess the content quality of concept maps, all propositions of all maps (7708 propositions) were rated by experts. The expert ratings were: "2" – correct proposition (CP); "1" – correct proposition, but shows everyday knowledge (EP); "0" – incorrect proposition (IP). To describe the overall quality of propositions, a new index – "Proposition Quality Index" ("PQI") was defined as:

$$PQI = 2CP + EP - IP \tag{1}$$

4   Results

4.1   Cmap Structure Characteristics of Different Active Learning Programs (ALP)

ALP "Fishes". The concept maps of this ALP are "thin", meaning they were created by just a few propositions per concept. Also, their structure is simple, e.g. the average number of branch points is just over 1.5 and the taxonomy level is lower that "2" (possible values "0"–"6"). A Taxonomy level of "2" indicates that there are many missing linking words between the concepts. After the ALP, the density (measured by number of propositions per concept) is a little higher, but for other characteristics of the structure there is no significant change (Fig. 3).

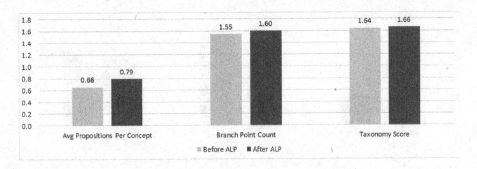

Fig. 3. Cmap characteristics of ALP "Fishes"

ALP "Vertebrates and Invertebrates". Before the ALP, the concept maps of this ALP has a relatively high "density", meaning that the number of propositions per concepts is relatively high. Also the number of branch points has a high value before carrying out the ALP. After the ALP this increases more. The values of taxonomy levels after the ALP decreases a little (Fig. 4).

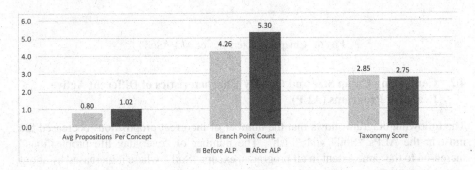

Fig. 4. Cmap characteristics of ALP "Vertebrates and Invertebrates"

ALP "Reptiles". Before the ALP, the concept maps of this ALP has a relatively high "density", meaning that the number of propositions per concepts is relatively high. The number of branch points increases significantly after carrying out the ALP. The taxonomy level does not show a significant increase after the ALP (Fig. 5).

ALP "Soil". The concept maps of this ALP are "thin" before the ALP, but after the ALP the number of propositions per concept increases significantly. Also, the other characteristics associated with the map structure develop significantly after the ALP (Fig. 6).

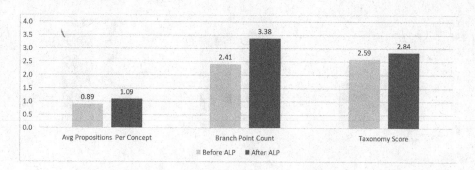

Fig. 5. Cmap characteristics of ALP "Reptiles"

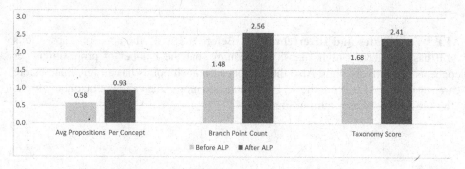

Fig. 6. Cmap characteristics of ALP "Soil"

4.2 Comparing Cmap Size and Quality Characteristics of Different Active Learning Programs (ALP)

The following diagram shows that the number of incorrect propositions decreased the most in the ALPs "Soil" and "Fish". The number of "everyday life propositions" increased to the same extent in all programs, except "Soil", where it increased by about twice as much. The number of "correct propositions" increased in all programs about one point (Fig. 7).

The number of incorrect propositions decreased after carrying out the ALPs, irrespective of the topic. The decrease was biggest for the ALP "Soil", followed by the ALP "Fishes". The number of correct propositions, after carrying out the ALPs, increased for all topics,. The increase was similar for all topics.

The smallest number of correct propositions was in the ALP "Soil" and the highest was in the ALP "Vertebrates and Invertebrates". The smallest number of propositions created per student was in the ALP "Reptiles" and the highest number was in the ALP "Vertebrates and Invertebrates".

The Proposition Quality Index (PQI) was calculated for all ALP concept maps (Fig. 8).

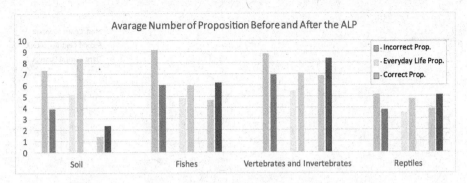

Fig. 7. Number of propositions before and after different ALPs

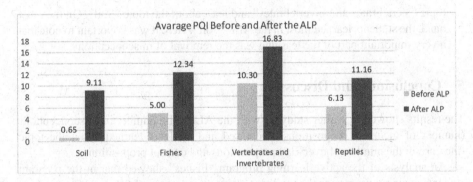

Fig. 8. Proposition quality index by different ALPs

The PQI shows a significant increase for all ALPs. After the ALPs, the PQI was significantly higher. (t-test with 95 % confidence level and p value for all APLs $p = 0.000$).

Figure 9 displays the frequencies of the three most central concepts. Where the centrality of concept is defined by the number of connections (linking phrases) from and to one certain concept. (It is assumed that concept, which are central, are more important in the concept map).

In all ALPs after the program, the number of connections with most central concepts increased. However, it was interesting to note that in the ALP ("Fishes"), one concept was much more central than the others, while for the other ALPs, the difference between the most central concept and the second central concept was not so big.

Summarizing the results, it can be said that:

1. Students learned during the active learning programs (ALP). The number of correct proposition in their concept maps increased significantly. In addition,, the Proposition Quality Index (PQI) was significantly higher for all ALPs.
2. Students had less misconceptions after the ALPs. The number of incorrect proposition decreased significantly.
3. The different ALPs (different topics) seemed to have different levels of complexity. The pre-knowledge about the different topic varied. Students knew most about the

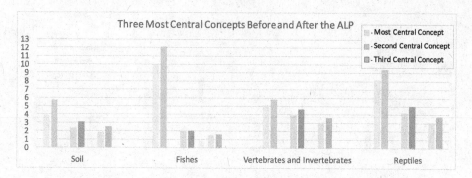

Fig. 9. Distribution of three most central concepts by different ALPs

topic "Vertebrates and Invertebrates" and least about the topic "Soil". On the other hand, the students learned most in the ALP "Soil". Here it was important to note that a very important part of the learning was the removal of misconceptions.

5 Conclusions and Discussion

The results showed that after studying with the ALPs, the number of misconceptions (number of incorrect propositions) decreased and students learned about the topic (increase in the number of everyday propositions and correct propositions).

An analysis of the active learning program "Fishes" showed that in the program students acquired professional knowledge about the anatomy of fish and learned about the role of fishes in our everyday life. On the other hand, the results of the analysis showed that the concept maps branching was low and therefore the program should strive to give more attention to the linking of different concepts.

The results of the active learning program "Vertebrates and Invertebrates" showed a very positive increase in subject knowledge acquisition (increase in the number of correct propositions). On the other hand, the big increase of everyday knowledge might indicate that the program was too easy for students.

The analysis of the active learning program "Reptiles" showed that changes in the correct and incorrect propositions were significant, but quite low. The reason might be in program duration (short time program), or in age appropriation.

The analyses of the active learning program "Soil" showed that the learner's misconceptions decreased and the everyday knowledge increased. The subject knowledge also changed significantly. From this program it was very clearly indicated that the learning process was also leading to lowering of misconceptions, not just an increase of new knowledge (increase of correct propositions).

In conclusion, the Tallinn Zoo active learning programs helped the students to acquire new knowledge and reduce misconceptions. The increase of new correct propositions per student was not very high, but the duration of the programs was just 1.5–2 h and therefore cannot be expected, in such a short time duration, for learners to acquire extensive new and complex knowledge. To increase the efficiency of the ALPs it is recommended to increase the duration and also compose one-class multi-day programs.

Appendix

Examples of Students' Concept maps
   Why the soil is important for the nature and humans? (Fig. 10)

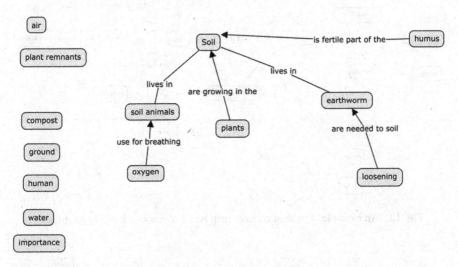

Fig. 10. An example of student concept map before the active learning program.

Why the soil is important for the nature and humans? (Fig. 11)

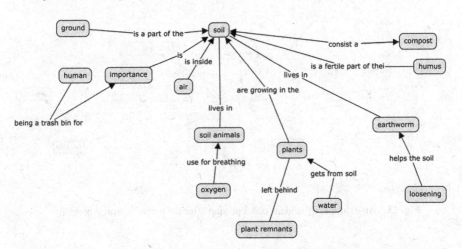

Fig. 11. An example of student concept map after the active learning program.

How are fishes adapted to the water? (Fig. 12)

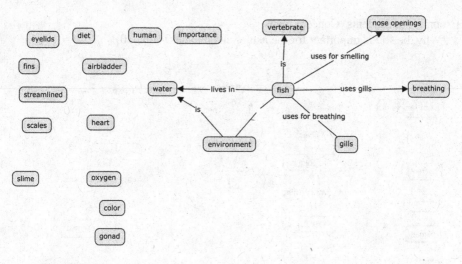

Fig. 12. An example of student concept map before the active learning program.

How are fishes adapted to the water? (Fig. 13)

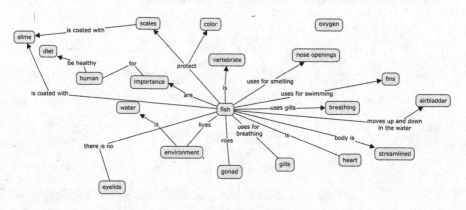

Fig. 13. An example of student concept map after the active learning program.

Examples of one experiment from ALP "Vertebrates and Invertebrates"

Experiment III: Characteristics of vertebrates based on turtle

Resources: turtle, cabbage leaves, carrot slices, water

Procedure	Observer notes
1. Observe the wildlife class turtle movements. Feed the turtle.	*Observe how the turtle:* Take food.. *grab suddenly / take slowly* Keep in mouth the cabbage leaves .... *with teeth / with sharp chin/ with tongue / with legs* *Place the bowl of the water into the cage of the turtle. How does he drink?* .... *Tap gently a turtle head* What's happened?..................................... Why did the turtle hides his head, legs and tail under the shield? How is it beneficial for him? .... Why can't turtle come out of his shield? ....

References

1. Bonwell, C.C., Eison, J.A.: Active learning: creating excitement in the classroom. ASHE-ERIC Higher Education report No.1, Washington, DC (1991)
2. Collins, J.W., O'Brien, N.P. (eds.): The Greenwood Dictionary of Education. Greenwood, Westport (2003)
3. Patrick, F.: Handbook of Research on Improving Learning and Motivation Through Educational Games: Multidisciplinary Approaches, 1st edn., p. 1003. IGI Global, Hershey (2011)

4. Moon, J.: A Handbook of Reflective and Experiential Learning: Theory and Practice, p. 126. Routledge Falmer, London (2004)
5. McCarthy, P.R., McCarthy, H.M.: When case studies are not enough: integrating experiential learning into business curricula. J. Educ. Bus. **81**, 201–204 (2006)
6. Kolb, D.: Experiential Learning: Experience as the Source of Learning and Development, p. 21. Prentice Hall, Englewood Cliffs (1984)
7. Jacobson, M., Ruddy, M.: Open to Outcome: A Practical Guide for Facilitating and Teaching Experiential Reflection, 2nd edn. Wood N Barnes, Bethany (2004)
8. Michael, J.A., Modell, H.J.: Active Learning in Secondary and College Science Classrooms: A Working Model of Helping the Learning to Learn. Erlbaum, Mahwah (2003)
9. Prince, M.: Does active learning work? A review of the research. J. Eng. Educ. **93**, 223–231 (2004)
10. Novak, J.D., Cañas, A.J.: The Theory Underlying Concept Maps and How to Construct and Use Them. Florida Institute for Human and Machine Cognition, Pensacola (2008). (Technical Report IHMC CmapTools 2008-1)
11. Ausubel, D.P.: Educational Psychology: A Cognitive View, pp. 45–46. Holt, Rinehart, and Winston, Inc., New York (1968)
12. Novak, J.D., Gowin, D.B.: Learning How to Learn. Cambridge University Press, New York (1984)
13. Mintzes, J., Wandersee, J., Novak, J.D.: Learning, teaching and assessment: a human constructivist perspective. In: Mintzes, J., Wandersee, J., Novak, J.D. (eds.) Assessing Science Understanding: A Human Constructivist View, pp. 1–13. Elsevier Academic Press, New York (2000)
14. Gouli, E., Gogoulou, A., Grigoriadou, M.A.: A coherent and integrated framework using concept maps for various educational assessment functions. J. Inf. Technol. Educ. **2**(1), 215–239 (2003)
15. Ruiz-Primo, M. A.: Examining concept maps as an assessment tool. In: Cañas, A.J, Novak, J.D., González,F.M., (eds.) Concept Maps: Theory, Methodology, Technology, Proceedings of the 1st International Conference on Concept Mapping, Vol. 1, pp. 555–563, Universidad Publica de Navarra, Spain (2004)
16. Watson, M.K., Pelkey, J., Noyes, C.R., Rodgers, M.O.: Assessing conceptual knowledge using three concept map scoring methods. J. Eng. Educ. **105**(1), 118–146 (2016)
17. Jablokow, K.W., DeFranco, JF., Richmond, S.S.: A statistical study of concept mapping metrics. Paper presented at the ASEE Annual Conference, Atlanta, GA (2013)
18. Besterfield-Sacre, M., Gerchak, J., Lyons, M.R., Shuman, L.J., Wolfe, H.: Scoring concept maps: an integrated rubric for assessing engineering education. J. Eng. Educ. **93**(2), 105–115 (2004)
19. Goldsmith, T., Johnson, P., Action, W.: Assessing structural knowledge. J. Educ. Psychol. **83**, 88–96 (1991)
20. Keppens, J., Hay, J.: Concept map assessment for teaching computer programming. Comput. Sci. Educ. **18**(1), 31–42 (2008)
21. DeFranco, J.F., Jablokow, K.W., Bilen, S.G., Gordon, A.: The impact of cognitive style on concept mapping: visualizing variations in the structure of ideas. Paper presented atthe ASEE Conference and Exposition, San Antonio, Retrieved from Cognitive Style and Concept Mapping Performance, 319 (2012)
22. Croasdell, D.T., Freeman, L.A., Urbaczewski, A.: Concept maps for teaching and assessment. Commun. Assoc. Inf. Syst. **12**, 396–405 (2003)

23. Reiska, P., Cañas, A.J., Novak, D., Miller, N.L.: Concept mapping as a tool for meaningful learning and assessment. In: Holbrook, J., Rannikmäe, M., Reiska, P., Ilsley, P., Lang, P. (eds.) The Need for a paradigm shift in science education for post-soviet societies (2008). Germany
24. Cañas, A.J., Bunch, L., Novak, J.D., Reiska, P.: CmapAnalysis: an extensible concept map analysis tool. J. Educ. Teach. Trainers **1**, 36–46 (2013). Universidad de Granada, Granada

Formative and Summative Assessment of Concept Maps

R.C.V. Marriott[1(✉)] and Patricia Lupion Torres[2]

[1] Universidade Tecnológica Federal do Paraná (UTFPR), Curitiba, Brazil
ritamarriott@yahoo.co.uk
[2] Pontifícia Universidade Católica do Paraná (PUCPR), Curitiba, Brazil
patorres@terra.com.br

Abstract. Concept maps are an excellent assessment tool when they have been used for teaching and learning [1]. This chapter presents the development of a Formative and Summative Assessment (FSA) Table for Concept Maps. The suggested table was developed in a large university in the South of Brazil as part of a doctoral research attached to a research group that focuses on Innovative Methodologies, Concept Mapping and Information, Communication and Technologies (ICT). The research that generated the proposed FSA Table was carried out with 7 groups of 'English as a Foreign Language' (EFL) students. The FSA Table was tested, improved and applied along the semesters of each of the 7 courses. The data gathered as well as the researcher's observation on students' pieces of work and assessments allows us to conclude that the FSA Table suggested can be a very useful tool to assist in the teaching and learning process.

Keywords: Formative assessment · Summative assessment · Concept mapping

1 Introduction

As important as the building of concept maps is their assessment. The student needs to know what is expected of him/her when he draws a concept map and how (and/or if) he/she will be provided with some constructive feedback [2]. To be able to assess using concept maps, concept mapping activities have to have been part of the course. Only when concept maps are used to facilitate learning can they be used to assess it and help learners learn to learn [1, 3]. So, assessments involving concept mapping activities should involve activities already developed in class and thus familiar to the students. They should not present anything new so that learners can focus on producing knowledge instead of spending their time trying to understand what they are supposed to do. Assessment activities using concept maps can be done individually or in groups of 2 or 3 students, as the knowledge exchange between peers can help correct mistakes and promote meaningful learning because students are very likely to be on the same level of understanding as their colleagues [4].

2 Assessment and Concept Maps

Concept maps (CMs) have both content and a graphic structure and when assessment is contemplated, both aspects have to be considered. The graphic structure can be assessed

© Springer International Publishing Switzerland 2016
A. Cañas et al. (Eds.): CMC 2016, CCIS 635, pp. 98–111, 2016.
DOI: 10.1007/978-3-319-45501-3_8

by the Topological Taxonomy [5] and the content can be analyzed by the Semantic
Scoring Rubric [6]. Both taxonomies are based on Bloom's learning taxonomy [1956,
apud 7], and were updated in more recent research by Beirute and Miller [8], Cañas et al.
[5] and Miller and Cañas [6]; they were grounded on Novak and Gowin's [9] initial
studies which were based upon Ausubel's cognitive learning theory.

The map structure and organization reveal the mapper's cognitive structure. Well
organized concept maps usually stem from a well-organized cognitive structure in which
content was learnt in a meaningful way [1]. The graphic structure offers the possibility
of an objective assessment of the concept map and experts tend to agree that a Cmap
can be considered 'good' "by just looking at its structure without considering its content"
[Carvajal et al., 2000, apud 1]. The assessment of the graphic structure – Topologic
Taxonomy – takes into account the Cmap structural complexity without giving importance to the meaning of the concepts and propositions and it can evaluate students'
progress in their initial learning phase, explain Cañas et al. [5]. Their Topologic
Taxonomy considers 5 criteria: the use of concepts instead of text; the establishment of
crosslinks between concepts; the level of ramification; the depth of the hierarchy of
concepts; and the presence of crosslinks. These 5 criteria have 7 different assessment
Levels, from 0 (non-existent) to 6 (for a perfectly fulfilled criteria). The first criteria

	Map type		
	Spoke	*Chain*	*Net*
Hierarchy	One level only	Many levels, but often incorrect – e.g. 'female parts' are shown as subordinate to 'male parts' in Figure 2(b)	Several justifiable levels
Processes	Simple association with no understanding of processes or interactions	Shown as a temporal sequence with no complex interactions or feedback	Described as complex interactions at different conceptual levels
Complexity	So little integration that concepts can be added without consequences for 'map integrity'	Map integrity cannot cope with additions, particularly near the beginning of the sequence	Map integrity is high. Adding one or more concepts has minor consequences as 'other routes' through the map are available
Conceptual development	Shows little or no 'world view'. Addition or loss of a link has little effect on the overview	Integrated into a narrow 'world view', suggesting an isolated conceptual understanding. Loss of a link can lose meaning of the whole chain	Can support reorganization to emphasize different components to appreciate a 'larger world view' or to compensate for a 'missing' link
Represents	National Curriculum structure	Lesson sequence	Meaningful learning

Fig. 1. Concept map analysis proposed by Kinchin, Hay and Adams [10]

(the use of concepts instead of text) and the second one (the establishment of crosslinks between concepts) reach their highest level in Level 3: There is no text and there are no linking words missing.

Another way to assess concept maps (CMs) according to their structure was proposed by Kinchin et al. [10] who studied the CMs created by a group of students in Year 8. Searching for a quick and practical way to evaluate the students' CMs, the researchers identified the three most common concept mapping shapes produced by the students in their research: spoke, chain and net, and proposed the classification in Fig. 1. The description for the categories in the three different layouts (Hierarchy, Processes, Complexity and Conceptual development) suggests that meaningful learning occurs with the CM type called net.

In more recent research, Buhmann and Kingsbury [11] proposed 6 classifications according to the CM's layout for assessment of its morphology. This classification indicates 6 different types: (i) broad; (ii) deep; (iii) imbalanced; (iv) disconnected; (v) interconnected; and (vi) normal (Fig. 2).

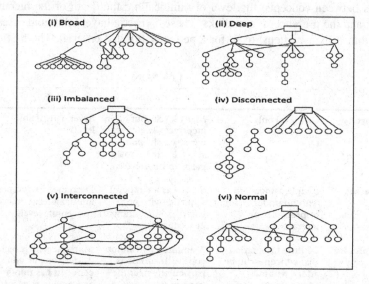

Fig. 2. Concept map global morphologies suggested by Buhmann and Kingsbury [11]

After considering the topological assessment, let's now consider how content can be evaluated.

Content assessment of CMs, based on the Semantic Scoring Rubric [6, 7], was further developed by Miller and Cañas in the Panama Conéctate Project [6]. For a semantic analysis to be carried out, the CM needs to have enough structural and semantic elements for CM reading to make sense, i.e., the CM needs to meet the following 2 criteria: (a) concepts, and not text, must predominate; and (b) linking words must be present. These semantic elements correspond to topological level 3 or higher in Miller and Cañas' Semantic Scoring Rubric which considers the following 6 criteria: concept relevance and completeness; correct propositional structure; presence of erroneous propositions (misconceptions); presence of dynamic propositions; number and presence of cross-links and presence of cycles [6].

As it can be observed, both taxonomies include crosslinks. However, the topological taxonomy is only interested in the presence of crosslinks while the semantic scoring rubric analyzes how many there are and their quality.

Still considering content and graphic structure in the assessment of a CM, Cañas, Novak and Reiska hold that not only content and graphic structure should be considered, but that the interaction between them should also be taken into account, i.e., if the graphic structure used is the best one to express the map content [1].

There is still another aspect that can influence and affect the creation of a CM and consequently its assessment: it is whether the information to create the map is provided by the teacher or selected by the student. Ruiz-Primo [12] systematized a way to classify this level of freedom and restriction and called it Degree of Directedness, i.e., whether it is the teacher or the student who is in charge of selecting how to create the Cmap. The Degree of Directedness (Fig. 3) is considered high when it is the teacher who: (a) provides the concepts; (b) indicates which concepts to link; (c) determines which linking words to use; and (d) states which structure of Cmap to use. The Degree of Directedness is considered low when it is the student who chooses this information, being, therefore, not directed.

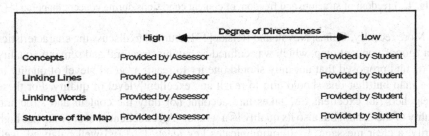

Fig. 3. Degree of directedness of a concept map presented by Ruiz-Primo [12]

The demands imposed on students by the higher or lower directedness of the activities promotes distinguished reasoning by the student, explains Ruíz-Primo, as for when the directedness is low there is more cognitive demand from the student as he/she needs to take more decisions.

Cañas, Novak and Reiska [1] also consider the levels of freedom and restriction in concept mapping activities concerning their content and structure. They created an image (Fig. 4) to illustrate where the activities are positioned in relationship to each other and also where they stand as regards their degree of freedom of structure (X-axis) and freedom of content (Y-axis). The closest the activity is to the X/Y origin, the more restricted the freedom of content and structure (this would happen when students are asked to memorize a Cmap) whereas the farthest it is to X/Y origin, the freer the activity is in relationship to content and structure (this is the case when students have the choice of theme, content and structure of the Cmap). In the image, the researchers place the Focus Question and the Root Concept as the second highest condition-free activities and activities to Fill-in Cmap as the ones that restrict freedom of content the most, after the memorization of a Cmap.

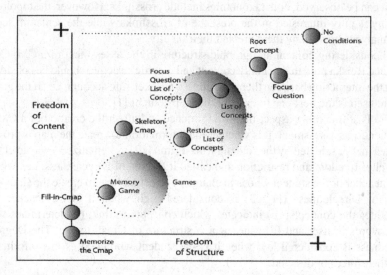

Fig. 4. Freedom of structure and freedom of content conditions during concept mapping [1]

More recently, Cañas, Novak and Reiska [13] returned to discuss the characteristics of a "good" concept map, which was defined as having structural and semantic quality [5, 6], and proposed that not only should one try to reach a "good" level of quality in the Cmap but that one should aim to reach an "excellent" level of quality. For these researchers, an excellent CM takes into account not only the content and structural quality of the Cmap, but also its quality as a whole: "An excellent concept map has high clarity, a clear message, [...] communicates key ideas. [...] [is] well balanced, well structured, [...] demonstrate[s] understanding, [...] [is] explanatory, not descriptive." (p. 15). An excellent concept map not only answers the Focus Question, but explains it in a clear way; it is concise, and it does not include unnecessary concepts, propositions or crosslinks (p. 14–15).

Another alternative to assessment, besides those covered above, which is also a methodological and an assessment option in Inquiry-based learning involving projects and holistic approaches, is the use of portfolios for assessment from a complexity perspective [14]. Portfolios could be used for the assessment of concept maps for satisfying the criteria of formative assessment and also for registering the steps of the methodological process, besides having their focus on meaningful learning. The portfolios could also promote the management and organization of individual and collaborative production, facilitating self-assessment.

The taxonomies and classifications reviewed in this paper explore the possibilities to assess a CMs content, structure and overall quality. To facilitate the assessment of CMs, we have put together a table which takes into account most of these aspects and categories; provides the teacher and students with a grade from 0 to 10 (summative assessment); and also offers the possibility of interaction between the teacher and student to help them understand the subject matter better and advance their learning (formative assessment [15]).

The creation and development of this table, named as Formative and Summative Assessment Table – FSA Table, is presented as follows.

3 Presentation of Pedagogical Assessment Experience

The assessment table presented at the end of this paper (Table 3) was developed in a large university in the South of Brazil, as part of a doctoral research. The researcher, the first author of this paper, was one of the members of a research group on Innovative Methodologies, Concept Mapping and Information, Communication and Technologies (ICT) in Education. The final table (Table 3) stems from a table (Table 1) proposed by Marriott and Torres [16] in which the assessment criteria combined both formative and summative assessment. This Formative and Summative Assessment Table – FSA Table (Table 1) allowed for points to be awarded to the different categories and levels and for their summing up (summative assessment) in a 4-level scale (from 2.5 to 0) totalizing to a maximum of 10 points, and for comments to be made by both the teacher and student (formative assessment). The FSA Table in Table 1 illustrates the evaluation of a student's concept map following these criteria.

Table 1. Formative and summative assessment table (FSA table), version 2008 [16]

Criterion	2.5 points	1.5 points	1 points	0 points	Number of points
Subject studied	Includes all the main concepts studied	Includes most of the important concepts studied	Many important concepts are missing, but the map shows that an effort was made	No effort made	1,5
Are links between concepts scientifically established? Do they show an understanding of the subject studied?	Shows relevant and significant links between concepts and an understanding of the content	Shows some relevant and significant links and an average understanding of the content	Shows little effort to link concepts in a relevant manner and poor understanding of the content	No effort made	1,0
Presentation, ramifications and hierarchy	Easy to read, clear and accurate, with ramifications and relevant structural hierarchy	An acceptable effort, but a bit difficult to read although the ramifications and hierarchy are shown	Very difficult to read, with few ramifications and showing difficulty in arranging concepts hierarchically	No effort made	1
Creativity	Shows a high level of creativity, with five or more relevant concepts and five or more cross-links, some distant, included	Shows average creativity with about three relevant concepts and three cross-links, some distant, included	Shows minimal creativity with only one relevant concept included and about one cross-link established	No effort made	0
Total number of points	3,5 / 10				
General comments on the map (with suggestions and questions)	In your map, you have included some key words from the text in a hierarchical way. Well done! However, you have not used any linking words to express how these concepts are linked. Do you think you could include them in your revised map? Also, could you establish a cross-link in your map?				
Result of the student / teacher discussion, with self-assessment	I will re-read the text and try and understand how the concepts are linked and I will try to establish at least one cross-link.				

After using Table 1 for some time, the final proposed FSA Table was developed from 7 groups of English as a Foreign Language (EFL) students, at 6 different proficiency levels (from Basic, Level 1, to Advanced – level 6), over a period of 2 years, with a total of 84 students. Lessons took place once a week for 1 h 40 min, for 16 weeks per group. To illustrate one of the last stages in the development of the table we share the end-of-term reading test activity, assessed using Table 2, applied to one of the groups of students.

Table 2. FSA table – E6b-01 – V1 & V2

Formative and Summative Assessment Table for Concept Maps (FSA Table)

Date:_____ 26.August.2014___ Focus Question: ___What does the text tells us about this research and about Andraka?___ Student: __[xxx]_____

Final grade = V1 (50 points) + V2 (50 points) = 100 points	Excellent! (100%-90%) 10/9-5/4,5	Good! (80%-70%) 8/7-4/3,5	Regular (60%-50%) 6/5-3/2,5	Poor (40%-30%) 4/3-2/1,5	Insufficient (20%-10%) 2/1-1/0,5	Not done (0%) 0	V1 +V2
Language Level → Content / Form (30 points)							
1(a) Do nouns /concepts appear in boxes and linking words / verbs (plus preposition) on lines to form propositions (noun+ verb + noun)? 1(b) Are all concepts connected with linking words? 1(c) Are there any duplicate nouns / concepts? 1(d) Are there boxes with too much information in them? (10 pts)	V2-10	V1-7					17
2. Are the propositions: (a) correct / meaningful (do they make sense)? and (b) context appropriate? (5 pts)	V2-5	V1-4					9
3. Have verbs been properly conjugated? (5 pts)	V2-5			V1-2			7
4. Was the (4a) concept; (4b) verb; (4c) preposition selected appropriately? (5 pts)	V2-5	V1-3,5					8,5
5(a) Are there any spelling mistakes? 5(b) Have the ambiguities in V1 been solved (or abandoned) in V2? (5 pts)	V1-5 V2-4,5						9,5
Cmap Level → Contend / Form (20 points)							
6. Does the Cmap: (a1) answer the Focus Question WELL? (a2) include the Focus Question? (5 or 10 points)	V2-5	V1-4					9
(b) use ALL terms in Parking Lot(s)? (5 or 0 points)	V1-5/V2-5						10
(c) include the number of concepts requested? (5 or 0 points)	V1-4/V2-5						9
6(d1) flow from the root concept? 6(d2) develop a hierarchical structure? 6(d3) present branches with branches (and not a line of concepts forming a sentence)? (5 or 10 points)	V1-5/V2-5						10
BONUS POINTS - Creativity							
7. Are there any appropriate crosslinks? (2 points each)					V2-2	V1-0	2
8. Is there any extra (own) information? (2 points each)						V1-0/V2-0	0
Total Number of Points	Bonus Points = 0					TOTAL Points = 91	

CM V1-T's comments / suggestions / questions → Well done, [xxx]! You included all the words in Parking Lot A & B, added other 15 concepts from the text and another 3 (out of 5) extra ones, well done!!! And the hierarchy on your Cmap is great! An excellent progress in the semester! We can see, however, that you have got some difficulty with verb conjugation (code 3), some of the concepts were repeated (code 1c), the meaning of some propositions were not clear (code 2a) and in some propositions, the concept (code 4a) and the verb (code 4b) were not well selected. Please, have a think on how you can better express these ideas more appropriately, and how this new version (V2) will affect your written text (that also needs to include your personal information). OK? Regards, [xxx]

St's comments

CM V2 –T's comments → Well done [xxx]! You have reflected and worked on the verbs and linking phrases, have established a crosslink and have applied the changes to the written text making it nearly flawless, congratulations! However, the written text, unlike the CM, needs articles and pronouns for reading to flow... do not leave them out, OK? Any questions, just ask! All the best, [xxx]!

In this end-of-term reading test activity, students worked individually on a piece of text titled 'Teen Googles his way to new cancer testing method' [17]. After reading the text, they answered some content and language related questions (involving prefixes, suffixes, comparatives, superlatives, active and passive voice).

They were then asked to create a CM following this sequence of steps: (1) answer the Focus Question: What does the text tell us about this research and about Andraka?; (2) chose a relevant root concept to start your Cmap; (3) use all concepts from Parking Lot A (Glee, advanced research, 2012 Intel Science fair, Google, lung cancer, lab access); (4) use all verbs from Parking Lot B (create, develop, conduct, earn, look up, detect); (5) add another 15 concepts (minimum) from the text; and (6) add another 5 extra concepts of your choice, establishing a link with any of the information on your Cmap.

The goal of asking students to add extra concepts to the Cmap is to promote mean-ingful learning when establishing a link between new information and their previous knowledge, and thus activate their encyclopedic knowledge [18]. After creating the Cmap, following the given information and the skeleton map provided (Fig. 5), students had to write a piece of text titled 'Andraka and his impressive research' only looking at the information expressed on the Cmap.

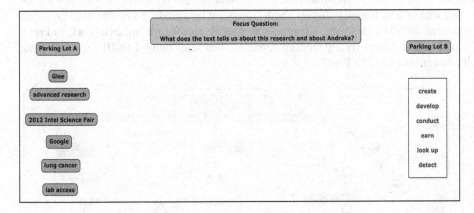

Fig. 5. Assessment 2 – skeleton map [19]

The skeleton map provided (Fig. 5) was available on the test sheet and was sent to students by email; they were free to draw the Cmap by hand or using CmapTools (installed in the university computer lab). All students used CmapTools. The concepts in Parking Lot A were meant to be dragged and used in the Cmap. The verbs available in the squared-angle single box in Parking Lot B, were meant to be removed from the box and used in the Cmap, appropriately conjugated.

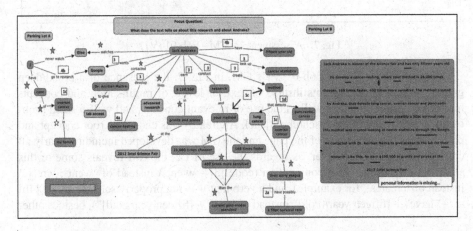

Fig. 6. Assessment 2 – overview of CM & narrative - E6b-01 (V1)

In the week after the test, students were handed in Version 1 (V1) of their CMs, marked according to the FSA Table (Table 2). V1 was worth 50 % of the total points available in the FSA Table. On their CMs (Figs. 6, 7 and 8), stars highlight some appropriate use of concepts or linking words, and numbers, followed (or not) by letters, refer to the criteria in the FSAT that needs to be looked into and reformulated.

To keep the piece of text next to the Cmap, students suggested writing the narrative in the Cmap itself. To facilitate marking, the teacher asked them to skip a line between each line of text. Figure 6 displays both Cmap and text produced by one of the students (student E6b-01). However, to provide an overall view of his finished work, in Fig. 6 Cmap and text were greatly reduced, affecting their readability. E6b-01's Cmap V1 can be better visualised in Fig. 7.

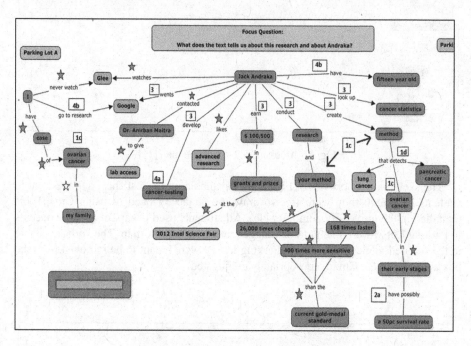

Fig. 7. Assessment 2 – CM - E6b-01 (V1)

It is possible to see in E6b-01 V1's CM, in Fig. 7, the presence of a broad/deep graphic structure, of concepts instead of text, of levels of ramification and concepts hierarchically presented as well as the use of relevant concepts and well-formed propositions. The name of the researcher ([Jack Andraka]) was chosen as root concept and placed at the top and centre of the page and the CM was developed including nearly all concepts requested. However, as regards the use of L2, the CM reveals some of this student's difficulties: verb conjugation (code [3] - \wents\ instead of 'went'; \create\ instead of 'creates', for example), and a verb that was not properly selected (code [4b] – "+\ have\ + [fifteen year/0/old" instead of "+ is + [fifteen years old]"), besides other ambiguities mentioned in the Teacher's Comments on V1 (CM V1)[1] in the FSA Table. In V1 of his narrative, which corresponds to V1 of his CM, the ambiguities present reflect the ones marked on his map.

With the assessed V1 of CM and narrative and the FSA Table, students could reflect about the marking and comments made, produce the second version (V2) of both CM and narrative, and submit them. Although this was an end-of-term test, and students do not normally get a second chance to redo any piece of work, we followed the same procedure as in a normal class activity to allow for students to reflect on their productions, learn and consolidate their knowledge of L2, developing their cognition and metacognition.

In E6b-01 V2's CM and narrative, in Fig. 8, it is possible to observe that most ambiguities were solved and a crosslink was established (to mention a case of ovarian cancer in his family). The Teacher's Comments on V2 (CM V2)[2] highlight his progress and achievements and remark on his CM and written work. With the V2 of CM and narrative, the student received the FSA Table completely filled in with grades and comments on both V1 & V2 (Table 2). This FSA Table now includes 4 categories in item 6 (6a, 6b, 6c e 6d) with 6a subdivided in 2 aspects (6a1 and 6a2) and 6d subdivided in 3 aspects (6d1, 6d2, and 6d3), and item 6c was reworded.

The 5 categories in the Language Level add up to 30 points and the 4 categories in the Cmap Level total 20 points (whether or not the activity includes a request to use "ALL terms in Parking Lot" (6b) or to include a number of concepts (6c)). In order to promote creativity and meaningful learning, Bonus Points can be awarded for the appropriate use of crosslinks and any extra, unprompted information.

After using this iteration of the FSA Table with this very group of students, we asked them how the table had helped them think in the target language and if it had helped them in the acquisition of L2. All students said they liked the table and/or found it very interesting and helpful, highlighting that "It helped us see our mistakes on the CM and it became easier to correct them" (E6b-08); "… it made clear what I got right and what I got wrong, and it helped me with V2 as I knew what I was doing" (E6-09); "… it shows us where we are making mistakes and we can avoid making them in future Cmaps"

---

[1] **CM V1**–T's comments/ suggestions/ questions → Well done, [xxx] ! You included all the words in Parking Lots A & B, added other 15 concepts from the text and another 3 (out of 5) extra ones, well done!!! And the hierarchy on your Cmap is great! An excellent progress in the semester! We can see, however, that you have got some difficulty with verb conjugation (code 3), some of the concepts were repeated (code 1c), the meaning of some propositions were not clear (code 2a) and in some propositions, the concept (code 4a) and the verb (code 4b) were not well selected. Please, have a think on how you can better express these ideas. Once you've made changes to your CM and produced the new version (V2) revise your written text and change it accordingly (do not forget to include your personal information), OK? Regards, [xxx].

[2] **CM V2** – T´s comments → Well done, [xxx]! You have: reflected and worked on the verbs and linking phrases; stablished a crosslink; and applied the changes to the written text making it nearly flawless, congratulations! However, the written text, unlike the CM, needs articles and pronouns for reading to flow… do not leave them out, OK? Have a look at my suggestions and if you have any questions, just ask! All the best, [xxx]!.

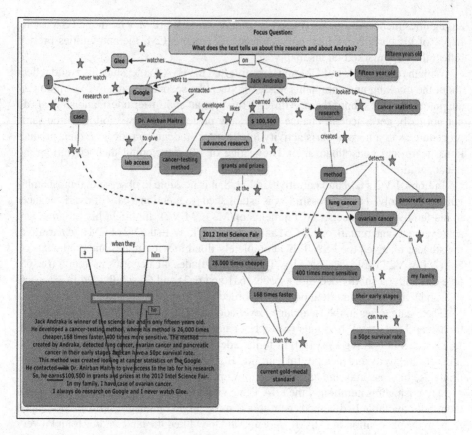

Fig. 8. Assessment 2 – CM & narrative - E6b-01 (V2)

(E6b-01); "… the feedback is very specific and there is also some personalised comment for each student at the end that helps us with L2 acquisition" (E6b-07); "… sometimes we don't realise we are making some mistakes and this way we can reassess the use of prepositions and concepts in L2" (E6b-06); and "With the use of the table it helped me see my mistakes with verb conjugation…" (E6b-05).

At the end of this research after applying concept mapping activities to 7 groups of students over a 2-year period we came to the final FSA Table iteration (Table 3). In this final table for the assessment of CM in language teaching, compared to the previous table (Table 2), we have simplified the marking system (displayed on the line at the top) from 7 columns to just 5: 2 columns for V1, 2 columns for V2 and a final column for the Final Grade (V1 = 50 % + V2 = 50 %). In the first column for V1 and V2, we decided to use percentages to indicate how much per cent each one of the 6 characteristic assessed (with their subdivisions) has been achieved; and in the second column the teacher awards a general grade (from 0 to 10) for each one of the 5 characteristics.

Table 3. Resulting FSA table for CMs

Formative and Summative Assessment Table for Concept Maps (FSA Table)

Date:_____ Focus Question: _____ Student: _____ CM No.:_____

Summative Assessment	% / (-)	V1 Mark	% / (-)	V2 Mark	FINAL Mark
Legend: % = percentage of item present in Cmap / (-) = item not requested / ? = award grade from 0 to 10 / ?? = partial grade / ??? = Final Grade					
Linguistic Level → Content / Form - 10 + 10 + 10 = 30 points					
1(a) Are there only concepts in the boxes?	%		%		
1(b) Are concepts linked with only verbs / linking words or prepositions?	%	?	%	?	??
1(c) Have concepts been mentioned only once (i.e., they were not duplicated)?	%		%		
1(d) Do boxes contain only 1 concept?	%	-	%		
2 (a) Have verbs been appropriately conjugated?	%	?	%	?	??
2 (b) Is word spelling correct?	%		%		
3(a) Do propositions reflect the content or text studied?	%		%		
As regards the propositions … Was there an appropriate selection of: 3(b) concept?	%	?	%	?	??
3(c) verb/linking word?	%		%		
3(d) preposition?	%		%		
CMap Level → Content / Form - 10 + 10 = 20 points					
Does the Cmap: 4(a) include the Focus Question and develops it?	%		%		
4(b) use ALL terms in Parking Lot(s)?	%	?	%	?	??
4(c) include the number of concepts (or information) requested?	%		%		
5(a) present features of a net, deep, interconnected or cyclic layout?	%		%		
5(b) flow from the root concept?		?		?	??
5(c) develop a hierarchical structure?	%		%		
5(d) present branches with branches (and not a line of concepts forming a sentence)?	%		%		
BONUS POINTS – Creativity - 2 points for each crosslink or concept					
6(a) Are there any appropriate crosslinks?					
6(b) Is there any extra (unprompted) information?					
V1 + V2 = FINAL MARK				??	???

Formative Assessment
V1–T's comments / suggestions / questions →
V1 -St's comments →
V2 – T's comments / suggestions / questions →
V2 -St's comments →

We have kept the 3 different levels: the Linguistic Level (with Content and Form), the Cmap Level (with Content and Form), and the Bonus Level (for extra points for student's Creativity and unprompted inclusion of extra information). We have excluded the adjective "well" from the question "Does the Cmap answer the Focus Question WELL?" for being difficult to express objectively what "well" actually means; and we have included a question on the type of layout "Does the Cmap (5a) present features of a net, deep, interconnected or cyclic layout?" to promote and foster these types of structures. The space for Formative assessment and Comments was kept at the bottom of the table where teacher and student can interact.

We conclude that the use of the resulting FSA Table to assess students' CMs helped students learn and consolidate their acquisition of L2 as well as contributed with the development of cognitive and metacognitive skills when thinking over the language used and observations made and assessing their own learning. The reflection over their learning in addition to the creation, analysis, redrawing of CMs and rewriting of narratives favoured both meaningful learning of the topics discussed and linguistic aspects involved due to anchorage with previous knowledge.

4 Summary

The resulting FSA Table (Table 3) allows for formative and summative assessment, combines items from both the Topological Taxonomy and the Semantic Scoring Rubric, considers Cmap layout and the Degree of Directness and aims to promote and foster the creation of an excellent CM. It is possible to observe a parallel between the general level of a CM, i.e., its overall structure [13] and the features of a holistic approach from a Complex point of view [20, 21] as both perspectives consider and aim to promote the comprehension and apprehension of the overall meaning and specific information. The understanding on the holistic and detailed levels can be reached via reflection and development of critical thinking. The practice of building Concept Maps involving analysis in V1 and V2 also has the potential to promote and foster meaningful learning and a change from a more traditional teaching proposal to a more innovative and holistic one with a higher level of broadness, depth and overall interconnectedness.

References

1. Cañas, A.J., Novak, J.D., Reiska, P.: Freedom vs. restriction of content and structure during concept mapping - possibilities and limitations for construction and assessment. In: Concept Maps: Theory, Methodology, Technology - Proceedings of the Fifth International Conference on Concept Mapping, Valletta, Malta (2012)
2. Marriott, R.C.V., Torres, P.L.: Concept Maps: a Tool for the Construction of a Knowledge Cartograpy, in Complexity - Networks and Connections in the Production of Knowledge (Mapas Conceituais uma Ferramenta para a Construção de uma Cartografia do Conhecimento, in Complexidade - Redes e Conexões na Produção do Conhecimento) Torres, P.L. (ed.), SENAR-PR, Curitiba (2014)
3. Novak, J.D.: Meaningful Learning for Empowerment, in Learning, Creating and Using Knowledge - Concept Maps as Facilitative Tools in Schools and Corporations. Routledge, New York (2010)
4. Novak, J.D., Cañas, A.J.: Building on new constructivist ideas and cmaptools to create a new model for education. In: IX Taller Educacional de Software Educativo TISE 2004. Memorias TISE 2004, Santiago (2004)
5. Cañas, A.J., et al.: Confiabilidad de una Taxonomía Topológica para Mapas Conceptuales. In: CMC2006 - Concept Maps: Theory, Methodology, Technology, Proceedings of the Second International Conference on Concept Mapping. Universidad de Costa Rica, San Jose (2006)

6. Miller, N.L., Cañas, A.J.: A semantic scoring rubric for concept maps: design and reliability. In: CMC 2008 - Concept Mapping - Connecting Educators, Proceedings of the Third International Conference on Concept Mapping. Tallinn University, Tallinn (2008)

7. Novak, J.D.: Learning, Creating, and Using Knowledge - Concept Maps as Facilitative Tools in Schools and Corporations, 2nd edn. Routledge, New York (2010). 317 p.

8. Beirute, L., Miller, N.L.: Interaction between topology and semantics in concept maps: a neurolinguistics interpretation. In: CMC 2008 - Concept Mapping: Connecting Educators, Proceedings of the Third International Conference on Concept Mapping. Tallinn University, Tallinn (2008)

9. Novak, J.D., Gowin, D.B.: Learning How to Learn. Cambridge University Press, Cambridge (1998)

10. Kinchin, I., Hay, D., Adams, A.: How a qualitative approach to concept map analysis can be used to aid learning by illustrating patterns of conceptual development. Educ. Res. 42(1), 43–57 (2000)

11. Buhmann, S.Y., Kingsbury, M.: A standardised, holistic framework for concept-map analysis combining topological attributes and global morphologies. Knowl. Manag. E-Learn. 7(1), 20–35 (2015)

12. Ruíz-Primo, M.A.: On the use of concept maps as an assessment tool in science: what we have learned so far. In: Revista Electrônica de Investigacíon Educativa (2000)

13. Cañas, A.J., Novak, J.D., Reiska, P.: How good is my concept map? Am i a good Cmapper? Knowl. Manag. E-Learn. 7(1), 6–19 (2015)

14. Behrens, M.A.: O portfólio como Procedimento Avaliativo, in Paradigma da Complexidade. Metodologia de Projetos, Contratos Didáticos e Portfólios Vozes: Petrópolis, pp. 103–110 (2008)

15. Trumbull, E., Lash, A.: Understanding Formative Assessment - Insights from Learning Theory and Measurement Theory. WestEd, San Franciso (2013)

16. Marriott, R.C.V., Torres, P.L.: Enhancing collaborative and meaningful learning through concept mapping. In: Okada, A., Shum, S.B., Sherborne, T. (eds.) Knowledge Cartography, pp. 47–72. Springer, London (2008)

17. UFPR, V.: Teen Googled his Way to New Cancer Testing Method (2012). http://www.nc.ufpr.br/concursos_institucionais/ufpr/ps2013/provas1fase/PS2013_conhecimentos_gerais.pdf

18. Dörnyei, Z., Kormos, J.: Problem-solving mechanisms in L2 communication. SSLA - Studies in Second Language Acquisition. 20(3), 349–385 (1998)

19. Marriott, R.C.V.: From the Language Learning Lab (LAPLI) to the Use of Concept Maps for the Development of Language Acquisition (MAPLI) (Do Laboratório de Aprendizagem de Línguas (LAPLI) ao Uso de Mapas Conceituais para o Desenvolvimento da Aquisição de Línguas (MAPLI)) thesis in Education, Pontificia Universidade Católica do Paraná – PUCPR, Curitiba, p. 448 (2016)

20. Behrens, M.A.: The Connection of the Complexity Paradigme from a Global Perspective, In Complexity Paradigme - Inquiry-based Learning, Teaching Contracts and Portfolios (A Conexão do Paradigma da Complexidade num Enfoque Globalizado, in Paradigma da Complexidade - Metodologia de Projetos, Contratos Didáticos e Portfólios) Vozes, Petrópolis, p. 11–27 (2008)

21. Larsen-Freeman, D.: Chaos/complexity science and second language acquisition. Appl. Linguist. 18(2), 141–165 (1997)

Improving the Teaching of Children with Severe Speech-Language Difficulties by Introducing an Authoring Concept Mapping Kit

Ria Kicken[1], Elise Ernes[1], Ilja Hoogenberg-Engbers[2], and Gloria Gomez[3(✉)]

[1] Vitus Zuid Mgr.Hanssen, Hoensbroek, Netherlands
{ria.kicken, elise.ernes}@mgrhanssen.nl
[2] Independent Scholar, Berkel-Enschot, Netherlands
i.hoogenberg@zichtoponderwijs.nl
[3] University of Southern Denmark, Odense M, Denmark
gege@iti.sdu.dk

Abstract. The paper reports on case studies in which an Authoring Concept Mapping Kit was incorporated as a didactic tool in the teaching of children with severe speech-language difficulties. The Kit was introduced to replace methods such as topic webs, or complement others such as conversation exchange. Three pilots were carried out between 2012 and 2015, with escalating numbers in participation and duration. The paper focuses on the teachers, their training, implementation, and their motivations for incorporating concept mapping in interactive learning language. The outcomes report on how the teachers' practice has been transformed and improved. The children's perspective on the topic comes through in the teachers' opinions. Concept mapping turned out to enhance meaning negotiation, active inquiry and collaboration during teaching interactive learning language. Teachers reported that it had great impact on children's language development, vocabulary and spontaneous speech, while it had minimal impact on the way activities were performed in everyday classes.

1 Background

This paper reports on three pilot studies in which the Authoring Concept Mapping Kit was used as a didactic method to teach children with severe speech-language difficulties at the Institute Vitus Zuid Mgr. Hanssen in the Netherlands. These studies were designed to research if this tool could be implemented to enhance performance or replace current didactic methods for teaching interactive language learning.

1.1 Concept Maps and the Authoring Concept Mapping Kit (Also Authoring Kit or the Kit)

Novak and his research team [1] developed concept maps in the 1970 s based on Ausubel's Theory of Assimilation. Concept maps are tools for organizing and

A. Cañas et al. (Eds.): CMC 2016, CCIS 635, pp. 112–127, 2016.
DOI: 10.1007/978-3-319-45501-3_9

representing knowledge. It has been demonstrated that they are effective for the promotion of meaningful learning as they facilitate knowledge retention, preservation and sharing. This tool is comprised of concepts that are enclosed in boxes or circles. These enclosed concepts are related to each other via connecting lines. The conceptual relationship between two or more concepts is given by linking phrases placed on the line. Novak also states that concepts can be labeled with words as well as symbols such as %, +, etc. Of great practical importance for the Institute's educational program is the core of Ausubel's theory that suggests we learn new concepts based on the concepts we already know. In interactive language learning it is highly important to collaboratively establish connections between known words and new words being learned.

Coffey and colleagues [2] tell us that if learning is to occur during the building of a concept map, the nature of the learner's mental interaction with the subject matter to be learned cannot be passive. A teacher or other facilitator, the learner himself or herself, a computer device or group learning, are all factors that activate learning during the building process. The learner's mental interactions with these factors promote active inquiry and organization by engaging them in a process that involves asking questions, prompting for explanation and justification, requesting clarification, embellishment, encouraging the learner to make connection among elements and formulate questions about the material, and so forth.

The Authoring Concept Mapping Kit [3, 4] was developed for enabling preliterate children to build Novak's concept maps with spoken words and visual representations, and for enabling early childhood experts to effectively investigate the significance and effectiveness of concept maps in the classroom. The Kit development was informed by Novak's concept mapping theory, early childhood education and learning, and human-centered design principles. It is comprised of blank cards and/or picture cards (with pre-determined topics), arrows, voice-recorders, and a magnetic whiteboard. These components facilitate preliterate and emergent writing children to make concept maps with voice, drawings or picture cards, and "kindergarten writing". The voice recorder enables the child to verbally establish the relationship between two drawings or pictures representing concepts, through spoken words (Fig. 1, right photo). Independently, a child can listen to the voice-recorded relationship any time during the activity by pushing the play button on the voice-recorders.

A small number of research studies [4] demonstrate that children who have not yet learned to read and write could independently make concept maps with the Kit. During the building process, they displayed enhanced autonomy, active inquiry and meaning negotiation, individually, in peer-to-peer interactions, and/or in company of teachers. These outcomes have provided sufficient evidence to inspire early childhood experts to undertake their own exploratory studies and suitably investigate teaching and learning with concept maps.

In the United States, Cassata-Widera [5, 6] examined ways in which concept maps may serve as mediating tools that facilitate development of metacognitive control skills, including planning, monitoring, and self-correction. Data gathered from an 8-week mixed-method study showed that 5-year old children's ability to independently make maps (on science concepts), and particularly planning behaviors increased over time. She also reported on implications for early literacy. In the Netherlands, Hoogenberg-Engbers [7] introduced the Kit during a workshop at a conference for primary school teachers on educational interventions for gifted children. The theory and guidelines relating to concept mapping with young children were presented. Concept mapping can be an effective educational activity to challenge children to stretch their thinking in the zone of proximal development, as it can help reconstruct and expand their conceptual knowledge, promote self-regulatory learning, and support the process of learning how to write.

1.2   Concept Mapping at the Institute Vitus Zuid Mgr. Hanssen

The Institute is constantly looking for opportunities to meet educational needs. It is often searching for challenging, stimulating, and achievable forms of teaching and learning for children with serious speech-language difficulties, as well as children who are deaf and hard of hearing, from ages 4 to 18. Kicken and Ernes are teachers who work as contractors of the Institute's external service. As part of the training to become a specialist in guiding gifted and talented children, they attended the concept mapping workshop run by Hoogenberg-Engbers and learned to encourage children to make their own connections between concepts using the Authoring Kit. They thought that this approach could also work for teaching interactive language learning. What commenced with an afternoon pilot, has evolved into a three-year engagement with two more pilots, which has culminated with the incorporation of concept mapping as a didactic tool at most grade levels.

This paper reports on the motivations, the pilots' implementation, and a summary of outcomes that illustrates how concept mapping was incorporated in the regular teaching at the Institute by the end of 2015. The summary does not explore in detail the learning claims made by the teachers, as such reporting would require a careful analysis of the activities recorded in the last three years. The paper concludes with a discussion that connects the study outcomes to related work, new development, and research plans.

2   Interactive Language Learning and Concept Mapping for Children with Severe Speech-Language Difficulties

In the education of children with severe speech and hearing problems, teachers mostly work according to the principles of interactive language learning. The first condition is that the education in language is interactive and should involve the following activities: conversation exchange, learning talk, storytelling, talking about the meaning of words, functional writing, arguing and debating, and lecturing. The last two activities are undertaken only with children in older groups. These activities indicate that during the lessons, children should be actively involved in their own language development, and that vocabulary expansion should take a prominent role [8]. One's own vocabulary then becomes part of a network of connected relationships in one's mind. New words are immediately placed in the current network.

The didactic approach of van den Nulft and Verhallen [9] is used as the starting point of the learning program at the Institute. The four steps (*Viertakt*) used in this approach match perfectly with concept mapping.

- **Step 1 - Pre-processing:** the teacher activates all knowledge so the children get involved in the subject. Concept mapping makes explicit to the teacher how children are understanding a subject of study, through asking questions about what they already know, and how concepts relate to the subject. The children are actively involved in the process.
- **Step 2 - Semantics:** the teacher explains the word clearly and suggests new words. A correct pronunciation is important. The teacher explains, depicts, and expands the new words. This happens also in concept mapping. There are also opportunities to make children responsible for their own learning (learning how to learn).
- **Step 3 - Consolidation:** this is the practice phase so the words can take root in memory and in the students' word network. In concept mapping, this is done by the mutual relationships of the words through a variety of ways (arrow, voice recorders). The children can check or revise their pronunciation and the relationship between words anytime by playing the voice recorders back.
- **Step 4 - Reviewing:** the final stage is to check that the children have acquired the new words. The teacher mainly performs this step, but the children can also do it themselves.

Concept mapping using concrete materials, pictures, or single words on a theme, enables children themselves to establish the relationships between certain concepts. The aim is to find the right vocabulary words to link two concepts together. This requires a creative way of thinking. A topic web (also called mind map) is a graphic tool for brainstorming and placing all concepts and knowledge in an overview [9] (Fig. 1, left photo). The difference between a topic web and a concept map is the emphasis on the relationships between the connected concepts in a concept map. The Authoring Kit makes the meaning of concepts visible (pictures and concrete objects represent concepts) and the children can verbally-label the relationships among them using the small voice recorders (Fig. 1, right photo).

Fig. 1. Making an overview and brainstorming with topic webs (left); concept mapping with the authoring kit (right)

3 Three Pilots Between 2012 and 2015

3.1 An Afternoon Pilot

After attending the workshop, Kicken, Ernes and Hoogenberg-Engbers decided to try the Authoring Kit with three children (ages 4, 5, and 9) during an afternoon in March 2012. In only a few hours, this method yielded unexpectedly beautiful results with these children. The 5-year old boy set intermediate steps (e.g. words, concepts) in telling the production process from milk to cheese, which is usually not done by such a young child. Furthermore, the relations between these words are not offered in the teaching program for this age group. The 9-year old talked about the full recycling process in dealing with a theme on "a waste container". Concept mapping enabled these children to show their own creative thinking and make explicit to adults what they knew about the topics. The findings motivated the teachers to undertake more practice, leading to the Institute's management authorizing an initial pilot.

3.2 Five-Month Pilot

From November 2012 to April 2013, a small group of teachers volunteered their time to learn and practice concept mapping with the Authoring Kit. Three research questions guided this pilot:

- **Question 1:** Can concept mapping be a didactic tool in a group of children with language development disorders?
- **Question 2:** Does concept mapping offer added value with regard to vocabulary education, specifically in expanding networks?
- **Question 3:** Does concept mapping offer children the ability to show more of their thinking?

Implementation. Teachers were introduced to the opportunities that concept mapping could have in the development of thinking and language skills. Kicken and Ernes shared their personal experience and encouraged teachers to practice independently. Five teachers practiced concept mapping on a particular theme, with their students, at least twice a week, for 4 weeks. One teacher represented the lower grades (ages 4 to 5), two teachers the middle grades (ages 7 to 9), and the last two teachers the upper grades (ages 11 to 12). The teachers were regularly observed and filmed.

The starting point was to use concept mapping for language teaching of word orientation instead of their current didactic method, a topic web or a conversation exchange. The practice was to show that concept mapping stimulates the interactive language use in children. The expected behaviors were:

- Children must think about the connections of two pictures in relation to the theme
- Children will have a conversation about it
- Children will hear their own speech, and then, they will improve their own speech
- Children will hear the sentences of their classmates, and then, they will talk about what is right or wrong

Through regular targeted observations, the teachers, Kicken and Ernes together reviewed and studied this new way of teaching the theme, and the effect that it had on the children. After the four weeks, the teachers completed an evaluation form providing data that could be used to answer the three research questions. The outcomes are discussed further below (Fig. 2).

Fig. 2. Upper grade class concept mapping on the theme "World War II" (left); middle grade class concept mapping on the theme "Work" (right)

3.3   One-Year Pilot

During the school year 2014–2015, a larger pilot was started with 18 groups with all the teachers of the middle and upper grades. The children were age 6 to 12. The research questions from the five-month pilot remained.

Implementation was broadly the same as the one of the five-month pilot, but there were two differences: (a) more teachers and their groups joined it and (b) internal counselors were involved which created the opportunity for shared responsibility. This time, the introduction also included an explanation to internal counselors during the pedagogical and educational consultation with teachers, and a good practice video. Then, Kicken and Ernes co-taught and practiced with teachers and counselors. Through their own experience, they were able to better assist teachers in the change in thinking and understanding of this approach. The internal counselors will take over the coaching job in the future. The same groups also discussed the final evaluations in June 2015.

4   A Summary of Outcomes from Both Pilots

Fragments of teachers' comments excerpted from completed evaluations and fragments of children's comments provide evidence to answer the three research questions. The benefits of the Authoring Concept Mapping Kit [4] are used to categorize the teachers and children's comments.

The answer for question 1 is yes; concept mapping fits the Institute's approach to language teaching. The Authoring Kit integrated as a good didactic tool with the current interactive language learning approach. There was no additional work for the teachers, just another way of teaching a theme. It transferred to the whole team, and co-teaching was possible. Table 1 includes supporting fragments.

The answer for question 2 is yes; concept mapping offers added value with regard to vocabulary learning, specifically in expanding the children's word networks. The practice phase showed that it took both the teachers and the children some effort to widen the word networks in this way. They had to let go of the old strategies such as stopping the use of a picture to inculcate a word, and stopping the repetition of this new word over and over. Some teachers had to learn to use open questions and even learn to listen to what the children meant by asking more questions. Table 2 includes supporting fragments.

The answer for questions 3 is yes; concept mapping offers children the ability to show more of their own thinking ability. The following transcripts illustrate that a conversation exchange with concept mapping is more child-initiated and interactive. The teacher and three young children (ages 5 and 6) are discussing the theme "ill" (Fig. 3). Children themselves are establishing relationships between concepts, and completing each other's sentences.

> Teacher: Child Z is ill, she is not at school
> Child X: If you're sick, the doctor comes
> Teacher: What does the doctor do?
> Child Y: You get a shot
> Child W: Then you get a squirt
> Child X: I've also had a squirt, did au [the child speaks this sentence in the voice
>   recorder]
> Child W: That hurt!

Another excerpt of the same conversation shows that children are completing each other's sentences or stories, and therefore learning from each other about the theme. Children can see the relationships that peers are offering, respond spontaneously and add their own ideas to the concept map.

> Teacher: What else can the doctor do?
> Child X: I've had a pill
> Child Y: It is called, medication, my mom said
> Teacher: Where does your mom buy this medication?
> Child Y: At the pharmacy
> Child X: You buy a pill at the "pharcy" [the child was meaning pharmacy. This
>   sentence was on the voice recorder]
> Child Y: I was in a pharmacy

Table 1. Fragments with evidence for question 1

The benefits of the authoring concept mapping kit [4]	Fragments of teachers and children's comments
Enabling teachers to diversify instruction	"It doesn't cost a lot of time to prepare the activities" [teacher, five-month pilot]
	"For me it was quite an experience and I absolutely see the added value of concept mapping. It is also nice to fit into the lessons" [teacher, five-month pilot]
	"There is a clear difference between teachers bound-concept mapping and independent children work" [teacher, one-year pilot]
	"Concept mapping is widely applicable in our education not only in language teaching. The visualization in concept mapping is good for our students" [teacher, five-month pilot]
	"I do understand my classmates better when using concept mapping" [child, one-year pilot]
Revisiting and sharing the elements of the map	"The interaction between children is increasing, the children ask more questions to each other. By talking together about the words, the words are better understood" [teacher, five-month pilot]
	"It is fun to work with concept mapping" [child, one-year pilot]
	"Children are highly motivated and grow in communication" [teacher, five-month pilot]
	"I can ask why somebody chooses a specific word and this is how I learn more words" [child, one-year pilot]
	"Children get more active. Concept mapping encourages collaboration and gives nice results" [teacher, one-year pilot]
	"Children learn from each other and complete each other words [sic] in their conversations" [teacher, one-year pilot]
Promoting children's autonomy during the building of a map	"Concept mapping encourages spontaneous conversations" [teacher, five-month pilot]
	"The absolute surplus value is that words are given multiple meanings by the children and therefore the children can remember the words better" [teacher, one-year pilot]
	"There is a lot of interaction because all the information during concept mapping derives from the children themselves" [teacher, one-year pilot]
	"Some children took more initiatives in talking and there is more interaction in the small groups during concept mapping in comparison to working with a didactic method used for a whole class" [teacher, one-year pilot]

Table 2. Fragments with evidence for question 2

The benefits of the authoring concept mapping kit	Fragments of teachers and children's comments
Making children's conceptual and propositional knowledge explicit	"By talking about different areas, you work more effectively on the development of the vocabulary. Children are encouraged to make better networks between words" [teacher, five-month pilot]
	"Concept mapping is an improvement in the methods used in vocabulary learning. In the way we were teaching words we focused on the connection of word with themes and not so much on the relationships between the words. There was also no connection between themes and that was a pity. Concept mapping is an asset to our education." [teacher, five-month pilot]
	"Concept mapping is a fine addition to learn, to have more and better conversations, and it expands vocabulary" [teacher, one-year pilot]
	"We work with many word networks. By using concept mapping everything is visual so the children can focus better. They can also look back [review] to what already has been said" [teacher, one-year pilot]
	"Word networks sometimes need to be restricted with concept mapping otherwise the risk of too much digression will work counterproductive for some children" [teacher, one-year pilot]
Promoting children's autonomy during map building	"The stronger students make the networks much more extensive and add their own words to it" [teacher, five-month pilot]
	"The better students get the chance to extend meanings of words. And so, therefore they can increase their vocabulary" [teacher, five-month pilot]
	"By using concept mapping I get the opportunity to add my words" [child, one-year pilot]
	"I can add my own words with concept mapping" [child, one-year pilot]

Fig. 3. Concepts mapping on the theme "ill"

5 Outcomes of an Opinion Poll on the Motivation of the Teachers Concerning Concept Mapping

As part of the one-year pilot, a questionnaire was designed for teachers on their motivations to use concept mapping and support its implementation at the Institute. It was designed based on three important pillars of education [10]. Every human being has a natural need for autonomy ("I can do it myself, though not always alone"), competence ("I am confident about my own abilities"), and relationship ("others appreciate me and want to deal with me"). When these three needs are met in education, students and teachers can grow and will show motivation and commitment for learning. The questionnaire was applied after three months of working with concept mapping. Of the 25 teachers, 19 completed the questionnaire consisting of three parts addressing the three pillars.

5.1 Autonomy

Regarding autonomy, it can be said that most teachers felt that concept mapping was not a forced didactic structure or method they had to use in their groups. They felt that they had the space to apply it in a different way, if they had wished to (Table 3).

Table 3. Teacher responses on autonomy

	Strongly disagree	Disagree	No opinion, I do not know yet	Agree	Strongly agree
Q1: I feel that I can be myself in shaping concept mapping	1	0	3	10	5
Q2: When shaping concept mapping, I often feel that I have to do what other people recommend me	8	8	0	2	1

(Continued)

Table 3. (*Continued*)

	Strongly disagree	Disagree	No opinion, I do not know yet	Agree	Strongly agree
Q3: If I could choose, I would do it in another way	10	5	3	1	0
Q4: My tasks with regard to concept mapping correspond to what I really want to do	1	1	3	12	2
Q5: I feel free to shape concept mapping as I think it is good	1	0	4	10	4
Q6: In the context of concept mapping, I feel compelled to do things I do not want to do	12	6	0	0	1

5.2 Competence

Results show that about a third of teachers found difficult to answer the questions on the topic of feeling confident in applying concept mapping in the classroom. Another third felt that they mastered the tasks related to concept mapping. A quarter did not feel totally confident about using concept mapping in their classrooms. One question was about teachers estimating the opportunities that the students have to show what they know during concept mapping. All the teachers, except one, reported that students have more opportunities to show what they know in contrast with other methods they have used (Table 4).

Table 4. Teacher responses on competences

	Strongly disagree	Disagree	No opinion, I do not know yet	Agree	Strongly agree
Q7: I do not really feel competent to concept mapping.	7	6	4	1	1
Q8: I have mastered the tasks for concept mapping.	1	3	8	7	0
Q9: I feel qualified for concept mapping.	1	2	6	9	1
Q10: I doubt whether I can perform concept mapping well	5	6	4	3	1
Q11: During concept mapping the student gets more space to show his/her knowledge	1	0	0	12	6
Q12: I feel that I can bring the difficult tasks around concept mapping to a successful end	1	4	7	6	1

5.3   Relationship

Almost all the teachers reported that their motivation was influenced by the effect concept mapping was having on the children's learning. Besides this, all the teachers reported that it had an added value. More than half of the teachers pointed out that it offered more opportunities for spontaneous interaction between students. Teachers declared that they did not feel alone working with this approach. Most of them also liked to work together with the speech therapist (Table 5).

Table 5. Teacher responses on relationship

	Strongly disagree	Disagree	No opinion, I do not know yet	Agree	Strongly agree
Q13: The learning effect on children affects my motivation	0	1	1	12	5
Q14: In working with concept mapping, I feel alone	8	5	4	1	1
Q15: Concept mapping offers more space for spontaneous interaction between students	1	0	6	5	7
Q16: I see no added value in concept mapping	18	0	0	0	0
Q17: I often feel alone when working with colleagues with concept mapping	11	4	3	0	0
Q18: I like to work on concept mapping together with the speech therapist/teacher	1	0	0	7	10

5.4   Survey Outcome Discussion

A cautious conclusion should be made regarding the teachers' proficiency to teach with concept mapping. About 15 of the 19 teachers reported that they could use concept mapping in their teaching, could do it by themselves, felt confident and motivated of doing so, and felt that they were supported by colleagues when help was needed. Four teachers had doubts relating to its implementation or were insecure about their own abilities.

6   Discussion, New Developments, and Conclusions

6.1   The Authoring Kit and Interactive Language Learning

Similar to Gomez's studies [4] with children aged 5 to 6, our studies showed that the Authoring Kit enabled children to enhance meaning negotiation, autonomy, and active inquiry during the building of concept maps in company of peers and with teachers. Opportunities for the children to individually build concept maps are still to be implemented. Cassata-Widera's [5, p. 1] studies showed that concept maps have potential in facilitating a wider range of literacy activities in young children for three reasons. Firstly, the visual, hands-on, and representational qualities of concept maps. Secondly, they provide a unique opportunity for children who are not yet readers to create, manipulate, share, and interact with text in a highly personal, meaningful fashion. Thirdly, the logic in the concept map structure allows children to become familiar with expository, information-bearing language structures important for later school success. Cassata-Widera's [5] three reasons were also observed in our studies and with children of several ages.

Hoogenberg-Engbers [7] has written and taught that the Authoring Kit can support expanding the conceptual knowledge of children. Children can show what they know with concept maps. Teachers can use this information as assessment for learning [11]. Teachers, or children mutually, can give feedback on the visual representations of knowledge. Feedback gives children the opportunity to reflect on their knowledge, reorganize it or expand it. This social interaction also supports the development of perspective taking. Children experience that other people can have a different per-spectives or ideas. This can promote cooperative learning, critical and creative thinking [12, 13]. The process of making a concept map can also help children to develop metacognitive skills. Children need to make a plan, monitor their process of making the concept map, solve problems, and evaluate the outcome. Concept mapping can help in the development of self-regulatory processes in learning. But, teacher scaffolding is needed to get the full benefits [6]. Concept mapping can also help children to develop phonemic awareness. In the process of learning to read and write, children need to learn that sentences are divided in segments. It can help children's conceptions of word boundaries in speech [14].

The studies' outcomes further support these claims, as they showed that introducing concept mapping in teaching children with severe speech-language difficulties can have positive effects. Concept mapping during group learning encourages more spontaneous conversation, and peer-to-peer learning interactions. Children become more active learners because by making a concept map together they get a better understanding of each other and a better understanding of the relationships between words/concepts. It helps them with the development of knowledge. For example, individual vocabulary networks are expanded and the meaning of words and vocabulary are learned in more depth. Due to the children using the voice recorders, a side effect was the improvement of articulation – the correct pronunciation of words, and the stimulation of sentence structure.

6.2   New Developments

Using The Authoring Kit as an inspiration, the teachers developed their own kits used in the three pilots. Due to frequent use, the photo cards became worn out and the voice-recorders' sound quality diminished and worsened. Therefore, the voice recor-ders have been replaced with alternative ones sold via talkingproducts.com. One teacher, Ger Wensink, developed a concept mapping application for the Interactive Whiteboard (Fig. 4). This application has allowed teachers to save the results and reuse the concept map in another learning activity. The teachers are extremely happy with the development of this digital application because it has multiple possibilities.

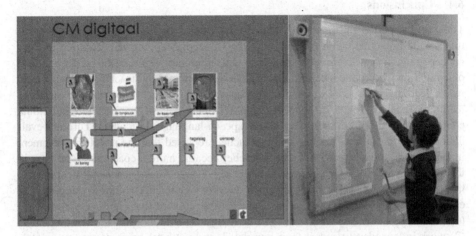

Fig. 4. Example flipchart on interactive Whiteboard (left); child making a concept map (right)

Dissemination activities have included visits by Hoogenberg-Engbers and Gomez in April 2013 and an article in the local media [15]. Gomez prepared an outcomes report for sharing with key people in the preschool concept mapping community and early childhood education. The replies of a number of colleagues were included in a message to the management encouraging the Institute to continue the work with a one-year pilot.

6.3 New Research Explorations

After consultation and sharing outcomes of pilots, the management, internal counselors and supervisors decided to introduce concept mapping as a mainstream didactic tool in the school year 2015–2016. Every grade will incorporate this tool into their teaching, except for the kindergarten groups (age 4 to 6), as they are currently implementing other methods. Next research explorations will involve studying the effects of concept mapping on passive vocabulary and how concept mapping could influence the learning of articulation. During the five-month pilot, it was noted that the voice-recorders enabled children to listen back to their own slurred pronunciation, and that they wanted to improve it. By listening back to own voice-recorded sentences, the children corrected the syntax during collaborative peer-conversations, and talked spontaneously about the word meaning. These outcomes should be researched in the future.

In parallel to the activities at the Institute, Kicken and Ernes are expanding the use of concept mapping to regular primary and secondary schools, and have given a workshop so more teachers in the Netherlands become familiar with the theory and can experience it. Hoogenberg-Engbers is also working at a primary school and has introduced concept mapping in the upper grades.

6.4   Conclusions

This paper reported on three consecutive pilot studies designed to research an Institute's wide implementation of the Authoring Concept Mapping Kit. This Kit enables concept mapping with verbal, symbolic, and emergent writing skills. The studies' outcomes showed that concept mapping matched perfectly the teaching methods used in the learning process of vocabulary expansion – an aspect of interactive language learning. Teachers found in concept mapping a new natural way to meet individual educational needs of children with severe speech-language difficulties. Through evaluation forms and a final teacher survey, teachers reported that the novel improvement in their teaching practice was that each teacher became more a coach and facilitator in the learning process of the children. It was a big change for the teachers to experience how the process of asking the right open questions enabled children to suggest concepts, and change the concept maps. The teachers reported that children were able to (1) make extensive networks of words representing concepts and relationships, (2) work independently and at their own level, and (3) have more peer to peer interactions and learn more from each other. Teachers freely adapted the Kit to own teaching activities, and felt that they could develop their own designs departing from the Kit idea, including the development of an application for the Interactive Whiteboard. Concept mapping is now considered a good addition to the already existing educational methods because concepts are visually supported. The representation of meanings with verbal and visual symbols was found to be very important for this type of learners.

Acknowledgements. This research project would have not been possible with out the support of the directors, internal counselors and supervisors, teachers and speech therapists of the Institute Vitus Zuid Mgr. Hanssen. Thanks also go to colleagues who provided support and technical advice, and especially to the Director of the External Service who strongly encouraged the undertaking of these pilot studies. Finally, thanks to Rodney Tamblyn for proofreading versions leading to this publication.

References

1. Novak, J.D., Gowin, D.B.: Learning How to Learn. Cambridge University Press, New York (1984)
2. Coffey, J.W., Carnot, M.J., Feltovich, P.J., Feltovich, J., Hoffman, R.R., Cañas, A.J., Novak, J.D.: A summary of literature pertaining to the use of concept mapping techniques and technologies for education and performance support. IHMC - Institute for Human and Machine Cognition, Technical report submitted to the Chief of Naval Education and Training, Pensacola, Florida (2003)

3. Gomez, G.: An authoring concept mapping kit for the early childhood classroom. In: Cañas, A.J., Novak, J.D. (eds.) Concept Maps: Theory, Methodology, Technology, Proceedings of the 2nd International Conference on Concept Mapping, pp. 32–38. Universidad de Costa Rica (2006)

4. Gomez, G.: Enhancing autonomy, meaning negotiation, and active inquiry in preschool concept mapping. In: Lupion Torres, P., Veiga Marriott, R.C. (eds.) Handbook of Research on Collaborative Learning Using Concept Maps, pp. 383–401. Information Science Reference, Hershey (2010)

5. Cassata-Widera, A.E.: Concept mapping and early literacy: a promising crossroads. In: Cañas, A.J., Reiska, P., Ahlberg, M., Novak, J.D. (eds.) Concept Maps: Theory, Methodology, Technology, Proceedings of the 3rd International Conference on Concept Mapping, pp. 189–196. Tallin University, Tallin (2008)

6. Cassata-Widera, A.E.: Concept Mapping with Young Children: From Representation to Metacognition. VDM Verlag, Saarbrücken (2009)

7. Hoogenberg-Engbers, I.: Concept Mapping met Kleuters/Leren Communiceren op Papier. Tijdschrift voor Remedial Teaching, vol. 21, pp. 20–24. Onderwijstijdschriftenplein (2013)

8. Damhuis, R., Litjens, P.: Mondelinge Communicatie: Drie Werkwijzen voor Mondelinge Taalontwikkeling. Expertisecentrum, Nijmegen (2003)

9. van den Nulft, D., Verhallen, M.: Met Woorden in de Weer. Uitgeverij Coutinho, Bussum (2009)

10. Stevens, L.: Zin in School. Uitgeverij EDG Thuiswinkel, Utrecht (2004)

11. Clarke, S.: Active Learning Through Formative Assessment. Hodder Education, London (2008)

12. Birbili, M.: Mapping Knowledge: Concept Maps in Early Childhood Education. ECRP 8 (2006). http://ecrp.uiuc.edu/v8n2/birbili.html

13. Gallenstein, N.L.: Never too young for a concept map. Sci. Child. **43**, 44–47 (2005)

14. Flanigan, K.: "Daddy, where did the words go?" How teachers can help emergent readers develop a concept of word in text. Read. Improv. **43**, 37–49 (2006)

15. van Veen, P.: Positieve resultaten met conceptmappen op Mgr. hanssenschool. VHZ: Van Horen Zeggen **55**, 6–7 (2014)

Is My Concept Map Large Enough?

Alberto J. Cañas[1(✉)], Priit Reiska[2], and Joseph D. Novak[1]

[1] Institute for Human and Machine Cognition, Pensacola, FL, USA
{acanas,jnovak}@ihmc.us
[2] Tallinn University, Tallinn, Estonia
priit@tlu.ee

Abstract. Users learning to concept map often confront the problem of when is it that their concept map is complete. They ask the question "Is my concept map large enough?". As they progress in their understanding of concept maps, users often stop asking themselves whether the concept map is the appropriate size, which is key when using concept maps as means to communicate and share knowledge. In this paper we examine what factors need to be taken into account when determining the proper size for a concept map, and examine the importance of the purpose of the concept map and its intended audience. The stages through which a new Cmapper goes are also examining, and propose that to reach a Level 3 Excellent Cmapper, the question to be asked is "Is my concept map small enough?".

1 Introduction

Since its inception in the 1970's by Joseph Novak and his research group at Cornell University, the concept mapping tool has extended throughout the world, reaching users of all ages and has been applied to all domains of knowledge [1, 2]. During this time, throughout our professional careers we have had the opportunity to introduce concept mapping to students, teachers, professors, and professionals from a large variety of knowledge areas and organizations and in a large number of countries, through workshops, courses, tutoring, academic supervision, consulting, and collaboration with colleagues. In this paper we present our insight into some of the stages users go through as they progress in their ability to construct better concept maps.

2 Concept Mapping: 'Easy' or 'Hard'

Concept mapping is both 'easy' and 'hard'. The drawing part is easy. You can draw a simple concept map in a few minutes, and show somebody the simple steps to construct a concept map just as fast. Two concepts connected by a linking phrase form a proposition. Keep on adding concepts and propositions and you have constructed your first concept map. The process of constructing and refining a concept map is further simplified by using concept mapping software tools such as CmapTools [3]. During the teacher training workshops at the Conéctate al Conocimiento Project in Panamá [4] we had the opportunity to work with teachers who had never used a keyboard, let alone a computer.

© Springer International Publishing Switzerland 2016
A. Cañas et al. (Eds.): CMC 2016, CCIS 635, pp. 128–143, 2016.
DOI: 10.1007/978-3-319-45501-3_10

Once they figured out in a few minutes how to use a mouse and the simple mechanics of building a map, they were off constructing first maps. Of course they were initially slower than their colleagues who were familiar with computers, but this difference disappeared by the second day of the workshop. We had a similar experience in a large scale research project that involved hundreds of Estonian high school students constructing a concept map about a science topic [5]. A large percentage of the participants had little or no experience building concept maps and using CmapTools, but were able to build their first concept maps without problems. In general, the reaction from most people to whom we show concept maps or knowledge models for the first time is that the maps look very 'simple' and 'easy to make'. So the initial learning curve of learning the mechanics of constructing a concept map is small.

However, getting to build *good* concept maps is 'hard'. Our experience tells us that once the user gets the mechanics right (concept, proposition, hierarchy of concepts, etc.), the problem turns into the difficulty of expressing his or her understanding of the topic in a concept map. The questions regarding the mechanics turn into questions regarding the content of the map. The non-linear nature of the concept map allows it to grow in 'any direction'. Concepts can be added just as easily if linked to the root of the concept map or to one of the leave concepts, in contrast to adding content to a text. It is therefore difficult to determine when the concept map is done. "Is my concept map large enough?" is a typical question. The user becomes aware that more concepts could be added, and that the concept map could continue growing forever. Sometimes, users stop after constructing a very simple, top-level map and feel that they are done, while it is clear that their knowledge about the topic being mapped is much broader and deeper than what has been expressed in the map. In other cases, they continue adding more and more concepts, and the concept map loses its focus. The user becomes aware that building a good concept map is 'hard'. Learning to determine when the concept is 'large enough' takes time, depends on a series of parameters that we will examine below, and is very personal in nature. In this paper we discuss these issues.

3   A Categorization Perspective

We define *concept* as a perceived regularity in events or objects, or records of events or objects, designated by a label [6]. There is a clear relation between a concept and a category, where "a concept can be defined as an idea or mental image that allows for things which share common properties to be grouped together or categorized" [7]. We could think of a concept map as a set of categories, and that the relationship between these categories is expressed through connections with linking phrases.

In this paper we take a different perspective: we will look at the concept map, not at each concept, as a category. The concepts within the concept map are the things, objects or elements of the category. Categorization is a task that we are all very familiar with: we are constantly categorizing items, people, events, etc. When we are categorizing we are continuously confronted with issues such as (a) how many categories should I create? and (b) in which category should I place each item? In most cases, we want to categorize items in a way that allows us to easily find or locate them afterwards. Intuitively, we look for a categorization scheme for which there is little or no ambiguity as to which category an item belongs to. That is, we want the categories to be distinct. We need to note that the level of distinction between categories cannot be inferred from the physical properties of the categories' structure [8]. We could initially think that the number of categories and their average size would be an indication of the level of distinction. But experience tells us that it's not just the number of categories, but the semantics of the categories – what each category is about – that allows us to discriminate between categories when categorizing an item. Cañas [9] has shown how the level of semantic distinction used in a set of categories can be calculated by measuring the *variability within a category* (V), that is, how close the category members are to each other, and how dissimilar the categories are from each other, which he calls the *variability between categories* (D). Without going into the details of how the measurements are obtained, the *variability ratio R = mean(V)/D* provides a measure of the overall level of distinction used to construct the set of categories. Low levels of R provide a large number of categories that are hard to distinguish from each other, while large values of R indicate categories with many irrelevant or unrelated elements. Results seem to indicate that, for a given task, that is, for a set of items and types of search for items, there is a range of R that will result in best retrieval performance as is shown in Fig. 1. This optimal value for R implies categories for which all items clearly belong in the corresponding category, and there are no items outside a category that should be in it; it means that categories are clearly distinct from each other. For a given set of retrieval tasks and items, the optimal value of R is the response to the question "How large should my categories be?".

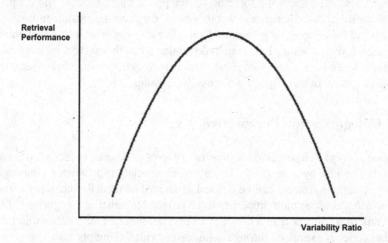

Fig. 1. Retrieval performance vs variability ratio for a set of categories and items

Retrieval, however, is not a common task in concept mapping. Rohani-Tabatabai [10] has shown that the variability ratio R is also a good predictor of the effectiveness of the task of communicating categories between persons. Additionally, the literature shows that when the ratio of variability within to variability between is high, the learners experience more difficulty in learning the categories, compared to learning the categories with low ratio of within to between variability [11, 12].

Extrapolating to a concept map as a category, these research results suggest that there might be an 'optimal size' for a concept map for a given task and purpose. We first need to clarify what 'size' means for a concept map, since a concept map has a more complex structure and semantics than a category.

4 The Size of a Concept Map

We saw that the semantic distinction within and between categories is more relevant than the number of categories and the number of items in the categories in predicting the effectiveness of tasks on categories. When discussing the *size* of a concept map we also have to distinguish between structure and content. A concept map consists of a graphical representation of a set of concepts, usually enclosed in ovals or rectangles of some type, and relationships between concepts indicated by a connecting line linking two concepts. Words on the line, referred to as linking words or linking phrases, specify the relationship between the two concepts. The two concepts with the linking phrases that join them form propositions. Propositions are statements about some object or event in the universe, either naturally occurring or constructed. Propositions contain two or more concepts connected using linking words or phrases to form a meaningful statement. Sometimes these are called semantic units, or units of meaning [13]. Concept maps therefore consist of "graphical structure" and "content".

When examining a concept map to determine its size, we need to look at both the content and the structure. In addition, we need to consider the task under which the concept was constructed. Cañas et al. [14] explain how the instructions or conditions under which a concept map is constructed influence and restrict the resulting concept map, as shown in Fig. 2. Under the conditions on the lower left quadrant of the graph, the reduced freedom in content and structure results in practically fixed size concept maps, both in content and structure. Even providing a fixed list of concepts only allows the freedom in the number of connections and linking phrases the concept map author can add. Therefore, for the analysis of the concept map size, we will consider only concept maps constructed under the tasks which are within the thick oval in Fig. 2, and thus more or less the top right quadrant of the graph.

The graphical nature of concept maps lends itself to counting graphical elements to determine the map's size. The more obvious measure is the number of concepts. This is reflected by the common question during workshops, "Should I add more concepts?", and by the frequent suggestion "You are missing concept *xxxx*" when commenting on a concept map. Other graphical measures, such as the hierarchical level or number of branching points are not usually considered when looking at the size of the concept map. The number of linking phrases, however, is an important component of the size measurement. The density of connections, that is, the average number of linking phrases per concept, does provide a measure of size. Notice that counting the number of propositions is not the same as a composite count of concepts and density of connections. Two concept maps could have the same number of propositions, but the one with the higher density

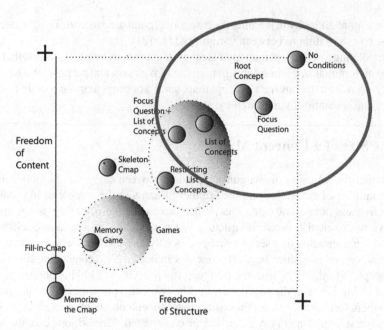

Fig. 2. freedom of structure vs. freedom of content conditions during concept mapping. Adapted from [14].

of connections would have a much smaller number of concepts. This leads us to the quality of the structure, which we'll discuss in the next section.

As we mentioned earlier, a concept map consists of structure and content. The content of the map is expressed through its concepts, its linking phrases, and the propositions they form. Not surprisingly, the list of criteria used to assess content reported by Strautmane [15] is based on these three elements. Additionally, the focus question provides a key criterion when assessing content. The content of a concept map is not countable. The size of a concept map could be increased because content is missing, or the size of a concept map may need to be reduced because it includes content that is not relevant to the focus question. That is, the tightness of the concepts (how closely related the concepts are), how well the concept maps and linking phrases answer the focus question, and the quality of the propositions, are the equivalent of the 'measure' of variability V for the concept map. This implies assessing the quality of the content of the concept map.

5   Quality of Structure and Content of a Concept Map

The categorization research described above informed us that just counting number of categories and items in the categories is not an effective way to predict performance in retrieval, communication and learning tasks involving categories. The semantic distinction between and within categories need to be measured [9–12]. In a similar way, assessing a concept map requires evaluating the quality of content as well as the quality of the structure of the concept map. Cañas et al. [16] discuss what makes a good concept map and present a classification of concept maps based on the quality of the structure, content and the quality of the concept maps, as shown in Table 1. A concept map that has good structural quality but poor content quality, or poor structural quality and good content quality is anyway considered a Poor, Level 1 concept map. A concept map with good structural quality and good content quality is classified as a Good, Level 2 map. A Level 3 concept map has good structural quality, good content quality, and good overall concept map quality.

Table 1. Classification of concept maps depending on the quality of the structure, content, and the quality of the concept map [16].

Quality level		Structural quality	Content quality	Concept map quality
1	Poor	✓		
			✓	
2	Good	✓	✓	
3	Excellent	✓	✓	✓

One could easily conclude that a Level 3 concept map is at the 'optimal' size. However, a Level 2 or even a Level 3 concept map may not be appropriate in terms of size, structure and/or content if the audience to which its presented or its intended purpose is changed. Derbentseva and Kwantes [17] report on how concept maps that received a positive reaction for their analytics support capability received a variety of reactions from decision makers when they were presented with critical information for decision making as a concept map. The decision makers were only map readers, and their reaction ranged from immediate embrace to the rejection of the use of concept maps. The authors continue to discuss the human factors aspects of concept map read-ability and flow, analyzing the design and layout of concept maps. In our experience, concept map authors seldom take into consideration the circumstances under which a concept map is going to be 'read' when constructing the map. As a result, the map could be Level 2 or 3, and thereby the right *size* from the author's perspective, but not the right *size* from the readers' perspective.

6   How Large Should a Concept Map Be?

The question "Is my concept map large enough" leads us to ask the question "How large should a concept map be?". The answer to this second question is a size-range that depends, in our experience, on one important set of criteria: the purpose of the map, what it is going to be used for, and by whom. Understanding this criteria is one of the characteristics of an Excellent Cmapper as described by Cañas et al. [16], as we will explain later. Figure 3 shows that Excellent Cmappers construct Level 3, Excellent concept maps.

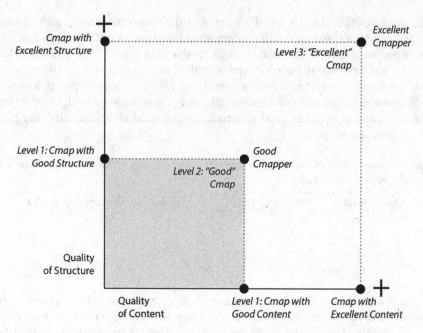

Fig. 3. An Excellent Cmapper constructs Level 3, "Excellent Cmaps" [16].

6.1   Concept Map Size Depending on the Intended Purpose of the Concept Map

A Level 3 Excellent concept map is probably of the right size for its intended purpose. But this does not mean all Excellent concept maps are of the same size, not even for the same Cmapper. Additionally, we have found that depending on the intended purpose of the concept map, there are size ranges that are recommended, or that have worked for us. Concept maps are being used for a large variety of purposes [2] and so we don't intend to provide an exhaustive list, nor do we pretend to have one. For the sake of explanation, we will examine a set of intended purposes as a way to present how the size of map could vary depending on its intended purpose and audience.

Student Assessment. Possibly the most common use of concept mapping is the assessment by instructors of student's understanding of a particular topic. In most cases the student has, unfortunately, only one shot at getting the concept map 'right' according to what the instructor expects; students don't get the opportunity to revise their maps based on the instructor's or peers' feedback. As was explained earlier, the task given may limit the student's freedom of structure and content, as is the case when given a list of concepts and asked not to add additional concepts [14], but we won't consider those cases. For other tasks, as shown in the top right quadrant of Fig. 2, given the heavy reliance of most concept mapping assessment rubrics on structural measurements [16], students may just as well add as many concepts as possible, many levels of hierarchy, and lots of cross links and branching points to make sure they cover all items in the rubric. Similarly, students will tend to add as much content as possible in terms of concepts and linking phrase with the hope that they will match what instructors expect. Students may presume the instructor will have a checklist of content and structure items and want to make sure all are marked as covered on the list. In this circumstance, there is no way for the student to know what the *right size* for the concept map is, and so they ask the instructor, the intended audience, "Is my concept map large enough?".

The students, mostly novices in the subject area, will mostly tend to add as many concepts as they can think of to the map. Experts with a better understanding will tend to build more concise maps, since they will tend to include only the more relevant, key concepts, describe the 'big ideas', and have a better conceptual hierarchy. In concept mapping, larger is not always better. As we will explain below, this is a natural progression towards becoming an Excellent Cmapper.

When the concept mapping in the classroom is a process, where students either individually or in groups iteratively work on their maps as they learn about a unit, and feedback from the instructor and peers facilitate the improvements of the maps [18], the students will evolve towards Good Cmappers and their interaction with the instructor will lead to determining the size of concept maps the instructor expects. As the concept maps integrate into knowledge models, the issue of variability between categories D comes to play: the need to make sure the concept maps are semantically distinct (the focus question for each concept map is of great aid in this distinction), and questions begin to arise such as in which concept map(s) should particular concepts be included. A good balance between number of concept maps and the size of each concept map will lead to a better knowledge model, just as a good variability ratio R led to better performance in categorization tasks.

Knowledge Elicitation and Archiving. We distinguish between the archiving and the sharing of knowledge as separate and distinct objectives when constructing concept maps. During knowledge elicitation for archiving, in particular when recording the understanding of an expert whose knowledge could be lost (e.g. because of retirement [19]), concept maps tend to be larger and denser. We want to make sure all details are included and nothing is lost. Figure 4 is an example of a concept map constructed by Joseph Novak after a set of interviews with several experts at NASA's Astrobiology Institute, where the intention was to capture the whole interviews and show how the experts' views of Astrobiology were interlinked. If this concept map was split into several maps some cross links may be lost (although CmapTools allows cross links between concepts in different Cmaps). For completeness purposes, this concept map was kept large – the purpose justified it. It was not meant for communication or knowledge sharing, for which a more concise version of the Cmap was made.

Knowledge Sharing and Communication. Derbentseva and Kwantes [17] reported how concept maps that were constructed at a group or committee were not always well received when presented to decision makers. We have similar experience with use of concept maps in organizations, both with maps we built and maps built by others. We recall in particular a colleague at a large worldwide leader technology company, an enthusiast of concept mapping, who was surprised that his concept maps were not well received by his colleagues. Looking at the maps it was clear that they were a great tool

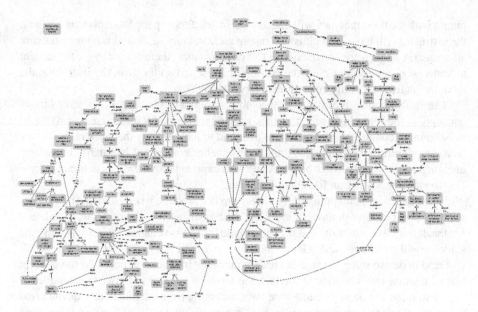

Fig. 4. Astrobiology concept map, by J. Novak.

for him, but were too complex and dense for a reader to follow. Derbentseva and Kwantes [17] propose readability and reading flow as key aspects to consider when constructing concept maps for communication purposes. This seems to be an important research topic that has not been addressed.

At IHMC we have collaborated for many years with NASA on a long series of Blue Sky meetings where leading scientists and researchers get together to brainstorm on innovative and often far-fetched ideas on Space exploration. From the very beginning concept mapping has been used as one of the means to record the ideas presented. Initially, large dense concept maps were constructed that included all the details discussed in the meetings. The concept maps tended to look like that in Fig. 4. However, one of the main objectives of concept mapping the meetings was to easily communicate the key, innovative ideas that were presented to NASA headquarters. The large, dense concept maps were useless for this purpose. We switched to constructing a set of concept maps, using an 8.5in × 11in page for a printed Cmap as a reference for the largest canvas space for each map and using CmapTools' default sizes for fonts, concepts and linking phrases (no cheating by using smaller fonts) (the concept maps are delivered as part of a printed report anyway). The new sized maps were very well received as they are much more readable and contain only the new key ideas, disregarding details, and serve well the purpose of communicating these ideas to NASA leaders. The recently added feature in CmapTools that limits the canvas size is a convenient way to keep the concept map within the desired space limits. Note that limiting the canvas size doesn't mean that one starts cramming concepts into the available space making the map unreadable. Readability is a key aspect of concept maps built for knowledge sharing.

Organizer Concept Maps. Concept maps are often used as 'organizers', whether as advance organizers [20], to present learning itineraries [21], or as navigational tools to organize large collections of media (e.g. [22–24]). In organizer concept maps the knowledge presented does not go as deep as in concept maps used for communication, and the concept maps tend to be smaller in terms of number of concepts and density of connections, facilitating the easily navigate through the maps and, when available, selecting from linked resources. These maps are not meant to be studied, but may present new knowledge that the reader can easily comprehend. Readability is of course, an issue.

Our experience has taught us to construct these maps smaller and simpler. As an example, in the first knowledge model we designed as an iPad app which was reported in Cañas et al. [25], the concept maps were about the same size as those used for communication in NASA Blue Sky meetings, after reducing them from larger concept maps resulting from knowledge elicitation meetings with NASA scientists. Even then, we found the concept maps to be too complex and dense for easy navigation on an iPad screen. For the next stage of the project which resulted in the NASA/IHMC Asteroid Retrieval Mission (ARM) iPad App available at the iTunes store [24], the size range for the maps was reduced to around 20–25 concepts per map. Figure 5 is an example of one of the concept maps in the App. For another knowledge model for the iPad involving users with low reading scores, the average number of concepts was reduced even further. It's important to note that in the majority of cases the removed concepts were not added to a new submap or to another concept map; they were discarded given the depth level

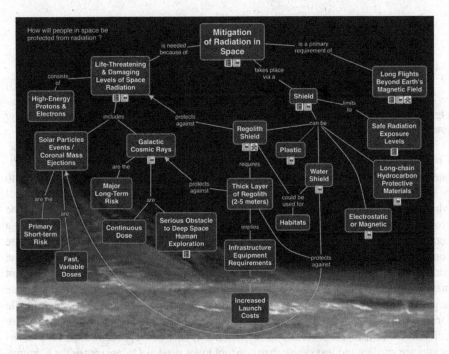

Fig. 5. Radiation Mitigation concept map from the NASA/IHMC Asteroid Redirect Mission (ARM) iPad app [24].

of the new concept maps that were being redone, or their explanation was covered by a linked resource.

Itinerary concept maps, such as those in the Learn section of the Cmap website, guide users in a non-linear way through the learning stages needed to learn a topic, such as Learning to Build Concept Maps as shown in Fig. 6. Itineraries organize learning objects and instructor's experience in using the learning objects, and tend to be small in size. These organizer maps tend to be within a similar range of size.

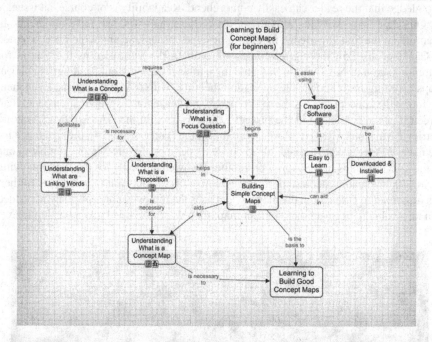

Fig. 6. Itinerary concept map on Learning to Build Concept Maps, by A.J. Cañas. From http://cmap.ihmc.us/docslearn.php

Concept Map-Based Presentations. The presentation module in CmapTools facilitates the step-wise display of concept map elements (concepts and linking phrases) to be used for oral presentations, e.g. at conferences. In front of a large audience, some of which are far away from the screen, concept maps need to be small and concise. The presenter does not want to have the audience trying to figure out and understand a complex, large concept map. Unfortunately, we have seen many presenters use large concept maps, with small fonts, during presentations in which it was impossible for the audience to read or understand the map. Once again, even if you already have a concept map about the topic you want to present but which was prepared for another purpose (e.g. a concept map that describes your project), this doesn't mean the map is suitable for usage in a presentation. Different audiences and different purposes may require different concept maps. Overall, our experience is that concept maps used for presentations are smaller and less dense than concept maps used as Organizers or for Communication. Figure 7 shows an example.

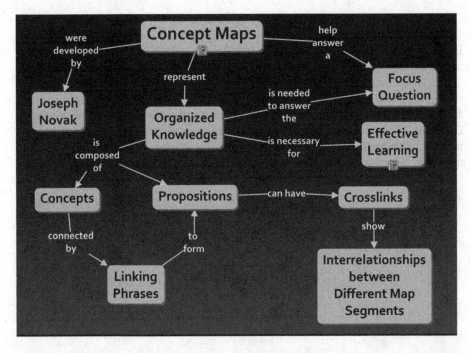

Fig. 7. A concept map part of a Cmap-based presentation using CmapTools presentation module.

Own Personal Use. We all construct concept maps for our own personal use. It could be for note taking, to organize our ideas on an academic paper, or to learn about a new topic, among a lot of other possible uses. For personal uses, the size of the concept map will be that which satisfies our interest in constructing the map. Given that the map creator is the map reader, it should be easy to determine when the concept map is large enough.

7 Building Concept Maps that are Large Enough

Even though we presented different size-ranges for the different purposes of concept maps, there are a few criteria that all concept maps should have to be of the *right size*. Notice that these are necessary (or recommended) but not sufficient conditions.

1. The concept map should answer the focus question
2. The concept map should be as concise as possible while fulfilling its objective; smaller is better
3. All concepts and propositions should be relevant to the topic of the concept map and to answering the focus question
4. There should be no 'unnecessary' concepts, propositions or crosslinks
5. The concept map should not be missing any key, relevant concepts, propositions or crosslinks

Not surprisingly, these are some of criteria for Level 3, Excellent concept maps.

Geoff Briggs, when describing the construction of the concept maps presented in Briggs et al. [26], commented that his problem wasn't an inability to find which concepts to link, but rather determining which propositions provided a clear explanation, and only those that contributed to the explanation.

Our experience has shown that new users' development as a Cmapper follow a graph similar to that in Fig. 8, from the time they start concept mapping to the time they reach Excellent Cmapper. This figure shows the size of the concept maps that Cmappers tend to build throughout this time period. Note that this graph is meant to show a general tendency, with no specific time periods or concept map sizes. Different users pass through these stages at a different rhythm.

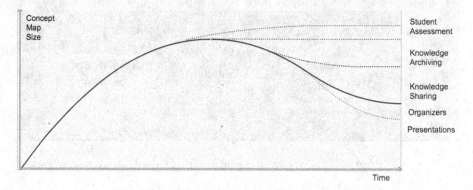

Fig. 8. Cmapper's concept maps size across time.

New users begin constructing small concept maps, trying to understand the mechanics of constructing the map, particularly if they are also learning to use concept mapping software such as CmapTools. By the time they start refining their first few concept maps and building subsequent maps, the size of their concept maps increases. During the construction of your first concept maps, it's hard to determine when you are done, and thus the question "Is my concept map large enough?". There is still no clear understanding of the importance of key concepts, crosslinks, and responding to the focus question.

Students who build concept maps only as a response to assessment questions seldom get beyond this point, often close to the peak of the curve. As discussed above, their maps are as large as possible in order to try to meet the instructor's expectations. Most students who continue to work on their maps as they learn their subject matter and get feedback from the instructor and peers will start to discriminate between key and irrelevant concepts, and their maps will become better built structurally and content-wise, and more concise, as has been reported by Dowd et al. [27].

Users who understand well the topic they are mapping will soon begin to comprehend the importance of the key concepts and big ideas, the importance of linking phrases, and will begin to revise and rethink their concept maps. As these users continue to build concept maps, they will evolve towards the right of the curve, towards becoming Good or even Excellent Cmappers. These are the users depicted by the solid line in Fig. 8. Some of them will reach the level of expertise in concept mapping where they recognize the importance of the target audience and the purpose of the concept map as a factor in determining the type and size of map they will construct, possibly having reached the level of Excellent Cmapper. In Fig. 8, on the right we have listed some of the purposes of the concept maps which we described in this paper ordered by the range of sizes of maps we discussed, without intending to link them particularly to the different curves. The intention is to show that an Excellent Cmapper will identify the purpose of the concept map and will build a concept map accordingly. The family of curves show that the concept maps for different purposes have different sizes. Not all Cmappers follow the curve all the way to the end. Some are stuck somewhere in the middle, constructing large concept maps or always maps of similar sizes. For many of them, some guidance or tutoring would help them move along the curve.

8 Summary

We have described the issues involved in determining the size, or range of sizes, of a concept map based on its intended purpose and audience, and have presented research results in categorization as a guidance in determining the importance of measuring beyond counting structural elements when determining the size of a concept map. Our experience has shown that new users, because of their novice status, often don't know when they are done building their concept map, and wonder whether they should continue adding more concepts. With time however, better Cmappers tend to build smaller, more concise maps. The questions users should be asking then, is "Is my concept map small enough"?

References

1. Novak, J.D., Cañas, A.J.: The origins of the concept mapping tool and the continuing evolution of the tool. Inf. Vis. J. **5**, 175–184 (2006)
2. Novak, J.D., Cañas, A.J.: The universality and ubiquitousness of concept maps. In: Sánchez, J., Cañas, A.J., Novak, J.D. (eds.) Concept Maps: Making Learning Meaningful. Proceedings of the Fourth International Conference on Concept Mapping, vol. 1, pp. 1–13. Universidad de Chile, Viña del Mar, Chile (2010)
3. Cañas, A.J., Hill, G., Carff, R., Suri, N., Lott, J., Eskridge, T., Gómez, G., Arroyo, M., Carvajal, R.: CmapTools: a knowledge modeling and sharing environment. In: Cañas, A.J., Novak, J.D., González, F.M. (eds.) Concept Maps: Theory, Methodology, Technology. Proceedings of the First International Conference on Concept Mapping, vol. I, pp. 125–133. Universidad Pública de Navarra, Pamplona, Spain (2004)
4. Tarté, G.: Conéctate al Conocimiento: Una Estrategia Nacional de Panamá basada en Mapas Conceptuales. In: Cañas, A.J., Novak, J.D. (eds.) Concept Maps: Theory, Methodology, Technology. Proceedings of the Second International Conference on Concept Mapping, vol. 1, pp. 144–152. Universidad de Costa Rica, San José, Costa Rica (2006)
5. Soika, K., Reiska, P.: Large scale studies with concept mapping. J. Educ. Teach. Train. **1**, 142–153 (2013)

6. Novak, J.D., Cañas, A.J.: The theory underlying concept maps and how to construct and use them. Technical report, Institute for Human and Machine Cognition (2008)
7. Oden, G.C.: Concept, knowledge, and thought. Annu. Rev. Psychol. **38**, 203–227 (1987)
8. Raymond, D.R., Cañas, A.J., Tompa, F.W., Safayeni, F.R.: Measuring the effectiveness of personal database structures. Int. J. Man Mach. Stud. **31**, 237–256 (1989)
9. Cañas, A.J.: Variability as a measure of semantic structure in document storage and retrieval. Ph.D., Department of Management Sciences, University of Waterloo, Waterloo, Ontario, p. 149 (1985)
10. Rohani-Tabatabai, M.: Effects of category structures on learning and communication of the learned categories. Ph.D., Department of Management Sciences, University of Wateloro, Waterloo, Ontario (2014)
11. Minda, J.P., Smith, J.D.: Prototypes in category learning: the effects of category size, category structure, and stimulus complexity. J. Exp. Psychol. Learn. Mem. Cogn. **27**, 775 (2001)
12. Kloos, H., Sloutsky, V.M.: What's behind different kinds of kinds: effects of statistical density on learning and representation of categories. J. Exp. Psychol. Gen. **137**, 52 (2008)
13. Cañas, A.J., Novak, J.D.: Concept mapping using CmapTools to enhance meaningful learning. In: Osaka, A., Shum, S.B., Sherborne, T. (eds.) Knowledge Cartography. Springer, London (2008)
14. Cañas, A.J., Novak, J.D., Reiska, P.: Freedom vs. restriction of content and structure during concept mapping - possibilities and limitations for construction and assessment. In: Cañas, A.J., Novak, J.D., Vanhear, J. (eds.) Concept Maps: Theory, Methodology, Technology - Proceedings of the Fifth International Conference on Concept Mapping, vol. 1. University of Malta, Valletta (2012)
15. Strautmane, M.: Concept map-based knowledge assessment tasks and their scoring criteria: an overview. In: Cañas, A.J., Novak, J.D., Vanhear, J. (eds.) Concept Maps: Theory, Methodology, Technology. Proceedings of the Fifth International Conference on Concept Mapping, vol. 2, pp. 80–88. University of Malta, Valletta, Malta (2012)
16. Cañas, A.J., Novak, J.D., Reiska, P.: How good is my concept map? Am I a good Cmapper? Knowl. Manag. E-Learn.: Int. J. (KM&EL) **7**, 6–19 (2015)
17. Derbentseva, N., Kwantes, P.: Cmap readability: propositional parsimony, map layout and semantic clarity and flow. In: Correia, P.R.M., Malachias, M.E.I., Cañas, A.J., Novak, J.D. (eds.) Proceedings of the Sixth International Conference on Concept Mapping, pp. 86–93. University of Sao Paulo, Santos (2014)
18. Novak, J.D., Cañas, A.J.: Building on constructivist ideas and CmapTools to create a new model for education. In: Cañas, A.J., Novak, J.D., González, F.M. (eds.) Concept Maps: Theory, Methodology, Technology. Proceedings of the 1st International Conference on Concept Mapping. Universidad Pública de Navarra, Pamplona, Spain (2004)
19. Hoffman, R.R., Lintern, G.: Eliciting and representing the knowledge of experts. In: Cambridge Handbook of Expertise and Expert Performance, pp. 203–222 (2006)
20. Ausubel, D.P.: The Psychology of Meaningful Verbal Learning. Grune and Stratton, New York (1963)
21. Cañas, A.J., Novak, J.D.: Itineraries: capturing instructors' experience using concept maps as learning object organizers. In: Sánchez, J., Cañas, A.J., Novak, J.D. (eds.) Concept Maps: Making Learning Meaningful. Proceedings of the Fourth International Conference on Concept Mapping, vol. 1. Universidad de Chile, Viña del Mar (2010)
22. Ford, K.M., Coffey, J.W., Cañas, A.J., Andrews, E.J., Turner, C.W.: Diagnosis and explanation by a nuclear cardiology expert system. Int. J. Expert Syst. **9**, 499–506 (1996)

23. Hoffman, R.R., Coffey, J.W., Ford, K.M., Carnot, M.J.: STORM-LK: a human-centered knowledge model for weather forecasting. In: Proceedings of the 45th Annual Meeting of the Human Factors and Ergonomics Society (2001)
24. IHMC: NASA Asteroid Redirect Mission iPad App (2016)
25. Cañas, A.J., Carff, R., Marcon, M.: Knowledge model viewers for the iPad and the web. In: Cañas, A.J., Novak, J.D., Vanhear, J. (eds.) Concept Maps: Theory, Methodology, Technology - Proceedings of the Fifth International Conference on Concept Mapping. University of Malta, Malta (2012)
26. Briggs, G., Shamma, D.A., Cañas, A.J., Carff, R., Scargle, J., Novak, J.D.: Concept maps applied to mars exploration public outreach. In: Cañas, A.J., Novak, J.D., González, F. (eds.) Concept Maps: Theory, Methodology, Technology. Proceedings of the First International Conference on Concept Mapping, vol. I, pp. 109–116. Universidad Pública de Navarra, Pamplona, Spain (2004)
27. Dowd, J.E., Duncan, T., Reynolds, J.A.: Concept maps for improved science reasoning and writing: complexity isn't everything. ICBE-Life Sci. Educ. **14**, ar39 (2015)

Learning from Static versus Animated Pictures of Embodied Knowledge

A Pilot Study on Reconstructing a Ballet Choreography as Concept Map

Bärbel Fürstenau[1(✉)], Maria Kuhtz[1], Boglárka Simon-Hatala[2], and Lenie Kneppers[3]

[1] Technische Universität Dresden, Dresden, Germany
baerbel.fuerstenau@tu-dresden.de, maria.kuhtz@gmx.de
[2] Semperoper Dresden, Dresden, Germany
boglarka.hatala@semperoper.de
[3] University of Amsterdam, Amsterdam, The Netherlands
H.C.Kneppers@uva.nl

Abstract. In a research study we investigated whether static or animated pictures better support learning of abstract pedagogical content about action-oriented learning. For that purpose, we conducted a study with two experimental groups. One group received a narration about learning theory and a supporting series of static pictures, the other a narration and animated pictures. As pictures we used ballet positions so that both static pictures, and animations display a ballet choreography. Ballet positions are specific pictures which show embodied abstract knowledge. Students were requested to reconstruct the content of the choreography as concept map. In addition, students completed a transfer test answering open questions. Both concept maps and answers to open questions were analyzed using content analysis procedures and were subsequently scored. The results do not show significant differences between the groups. Static pictures can be as effective as animation in promoting learning.

Keywords: Concept map · Ballet · Static picture · Animated picture

1 Introduction

Students should be supported in acquiring complex knowledge in order to adequately understand complex content, and cope with complex situations, both in professional and daily life. However, learning and structuring complex knowledge is a challenge, and not always successful. Instructional support is necessary in order to foster meaningful learning. One option for this instructional support are multimedia presentations in which texts or verbal information is provided together with pictures (static graphics, e.g. graphs, photos, or dynamic graphics, e.g. animations or videos) [1]. Research shows that in general learning can be better supported if pictures are used in addition to verbal material [2].

© Springer International Publishing Switzerland 2016
A. Cañas et al. (Eds.): CMC 2016, CCIS 635, pp. 144–158, 2016.
DOI: 10.1007/978-3-319-45501-3_11

Pictures are one crucial part of multimedia learning materials. Especially, informative pictures which aim at coding information in a way that learners can capture the meaning as completely and exactly as possible, are of major interest for learning purposes. Informative pictures can represent the learning material, and/or organize, interpret, and transform the information given (e.g. as charts or graphs do). Independent of their functions, one can distinguish among static and animated pictures. In general, animated pictures are advantageous, especially when movements of humans or objects are to be learned.

So far, pictures of embodied knowledge have not or only hardly been used as informative pictures and have not been taken into account as an aid to support students in learning abstract complex content. The idea of using embodiments aligns with research on embodiment and embodied design according to which conceptual reasoning has its origin in physical (inter)action or perceptuomotor activities. Thus, physical (inter)action and conceptual reasoning interrelate [3]. Presumably, pictures about embodiments can have the same function and stimulate retention and conceptual understanding.

Against this background, in our research study we aim at investigating whether static or animated pictures of embodied knowledge better support learning of abstract pedagogical content, in this case action-oriented learning. We used different ballet positions as specific embodiments of key concepts of action-oriented learning. Firstly, students learned how to associate key concepts and their embodiments. This is in line with research in the field of visual mnemonics that requests learners to associate verbal information (often vocabulary of a foreign language) with pictures and thus help them improve retention [4]. Secondly, after learning the concepts, the students were provided with a ballet choreography showing a series of ballet positions (either static or animated), and in addition with an explanatory narration of the choreography. Based on that, they should learn how the positions respectively the theoretical concepts are interrelated, by that generate an understanding of the theory, and thus develop complex knowledge.

2   Learning from Text and Pictures

The Cognitive Theory of Multimedia Learning (CTML) explains why learning with text and pictures is more effective than with only one medium [5]. CTML is based on three major assumptions: dual-channel assumption, limited-capacity assumption, and active-processing assumption. The dual-channel assumption presupposes that information in working memory is processed in two channels, a pictorial and verbal one [2]. Processing information in two channels increases probability of retrieval and recall [6]. The limited-capacity assumption means that the capacity of the working memory is limited, and that the limitation is influenced by different kinds of cognitive load: intrinsic cognitive load (dependent on complexity of content to be learned), extraneous cognitive load (dependent on design of learning material), and germane cognitive load (dependent on learning activities). Learning is endangered if no or only a small portion of working memory capacity is left over for relevant learning activities (germane load). Thus, the design of learning material should aim at enhancing germane, and reducing extraneous cognitive load [7]. The active-processing assumption refers to the fact that the learner should select and organize relevant information, and integrate it with prior knowledge from working memory. The design of multimedia learning environments should take into account human information processing and should keep necessary (germane) cognitive load at a maximum. For that purpose, principles for designing multimedia (i.e. verbal and pictorial material) were defined and in many studies empirically tested [8].

Because pictures are of major interest in our study, it seems worthwhile to have a closer look at pictures. Weidenmann [9] distinguishes among three types of pictures: entertaining pictures, artistic pictures, and informative pictures. Entertaining and artistic pictures are not as useful as informative pictures for information and learning purposes. Informative pictures can be further divided into representations and logical pictures. Representations are for example photographs or drawings which are highly realistic. Logical pictures are graphs or charts that visualize relationships not or not easily to be perceived in reality. Closely connected with the types of pictures are their functions. Pictures can have a decorative function which means that they direct attention, stimulate and motivate the learner, but do not support him or her in learning. Other functions to be mentioned are: representation, interpretation, organization, and transformation [10]. Representation means that pictures show almost exactly information given in texts or narrations. Interpretation means that new and already given information is connected. This is especially true when abstract concepts and complex issues are visualized in a way that the learner can combine it with experiences and his or her prior knowledge. Organization refers to illustrating structures, or spatial, and temporal relations. Transformation means that pictures should support human information processing and thus facilitate recall.

Pictures can be static or dynamic. Dynamic visualizations can be regarded as animations either in the sense of computer-based (somehow artificial) animations or in the sense of videos (e.g. movies) which are closer to reality. Dynamic visualizations can better represent motion sequences, transitions from one state to another, and changes over time than static pictures. Thus, animations or videos link individual pictures which might better support learners [11]. In addition, animations comprise higher information load which can be advantageous on the one hand but may lead to cognitive overload on the other hand. In addition, the Transient Information Effect [12] is likely to occur. This effect points to the problem of short life presentation: If the learner misses or does not comprehend one piece, comprehension of the following information might be hindered or endangered.

Many research studies have been carried out in order to investigate the learning potential of pictures, and multimedia material. Some results are reported in the following. A meta-analysis by Carney and Levin [13] confirms that learning from text and pictures is more effective than learning from text alone. Only pictures with a decorative function do not seem to effectively support learning whereas pictures with a transformative function usually have a big positive effect on learning. Michas and Berry [14] found that signals such as arrows support learning because they hint to important information and can indicate dynamic sequences. Arguel and Jamet [15] found that it is better to use only a limited number of key pictures representing important information than too many pictures. Concerning animations Höffler and Leutner [16] conclude based on a meta-analysis that realistic and representative videos are the most effective ones with regard to learning. Furthermore, a representative design is more important than a decorative one. Concerning the comparison of static and animated pictures the results are not conclusive. When learning motor skills such as bandaging a hand, knotting in different ways, or learning about the trajectory of a ball, static pictures and videos can either almost be equally effective, or animation is superior to static pictures [14, 17, 18]. One influence factor might be learner control in the sense of interactivity.

In order to complement previous research, in a study we investigated whether static or animated pictures better support learning of abstract content. We go beyond the current research in that we used ballet positions as pictures–either a sequence of static photos or a video show a choreography. Ballet positions can be interpreted as informative and logical pictures which embody and by that represent the learning content. Thus they can be regarded as pictorial analogies which have the function of interpretation, organization, and transformation.

3   Method

3.1   Research Questions and Design of the Study

Based on the considerations mentioned above, the following research question guided our pilot study:

General research question: Is learning from animated pictures superior to learning from static pictures short-term and in the long run? Or, to put it more specific: Is learning from animated pictures superior to learning from static pictures when students have to learn abstract pedagogical content and associate it with embodied visualizations?

Twenty-seven students of business education aiming at receiving a university's bachelor degree took part in the study. They were 22.7 years on average. The students were randomly assigned to one of two experimental groups, i.e. either learning with static pictures or learning with animated pictures (video). The students took part in a learning unit on the pedagogical content of action-oriented learning. The concepts of the learning unit and their order were displayed as words and pictures, in this case ballet positions. The content had to be reconstructed as a concept map by the students either from a series of static pictures or from a video of ballet positions. Concept maps are two-dimensional structural representations of a topic consisting of nodes and labeled lines between the nodes. The nodes represent important concepts; the lines are relations between the concepts. The combination of two nodes and a labeled line in between is called a proposition. A proposition is a basic semantic unit which can be assessed true or false [19, 20]. Concept maps can be regarded as scaffolds that help students in acquiring complex knowledge in order to adequately understand content to be learned. Often, students have difficulty understanding main ideas and complex interrelationships of relevant topics. However, a structured knowledge base may result in better memory and better understanding of the learning material.

The study had a pretest-posttest design. In addition, one week after finishing the learning unit a delayed test was administered by the students. Only 16 out of the 27 students took part in the delayed test. Before starting the study, the students were asked about their knowledge about ballet positions, and their interest in ballet, and dance. Furthermore, the concept mapping technique was introduced (Table 1).

Table 1. Design of the study

Group	Preparation Phase		Tes-ting Phase	Learning Unit	Imm e-diate Testing Phase	De-layed Testing Phase
Static	Questionnaire on knowledge about ballet and interest in ballet and dance	Introduction to concept mapping	Pretest	Learning unit on action-theory and action oriented learning using static pictures and narration	Posttest	Delayed test
Video				Learning unit on action-theory and action oriented learning using video and narration		

3.2 Materials

The learning unit aims at introducing the students to foundations of action-oriented learning. Action-oriented learning is based on action theory or action-control theory (in German: Handlungstheorie or Handlungsregulationstheorie). Action-control theory provides hints for effective learning. It is largely compatible with constructivist learning conceptions based on the idea of situated learning. According to this theory actions play a decisive role in learning and developmental processes. Acting is seen as a conscious, goal-oriented and cognitively controlled process. In order to act, individuals must, at a minimum, be rational, reflective, self-regulated, and have the ability to participate in social processes. Actions can be enabled by action-oriented instruction using complex learning environments such as simulation games, case studies, etc. Action-oriented instruction aims at supporting students in developing action competence. Action competence, then, is the ability to plan, carry out, control and generate actions on the basis of available declarative (subject matter, facts, objects) and procedural (cognitive operations and transformations) knowledge [21, 22], the current state of emotion, motivation, and environmental conditions. Action competence presupposes an adequate (e.g. structured, complete and sophisticated) internal representation of the situation, and the ability to plan, and carry out actions [23].

Ballet positions were assigned to the key concepts of action-oriented learning respectively action theory in order to illustrate them and enable the student to generate associations between abstract knowledge and its embodied counterpart (as is intended by visual mnemonics). For example, the concept "Microsequence" is associated with the ballet position "Plié" which in this case can be interpreted as being small (micro) but somehow upwards oriented (microsequence hinting to macrose-quence, of which it is part). Contrastingly, the concept "Macrosequence" is associated with and embodied by the position "Developpé". It shows an upright posture of a person which can be interpreted as something big (macro) (Fig. 1). The ballet positions thus have an interpretative and transformative function. The whole structure of the concept map is represented by the sequence of ballet positions (which are part of the choreography). Thus, the choreography has an organizing function.

Microsequence (Plié)   Macrosequence (Developpé)

Fig. 1. Association of ballet positions and key concepts (Photos by Ian Whalen)

Based on this, two learning units using identical information were developed. They differed in that one unit used a series of static positions and the other one an animated sequence of positions in form of a video. At the beginning, the aims of the unit were introduced to the learners and they were given basic information about characteristics of ballet. While listening to the characteristics, the students watched the choreography either as video or as series of static pictures. Then, they learned which key concept of action-oriented learning is assigned to which ballet position. Students of the static group saw a picture and the written name of the position. Simultaneously, they listened to the spoken concept. Students of the animation group saw a danced element, the written name of the position, and also simultaneously listened to the spoken concept. This part of the training can be regarded as a pre-training [2]. Subsequently, students watched the complete dance choreography either as animation (video) or as series of static pictures (static). If a position appears more than once, students know that this position is connected with more than one other. In the static series and in the video, a narration went along with the pictures. In addition, the key concepts of action-oriented learning were displayed. The final part of the learning unit aimed at supporting students in consolidating and reflecting content just learned. For that purpose, students could listen again to a narration as well as a pictorial and verbal display of the key concepts. In addition, they could watch again the respective choreography (static or dynamic). Lastly, they could watch again the complete choreography without narration.

3.3 Data Gathering and Analysis

Before starting the learning unit, the students completed a questionnaire on prior knowledge about ballet and on interest in ballet and dance. The knowledge test on ballet consists of three open answer questions concerning ballet positions. The interest test was developed according to Schiefele's [24] conceptualization of interest. It consists of

6 items (3 for interest in ballet and 3 for interest in dance), which could be rated on a 4-point Likert scale (from 0 = no interest to 3 = high interest). Both knowledge and interest in ballet and dance can have an influence on learning. In addition, students received training in concept mapping.

Before and after studying the material, the students took a knowledge test comprising structural knowledge and transfer questions. In addition, a delayed test was given to the students one week after finishing the learning unit. For measuring structural knowledge, the students had to construct a concept map on action-oriented learning using paper and pencil. Eleven concepts and 11 relations were given as an aid. The concepts were displayed as picture of a ballet position and the corresponding name of action theory. The relations were given as a list of linking phrases. The decision to support students by providing concepts and relations was made in order to reduce cognitive load [7] caused by the need to learn both ballet positions and a pedagogical content, and to combine the two of them. The transfer test consists of two open answer questions concerning action-oriented learning and how to put it into instructional practice.

The open answers of the students were analyzed using a qualitative content analysis. A qualitative content analysis is a systematic, replicable technique for assigning words or phrases of a text to content categories based on explicit rules of coding [25]. For example if students express "when planning a lesson, the teacher should take into account students' knowledge structure" or "it is important that the teacher knows about how knowledge of students is structured and regards it in instruction" both are categorized under "instruction has to adapt to students' knowledge structure". Based on coding regulations, two coders coded independently. The intercoder reliability rates ranged from $\rho = .7$ to $\rho = .9$ (Spearman rank correlation coefficient) for the different tests. After independent coding, the coders compared the results, discussed differences and found a consensus. On the basis of the consensus, a test score was calculated for each student. For the 3 open answer questions measuring prior knowledge about ballet, the students could get 3 points at a maximum, for the transfer test 4 points as a maximum. For the rating scales concerning interest in ballet and dance, the mean was calculated. Due to the small sample size and the pilot character of the study, mainly descriptive statistics were used.

In order to enable the comparison of individual concept maps, again, a content analysis was conducted. The content analysis aimed at aggregating both concepts and relations according to their semantic similarity. In addition, it was necessary to make the concept maps comparable regarding their structure. The unit of analysis here was the complete proposition in the form concept-relation-concept. In some cases the direction of relations was changed, e.g. when passive voice was transferred into active voice [26]. To assess the quality of the concept maps, we constructed a reference concept map (Fig. 2) which consists of 12 propositions. In order to determine the quality of the individual maps, we calculated the percentage of agreement between individual concept map and a reference concept map based on the propositions as unit of analysis. In case a student's proposition matched the reference proposition we coded a "1", otherwise a "0". Consequently, the score of a student's concept map could range between 0 and 12 points, so the higher the score, the closer the summary or the concept map comes to the reference concept map. The degree of correspondence of a student's concept map and the reference concept map could be expressed as distance measure. For the calculation of the distances we used the Galanter-Metric, a relative distance measure that shows how many of all propositions that occur in two concept maps do not have a corresponding counterpart in the other concept map. This number is divided by the union of sets of propositions in two concept maps. The resulting value stands for the degree of inequality of two concept maps. Whereas a "0" means total equality, a "1" says that the two compared concept maps do not have a single proposition in common. Thus, the smaller the value of the distance measure, the higher the quality of the concept map.

4 Results

4.1 Prior Knowledge About Ballet, Interest in Ballet, and Dance

Students of both groups almost had no prior knowledge about ballet. The mean points were about .38 (SD = .65) for the static group and .43 (SD = .76) for the video group out of a maximum score of 3. The mean value for interest in ballet was 1.37 (SD = .74) for the static group, and 1.10 (SD = .71) for the video group. The means were below the theoretical mean of 1.50, indicating that the students were in general not very interested in ballet. The mean value for interest in dance was in both groups higher than the one for interest in ballet. It was 1.68 (SD = .80) for the static group, and 1.55 (SD = .77) for the video group. It can be concluded that the students of both groups slightly tended to be interested in dance. The means were just above the theoretical mean of 1.50.

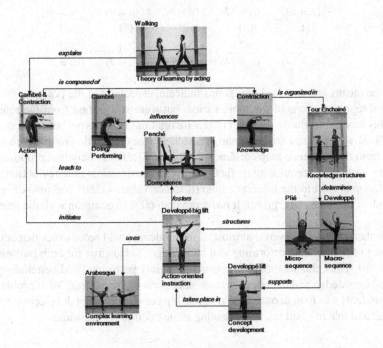

Fig. 2. Reference concept map (Photos by Ian Whalen)

4.2   Structural Understanding Based on Quality of Concept Maps

Structural understanding was measured by the distance (based on the Galanter metric) between students' concept maps and reference concept map. The results show that in both groups students increased the quality of their concept maps from pre- to ·posttest indicated by the smaller mean distance values. Students in the static group reached better results than students in the video group. However, an ANOVA showed no significant difference between the groups for the interaction effect between the factors time and group, $F(1, 25) = 1.76$, $p = .197$. That means, the groups did not differ in their development of the quality of concept maps from pretest to posttest. Looking at the delayed test, the scores increased again and almost equal the initial ones shown in the pretest. Thus, no long-term retention effects could be detected (Table 2). An ANOVA also showed no significant difference between the groups concerning the interaction of the factors time and group, $F(1, 14) = .04$, $p = .842$). The groups also did not differ in their development of quality of concept maps from pretest to delayed test.

Table 2.   Mean distances between individual concept maps and reference concept map

Group		Pretest	Posttest	Pretest	Posttest	Delayed test
		Based on 27 participants taking part in two tests		Based on 16 participants taking part in all three tests		
Static	M	.924	.749	.917	.770	.897
	SD	.057	.171	.061	.157	.098
		(n = 13)	(n = 13)	(n = 9)	(n = 9)	(n = 9)
Video	M	.911	.820	.912	.854	.903
	SD	.076	.162	.087	.094	.103
		(n = 14)	(n = 14)	(n = 7)	(n = 7)	(n = 7)

As the means and standard deviations indicate, especially in the posttest, students' structural representations of the topic varied, but were still distant from the reference map. This was mainly due to wrong or unprecise relations students put between concepts. Figure 3 shows a posttest concept map of a student from the static group which is very distant from the reference map (distance value = .917). It has only one proposition in common with the reference map (action-oriented instruction initiates action). The concept map closest to the reference map (distance value = .389) was also developed by a student from the static group. It has more than 60 % in common with the reference map.

A further analysis showed that most of the students could reconstruct that action is composed of both doing/performing and knowledge. This is true for both posttest, and delayed test. Thus, this relationship seems intelligibly performed and better aligned to students' knowledge and experiences than other parts of the content. Most problematic for the students was to understand the relationship between concept development on the one hand and macro-, and microsequencing of instruction on the other.

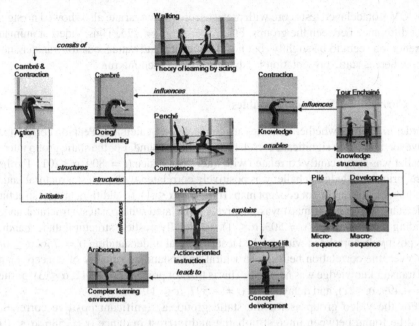

Fig. 3. Posttest concept map of static group student (Photos by Ian Whalen)

4.3 Transfer Knowledge

Concerning transfer questions, it becomes obvious that both groups improved their transfer knowledge from pre- to posttest (Table 3).

Table 3. Transfer knowledge

Group		Pretest	Posttest	Pretest	Posttest	Delayed test
		Based on 27 participants taking part in two tests		Based on 16 participants taking part in all three tests		
Static	M	.69	1.77	.77	1.55	1.44
	SD	1.18	1.69	1.3	1.74	1.01
		(n = 13)	(n = 13)	(n = 9)	(n = 9)	(n = 9)
Video	M	.29	1.43	.14	1.43	1.14
	SD	.61	1.34	.38	1.51	.69
		(n = 14)	(n = 14)	(n = 7)	(n = 7)	(n = 7)

Though the level of knowledge was remarkably higher in the static group (especially concerning pretest scores), the increase in knowledge from pre- to posttest was higher in the video group. An ANCOVA on posttest score with pretest score as a covariate showed no significant difference between the groups, $F(1, 24) = .09$, $p = .761$. With regard to long-term effects, one can say that the level of transfer knowledge decreased in both groups. In contrast to the structural understanding test (concept map), the level of knowledge was in both groups higher in the delay-test than in the pretest. An

ANCOVA on delayed test score with pretest score as a covariate also showed no significant difference between the groups, $F(1, 13) = .09$, $p = .775$. Thus, video or animated presentation seem to be slightly (but not significantly) advantageous for transfer short-term, whereas static presentation is advantageous in the long run.

4.4 Correlations Between Variables

In order to identify whether variables are connected we calculated Pearson correlations. However, almost no significant correlations could be found. For the static group interest in ballet was significantly correlated with interest in dance ($r = .809$, $\alpha \leq .01$). Furthermore, prior knowledge in ballet was positively correlated with pretest structural understanding, i.e. the quality of concept maps ($r = .485$, $\alpha \leq .1$). In addition, pretest structural understanding (concept map) was positively correlated with posttest structural understanding (concept map) ($r = .503$, $\alpha \leq .1$), and finally posttest structural understanding was positively correlated with delayed test structural understanding ($r = .756$, $\alpha \leq .05$). However, the correlation between structural understanding (quality of concept maps) and transfer knowledge was negative. This is true for pretest ($r = -.312$, $\alpha \leq .3$), posttest ($r = -.499$, $\alpha \leq .1$), and delayed test ($r = -.597$, $\alpha \leq .1$).

For the video group as for the static group, a significant positive correlation could be found between interest in ballet and interest in dance ($r = .586$, $\alpha \leq .01$). In addition, for this group, a significant positive correlation could be found between interest in ballet and prior knowledge in ballet ($r = .635$, $\alpha \leq .01$), and a significant negative correlation between interest in ballet and structural knowledge in the delayed test ($r = -.870$, $\alpha \leq .05$). A further almost significant negative correlation could be found between prior knowledge in ballet and transfer knowledge in the delayed test ($r = -.745$, $\alpha \leq .1$). Similar to the static group, structural understanding in the posttest was negatively correlated with transfer knowledge ($r = -.553$, $\alpha \leq .05$). More obvious than in the static group transfer knowledge in the pretest positively correlated with transfer knowledge in the posttest ($r = .495$, $\alpha \leq .1$).

5 Summary and Conclusions

Students of both groups had almost no prior knowledge about ballet, comparatively low interest in ballet, but some interest in dance. In addition, structural knowledge about the content to be learned (action-oriented learning), and transfer knowledge were comparatively low in the beginning. Both learning units contributed to the development of structural knowledge and transfer, which is especially true for immediate testing (posttest). The delayed test showed that structural knowledge decreased remarkably whereas transfer knowledge only slightly decreased. Taking research about learning from static versus learning from animated pictures into account, this again confirms that results are not conclusive though animations more often tend to better support learning than static pictures. Concerning the study presented here, a slight advantage of the static group could be explained by the fact that reconstructing a concept map from a danced choreography causes higher extraneous load for the following reasons: 1. It might be too difficult for the students to concentrate both on associating ballet positions with pedagogical concepts, and on comprehending their interrelationships that is to say the whole structure of the theory. 2. Closely connected with the argument just mentioned is that students of the video group watched a complete choreography. In addition to the individual elements (concepts), they watched their performed linkages, and listened to the narration of their linkages. Thus, in this case the dynamic character might have caused additional cognitive load. 3. The students might have focused on enjoying the dance performance instead of concentrating on comprehending the content.

Further results showed that for the static group high quality of concept maps in the pretest went by trend along with high quality concept maps in the posttest, and the delayed test. The same stable results could not be replicated for the concept map measurement of the video group. But, by trend the results hint in the same direction. Also, the transfer knowledge measured at the different points in time correlated positively, which is true for both groups. The respective values were higher in the video group than in the static group. To sum up, these results seem to be consistent with findings showing that prior knowledge has a significant influence on learning.

The correlations between structural understanding (quality of concept maps) and transfer knowledge, however, were negative. This means that structural knowledge and transfer knowledge somewhat impeded each other what might be due to the fact that students could only focus on structuring knowledge, or on deep understanding, not on both. Possibly, if they focused on reconstructing structured knowledge from the choreography, they did not have free cognitive capacities for deep understanding, or the other way round. Because of the missing prior knowledge about ballet, they were not able to connect ballet positions with action-oriented learning. The challenge of concentrating on ballet, on learning ballet positions, on associating these positions with the topic of action-oriented learning, and on deeply understanding it was too high. Thus, the task very likely caused extraneous cognitive overload especially due to the fact that students were not familiar with ballet. Consequently, students might have focused on understanding and structuring positions and not on deep understanding.

This assumption can be supported by the fact that interest and prior knowledge in ballet inconsistently (sometimes positively, sometimes negatively) correlated with structured knowledge (quality of concept maps) but by trend negatively with transfer knowledge. This was in general more obvious for the video group. An exception was the posttest transfer knowledge which positively correlated with prior knowledge in ballet in the static group.

To sum up, in the example presented here, too much cognitive load might have been caused by requesting the students to learn both ballet positions and scientific content, and combine the two different worlds. The combination of learning content with ballet movements might have distracted concentration on content [27]. In addition, too many movements might have hindered knowledge acquisition [15]. Possibly, the pictures of ballet positions were too unfamiliar and not intuitively enough be connected with the scientific concepts of action-oriented learning. Thus, pictures might have not matched the experiences of the students [28] and could not well be associated with the learning content [4]. Consequently, the informative, organizing, and transformative functions of pictures were contradicted and association effects known from visual mnemonics could not be exploited. In addition, the Transient Information Effect [12], meaning that students missed pieces of the performance, might have hindered learning. Concerning the concept maps, their low quality might have been caused by the fact that students were not familiar enough with the technique so that they could not apply it confidently. Thus concept mapping might also have caused extraneous cognitive load. Continuous training in concept mapping previous to the study might have led to other results.

In further studies, a more comprehensive pre-training should be considered. The students should learn more about ballet, the meaning of individual ballet positions, and the background of why a specific position is assigned to a specific scientific concept. Subsequently, the students can design the positions themselves, and thus actively construct verbal and pictorial connections. Alternatively, other positions better corresponding the students' experiences and that are therefore familiar can be implemented, or designed. Last, but not least, it might be an option that the students perform the positions themselves, and thus not only learn from words and pictures but from embodiment, and by that from using the haptic sense [3, 29]. Further ideas are that it would be useful to measure cognitive load, though a reliable measurement seems to be difficult [30]. However, DeLeeuw and Mayer [31] report some success.

Acknowledgements. We would like to heartly thank the Semperoper Dresden (Germany) to make the project possible, especially: István Simon (Dancer, Semperoper Ballet), and Anna Merkulova (Dancer, Semperoper Ballet) for performing the choreography, further (in alphabetical order) Adi Luick (Ballet Company Manager), Jörg Rieker (Head of Press Department, Semperoper), Aaron Watkin (Artistic Director, Semperoper Ballet), Ian Whalen (Photographer, Semperoper) for supporting the project. Furthermore, we would like to express our special gratitude to Michael Steinbusch (TU Dresden, Center for Knowledge Architecture) who initiated the collaboration between the scientific research and arts, in our case (business) education, and ballet. Last, but not least, we would like to thank the anonymous reviewers for their helpful comments.

References

1. Mayer, R.E.: Introduction to multimedia learning. In: Mayer, R.E. (ed.) The Cambridge Handbook of Multimedia Learning, pp. 1–16. Cambridge University Press, Cambridge (2005)
2. Mayer, R.E.: Multimedia Learning, 2nd edn. Cambridge University Press, New York (2009)
3. Abrahamson, D., Lindgren, R.: Embodiment and embodied design. In: Sawyer, K.R. (ed.) The Cambridge Handbook of the Learning Sciences, 2nd edn, pp. 358–375. Cambridge University Press, New York (2014)
4. Soemer, A., Schwan, S.: Visual mnemonics for language learning: static picture versus animated morphs. J. Educ. Psychol. **104**(3), 565–579 (2012)
5. Mayer, R.E.: Cognitive theory of multimedia learning. In: Mayer, R.E. (ed.) The Cambridge Handbook of Multimedia Learning, pp. 31–48. Cambridge University Press, Cambridge (2005)
6. Paivio, A.: Mental Representations: A Dual Coding Approach. Oxford University Press, New York (1986)

7. Sweller, J.: Implications of cognitive load theory for multimedia learning. In: Mayer, R.E. (ed.) The Cambridge Handbook of Multimedia Learning, pp. 19–30. Cambridge University Press, Cambridge (2005)

8. Mayer, R.E. (ed.): The Cambridge Handbook of Multimedia Learning. Cambridge University Press, Cambridge (2005)

9. Weidenmann, B.: Lernen mit Bildmedien – psychologische und didaktische Grundlagen. Beltz, Weinheim (1994)

10. Levin, J.R.: A transfer-appropriate-processing perspective of pictures in prose. In: Mandl, H., Levin, J.R. (eds.) Knowledge Acquisition from Text and Pictures, pp. 83–100. Elsevier, Amsterdam (1989)

11. Ballstaedt, S.-P.: Bildverstehen, Bildverständlichkeit – Ein Forschungsüberblick unter Anwendungsperspektive. In: Krings, H.P. (ed.) Wissenschaftliche Grundlagen der technischen Kommunikation, pp. 191–233. Narr, Tübingen (1996)

12. Singh, A.-M., Marcus, N., Ayres, P.: The transient information effect: investigating the impact of segmentation on spoken and written text. Appl. Cogn. Psychol. **26**(6), 848–853 (2012)

13. Carney, R.N., Levin, J.R.: Pictorial illustrations still improve students' learning from text. Educ. Psychol. Rev. **14**(1), 5–26 (2002)

14. Michas, I.C., Berry, D.: Learning a procedural task: effectiveness of multimedia presentations. Appl. Cogn. Psychol. **14**(6), 555–575 (2000)

15. Arguel, A., Jamet, E.: Using video and static pictures to improve learning of procedural contents. Comput. Hum. Behav. **25**, 354–359 (2009)

16. Höffler, T.N., Leutner, D.: Instructional animation versus static pictures: a meta-analysis. Learn. Instr. **17**, 722–738 (2007)

17. McCloskey, M., Kohl, D.: Naïve physics: the curvilinear impetus principle and its role in interaction with moving objects. J. Exp. Psychol. Learn. Mem. Cogn. **9**(1), 146–156 (1983)

18. Ayres, P., Marcus, N., Chan, C., Qian, N.: Learning hand manipulative tasks: when instructional animations are superior to equivalent static representations. Comput. Hum. Behav. **25**, 348–353 (2009)

19. Ruiz-Primo, M.A., Shavelson, R.J.: Problems and issues in the use of concept maps in science assessment. J. Res. Sci. Teach. **33**(6), 569–600 (1996)

20. Novak, J.D., Cañas, A.J.: The theory underlying concept maps and how to construct and use them. Technical report IHMC CmapTools. Florida Institute for Human and Machine Cognition (2008)

21. Aebli, H.: Denken: Das Ordnen des Tuns. Band 1: Kognitive Aspekte der Handlungstheorie. Klett-Cotta, Stuttgart (1980)

22. Aebli, H.: Denken: Das Orden des Tuns. Band 2: Denkprozesse. Klett-Cotta, Stuttgart (1981)

23. Tramm, T., Rebmann, K.: Veränderungen im Tätigkeitsprofil von Handelslehrern unter dem Signum handlungsorientierter Curricula. In: Tramm, T., Sembill, D., Klauser, F., John, E.G. (eds.) Professionalisierung kaufmännischer Berufsbildung, pp. 231–259. Lang, Frankfurt am Main (1990)

24. Schiefele, U.: The Influence of topic interest, prior knowledge, and cognitive capabilities on text comprehension. In: Pieters, J.M., Breuer, K., Simons, P.R.J. (eds.) Learning Environments. Contributions from Dutch and German Research, pp. 323–338. Springer, Heidelberg (1990)

25. Mayring, P.: Qualitative Inhaltsanalyse. Beltz, Weinheim u. a. (2010)

26. Fürstenau, B., Oldenbürger, H.-A., Trojahner, I.: Prior knowledge of potential entrepreneurs. In: Weber, S., Oser, F.K., Achtenhagen, F., Fretschner, M., Trost, S. (eds.) Becoming an Entrepreneur, pp. 77–89. Sense, Rotterdam (2014)

27. Tversky, B., Morrison, J.B., Bétrancourt, M.: Animation: can it facilitate? Int. J. Hum.-Comput. Stud. **57**, 247–262 (2002)

28. Schnotz, W., Bannert, M.: Construction and interference in learning from multiple representation. Learn. Instr. **13**, 141–156 (2003)
29. Mayer, R.E., Moreno, R.: Interactive multimodal learning environments. Educ. Psychol. Rev. **19**, 309–326 (2007)
30. Schnotz, W., Kürschner, C.: A reconsideration of cognitive load theory. Educ. Psychol. Rev. **19**, 469–508 (2007)
31. DeLeeuw, K., Mayer, R.E.: A comparison of three measures of cognitive load: evidence for separable measures of intrinsic, extraneous, and germane load. J. Educ. Psychol. **100**(1), 223–234 (2008)

Russian Experience in Application of Concept Maps in Education

Svetlana Kostromina and Daria Gnedykh[✉]

St. Petersburg State University, Saint-Petersburg, Russia
lanank68@gmail.com, d.gnedyh@spbu.ru

Abstract. The paper describes an experience of Russian researchers and teachers in using of concept maps at classes. Concept maps are considered by Russian scientists as a tool of evaluation of information acquisition and as learning technique. The main objectives of application of CM in learning process are defined at the paper. Individual cases of using concept maps and its combination with other teaching techniques to achieve the best students' learning outcomes are described. Differentiated approach in selection of different kinds of CM as evaluation tool for students' knowledge is emphasis. The problems faced by teachers when using concept maps are summarized and highlighted. The developmental potential of CM as learning technique and as formation of students' conceptual framework is discussed.

Keywords: Concept maps · Russian education · Acquisition of information by students

1 Introduction

The aim of the learning process is to form a generalized conceptual structure of academic field at students and to provide a scientific understanding of concepts by students. In order to determine the quality of students' assimilation of learning material teachers often use such methods as tests or oral presentation at an exam. In this case the dynamics of formation of students' conceptual framework of academic field is left out of account. To better examine students' understanding of a topic and to correct misconceptions in time teacher could apply a technique of concept maps (CM) in his practice.

Traditionally, concept maps are used as a teaching tool. The experiments indicated that subjects which were studied using CMs, created by a teacher or experts, were learned by students better than courses where this method was not applied [24]. In the meantime, CM can be used as a method of evaluation of students' learning outcomes - representation and visualization of their knowledge [23]. The structuring of reasoning in concept maps reflects student's understanding of any problem or topic [3, 11].

The main objectives of the article are:

- To describe studies on the application of concept maps at lessons in Russian universities;

A. Cañas et al. (Eds.): CMC 2016, CCIS 635, pp. 159–168, 2016.
DOI: 10.1007/978-3-319-45501-3_12

- To highlight and summarize the main problems faced by professionals in the field of education when they use CMs;
- To denote directions of further research in application of CMs in Russian.

The paper contains a brief summary of beliefs of Russian scientists about why use CMs in education, a description of studies in evaluation of students' knowledge via CMs and a discussion of three main problems in application of CMs in Russia – theoretical issue, methodological problem and technical difficulties. There are also guidelines of Russian scientists and teachers for use CMs in educational process.

2 Russian Beliefs About Reasons to Use Concept Maps in Education

The authors often point to the following objectives of application of CMs at classes:

- regulation of thinking process, development of associative thinking, solving creative problems [6];
- awareness and understanding of a subject, a relevance of using CMs at the moments of integration of new concepts during the course [33];
- development of students' skills in analytical reading [30];
- to improve memory and orientation in increasing flow of information [26], etc.

Gavrilova with her colleagues made the classification of visual models by type of knowledge (WHAT-, HOW-, WHY-, WHO-, WHERE- and WHEN-knowledge) and came to the conclusion that concept maps can illustrate any of these types because it does not impose restrictions on semantics of a chart elements [15]. By means of CM we can present a definition of a concept and its properties (WHAT- or WHO-knowledge), illustrate causes that led to current situation or causal relationships in a subject area (WHY-knowledge), present variants and ways to achieve goals or solve problems (HOW-knowledge) or relationships between events (WHEN- and WHERE-knowledge).

Ammosova and Zilinskaia [2] consider concept maps as a mean of understanding learning materials that were presented in the forms of speech and text. In their study the authors taught students an algorithm for creating concept maps. During the semester students were drawing CMs on six themes of the course and then they were tested to identify their level of knowledge on a subject. It was revealed that the students' mastery of technique to create CM and their learning achievement were interrelated – the better developed students' skill of creation of CM, the higher their academic results. Thus, concept maps can be considered as a tool of learning process allowing to improve the understanding and acquisition of learning materials.

The research of Ammosova and Zilinskaya is the most frequently way of application of concept maps in Russian education to present an understanding of text or oral speech of teacher. We suggest that it would be interesting to look at concept maps created after studying pictures or images. When we look at a picture we mentally define drawn objects as concepts and a plot of a picture helps to identify relationships between them. Thus, we can create CM based on pictures and figures too.

From a brief review we can conclude that concept map is a tool for wide application that allows to evaluate a correct representation of all types of knowledge and can improve students' memory, analytical thinking, abilities to solve problems, etc. However, in Russia CMs are usually used not as independent tool. Russian scientists look for additional assessment techniques that could be used in a complex with concept maps. The examples of its application are presented in the following part of the paper.

3 Russian Experience of Application of CMs in Evaluation of Students' Knowledge

Degtyarev [14] proposes to combine the advantages of CM (words and arrows showing their relationships) with the advantages of mind maps (pictures and symbols) and a result of this combination to define as divergent maps (due to activation of divergent thinking). *Divergent map* is graphical, with nodal structure presentation of knowledge and experience of a person, logical and associative connections which are actualized in a process of multidimensional, nonlinear (divergent) thinking around some central concept (stimulus word) [34]. The purpose of creation of divergent maps is to reveal the structure and content of a subject (or section of curriculum) presented through the central concept (image) and key concepts, where relations between them form a structure of this subject.

Divergent maps can be created independently by students or students are given a half-finished test-map – a map where relationships and a logical chain are indicated but some elements are absent (Fig. 1). These elements have to be filled by students in the

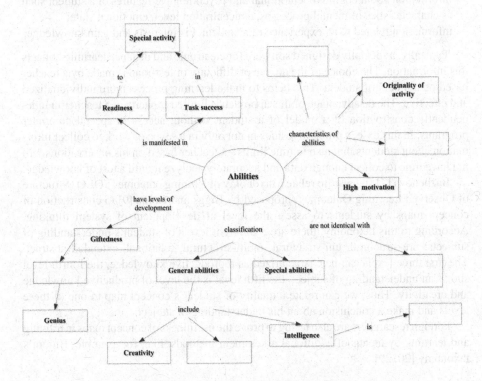

Fig. 1. An example of a half-finished test-map

process of working with map [12]. In the study which was carried out by Degtyarev [12] one group of students was given test-map directly before general test, the other group immediately started to do the general test. As a result the first group solved the certain kinds of tasks in the general test better than the second one. This led to the conclusion that divergent test-map was as a mean of expanding of attention focus – an important information for right decision of tasks occurred in a field of operative memory of students.

The advantage of this approach is that half-finished test-maps allow to activate a process of information analysis – when a student looks at a map and notes a missed item he needs to analyze a whole picture to understand how to fill a gap. However, he is given a scientific understanding of a topic before and there is no need to build relationships and understand logic himself. From our point of view, application of unfinished test-maps is allowed as an additional method of evaluation of acquisition of learning infor-mation.

Anokhina-Naumets and Lukashenko [5] also propose to evaluate a structure of students' knowledge by using test-CMs (concept maps created by a teacher but with missing concepts or links that a student has to define and insert into maps). But the selection of test-CM should be individual for each student on the basis of his personal characteristics – a model of student. This model includes:

– information about learning process and level of knowledge and skills of a student;
– information about cognitive, emotional and psychological features of a student such as characteristics of mental processes, concentration level, emotional state;
– information related to an experience of a student, his interests and gain knowledge.

Typically, a specially designed software for electronic and distance learning collects this information. The choice of the degree of difficulty of test-map is made by a teacher based on a model of student. This helps to make learning process more individualized and effective. The disadvantage of this approach is limited capacity of a teacher in inde-pendently construction of a model of a student without access to special computer programs. In this case, a problem resides in not only in a scope of work to collect infor-mation about students, but also in time limits - a teacher based on his observations will not have time to collect enough data and accurately analyze it until a test of knowledge.

Bazhenova [7] suggests to relate a taxonomy of learning outcomes SOLO (Structure of Observed Learning Outcomes) proposed by Biggs and Collis [9] to construction of concept maps by students to assess the level of development of system thinking. According to this taxonomy, there are 5 different levels of student's understanding of subjects: pre-structural, uni-structural, multi-structural, relational, extended abstract. The first three levels can be characterized as reproductive knowledge, the fourth level shows an understanding of subject, the fifth level is the level of productive knowledge and creativity. Thus, we can relate a quality of student's concept map to one of these levels and make a conclusion about his understanding of subject.

Foreign researchers are also trying to prove the usefulness of concept maps in training and learning by means of additional assessment methods, like, for example, Bloom's taxonomy [20, 29].

From our point of view, there is a problem of correlating results of evaluation of CM with other assessment tools (tests, case studies, etc.). Most often concept maps are evaluated qualitatively: correctness of use of certain concepts and relationships between them is analyzed. Correlation of these indicators with tests results is a challenge. For instance, how can we estimate whether a student learned information if he has high points for test and low points for concept map? How do these results relate to each other? Therefore, we think it is important to search ways to create CM based on different taxonomies, such as in the articles of Bazhenova, Mirzaie and Tavares.

In our opinion, concept maps can be used not only for evaluation of students' knowledge structure at the end of subject learning. CM allows to reveal the efficacy of any teaching technique. For example, in our recent study (the study design and other results are described in detail in: [18, 19]) we revealed that different forms of learning material (text, charts and comics) presented by means of PowerPoint presentations can effect in different ways on a formation of conceptual framework of a subject at students. The following significant differences were found (U-Mann-Whitney):

- Students of the *Faculty of Applied Mathematics and Control Processes* characterized by the growth of concrete concepts in concept maps created after studying a subject in the form of Charts compared with Comics ($p \leq 0.01$). The use of PowerPoint presentation in the form of Charts or Text provided the increase of the number of abstract concepts compared with Comics ($p \leq 0.01$). Learning material in the form of Comics due to the illustrations of studied concepts increased the number of special ($p \leq 0.03$) and concrete ($p \leq 0.01$) concepts compared with Text.
- Students of the *Faculty of Biology* have such difference only by one characteristic - after studying a subject in the form of Charts the number of abstract concepts in CMs increased in comparison with Text ($p \leq 0.05$).
- After studying a subject in the form of Text ($p \leq 0.04$) or Comics ($p \leq 0.07$) by students of *Psychology Faculty* the number of special concepts in their CMs increased in comparison with Charts. Text provides the increase of the number of concrete concepts compared with Comic ($p < 0.01$) and Charts ($p < 0.01$). Comics increased the number of abstract concepts, compared with Text ($p < 0.01$).

Thus, concept maps can be interesting as a method of diagnostics of teaching efficiency. This approach can be taken into account by researchers in a field of didactics to identify more useful instructional devices in different conditions.

4 Problems in Application of CMs in Russia

The review of Russian scientific articles allowed us to summarize and highlight the problems that often arise when applying concept maps in teaching practice. We can divide them into three groups - theoretical, methodological and technical problems.

4.1   Problem 1 - Incorrect Understanding of a Meaning of Used Terms

This kind of theoretical problem relates with quite frequent mistake in using concepts such as «concept maps», «mind maps», «cognitive maps», etc. They can be used as synonymous in Russian scientific literature. For instance, an author means CMs but uses the worlds «mind maps» or «cognitive maps» [10, 32]. Savuk [26] summarizes the most diagrams of links (in particular concept maps) under the name «associative-conceptual maps», but she does not determine differences between various kinds of graphical information. Degtyarev [13] notes that «mental maps», «cognitive maps», «memory maps», etc. are just different definitions describing «mind maps». Thereby, readers could think that they are all synonymous and henceforth use these concepts incorrect.

Another reason of this problem is that in spite of the fact that these terms have clear definitions in foreign publications, there could be their incorrect translation in Russian. The English term «concept» in Russian sometimes is defined as «mental», and «mental» is a synonymous of «intelligence» or «mind». Thus, in a similar vein concept maps can be nominally equated to mind maps (as, for example, in: [27]).

Thus, it could lead to misunderstanding and readers should be more attentive when they read such articles.

4.2   Problem 2 - the Absence of a Clearly Defined Algorithm or Guidelines for Creation of Concept Maps

Another problem is in a field of methodology of creation of CMs. The articles review indicated that the most common technique in Russia is mind mapping in comparison with concept mapping. This technique is quite well described by foreign authors and is actively used in education in Russia. According to some authors there are no universal recommendations for a formation of concept maps in national science. Therefore, many researchers propose their own algorithms for creating CM confirmed by practice and their experience. For example, Gavrilova et al. [16] suggest the following step-by-step method of CM creation for teachers:

1. A glossary of subject area (there are basic concepts from all sources used in a course).
2. Making connections between concepts of a glossary (concepts are grouped "from up to down", categories are created).
3. Visualization of hierarchical levels in a system of concepts (from a central idea).
4. If necessary, to elaborate and to detail categories.
5. Reengineering of content -1 (restructuring, clarification, correction of redundancy and synonymy, integration of new concepts).
6. Reengineering of design -2 (creation of balanced "picture").

Zelinskaia and Zelinsky [35] consider that the most important stages in creation of CM are:

Step 1 – selection of concepts related to a specific field of knowledge.
Step 2 – ranking of concepts: the central issue (central concept); key concepts; other concepts; examples and/or details.

Step 3 – concept mapping. On the top of a sheet a central issue is written. Key concepts, then other concepts and examples or details are below.
Step 4 – drawing lines: from a central concept to key concepts; then from key concepts to other concepts; from concepts to examples or details.
Step 5 – marking lines with verbs.

When developing concept maps it is possible to use projective-recursive strategy proposed in [25]. In this book the definition of projective methodical system as an open system modeled and developing as a project with certain characteristics and behavior in the present and the future is presented. The principle of projectivity is that a future professional activity of students is projected on a real learning process where conditions for solution of possible professional tasks are simulated [7]. The principle of recursivity suggests that in a process of learning students create and use electronic learning resources. The initiation, modeling and realization of projective methodical system of training consider designing and dynamic development of all components of the system with involvement of all project participants: students, teachers, potential employers. This strategy leads to a reduction in a number of students with low learning outcomes.

Projective-recursive strategy in a process of creation mental and concept maps consists from following stages [8]:

- mental map on a topic is created by referring to previously developed maps with the use of hyperlinks;
- modernization of concept map by integration of new concepts (algorithm, course unit);
- unification of concept and mind maps: concept map is created as a hierarchy of concepts each of which will be presented by mental map.

It should be noted that mental and concept maps are combined in this model: CM is as a basis and mental maps are as parts of CM.

There are foreign publications which contain clear guidelines for creation and scoring of concept maps [3, 4, 22]. But due to the lack of their translation in Russian or ignorance of foreign language Russian scientists are trying to develop their algorithms which are not always consistent with each other.

Thus, the highlighted problem indicates, on the one hand, that knowledge and data obtained by researchers in the field of CM application are segmentary, on the other hand, there is undying interest and tendency to development and improvement of this technique.

Additionally, we have to note that development and approvement of its own algorithms for creating CM require a lot of time from specialists. This is relevant to the third problem.

4.3   Problem 3 - Time Expenditure and Complexity of CM-Technique

It is required from teacher to spend additional time at lessons to ensure that students have mastered the skill of creating of concept maps. Many teachers can be not ready for it.

Some teachers want to give students as much as possible learning information on lectures and not ready to spare time for teaching students an algorithm of creation of CM.

A process of creation of concept maps by a teacher on topics of his subject is also time-consuming. First, studying the existing work-books for creating CMs [21, 32] requires from teachers mental energy and time expenditure. Secondly, to create a CM on a topic of subject teacher has to be able to generalize, categorize, classify – in other words to elaborate learning material. The complexity and ambiguity of processes of concepts categorization are consistently stressed in the papers of leading Russian and foreign researchers in the area of cognitive processes [1, 17, 28, 31], etc. It is much easier to teach a course not making such generalizations. Therefore, not every teacher chooses CM- technique when preparing for his lessons.

Nevertheless, Russian scientists recognize the developmental potential of CM- technique in learning process. For instance, Bogdanova and Bogdanova [10] point that concept maps can be used for:

- Organization and systematization of existing knowledge and creation of conditions for integration of new knowledge;
- Facilitation a deep understanding of concepts content and a background of applying theoretical knowledge in practice;
- CM is an effective pedagogical tool for shift in emphasis from passive mechanical processes of memorization and reproduction of information on processes of active and conscious learning;
- Development of skills of evaluation and self-evaluation, group work, critical and creative thinking.

5   Conclusion

CM as a learning technique actively used in educational process in Russia. However it has limitations in application at classes and requires additional estimating methods for objective evaluation of students' acquisition of information. From our point of view, the main objective of Russian researchers has to be the following: to summarize and structure national experience in applying of concept maps and to make it more intelligible and comprehensible for teachers.

If we suggest directions of further research in application of CM, it is important to note the following. At the moment there are not enough comparative or longitudinal studies dedicated understanding of learning information by children of different ages by means of concept maps. That would allow to trace the dynamics of formation of conceptual thinking.

In addition, we see prospective studying of relationship of students' psychological characteristics and specifics of creation process and content of their CM. Traditionally, CM is a result of understanding of a topic but we don't know the impact of certain factors on this result - why a student has some kind of concept map. Examining cognitive or personality characteristics of student and correlating them with meaningful analysis of concept maps we will be able to get an explanation of mechanisms of assimilation and understanding of concepts.

Acknowledgements. The study was supported by the Russian Foundation for Humanities, project 14-06-00521 «Neuropsychological mechanisms of complicated kinds of intellectual activity developing in the higher school education».

References

1. Allakhverdov, V.M.: Experimental Psychology of Cognition. The Logic of Conscious and Unconscious. Izd-vo S.-Peterb. un-ta, Saint-Petersburg (2006). (in Russian)
2. Ammosova, N.V., Zelinskaia, G.A.: Concept maps as a means of understanding learning materials in university. Vestnik KGU im. N.A. Nekrasova **15**, 67–75 (2009). (in Russian)
3. Anohina, A., Grundspenkis, J.: Scoring concept maps: an overview. In: International Conference on Computer Systems and Technologies. CompSysTech 2009 (2009). http://stpk.cs.rtu.lv/sites/all/files/stpk/alla/IV.8.pdf
4. Anohina, A., Vilkelis, M., Lukasenko, R.: Incremental improvement of the evaluation algorithm in the concept map based knowledge assessment system. Int. J. Comput. Commun. Control **4**(1), 6–16 (2009)
5. Anokhina-Naumets, A.V., Lukashenko, R.S.: Intelligent system of knowledge evaluation: a model of student and the method of experimental verification of adaptation algorithm. Obrazovatelnye tehnologii i obshhestvo **2**(14), 346–362 (2011). (in Russian)
6. Balina, O.G.: Graphic techniques of information visualization as a means of activation of students' learning and cognitive activity (on the example of studying "Pedagogy"). Psihologija i pedagogika: metodika i problemy prakticheskogo primenenija **48**, 109–116 (2016). (in Russian)
7. Bazhenova, I.V.: Projective-recursive strategy and cognitive technologies in teaching programming to math students. Pedagogicheskoe obrazovanie v Rossii **3**, 52–57 (2015). (in Russian)
8. Bazhenova, I.V.: The design of learning content and outcomes of programming to math students. Vestnik KGPU im. V.P. Astafieva **2**(24), 79–82 (2013). (in Russian)
9. Biggs, J.B., Collis, K.F.: Evaluating the Quality of Learning: The SOLO Taxonomy (Structure of the Observed Learning Outcome). Academic Press, New York (1982)
10. Bogdanova, E.L., Bogdanova, O.E.: Developmental potential of method of construction of cognitive maps in educational practice of higher school. Vestnik Tomskogo gosudarstvennogo universiteta **353**, 161–165 (2011). (in Russian)
11. Cañas, A.J.: A summary of literature pertaining to the use of concept mapping techniques and technologies for education and performance support. Technical report, Pensacola, FL (2003)
12. Degtyarev, S.N.: Didactic tool for activation of creative potential of students in the process of solving creative problems. Vestnik Tjumenskogo gosudarstvennogo universiteta **9**, 56–63 (2012). (in Russian)
13. Degtyarev, S.N.: Divergent map: developmental and diagnostic capabilities. Problemy i perspektivy razvitija obrazovanija v Rossii **2**, 241–247 (2010). (in Russian)
14. Degtyarev, S.N.: Improvement of the control and assessment activity as a component of teacher's training. Teorija i praktika obshhestvennogo razvitija **8**, 228–232 (2015). (in Russian)
15. Gavrilova, T.A., Kudrjavcev, D.V., Leshheva, I.A., Pavlov, Y.Y.: About the method of visual models classification. Biznes-informatika **4**(26), 21–34 (2013). (in Russian)
16. Gavrilova, T.A., Leshcheva, I.A., Strakhovich, E.V.: The use of visual conceptual models in teaching. Vestnik S.-Peterb. un-ta. kSeria Menedzhment **4**, 124–150 (2011). (in Russian)

17. Kholodnaia, M.A.: Structural-integrative methodology in the study of intellect. Psihologicheskie issledovanija **1**(3), 195–204 (2009). (in Russian)
18. Kostromina, S., Gnedykh, D.: Lecture with multimedia presentation: how to choose the best visual tools. Otkrytoe obrazovanie **4**, 73–80 (2015). (in Russian)
19. Kostromina, S., Gnedykh, D.: Type of visualization and quality of digest ion of educational information by students. Procedia – Soc. Behav. Sci. **171**, 340–349 (2015)
20. Mirzaie, R.A., Abbas, J., Hatami, J.: Study of concept maps usage effect on meaningful learning frontier in Bloom's taxonomy for atomic structure mental concepts. In: Proceeding of the Third International Conference on Concept Mapping, vol. 3, pp. 226–229. OÜ Vali Press, Estonia (2008)
21. Muller, H.: Designing of Mental Maps: The Method of Generating and Structuring Ideas. OMEGA-L, Moscow (2009)
22. Novak, J.D., Cañas, A.J.: Theoretical origins of concept maps, how to construct them and uses in education. Reflecting Educ. **3**(1), 29–42 (2007)
23. Novak, J.D., Cañas, A.J.: The Theory Underlying Concept Maps and How to Construct Them. Institute for Human and Machine Cognition, Pensacola (2006). http://cmap.ihmc.us/Publications/ResearchPapers/TheoryCmaps/TheoryUnderlyingConceptMaps.htm
24. Novak, J.D., Gowin, D.B.: Learning How to Learn. Cambridge University Press, New York (1984)
25. Pak, N.I.: The Projective Approach in Learning as an Information Process: Monograph. RIO KGPU, Krasnojarsk (2008). (in Russian)
26. Savuk, L.A.: Conceptual basis for design of distance courses. Obrazovatelnye tehnologii i obshhestvo **3**(15), 492–501 (2012). (in Russian)
27. Simoniva, M.V.: Use mental maps to ensure a quality of knowledge at different stages of learning. Nauchnye issledovanija v obrazovanii **6**, 44–47 (2008). (in Russian)
28. Solso, R.: Cognitive Psychology. Piter, Saint-Petersburg (2006). (in Russian)
29. Tavares, R., Tavares, J.: Concept map under modified bloom taxonomy analysis. In: Proceeding of the Third International Conference on Concept Mapping, vol. 2, pp. 34–39. Viña del Mar, Chile (2010)
30. Urunova, H.: Forming critical reading skills in the process of teaching humanities. Uchenye zapiski Hudzhandskogo gosudarstvennogo universiteta im. akademika B. Gafurova. Gumanitarnye nauki **3**(23), 129–140 (2010). (in Russian)
31. Velichkovsky, B.: Cognitive Science: The Bases of Cognition Psychology. Smysl, Moscow (2006). (in Russian)
32. Vorobieva, V.M., Churikova, L.V., Budunova, L.G. (eds.): Effective Use of the Method of Mind Maps in Classroom: Textbook of Methodics. GBOU «TemoCentr», Moscow (2013). (in Russian)
33. Yadrovskaia, M.V.: The models of pedagogical communication in e-learning conditions of university. Obrazovatelnye tehnologii i obshhestvo **2**(16), 469–488 (2013). (in Russian)
34. Zagvjazinskij, V.I., Zakirova, A.F. (eds.): Pedagogical Dictionary: A Manual for Students of Higher Education Institutes. Akademia, Moscow (2008). (in Russian)
35. Zelinskaia, G.A., Zelinsky, M.M.: The Technology of Using Concept Maps in Teaching: A Training Manual. AGTU, Astrahan' (2011). (in Russian)

Select-and-Fill-In Concept Maps
as an Evaluation Tool in Science Classrooms

Javad Hatami$^{(\boxtimes)}$, Mohammadreza Farrokhnia,
and Mohammad Hassanzadeh

Tarbiat Modares University, Tehran, Iran
{j.hatami, M.Farokhnia, hasanzadeh}@modares.ac.ir

Abstract. Much research has been done on the application of concept maps as means for learning assessment. Similarly, different types of Concept-Map Based Assessments (CMBA) and their validity have been examined as well in many studies, but to a far less extent. The present study uses a descriptive quantitative method and mainly aims to put forward the idea that the select-and-fill-in (SAFI) concept maps could be used as a valid instrument to assess the conceptual understanding of science among thermodynamics students. For this purpose, the concurrent validity of the SAFI concept map was evaluated according to the last version of the Thermodynamic Concept Survey (TCS) in order to develop a standard conceptual survey in thermodynamics. The TCS has a total KR-20 of approximately 0.78, an acceptable value, which could be employed as a valid test to assess teacher-made SAFI concept maps. The study population includes 60 students from two physics classes. An evaluation of the conceptual understandings of thermodynamics students were made concurrently using two assessment tools. Based on the study findings, there is a moderate to strong correlation (0.6) between the Teacher-made SAFI concept map and TCS. This leads us to the conclusion that SAFI concept maps are valid tools, at least, for evaluating conceptual understanding in thermodynamics. Moreover, the results of this study are confirmed a significant relationship between a student's ability to read and comprehend a given question and his/her ability to solve it.

Keywords: Conceptual mapping · Science classroom · Evaluation tool

1 Introduction

Science is the use of valid and reliable observation for the study of phenomena, and the generation of theories in order to explain all that is observed. Therefore, science is both a process and a product. As a process, science entails observation and inductive reasoning, while its immediate products include the branches of physical, biological, and social sciences, and at a greater distance, they incorporate technological developments [1].

As a result, Science instruction is mainly aimed at pursuing one of three general goals: (1) acquiring organized knowledge of a particular branch of science (conceptual knowledge), (2) enhancing the problem-solving ability in a certain scientific domain (procedural knowledge), and (3) enhancing general skills of reasoning [1]. According to the Ausubel's theory [2], students can meaningfully integrate new knowledge into

© Springer International Publishing Switzerland 2016
A. Cañas et al. (Eds.): CMC 2016, CCIS 635, pp. 169–180, 2016.
DOI: 10.1007/978-3-319-45501-3_13

their existing knowledge structure, if there are relationships between conceptual knowledge following instruction and achievement [3]. Assuredly, the results show that conceptual knowledge can accurately predict the problem-solving performance as an ultimate aim of science classes [4, 5].

Although researches suggest that expert and novice problem solvers are not very different as regards the general strategies they employ, an important question is raised here: how are they different then? The answer is that they appear to differ significantly with regard to both the quality and the quantity of the domain-specific knowledge that they have. That is to say, experts are likely to possess more and better organized long-term memory structures for their respective fields of expertise [6, 7, 9]. Furthermore, the activation and application of knowledge in new situations is mediated by the organization of knowledge which is referred to as the core of successful problem-solving. Based on Kempa [10, 11], there is a direct relationship between conceptual knowledge and problem-solving difficulties. These difficulties typically arise owing to one or more of the factors below:

- A student's memory structure lacks the knowledge elements.
- A student's memory structure has wrong or inappropriate links between the knowledge elements.
- A student's memory structure lacks the essential links between the knowledge elements.
- A student's memory structure has false or irrelevant knowledge elements.

It is obvious that testing and evaluation play a vital part in education. The process of teaching and learning is well-planned if the real outcomes of the teaching process can be determined and if one can really determine whether the things that one has taught have been understood by the students. Studies that have used a most suitable approach for evaluating the outcomes of the teaching process, have taken into account the fragile part of testing and evaluation. That is to say, every assessment tool and every type of knowledge need their own methods of evaluation. Be that as it may, there are various approaches to gathering assessment evidence from students: minute papers to gain quick insight into student thinking, reflective journal writing to promote metacognition and reveal confusions, and concept mapping to examine the structure of student's knowledge or conduct assessment tests such as the Concept Inventory testes. These various assessment approaches for monitoring the student thinking and knowledge structure, each has its own merits and demerits, and some instruments appear to be more suitable for some topics or for some instructors [12]. As a result, according to what was said, to ensure that student could be as an expert in science learning and would be a skilled problem solver, we should find a valid way to assess his/her conceptual knowledge of a domain. So the present study is focused on assessing student's learning outcomes in one of the important branches of science, i.e. thermodynamics.

Thermodynamics is concerned with the physical universe and is pivotal to our understanding of physics, chemistry, and biology. As an essential course, thermodynamics has been a fundamental part of k-12 student's curricula [13]. Although important, much research has indicated that students find thermodynamics hard to learn. This argument is supported by Hassan and Mat [13] and Patron [14] who maintain that even following instruction, students have considerable misconception about the principles of thermodynamics. Patron [14], Junglas [15], Anderson et al. [16], Meltzer [17], Cotignola et al. [18] argue that many students experience a hard time understanding the basic concepts in thermodynamics. Huang and Gramoll [19], and Cox et al. [20] argue that topics in thermodynamics are not concrete and hence hard to picture. Moreover, many studies have shown that students are often able to use their procedural skills for solving science numerical problems; however, they may not be able to answer non-numerical questions about basically the same content [21, 22]. These observations underpinned a well-established hypothesis that the conceptual understanding of science is not necessarily as well formed for many students as their numerical problem-solving.

1.1 The Research Problem

It is not a common practice to use concept mapping for evaluating the conceptual understanding of scientific subject matter. In this light, we should ask this question as the present research problem which we intend to address: "Is it appropriate to use concept mapping for testing and evaluation of the subjects in thermodynamics?" If not, what suggestions can be accordingly offered to address this problem?

1.2 Purpose of Study

Concept mapping has been regarded as a powerful tool for promoting meaningful learning (e.g., [23, 24]. Novak [25] proposed four major applications for concept mapping: learning, instruction, planning, and assessment. However, concept mapping has not been as popularly used for instruction as it has been for assessment [26]. The aim of concept mapping tasks when they are used for assessment is mainly to evaluate the mapper's knowledge structures. Validity studies have mostly focused on this aim. Although, if concept mapping is to be used for assessment, decisions should be made regarding the three assessment-related aspects of a concept mapping framework proposed by Ruiz-Primo and Shavelson: (1) task for the respondent, (2) format of the response, and (3) a scoring system that generates reliable and valid results [26].

The focus of the present study is on the response format of the concept map assessment and attempts to assess the validity of SAFT concept maps for evaluating the conceptual understanding of thermodynamics in k-12. This is done by making a comparison with the Thermodynamics Concept Inventory as a valid test for evaluating the students' conceptual understanding about this domain.

1.3 The Research Hypotheses

- There is a meaningful correlation between the SAFT concept map's score and the TCI's score.
- SAFT concept maps can be used as an alternative or supplementary testing and evaluation method in teaching science, especially in the field of thermodynamics.

2 Concept Inventory Tests

Concept inventories appear to be a powerful instrument at hand that support iterative improvement in science teaching and improve the scientific literacy of students. The concept inventories have changed in terms of their objectives: to evaluate and develop scientific literacy [27], to facilitate curriculum reform [28], and to identify the students' weak spots [29]. In other words, a concept inventory includes a sketch of core knowledge and concepts for a given field and a set of multiple-choice questions which are intended to investigate the student's understanding of these underlying concepts [30]. A concept inventory involves individual questions which often spring from previous qualitative research by way of open-ended essay questions or interviews that reveal a student's incorrect thinking, misconceptions, or incomplete understanding with respect to basic principles or concepts. After that, these common misconceptions are integrated into the choices of the multiple-choice questions as "distractors." When a student chooses a certain distractor, it gives instructors to see where a student is "stuck" in gaining command over a particular concept [29].

The present study employs a concept inventory test which is the product of a study carried out by Wattanakasiwich and her colleagues [31]. In their study, they have developed a Thermodynamics Concept inventory containing 35 multiple-choice questions that evaluate the students' understanding of the underlying principles of thermodynamics called TCS. This inventory is categorized into two parts: Part (1) deals with temperature and heat transfer, and the ideal gas law; and Part (2) deals with processes and the first law of thermodynamics.

2.1 Reliability and Validity of TCS

A test needs to be both reliable and valid in order to be proved effective. In this line, Wattanakasiwich and his colleagues utilized Kuder-Richardson formula 20 (KR-20) for determining the reliability (internal consistency) of the whole survey. According to Ding and Beichner [32], the KR-20 criterion is ≥ 0.70. The majority of groups in their study had a value higher than this criterion and the total KR-20 for the TCS was around 0.78, which is an acceptable value. Ferguson's Delta (δ) determines the discriminating ability of the whole survey by measuring how broadly it spreads the distribution of scores. The valid value range from 0.0 to 1.0 and the survey is considered to adequately discriminate provided $\delta > 0.9$ [32]. Each group had TCS values above 0.9, therefore, based on both the item analysis and the whole survey analysis; the TCS tool is valid and reliable. Furthermore, in order to verify the reliability of TCS when KR-20 is used for the data which is derived from implementation of TCS in present study, the KR-20 for the test is 0.717, which is an acceptable value.

3 SAFT Concept Maps

The patent need to evaluate the organization of student's knowledge, particularly in science classes triggered the emergence of different instruments for visual representation of the knowledge structure. Concept maps, as one of these instruments, can encourage the learning of well-embedded structural knowledge and lay the groundwork for externalization of the conceptual knowledge, both correct and erroneous, which learners have in a knowledge domain. During his research program, Novak developed Concept Maps to monitor and understand changes in children's knowledge of science. He used Ausubel's learning psychology as a basis of his work. The underlying idea behind Ausubel's cognitive psychology is that learning occurs when new propositions and concepts are assimilated into existing propositional and conceptual frameworks held by the learner [33, p. 108].

Concept map as an assessment task may vary in relation to the limitations it forces on a student in bringing forth her/his representation of structural knowledge. Previous research suggests that the task demands forced on students via high- and low-directed techniques are different as students are required to make more informed decisions in a low-directed technique. It seems that the cognitive demands imposed by a low-directed technique are higher than those imposed by a high-directed one [34].

By focusing on both extremes of the continuum by studying, high- and low directed techniques, in the left side of this continuum we have SAFT concept map technique and in the opposite side we have construct-a-map (CAM). Concept maps have many applications, and the CAM technique is the most popular one (e.g., [26, 35]). Students typically use this format to make an arrangement of important concepts into a map and tie them with links which they label. Moreover, it allows students to represent their connected understanding of a domain with many different maps. As students draw their maps, they can see a representation of the domain take shape.

It is important to stress that as an effective format to assess learning; CAM suffers from at least three limitations. First, students need to learn how concept maps are drawn and then draw them. These processes take a lot of time and thus they can be dull and discouraging. As it happens, some students and occasionally instructors dislike and hence will not draw concept maps (e.g., [36]). Second, no simple and universally accepted scoring system has been suggested for produced concept maps [35]. Third, the quality of maps produced by students is greatly contingent on the individual's communication skills [37]. Furthermore, some studies (e.g., [37]) have suggested that if one immediately asks students to draw a map, it forces too much a cognitive demand on them for generating a meaningful representation of their knowledge. Therefore, SAFT concept maps are helpful, particularly when we dealing with students who are not sufficiently interested or lack the skill for drawing a concept map. In this line, we utilized the SAFT concept map produced by experts of the given domain. This map serves as a criterion map for measuring student's conceptual knowledge about thermodynamics. In generating a SAFT reference map, it is assumed that: (1) there is some "agreed-upon organization" that sufficiently demonstrates the structure of a content domain, (2) "experts" in that domain can settle on the structure, and (3) concept maps of the expert offer an acceptable representation of the subject domain (e.g., [38]). The purpose of developing a criterion map is to determine those propositions (nodes and links) that are deemed "substantial" to the domain and students are expected to know about a topic at a particular point. In light of the study by Ruiz-Primo et al. [26], we followed seven steps which are presented in their study to develop our criterion map (Fig. 1).

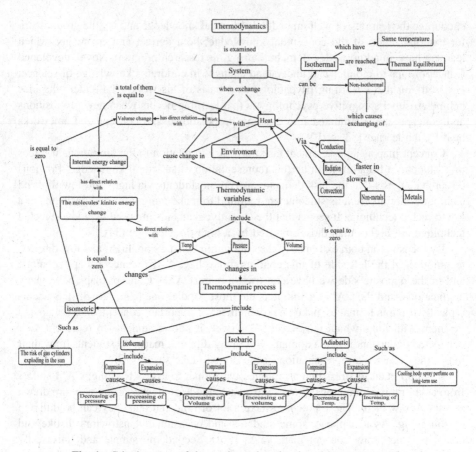

Fig. 1. Criterion map of thermodynamics, developed by expert panel.

In general, SAFI formats are created in two steps: (1) the creation of a reference map by an expert panel, and (2) the omission of some or all of the concepts or linking phrases by the experts. After that, the students are asked to fill in the blanks by choosing from a list of provided concepts [37]. As a result, we omitted 33 concepts from the original map to develop a conceptual assessment tool for the field of thermodynamics (Fig. 2).

3.1   Reliability of the SAFT Concept Map

KR-20 was used to evaluate the reliability of the final SAFT concept map. Hence, the map was examined with 35 students who had not participated in our study. The measured reliability was 0.887, which is an acceptable value.

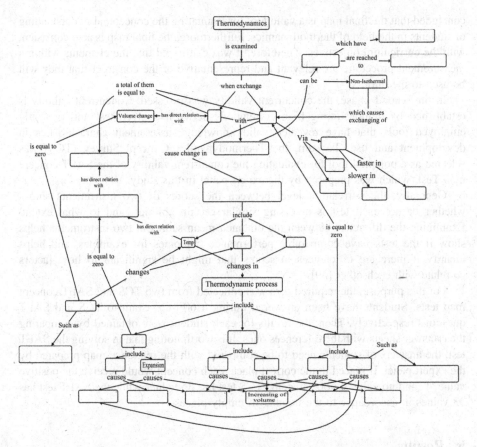

Fig. 2. Select and fill in (SAFT) concept map for the field of thermodynamics

4 Method

4.1 Sample Description

This study includes 60 K-12 male students who studying physics in the same school but in different classes, who were randomly selected from a mid-sized city in Tehran, Iran. The data collection was carried out by the school staff in the school, especially in designated areas for assessment.

4.2 Procedures

As previously mentioned in the introduction, the main goal of this study is to examine the validity of the SAFT concept map as an evaluative tool for assessing the conceptual understanding of thermodynamics at the high school level. Generally, the validation was assessed in two phases. In the first phase, the content validity was assessed. As the SAFT concept map was made by the expert panel that validated the TCS, it can be concluded that the final map is a valid tool for evaluating the conceptual understanding of students in the field of thermodynamics. Furthermore, the final map is also consistent with the curriculum objectives. Therefore, it was confirmed that the elements within a measurement procedure are relevant and representative of the construct that they will be used to measure.

In the second phase, the concurrent validity was assessed. Concurrent validity is established by demonstrating high correlations between a given test and presently employed tools that have revealed valid knowledge assessment characteristics in development and use. To sum, the Thermodynamics Concept Survey (TCS) was selected as a potential tool for evaluating the concurrent validity of the SAFT concept map Test, which was prepared by the expert panel in this study.

Generally, the correlation level between the scores of two instruments shows whether or not each test is assessing similar certain abilities, and to what extent. Examining the difference between the obtained mean scores in two instruments helps show if the tests have comparable performance outcomes for examines, and helps identify if there are differences in scores that might be significant to how factors correlate with each other [39].

For this purpose, the required data was collected from two TCS and SAFT concept map tests. Students have been answered during a 60 min' exam to TCS and SAFT questions respectively. Then, the results for each student were obtained by comparing their answer sheets with the references ones. It is worth noting that in solving the SAFT test, the answers of students need to be compared with the reference map prepared by the expert panel. If placed in the correct place, each concept would receive the positive value '1' and no value if not. Thus, the TCS test has 35 values while the SAFT test has 33 values in accordance to the number of empty places.

5   Results

The final scores obtained from the two tests for each student are illustrated in Fig. 3. As the scores of the two tests have been measured on an interval scale, we have used Pearson's Correlation Coefficient in order to calculate the correlation coefficient between TCS and SAFT in the current study. Of course, first we examined the normality of the data (Table 1).

After reviewing the data normality, the correlation between the scores was examined using the Pearson's correlation coefficient. The final results are shown in Table 2.

5.1   Data Analysis

Based on the data shown in Table 1, the scores of both concept map tests, i.e. TCS and SAFT, are normally distributed at the 5 % significant level ($p > 0.05$). Also, the correlation between TCS and SAFT concept map scores is 0.611 at the 0.01 level ($p < 0.01$). This suggests a moderate to high positive correlation between the designed test (SAFT concept map) scores in thermodynamics and the standard test in this field (TCS).

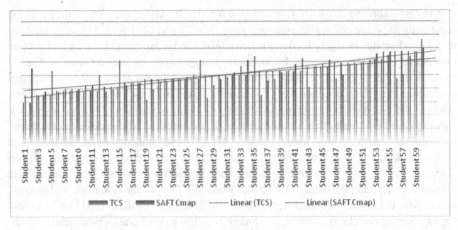

Fig. 3. The final scores obtained from the two tests for each student

Table 1. Tests of normality

	Kolmogorov-Smirnov			Shapiro-Wilk		
	Statistic	df	Sig.	Statistic	df	Sig.
TCS	.089	60	.200	.980	60	.422
SAFT Cmap	.095	60	.200	.967	60	.109

Table 2. Pearson correlation results which is calculated by SPSS V23

	TCS	SAFT Cmap
TCS pearson correlation	1	.611
Sig. (2-tailed)		.000
N	60	60

6 Conclusion

As the research data analysis indicates, fill-in concept maps are a suitable instrument for measuring conceptual learning in students in physics and thermodynamics. In fact, as these maps are simple to use and do not require instruction as how to be used, two features of a suitable test, they can be helpful in measuring the conceptual knowledge of students. Furthermore, it is recommended that due to their correlation with common conceptual knowledge tests, these tests can be used as a supplementary or even a predicting instrument. The results from the fill-in concept mapping tests can provide a good basis for measuring conceptual learning in students. Furthermore, in view of the obtained results from such tests, the misconceptions or misunderstandings of students can be identified and before giving classroom or problem-solving tests, they can be provided with separate and remedial instruction.

Among other findings of this study which is highly consistent with result of comparing the scores of the international tests, TIMSS and PIRLS (2011), is that failing to get good grades or doing badly at science tests can be explained by a lack of proper understanding of the questions by students. For example, as can be seen in Fig. 3, students number 2, 5 and 15 have obtained very good scores at the concept mapping test, while they have obtained very low scores at the TCS test which indicates these students did not have a proper understanding of thermodynamics. This inconsistency was explained by conducting an interview with each student whose descriptions threw light on the cause of this inconsistency. All of these students believed that their weakness at the TCS test was because they did not understand its questions. While some of the students were able to understand this test's questions well, others had difficulty understanding them. The results from this part of the study are highly consistent with the results obtained from the test by TIMSS and PIRLS (2011) where they found a strong correlation between a student's ability to read and comprehend a given question and his/her ability to solve it [40]. Therefore, concept maps and particularly fill-in concept maps can be utilized as a supplementary instrument for measuring knowledge in learners; and rather than relying only on classroom tests for analyzing a student's weaknesses, the results from this concept maps can be used to form more comprehensive and appropriate judgments.

7   Research Limitations

One of the main limitations of this study is its 60-student statistical population. In fact, the larger the population of students, the more valid would be the calculated correlation coefficient between the scores. These 60 students were selected as the sample at hand, as conducting a random sampling was not possible for the author.

8   Recommendations

It is recommended that other studies be done for measuring the validity and reliability of fill-in concept mapping tests in other domains of science and with larger statistical populations. Moreover, this instrument can be used more often for measuring students' understanding of conceptual knowledge who are generally weak at literature and reading comprehension, and for assessing their competence in these circumstances.

References

1. Gagné, E.D.: The Cognitive Psychology of School Learning. Little, Brown, Boston (1985)
2. Ausubel, D.P., Novak, J.D., Hanesian, H.: Educational Psychology: A Cognitive View. 2nd edn. (1978)
3. Pendley, B.D., Bretz, R.L., Novak, J.D.: Concept maps as a tool to assess learning in chemistry. J. Chem. Educ. **71**(1), 9 (1994)

4. Friege, G., Lind, G.: Types and qualities of knowledge and their relations to problem solving in physics. Int. J. Sci. Math. Educ. **4**(3), 437–465 (2006)
5. Solaz-Portolés, J.J., Sanjosé, V.: ¿Podemos predecir el rendimiento de nuestros alumnos en la resolución de problemas? In: Revista de Educación, vol. 339, pp. 693–710 (2006). http://www.revistaeducacion.mec.es. Accessed Jan 2007
6. Akin, O.: Models of Architectural Knowledge: An Information Processing View of Architectural Design. University Microfilms International, Ann Arbor (1980)
7. Chase, W.G., Simon, H.A.: Perception in chess. Cogn. Psychol. **4**(1), 55–81 (1973)
8. Chase, W.G., Simon, H.A.: The mind's eye in chess. Vis. Inf. Process. 215–281 (1973)
9. Egan, D.E., Schwartz, B.J.: Chunking in recall of symbolic drawings. Mem. Cogn. **7**(2), 149–158 (1979)
10. Kempa, R.F.: Students' learning difficulties in science. Causes and posible remedies. Enseñanza de las Ciencias **9**, 119–128 (1991)
11. Kempa, R.F., Nicholls, C.E.: Problem-solving ability and cognitive structure-an exploratory investigation. Eur. J. Sci. Educ. **5**(2), 171–184 (1983)
12. Smith, J.I., Tanner, K.: The problem of revealing how students think: concept inventories and beyond. Cell Biol. Educ. **9**(1), 1–5 (2010)
13. Hassan, O., Mat, R.: A comparative study of two different approaches in teaching thermodynamics. In: 2005 Regional Conference on Engineering Education, Johor (2005)
14. Patron, F.: Conceptual understanding of thermodynamics: a study of undergraduate and graduate students. Ph.D. thesis, Purdue University (1997)
15. Junglas, P.: Simulation programs for teaching thermodynamics. Global J. Eng. Educ. **10**(2), 175–180 (2006)
16. Anderson, E., Taraban, R., Sharma, M.P.: Implementing and assessing computer-based active learning materials in introductory thermodynamics. Int. J. Eng. Educ. **21**(6), 1168–1176 (2005)
17. Meltzer, D.E.: Investigation of students' reasoning regarding heat, work, and the first law of thermodynamics in an introductory calculus-based general physics course. Am. J. Phys. **72**(11), 1432 (2004)
18. Cotignola, M.I., Bordogna, C., Punte, G., Cappannini, O.M.: Difficulties in learning thermodynamic concepts: are they linked to the historical development of this field? Sci. Educ. **11**, 279–291 (2002)
19. Huang, M., Gramoll, K.: Online interactive multimedia for engineering thermodynamics. In: 2004 American Society for Engineering Education Annual Conference and Exposition, Salt Lake City (2004)
20. Cox, A.J., Belloni, M., Dancy, M., Christian, W.: Teaching thermodynamics with physlets® in introductory physics. Phys. Educ. **38**(5), 433–440 (2003)
21. Sawrey, B.A.: Concept learning versus problem solving: revisited. J. Chem. Educ. **67**(3), 253 (1990)
22. Cracolice, M.S., Deming, J.C., Ehlert, B.: Concept learning versus problem solving: a cognitive difference. J. Chem. Educ. **85**(6), 873 (2008)
23. Novak, J.D., Gowin, D.B.: Learning How to Learn. Cambridge University Press, Cambridge (1984)
24. Novak, J.D., Cañas, A.J.: The theory underlying concept maps and how to construct and use them. Technical report IHMC CmapTools 2006-01 Rev 01-2008, Florida Institute for Human Cognition (2008). http://cmap.ihmc.us/docs/theory-of-concept-maps
25. Novak, J.D.: Concept mapping: a useful tool for science education. J. Res. Sci. Teach. **27**(10), 937–949 (1990)
26. Ruiz-Primo, M.A., Shavelson, R.J.: Problems and issues in the use of concept maps in science assessment. J. Res. Sci. Teach. **33**(6), 569–600 (1996)

27. Klymkowsky, M.W., Garvin-Doxas, K., Zeilik, M.: Bio literacy and teaching efficacy: what biologists can learn from physicists. Cell Biol. Educ. **2**(3), 155–161 (2003)
28. Smith, M.K., Wood, W.B., Knight, J.K.: The genetics concept assessment: a new concept inventory for gauging student understanding of genetics. Cell Biol. Educ. **7**(4), 422–430 (2008)
29. Garvin-Doxas, K., Klymkowsky, M., Elrod, S.: Building, using, and maximizing the impact of concept inventories in the biological sciences: report on a national science foundation sponsored conference on the construction of concept inventories in the biological sciences. Cell Biol. Educ. **6**(4), 277–282 (2007)
30. Redish, E.F.: Discipline-based education and education research. J. Appl. Dev. Psychol. **21** (1), 85–96 (2000)
31. Wattanakasiwich, P., Taleab, P., Devi Sharma, M., Johnston, I.: Development of thermodynamic conceptual evaluation. Int. J. Innov. Sci. Math. Educ. **21**(1), 29–53 (2013)
32. Ding, L., Beichner, R.: Approaches to data analysis of multiple-choice questions. Phys. Rev. Spec. Top. – Phys. Educ. Res. Phys. Rev. ST Phys. Educ. Res. **5**(2), 1–17 (2009)
33. Cañas, A.J., Coffey, J.W., Carnot, M.J., Feltovich, P., Hoffman, R.R., Feltovich, J.: A summary of literature pertaining to the use of concept mapping techniques and technologies for education and performance support - Technical report Submitted to the Chief of Naval Education and Training, P. 108 (2003)
34. Schau, C., Mattern, N., Zeilik, M., Teague, K.W., Weber, R.J.: Select-and-fill-in concept map scores as a measure of students' connected understanding of science. Educ. Psychol. Measur. **61**(1), 136–158 (2001)
35. Shavelson, R.J., Lang, H., Lewin, B.: On concept maps as potential "authentic" assessments in science (CSE Technical report No. 388). University of California, Los Angeles, Center for Research on Evaluation, Standards, and Student Testing (CRESST) (1994)
36. Barenholz, H., Tamir, P.: A comprehensive use of concept mapping in design instruction and assessment. Res. Sci. Technol. Educ. **10**(1), 37–52 (1992)
37. Schau, C., Mattern, N., Weber, R.J., Minnick, K., Witt, C.: Use of fill-in concept maps to assess middle school students connected understanding of science. Paper Presented at the Annual Meeting of the American Educational Research Association (1997)
38. Ericsson, K.A.: The Road to Excellence: The Acquisition of Expert Performance in the Arts and Sciences, Sports, and Games. Lawrence Erlbaum Associates, Mahwah (1996)
39. Anastazi, A., Urbina, S.: Psychological Testing. Prentice Hall, Upper Saddle River (1997)
40. Martin, M.O., Mullis, I.V.: TIMSS and PIRLS 2011: Relationships Among Reading, Mathematics, and Science Achievement at the Fourth Grade - Implications for Early Learning. Boston: TIMSS and PIRLS International Study Center, Lynch School of Education, Boston College (2003)

Structural Equation Modeling (SEM):
Simply a Rotated Concept Map

Heather Monroe-Ossi[✉], Stephanie Wehry, and Cheryl Fountain

Florida Institute of Education, University of North Florida, Jacksonville, USA
{h.monroe-ossi,swehry,fountain}@unf.edu

Abstract. The purpose of this paper is to illustrate the connections between the uses of concept mapping and structural equation modeling (SEM). Concept maps can also be used to help authors organize and structure reviewed literature in a manner that may help them find their voice when adding to the existing conversation on a particular topic. A discussion of the process recently utilized for a doctoral dissertation is presented to provide an example of this organizational process by presenting a summary of the literature review with a concept map of the review and the supporting documents attached to the appropriate concepts as re-sources. Dissertation examples are then used to further demonstrate how the connections between concept mapping the review of literature and using a concept map to visualize the analyses can help students demystify research methodology, especially, the use of SEM.

Keywords: Structural equation modeling · Concept mapping · Dissertation literature review

1 Introduction

The purpose of this paper is to illustrate the connections between using concept mapping and structural equation modeling (SEM). A recent doctoral dissertation, Complexities of Technology Integration in the Elementary Classroom Context: A Structural Equation Model Study [18], is used as an example by presenting a summary of the literature review with a concept map of the literature review summary and the supporting documents attached as resources to the appropriate concepts. Then, the concept map of the literature review is transformed to resemble a SEM diagram, and finally the SEM diagram used in the final analyses of the data in the dissertation is presented. A brief discussion of concept mapping and SEM diagrams follows next to help the reader begin to see the similarities between the two visualizations. CmapTools, version 6.01.01, created by the Institute of Human and Machine Cognition [9], was used to produce the review of literature concept map as well as all SEM diagrams. The purpose of this paper is to show how the connections between concept mapping the review of literature and using the concept map to visualize the analyses can help students demystify research methodology, especially the use of SEM techniques.

© Springer International Publishing Switzerland 2016
A. Cañas et al. (Eds.): CMC 2016, CCIS 635, pp. 181–191, 2016.
DOI: 10.1007/978-3-319-45501-3_14

1.1 Concept Mapping

Researchers have described concept maps as graphical tools for representing knowledge. Concept maps include concepts shown by ovals, relationships between concepts shown by linking lines with a directional arrow, and by words on the linking lines that state the relationship between the linked concepts. Two linked concepts form a proposition, and propositions form meaningful statements when read. Concept maps generally represent concepts in a hierarchical fashion with the most general concepts at the top. Concept maps can also have cross-links, which connect concepts in different segments of the map. See for more background, e.g., [19, 25].

1.2 Structural Equation Modeling (SEM)

Standard analytic methods such as multiple regression, ANOVA, correlation, and factor analysis are all special cases of SEM. A unique property of SEM is the ability to model the relationship between observed and latent variables and to simultaneously model a variable as an independent and dependent variable, thus, allowing researchers to test a variety of hypotheses [11]. Researchers use graphic representations (diagrams) to explain both observed and latent variables and their associations. These diagrams are essential to the SEM process because they "allow the researcher to display the hypothesized set of relations among variables" [22, p. 36]. Ovals in SEM diagrams represent latent variables. Rectangles represent observed variables. Lines specify relationships between variables. The lack of a line connecting variables indicates that no relationship is hypothesized. Lines have either one or two arrows. Lines with one arrow represent a direct relationship between variables, and lines with two arrows represent correlations between the variables.

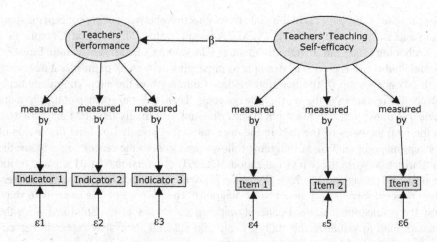

Fig. 1. The SEM diagram for the hypothesized research. When analyzed, the measured by statements would be factor loadings and the ε are replaced by the amount of measurement error in the item. The path between the two latent variables is a regression analysis, which produces the regression coefficient, β.

For example, suppose that a researcher hypothesizes that teachers' self-efficacy predicts teachers' performance evaluations. Both of these concepts are latent variables and are measured by observed or perceived behaviors. Teachers' self-efficacy is measured by three items on a survey and teachers' performance is measured by ratings on the three indicators of an observational rubric. The analysis could use multiple regression or multivariate models, but the researcher preferred to use SEM as the measurement model eliminates measurement error and some SEM statistical packages also account for the fact that the measured items are ordered categorical rather than continuous variables. Figure 1 shows the SEM diagram for this hypothesized study. Note that in the diagram the errors, the ε's, are not carried to the latent variables, but remain with the observed item or indicator. Thus, the latent variables are measured without error.

2   Concept Mapping and the Dissertation

Section two describes how concept mapping was used to organize a literature review and provides examples of primary concepts relevant to the doctoral student's research that were then used to develop an SEM. A review of relevant literature is necessary when writing any scholarly work, including dissertations. A quality dissertation requires the doctoral student to conceptualize and write his or her understandings of the literature related to the topic under investigation [2]. However, many students struggle to determine a method for analyzing, synthesizing, and evaluating empirical studies in a manner that helps organize their thinking [5, 15]. Martello explained,

> In other words, it is possible that the reviewer has all the key authors for a particular topic, and that in the write-up, he/she is able to provide the different perspectives about a contested topic. However, determining how to create new relationships with the existing perspectives is probably the most common challenge for many doctoral students [15, p. 62].

Concept mapping offers students a tool to help them organize their sources and provides a visual representation of the connections among concepts. In this way, concept mapping a literature review helps students organize and structure their knowledge, which promotes meaningful learning [19].

An example of a concept mapped literature review is provided in the following section. As reported in the dissertation [18] the purpose of the study was to extend the work of Kabakci-Yurdakul et al. [10] in which they reported on the development and early validation of their TPACK-deep, a scale measuring teachers' perceptions of the integration of technology into their practice. The subjects in their study were pre-service teachers in Turkey. In the dissertation study, the student used a sample of in-service elementary school teachers in Florida and included "additional constructs hypothesized to impact teachers' beliefs about their technology integration abilities" [18, p. 1]. The constructs under investigation were determined by how those concepts were associated with teachers' beliefs about their technology integration abilities as identified in the review of literature. The following sections present a summary of the dissertation literature review, and, as such, do not necessarily represent direct quotations from the dissertation.

2.1   Technology in Education

Technology has altered the way that we live, work, and learn. The 21st century will see fundamental transformation of 20th century schooling, which had changed little during the previous century. As Angeli and Valanides [1] pointed out,

> Technology has extensive pedagogical affordances and great potential for transforming the teaching and learning environment when it is used appropriately. Thus, the issue is no longer whether teachers should integrate technology in their existing practices, but how to use technology to transform their teaching with technology and create new opportunities for learning. (p. 154)

However, barriers to the integration of technology in education do not result from a lack of access to technology in the classroom or from mechanical issues regarding software and hardware, instead they lie in the traditional goals of education, interactions between teachers and students, resources, and the curricula [6, 23].

2.2   Technological, Pedagogical, and Content Knowledge (TPACK) Framework

In visualizing technology integration in education, the TPACK framework [13] shows that technology, pedagogy, and content have roles to play individually and together. The theoretical TPACK diagram (Fig. 2) is a Venn diagram having overlapping circles, one circle each for teachers' technological knowledge, pedagogical knowledge, and content knowledge and the three circle-overlaps representing teachers' pedagogical content knowledge, technological content knowledge, and technological pedagogical knowledge. The intersection of these two-way overlaps is the heart of the model and represents TPACK. However, "Good teaching is not simply adding technology to the existing teaching and content domain. Rather, the introduction of technology causes the

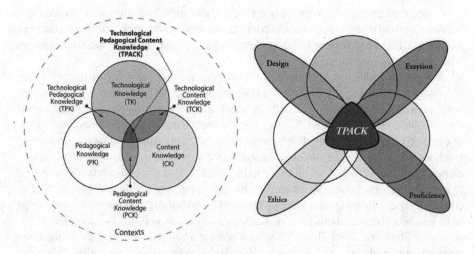

Fig. 2. TPACK model for technology integration (left), reproduced by permission of the publisher, © 2012 by tpack.org and the TPACK-deep model (right) reproduced by permission of Kabakci-Yurdakul et al. (2012).

representation of new concepts and requires developing a sensitivity to the dynamic, transactional relationship between all three components suggested by the TPCK framework" [12, p. 134].

Recently, literature has shifted to a more holistic approach in what Kabakci-Yurdakul et al. [10] described as technology-pedagogy integration (using technology in the pedagogical/content process). The approach is an integrative process that helps teachers develop their pedagogical knowledge and skill as they embed technology into practice. Kabakci-Yurdakul et al. developed TPACK-deep, which measures TPACK as a whole and includes four factors: design, exertion, ethics, and proficiency. Design is teachers' ability to design teaching that includes technology with their pedagogical and content knowledge. Exertion is teachers' ability to use technology in their classroom teaching. Ethics is teachers' abilities to behave ethnically when using technology. Proficiency is teachers' ability to integrate technology into content and pedagogy by becoming models for other teachers and to solve technology related problems.

2.3 TPACK Situated in Context

Teachers' planning for instruction is often complex, situated in classroom practice, and acquired through years of experience. However, as Angeli and Valanides [1] pointed out, the TPACK framework,

> … does not take into consideration other factors beyond content, pedagogy, and technology, such as, for example, teachers' epistemic belief and values about teaching and learning that may be also important to take into account. This simplified or general view, one might argue, may lead to possible erroneous, simplistic, and naïve perceptions about the nature of integrating technology in teaching and learning. (p. 157)

Furthermore, the integration of technology into teaching practice often happens in silos at the school level, with motivated teachers actively embracing advances in technology (often on their own time) and mastering the skills required to integrate technology in their practice [8, 14, 24]. The complexity of teaching with technology is situated in contextual factors that influence teaching practice and, therefore, student learning—including teaching self-efficacy, traditional beliefs about children, and leadership support for technology use. Measuring teachers' beliefs about children and examining how beliefs about children may influence their technology use in the classroom are critical to understanding the factors that are associated with effective technology use.

Tschannen-Moren and Hoy defined teacher's efficacy belief as "… a judgement of his or her capabilities to bring about desired outcomes of student engagement and learning, even among those students who may be difficult or unmotivated" [21, p. 783]. Moersche [17] reported that individuals with high levels of self-efficacy are most inclined to accept change and choose the best option. Brinkerhoff [3] examined the influence of professional development on teachers' self-assessed technology skills, computer self-efficacy, and technology integration beliefs and practice and found that teaching self-efficacy had a considerable impact on the use of technology, particularly for beginning users. Tschannen-Moren and Hoy's Teacher Sense of Efficacy Scale [21] is used to measure teacher's self-efficacy relative to student engagement, instructional strategies, and classroom management.

Zhao and Cziko [26] found that teachers use their existing beliefs and prior knowledge when adopting technology in the classrooms. Mascolo [16] indicated that understanding how to support teachers as they create technology-rich, child-centered classrooms is of great importance as student-centered methods have been reported more effective than the traditional, adult-centered approach to instruction. Several items measuring traditional beliefs from the Ideas about Raising Children scale, also known as the Modernity scale [20], can be used to assess adults' attitudes about childrearing and education including the nature of children (good or bad) and their learning (passive or active), the role of the teacher (to transmit knowledge or let children make their own meaning), and teachers' treatment of children (uniformly or individually).

The rapid change of technology is compounded by the intricate nature of change as it relates to reforming principal and educator practice. Principals must now lead faculty and staff to incorporate technology into the teaching and learning process by allocating time and resources, by inspiring teachers, and by setting expectations and directions for the integration of technology into the curricula [7]. A key role of principals is to provide the kind of support and continued education that teachers need in order to be willing to take risks, learn new strategies, and employ current technology most effectively in the classroom. Chang et al. [4] developed a questionnaire, the Elementary School Principals' Technology Leadership Questionnaire, which includes a 4-item scale, interpersonal and communication skills, that measures attributes of leadership that most directly relate to technology integration.

3   Concept Mapping the Literature Review and the Transition to an SEM Diagram

Next, we developed a concept map of the summary of the literature review presented above. Using the main concepts of the summary, we developed the concept map shown in Fig. 3. The concept map begins with Integrating Technology in Education and ends with measures of three contextual variables that might influence teaching self-efficacy as measured by the four scales of TPACK-deep. To make the concept map more closely resemble a SEM diagram, we chose to use ovals for concepts (constructs) that are not directly measured (thus, latent) and rectangles for observed variables (survey items used to measure latent concepts). Note, on the right side of the concept map, the concepts with the heavy lines represent the latent and observed variables at the heart of the SEM analyses.

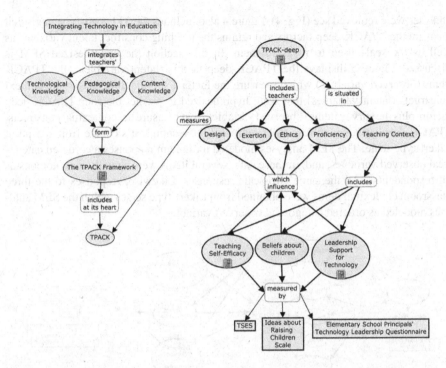

Fig. 3. Concept map representation of the literature review. Concepts in ovals using heavy lines represent latent variables in the study and concept in rectangles with heavy lines represent observed variables that measure the latent variables.

4   Data and the Hypothesized Structural Equation Model

4.1   Measures and Participants

Items from the four instruments, TPACK-deep, Teacher Sense of Efficacy Scale, Ideas about Children (Traditional Beliefs about Children), and the four items measuring interpersonal and communication skills from the Elementary School Principals' Technology Leadership Questionnaire (Leadership Support for Technology) were combined into one survey that also included demographic items. The link to the web-based survey was delivered via email to all eligible respondents (those whose districts and schools agreed to their participation). Data were collected from in-service southeastern USA elementary school teachers employed in 13 public school districts at 42 elementary schools. The participants consisted of 75 elementary school teachers who volunteered to participate in the study and completed the web-based survey.

4.2   Hypothesized SEM

The concept map in Fig. 3 was then rotated a quarter turn counter-clockwise to more closely resemble the hypothesized SEM diagram, and all concepts not linked to the SEM analyses were removed see (Fig. 4). Figure 4 also includes the 33 Likert-type items that measure the TPACK-deep factors and retains the teaching construct latent variables as well as the scale used to measure them. In this section the hypothesized SEM is discussed. Figure 5 displays the TPACK-deep factors (latent variables), the TPACK items (observed variables) which measure the factors, and the three classroom context constructs (latent variables) that were hypothesized to predict the four TPACK-deep factors plus the survey items (observed variables) that measure the contextual constructs. TPACK-deep survey item responses represent the respondent's choice from a 5-point Likert-type scale. The SEM analyses modeled these item responses as ordered categorical observed variables, and, in these data, several items were actually dichotomous as all respondents used the same two-scale responses. Likewise, responses to the three classroom contextual items were obtained from Likert-type scales which the SEM analyses modeled as ordered categorical observed variables.

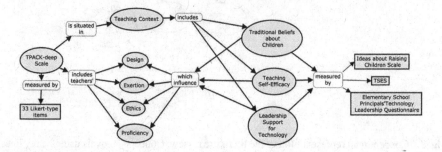

Fig. 4. Concept map indicating what concepts/constructs will be used in the SEM hypothesized model. TSES is Teacher Sense of Efficacy Scale.

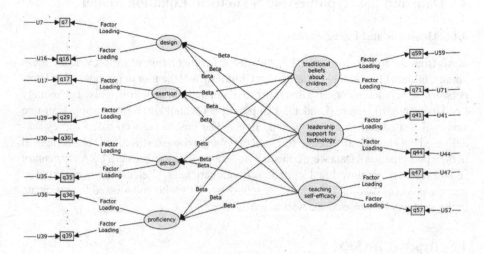

Fig. 5. Hypothesized SEM diagram.

4.3 Analyses and Results

The first step in the analyses was to confirm the four-factor structure of TPACK-deep and then determine whether or not teaching context variables, teachers' traditional beliefs about children, teaching self-efficacy, and leadership support for technology predict teachers' TPACK-deep self-efficacy. Results from the dissertation study suggest that the TPACK-deep scale has potential as a measure of teachers' beliefs about their technological, pedagogical, and content knowledge. Further, these findings posit that the scale could be used as a four-factor measure of teacher efficacy in technology use. Regression results indicated that both teaching self-efficacy and leadership support for technology predict teacher's self-efficacy relative to technology integration. Of particular interest were teachers' beliefs about their design abilities using technology, their exertion abilities implementing instruction with technology, and their behaviors related to ethical uses of technology, as well as teachers' beliefs about their technology integration proficiency. Furthermore, the dissertation study's findings indicate positive predictive relationships between leadership support for technology and teachers' beliefs about using technology in their classrooms. Based upon results from the dissertation study, more efficacious teachers and teachers who think that the school principal supports technology in the school are also more efficacious about their ability to integrate technology in their classroom practice. While positive predictive relationships between teachers' teaching self-efficacy and their beliefs about technology integration in classroom practice were found, no statistically significant association between teachers' beliefs about using technology and their traditional beliefs about children could be established for three (Design, Exertion, Ethics) of the four TPACK-deep factors under investigation.

5 Conclusions

Concept maps provide researchers with the tools to organize and structure their knowledge [19]. The example presented in this paper demonstrates how academic writers, particularly doctoral students, might use concept mapping to organize and structure the reviewed literature. This paper describes how one doctoral student further extended the concept mapping of a literature review to create a personalized visualization of the planned analyses of the data. In academic research, highly structured input is key to highly structured output. Doctoral students often struggle with strategies for organizing their dissertation study. The example presented in this paper details how concept mapping has the potential to help students design a highly organized structure for their dissertation.

Additionally, novice researchers, such as doctoral students, usually know more about the research topic than about the research methodology when it is not the familiar F- and t-tests. Methodologies, such as SEM, have recently become more popular. The newer statistical packages allow the researcher to analyze a drawn diagram, which can make the process simpler, but may not provide deep understanding for the novice researcher. This paper provides an example of using concept mapping of the literature to form a diagram that leads to a SEM diagram that represents the connections among latent and observed variables, which are often difficult for researchers to explain in concrete terms. In fact, the SEM in this paper and all diagrams in the sample dissertation were made using CmapTools. In the case of this doctoral dissertation, concept mapping was used as a method to organize the review of literature and illustrate the similarities among concepts identified as well as identify and connect the latent variables analyzed using structural equation modeling. This paper suggests ways in which doctoral students can potentiality improve the dissertation process though the use of concept mapping.

References

1. Angeli, C., Valanides, N.: Epistemological and methodological issues for the conceptualization, development, and assessment of ICT–TPCK: advances in technological, pedagogical content knowledge (TPCK). Comput. Educ. **52**, 154–168 (2009)
2. Boote, D.N., Beile, P.: Scholars before researchers: on the centrality of the dissertation literature review in research preparation. Educ. Res. **34**(6), 3–15 (2005)
3. Brinkerhoff, J.: Effects of a long-duration, professional development academy on technology skills, computer self-efficacy, and technology integration beliefs and practices. J. Res. Technol. Educ. **39**(1), 22–43 (2006)
4. Chang, I.H., Chin, J.M., Hsu, C.M.: Teachers' perceptions of the dimensions and implementation of technology leadership of principals in taiwanese elementary schools. J. Educ. Technol. Soc. **11**(4), 229–245 (2008)
5. Combs, J.P., Bustamante, R.M., Onwuegbuzie, A.J.: An interactive model for facilitating development of literature reviews. Int. J. Mult. Res. Approaches **4**(2), 159–182 (2010)
6. Cuban, L.: Frogs Into Princes: Writings on School Reform. Teachers College Press, New York (2008)
7. Flanagan, L., Jacobsen, M.: Technology leadership for the twenty-first century principal. J. Educ. Adm. **41**, 124–142 (2003)
8. Franklin, C.A.: Factors that influence elementary teachers' use of computers. ERIC Clearinghouse (2005). http://files.eric.ed.gov/fulltext/ED490605.pdf
9. Cañas, A.J., Hill, G., Carff, R., Suri, N, Lott, J., Gómez, G., Eskridge, T., Arroyo, M., Carvajal, M.: CmapTools: a knowledge modeling and sharing environment. In: Cañas, A.J., Novak, J.D., González, F.M. (eds.) Concept Maps: Theory, Methodology, Technology, Proceedings of the First International Conference on Concept Mapping. Universidad Publica de Navarra, Pamplona (2004)
10. Kabakci-Yurdakul, I.K., Odabasi, H.F., Kilicer, K., Coklar, A.N., Birinci, G., Kurt, A.A.: The development, validity and reliability of TPACK-deep: a technological, pedagogical content knowledge scale. Comput. Educ. **58**, 964–977 (2012)
11. Kline, R.: Principles and Practice of Structural Equation Modeling. The Guilford Press, New York (1998)
12. Koehler, M.J., Mishra, P.: What happens when teachers design educational technology? The development of technological pedagogical content knowledge. J. Educ. Comput. Res. **32**(2), 131–152 (2005)
13. Koehler, M.J., Mishra, P.: What is Technological, Pedagogical Content Knowledge? Contemp. Issues Technol. Teacher Educ. **9**(1), 60–70 (2009)
14. Lowery, N.V.: Teachers, professional development, and technology. In: Society for Information Technology and Teacher Education International Conference Proceedings, vol. 2003, no. 1, pp. 2934–2936. EditLib Database (2003). http://www.editlib.org

15. Martelo, M.: Use of bibliographic systems and concept maps: innovative tools to complete literature review. Res. Sch. **18**(1), 62–70 (2011)
16. Mascolo, M.F.: Beyond student-centered and teacher-centered pedagogy: teaching and learning as guided participation. Pedag. Hum. Sci. **1**(1), 3–27 (2009)
17. Moersch, C.: Levels of technology implementation (Loti): a framework for measuring classroom technology use. Learn. Lead. Technol. **23**(3), 40–42 (1995). http://loticonnection.cachefly.net/global_documents/1995_11NOV_LoTiFramework.pdf
18. Monroe-Ossi, H.: Complexities of Technology Integration in the Elementary Classroom Context: A Structural Equation Model Study (Unpublished doctoral dissertation). University of North Florida, Jacksonville (2016)
19. Novak, J.D., Cañas, A.J.: The theory underlying concept maps and how to construct and use them. Technical report IHMC CmapTools 2006-02 Rev 01-2008. Institute for Human and Machine Cognition, Pensacola (2008). http://cmap.ihmc.us/docs/theory-of-concept-maps. Accessed Apr 2016
20. Schaefer, E.S., Edgerton, M.: Parent and child correlates of parental modernity. In: Sigel, I.E. (ed.) Parental Belief Systems: The Psychological Consequences for Children, pp. 287–318. Erlbaum, Hillsdale (1985)
21. Tschannen-Moran, M., Hoy, W.A.: Teacher efficacy: capturing an elusive construct. Teach. Teach. Educ. **17**, 783–805 (2001)
22. Ullman, J.B.: Structural equation modeling: reviewing the basics and moving forward. J. Pers. Assess. **87**(1), 35–50 (2006)
23. Voogt, J., Pelgrum, H.: ICT and curriculum change. Hum. Technol. **1**(2), 157–175 (2005). doi:10.17011/ht/urn.2005356
24. Watson, G.: Models of information technology teacher professional development that engage with teachers' hearts and minds. J. Inf. Technol. Teach. Educ. **10**(1–2), 179–190 (2001)
25. Wehry, S., Algina, J., Hunter, J., Monroe-Ossi, H.: Using concept maps transcribed from interviews to quantify the structure of preschool children's knowledge about plants. In: Cañas, A.J., Reiske, P., Åhlberg, M., Novak, J.D. (eds.) Concept Maps: Connecting Educators, Proceedings of the Third International Conference on Concept Mapping. Tallinn, Estonia and University of Finland, Helsinki (2008)
26. Zhao, Y., Cziko, G.A.: Teacher adoption of technology: a perceptual control theory perspective. J. Technol. Teach. Educ. **9**(1), 5–30 (2001)

Teaching Science for Understanding: The Positive Impact of Simultaneous Use of Concept Mapping and Computer Simulations

Mohammad Hassanzadeh[(✉)], Javad Hatami, Saeed Latifi,
Mohammad Reza Farrokhnia, and Tahereh Saheb

Tarbiat Modares University, Tehran, Iran
{hasanzadeh, j.hatami, M.Farokhnia,
t.saheb}@modares.ac.ir,
saeed.latifi@gmail.com

Abstract. Concept map as an effective tool allows learners to deal with an in depth analysis rather than keeping more information which is transferred through lecture based teaching. Concept map also improves the efficiency of computer assisted simulation techniques in learning environments. This research especially focuses on effectiveness of a computer simulated environment and concept mapping and its effect on conceptual understanding of science. In this study, we selected 60 high school students and divided them into two groups (30 students in Group A and 30 students in Group B). The goal of this research is to investigate how the concept maps influence the learning of Direct Current (DC) concept in electric circuits. We collected data by using Determining and Interpreting Resistive Electric Circuit Concepts Test (DIRECT). Covariance analysis indicates significant difference between two groups. Adjusted pretest scores also approve the significant effect of learning with simulation plus concept map in comparison with the sole simulation among learners (Partial eta Squared = 0.08; F = 4.84; p < 0.03). We conclude that students who used simulation along with a concept map (group B) showed better learning than students who used only a simulation software.

Keywords: Concept mapping · Science education · Computer simulation

1 Introduction

One of the main challenges of science education is the lack of public understanding of science. Previous studies indicate that despite of having previous knowledge on a subject, students express difficulties in understanding scientific concepts. Tunnicliff [1] for example, in an investigation found that students between 9–10 years old shows difficulties in understanding of repercussion and digestion systems. Another study indicates that students have different perspectives on what is happening in our body when we drink a glass of water [2]. In another research, students expressed various perceptions regarding what happens when they have a meal [3]. Some of students have

© Springer International Publishing Switzerland 2016
A. Cañas et al. (Eds.): CMC 2016, CCIS 635, pp. 192–202, 2016.
DOI: 10.1007/978-3-319-45501-3_15

little understanding that there are different systems for meals and beverages in our body. In this study, there was no sign that shows students have knowledge about chemical change of food [3]. Physics also as a branch of science permanently encounters with this kind of challenges. In the last two decades, research on physics training in schools indicates that most of science students have problem understanding concepts of physics. Traditional Physics training causes little change on a student's' conceptual knowledge of physics. Students may have knowledge on how to use a formula or to solve calculative problems but they had little success in understanding the concepts of physics [4]. Many education professionals believe that this problem is caused due to the utilization of traditional teaching methods, such as a one-way lecture by the teachers [5]. Instead of engaging students with the problem, teachers give lectures and teach materials that are disconnected [6, 7]. As a result, the student only memorizes the information in order to pass the final exam successfully. The essential hypothesis of lectures in a class is to diminish the course materials into facts so to transfer it into a student's mind and a student memorizes the concepts without fully understanding the scientific concepts [8]. This educational approach is in contrast with an educational system that considers education not as a transferring process to transmit a series of abstract and difficult facts into a student's mind. Learning is a process which requires to nurture a set of skills and competencies among students to use resources for better discovering, evaluating and using of the information [9]. Moreover, learning should be a two-way communication process so that intriguers the active involvement and participation of both teachers and learners [10]. Unfortunately, in the contemporary teaching environment, scientific concepts are still taught through one way lectures in the form of a series of abstract and difficult facts to the students and students are only required to memorize these facts [6]. Hardly any sophisticated techno-centered methods, such as labs or simulation techniques are incorporated throughout the teaching process. As a result, we observe that many students experience academic failure [11]. It is obvious that traditional method of teaching does not assist a student to understand scientific concepts comprehensively, therefore, s/he gain a superficial understanding of the concepts. To facilitate an effective learning process, students should be able to build a knowledge through an active involvement and gaining experience in the learning process instead of playing an inactive role in the process. Of solutions that are developed and emphasized in recent years to increase the engagement of students in the learning process are cognitive tools, such as simulation and concept mapping. This paper is a scientific attempt to demonstrate the efficiency of these cognitive tools in the enhancement of students' learning process.

1.1 Cognitive Tools

Cognitive tools are designed to facilitate the process of learning with information processing technologies not from these technologies [12]. Learning with technology improves cognitive process of a learner. Therefore, cognitive tools and environments based on computers are tools for the improvement of cognition. If a learner and a computer are counted as major components of a learning system, the purpose should be distributing cognitive responsibilities among different components of the system.

Studies recommend that instead of forcing learners to store and retrieve information, a learner should be required for pattern recognition, organizing them and then developing them by information combination. Mental tools distribute cognition task in an efficient way among different components of the system. It should be mentioned that mental tools are not necessarily considered for reducing the information processing tasks but for simplifying the learning process through providing a more engaging environment throughout the learning cycle. They are also tools learners naturally use in a simple and efficient manner [13].

1.2 Concept Map and Computer Simulation

Different kinds of cognitive tools for helping student to construct their knowledge are identified and are used in education [14]. Among the main innovations for representing a natural phenomenon is interactive computer simulation [15] and concept mapping. Theoretical framework of concept map training method is based on Ausubel's Meaningful Learning Theory [16]. Ausubel proposes that learning occurs when the learner is able to organize new concept and information with his/her cognitive capabilities. Based on meaningful learning theory, Novak [17] introduced their concept map education method [18]. Concept maps are a subset of collection of tools and under main topic mind ware that relates to how we organize our knowledge and apply it [19]. The concept map is known as a cognitive tool which is affected by learning and education technologies in theory and action. A concept map is an imagined representation of meaningful relations among concepts that are interrelated in learners' mind. In some aspects, they represent our knowledge and the way we apply it. Concept map as a tool enables learner to see and to understand what is important for him/her. This tool allows learners to represent the knowledge and manipulate it precisely and to improve more abstract and challenging concepts and to link them together all together [19]. Knowledge, which is learned meaningfully through a concept map, will be sustained in a learner's mind for longer period and will nurture critical thinking skills and problem solving competencies among students [20].

There are many research evidences indicate the priority of concept maps for traditional methods of learning and education (e.g. [21–25]). While some studies did not report the positive impact of concept maps (e.g. [26–29]) some other studies confirm the positive impact of concept maps.

One of the other main tools is computer simulation. Utilizing simulation in education is one of the principles of cybernetics. However, it was first emerged in the form of simulated games in the 18th century, its new role and form emerged in the 1930s and 1940s [30]. Simulation mostly is implemented in natural and human systems and versions of some real tools or work environment attempting to show behavioral dimensions of a physical or abstract system through the behavior of another system [31]. The goal of these simulations is to increase the learners' activities, learning process, and the thoughts and approaches of the students, and to provide a rich environment wherein learners are able to achieve an in depth and conceptual understanding of science. Research shows that when simulation is designed and used based on learning foundations, it will be more effective and useful. In contrast, if a student becomes diverted from the learning path, s/he will achieve less or even negative outcomes. Wieman [32] introduces a new generation of simulations that were designed and created by group of researchers on physics and science education department of university of Colorado. This paper explains that interactive simulations, which are well-designed based on cognitive and education principles, can be used as efficient and engaging tools for physic education.

Generally, most of the previous research emphasize the effectiveness of simulations in understanding the concepts of physics (e.g. [33, 34]).

Physics is a branch of science which its learning is not limited to gaining knowledge regarding a phenomenon. In physics, a learner should understand the relation between different concepts. Considering the aforementioned statements, this research attempts to compare the impact of two different cognitive tools in a learning improvement.

2   Methodology

In this experimental research, we used accidental sampling in order to select samples that are readily available and convenient. The test and control groups were selected by using randomized appointment so members of both groups have equal chance to be selected. The research population are high school students studying mathematics and physics in the 3rd grade. Around 60 students were selected randomly and divided into two 30 member groups. In the group A, training based on computer simulation was carried out and in the group B, in addition to using simulation, we asked the students to draw a concept map based on predefined objectives of the session. The students finished these tasks in interaction with their teacher.

2.1   Implementation

We employed the pretest and posttest method in order to carry out the research. After appointing classes of students, all participants attended in a 20-minute introduction session. Then, they passed a conceptual understanding test of the exam textbooks. We continued the study for 3 months (equal to 8 one-hour training session). At the end, we hold a predefined exam text about "direct current circuits" and pertinent to measurement purposes of the learning test. We asked the students to answer the tests by using circuit simulating software (this software have been explained more in next section). As mentioned before, the only different task among group B and A was that group B were asked to depict the concept map of each session and finalize it with the help of their teacher. We gave the students of both groups homework for more exercise to use the simulation software in order to receive the teacher's feedback in the classroom. We asked the students of the group B after the last session to manipulate eight concept maps of all sessions and to create a final map with the help of their teacher (Fig. 1).

After 8 sessions and covering all of the materials, we conducted a conceptual understanding test for both groups. The results were compared by using covariance analysis.

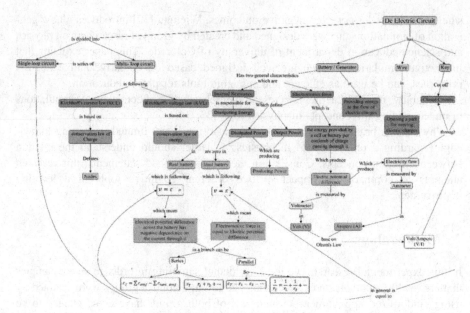

Fig. 1. Part of a final concept map

2.2 Measurement Tools

Learning Test. The extent which learners understand was very crucial for this research. This task was carried out by using a standard test of electric circuits (EC). Determining and Interpreting Resistive Electric Circuit Concepts Test (DIRECT) has been initially introduced by Paula Vetter Engelhardt (1997) on her PhD thesis [35]. The main objective of this test was to provide schools with a standard tool to measure the extent of conceptual understanding of students regarding electric circuit concept in direct current. This tool was consolidated in a sample of students: 454 high school students and 681 college students. After 3 editions, version 1.2 was used in this research. This test contains 29 questions, each pertaining to an educational objective of electric circuits (Table 1).

For the purpose of covering all of the educational objectives which would have been measured in learning test in 8 sessions, we added information included in the manual form for both groups (Fig. 2). We advised two expert teachers to achieve consistent objectives and a course plan for each session.

Please draw a circuit in PhET[1] software based on the following schematic chart and use voltmeter to measure potential variance between two ends of all components in circuit and write them in the following table. Please be careful while using voltmeter, the priority of cables for all components equally. For example, if there were a negative (black) cable for the valve and the positive cable (red in right side), take this priority for next valves and power resource. Then, according to the table answer the following questions.

---

[1] Physics Education Technology (PhET).

Table 1. Test questions and the educational objectives

Questions number	Objectives
	Visual aspects of electric circuits
11, 21, 11	1. Identifying and explaining short connection in EC
20, 10	2. Identifying and understanding circuit elements which are connectable from two sides
	3. Understanding a complete circuit and its necessity in electric flow
29	4. Combination of objectives 1 to 3
25, 15, 5	5. Using the concept of resistance including the fact that resistance is a characteristic of each material (body structure and raw materials) as well as the fact that in the sequence mode with the addition of each element in circuit, the resistance increases, and in parallel by adding an element to circuit, the resistance decreases
24, 14, 4	6. Interpretation of circuit figures ranging from series, parallel or mixed
	Energy
13, 2	1. Applying the concept of power (work done (Energy) per time unit) on various circuits
23, 3	2. Applying the conceptual understanding of Kirchhoff's law of energy conservation concept including the ring (which with each cycle of the electrical circuit is $\sum V = 0$) and the fact that battery is a source of energy
	Electric flow
28, 19, 18, 9, 8, 22	1. Understanding and applying the law of conservation of electric current (law of conservation of charge in a steady and uniform conditions) on different circuits
1, 12	2. Explaining Microscopic aspect of electric current in a circuit using this type of electrostatic because of low electric field, the potential difference and the interaction of forces on charged particles
	Potential (voltage) variance
7, 17, 7	1. Applying the knowledge on the impact of a potential difference on electric current
28, 26, 16, 6	2. Applying the concept of potential difference on the different circuits that include knowledge that the potential difference is accumulated in a row circuits and the circuit remains the same

DC Simulation Software. As mentioned in the previous sections, in the virtual session of electricity circuit labs, we used Phet application. It was developed by the University of Colorado (Fig. 3).

Of the properties of this simulation technology, which differentiate it from other same technologies, are:

- Attractive environment that employs graph and animations to attract learners for doing tests and leaving ideas.
- Visualizing models (such as electrons motion in electric circuits), which are useful in realizing concepts in learners' mind.
- A very simple function, which does not require sophisticated skills.

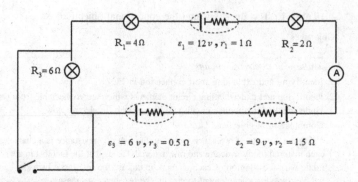

Component Name	Valve 1	Source 1	Valve 2	Source 2	Valve 3	Source 3
Current Intensity						
Potential Variance						

Fig. 2. A sample manual for each group

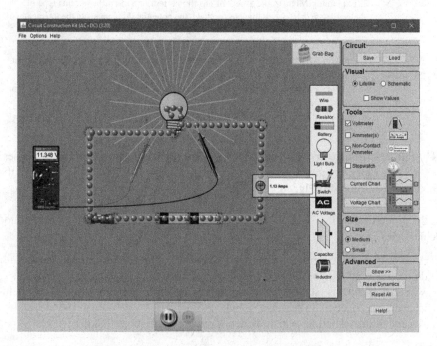

Fig. 3. Electric circuit simulating application interface

3   Findings

Table 2 enlists descriptive indicators of both groups. For each group, same pretest and posttest were carried out.

As shown in Table 2, means for two groups don't differ significantly in pretest. But the difference in test stage is significant (4.56). Since it is possible that the difference can be caused by sampling error or etc., we carried out a covariance test as well. Therefore, pretest results were controlled and test results were compared. For conducting covariance analysis, we ensured that variance of both groups are equal. We conducted Levin's test for that end. Results presented in Table 3.

Table 2. Descriptive statistics for both groups in conceptual understanding test

		Simulation (group A)	Simulation + concept map (group B)	N
Pretest for conceptual understanding	Mean	7.53	7.76	30
	Standard deviation	2.63	2.90	
Posttest for conceptual understanding	Mean	17.00	21.56	30
	Standard deviation	2.57	3.64	

Table 3. Levin test for equality of variances

F	df (1)	df (2)	P value
0.6	1	58	0.43

Since P value is greater than 0.05, we conclude that there is no significant difference between variances and they are almost equal. Table 4 presents results achieved by co variance analysis test.

After adjusting pretest scores, we observed that the simultaneous use of simulation and concept map can have a great impact on the learning process in comparison with the sole use of simulation (Partial eta Squared = 0.08; F = 4.84; p < 0.03). Adjusted means (Table 5) also approves this. We conclude that the members of group B that used simulation and concept map at the same time had better understanding of this scientific concept compared to the members of the group A, who only used the simulation software. It should be highlighted that their learning different was highly significant.

Table 4. Covariance analysis test to comprise groups mean controlling pretest effect

	Sum of squares	df	Squares mean	F	P value	Partial eta square
Group	14/99	1	14.99	4.84	0.03	0.080
Pretest	389/214	1	389.214	125.638	0.000	0.69
Group* Pretest	0/510	1	3.510	1.13	0.29	0.020
Error	173/48	56	3.09			
Total	23201/00	60				

Table 5. Adjusted means for experimental groups A and B

Learning style	Adjusted mean	Mean standard error
Group A	17.09	0.32
Group B	21.44	0.32

4 Conclusion

This research aimed to investigate the effectiveness of concept mapping as a tool for summarization of concepts in computer simulated environment. As covariance analysis showed, there was a significant difference between groups A and B in regards to their understanding of scientific concepts. Students who used concept mapping and simulation at the same time showed greater efficiency in comparison to the students who only used the simulation software. The reason lies behind the fact that simulation tools improves knowledge structures and knowledge construct of learners. In fact, meanwhile students were doing their tasks and learning concept, they attempted to know their relation with each other as well We conclude that a student with an understanding of meaningful relations among two or several concepts, depicts it in a form of conceptual map and at the end of the class complete all relations. As a result, s/he can achieve a more comprehensive and accurate understanding of relations among concepts, and even experience a lesser level of cognitive difficulty. On the other hand, a student whose mind is filled with abstract concepts and relations will be confused and cognitively overwhelmed. Students' mind is filled with information that will prevent her/him from effective analysis and correlation among concepts. Therefore, the conceptual map will assist a student as a cognitive and mind tool for understanding the course materials. This is the unique functionality of concept map that provides learner with more potential to analyze what he/she learns. A close collaboration between information professionals and education technologist may improve the functionality of conceptual maps in science education.

References

1. Tunnicliffe, S.D.: Where does the drink go? Prim. Sci. Rev. **85**, 8–10 (2004)
2. Granklint Enochson, P., Helldén, G., Lindahl, B.: Students' understanding about the function of the human body in relation to their own health. In: Paper Presented at the Conference ESERA, Malmö University, Sweden (2007)

3. Rowlands, M.: What do children think happens to the food they eat? J. Biol. Educ. **38**(4), 167–171 (2004). Skolverket (two thousand and seven). http://www3.skolverket.se/ki/eng/comp.pdf

4. Lichtenberger, A., Vaterlaus, A., Wagner, C.: Analysis of student concept knowledge in kinematics. In: Constantinou, C.P., Papadouris, N., Hadjigeorgiou, A. (eds.) Proceedings of the ESERA the 2013th E-Book Conference: Teaching and Coherence in Learning Science Education Research for Evidence Based, Part 11 (Millar, R. & Dolin, J.), pp. 38– 50. ESERA, Nicosia (2014)

5. Gardner, J.: Testing the efficacy of Merrill's first principles of instruction in improving student performance in introductory biology courses. All graduate theses and dissertations, Utah State University (2011)

6. Michael, J.: Where's the evidence that active learning works? Adv. Physiol. Educ. **30**(4), 159–167 (2006)

7. Halpern, D.F., Hakel, M.D.: Learning that lasts a lifetime: teaching for long-term retention and transfer. New Dir. Teach. Learn. **89**, 3–7 (2002)

8. Mayer, R.E.: Thinking, Problem Solving, Cognition, 2nd edn. WH Freeman, New York (1999)

9. DiCarlo, S.E.: Cell biology should be taught as science is practiced. Nat. Rev. Mol. Cell Biol. **7**(4), 290–295 (2006)

10. Ebert-May, D., Brewer, C., Allred, S.: Innovation in large lectures: teaching for active learning. Bioscience **47**, 601–607 (1997)

11. Freeman, S., O'Connor, E., Parks, J.W., Cunningham, M., Hurley, D., Haak, D., Dirks, C., Wenderoth, M.P.: Prescribed active learning increases performance in introductory biology. CBE Life Sci. Educ. **6**(2), 132–139 (2007)

12. Salomon, G., Perkins, D.N., Globerson, T.: Partners in cognition: extending human intelligence with intelligent technologies. Educ. Res. **20**(3), 2–9 (1991)

13. Perkins, D.N.: PERSON PLUS: a distributed view of thinking and learning. In: Salomon, G. (ed.) Distributed Cognitions. Cambridge University Press, Cambridge (1993)

14. Kuhn, D., Dean, D.J.: Is developing scientific thinking all about learning to control variables? Psychol. Sci. **16**(11), 866–870 (2005)

15. Abdullah, S., Abbas, M.: The effects of inquiry-based computer simulation with cooperative learning on scientific thinking and conceptual understanding. Malays. Online J. Instr. Technol. (MOJIT) **3**(2), 1–16 (2006)

16. Ausubel, D.P., Novak, J.D., Hanesian, H.: Educational Psychology: A Cognitive View, 2nd edn. Holt, Rinehart and Winston, New York (1978)

17. Novak, J.D., Gowin, D.B.: Learning How to Learn. Cambridge University Press, New York (1984)

18. Raisa, B.G., Jeanette, A.B.: Concept mapping a strategy for teaching and evaluation in nursing education. Nurse Educ. Pract. **6**, 196–203 (2006)

19. Jonassen, D.H., Marra, R.M.: Concept mapping and other formalisms as mindtools for representing knowledge **2**(1) (1994)

20. Materna, L.: Impact of concept mapping upon meaningful learning and metacognition among foundation level associate degree nursing students. Dissertation, Capella University. (2000)

21. Horton, P.B., McConney, A.A., Gallo, M., Woods, A.L., Senn, G.J., Hamelin, D.: An investigation of the effectiveness of concept mapping as an instructional tool. Sci. Educ. **77** (1), 95–111 (1993)

22. McCagg, E.C., Dansereau, D.F.: A convergent paradigm for examining knowledge mapping as a learning strategy. J. Educ. Res. **84**(6), 317–324 (1991)

23. Chiou, C.C.: The effect of concept mapping on students' learning achievements and interests. Innov. Educ. Teach. Int. **45**(4), 375–387 (2008)
24. Abbasi, J., Abdullah Mirzaee, R., Hatami, J.: Usage of concept maps in teaching high school chemistry. J. Educ. Train. (97), 29–52 (2009). New Courses, Spring 1388
25. Zare, M., Zrbkhsh, C., Sarikhani, R.: Effect of concept mapping on academic achievement and high levels of self-regulated learning in physics lessons. Media Mag. **4**(4), 18–24 (2012). Winter 92
26. Huber, F.E.: Effects of concept mapping on learning anatomy and transfer of anatomy knowledge to kinesiology in health sciences students. Doctoral dissertation, West Virginia University (2001)
27. Markow, P.G., Lonning, R.A.: Usefulness of concept maps in college chemistry laboratories: students' perceptions and effects on achievement. J. Res. Sci. Teach. **35**(9), 1015–1029 (1998)
28. Beissner, K.L.: Use of concept mapping to improve problem solving. J. Phys. Ther. Educ. **6**(1), 22–27 (1992)
29. Rahmani, A.: Effect of concept mapping in the second semester nursing student nurses learning process. End of a Master, Tabriz University of Medical Sciences (2005)
30. Bremner, M.N., Aduddell, K., Bennett, D.N., VanGeest, J.B.: Usage of human patient simulators: best practices with novice nursing students. Nurse Educ. **31**(4), 170–174 (2006)
31. Rodgers, D.L.: High-Fidelity patient simulation: a descriptive white paper report. Healthcare Simulation, Charleston (2007). http://simstrategies.com/downloads/Simulation%20White%20Paper2.pdf
32. Wieman, C.E., Perkins, K.K., Adams, W.K.: Interactive simulations for teaching physics: what works, what does not, and why. Am. J. Phys. **76**(4&5), 393–399 (2008)
33. Mustafa, M.I., Trudel, L.: The impact of cognitive tools on the development of the inquiry skills of high school students in physics. Int. J. Adv. Comput. Sci. Appl. (IJACSA) **4**(9), 124–129 (2013)
34. Finkelstein, N.D., Adams, W.K., Keller, C.K., Kohl, P.B., Perkins, K.K., Podolefsky, N.S., Reid, S., LeMaster, R.: When learning about the real world is better done virtually: a study of substituting computer simulations or laboratory equipment. Phys. Rev. Spec. Top. - Phys. Educ. Res. **1**, 010103 (2005)
35. Engelhardt, P.V., Beichner, R.J.: Students' understanding of direct current resistive electrical circuits. Am. J. Phys. **72**(1), 98–115 (2004)

The Educational Multimedia Clip
as a Tool for Students' Self-learning
on Concept Mapping

Alla Anohina-Naumeca[1,2]([✉])

[1] Riga Technical University, Riga, Latvia
alla.anohina-naumeca@rtu.lv
[2] University of Latvia, Riga, Latvia

Abstract. It has been already justified that concept mapping is an exceptionally suitable tool for formative assessment of structural knowledge. However, before the implementation of such type of assessment, the teacher should decide on a reasonable students' training strategy, its implementation way, and content to be delivered. The paper focuses especially on the last mentioned issue - the selection of the content and its representational forms for an educational multimedia clip that has been developed as a main tool for students' self-learning on concept mapping before the regular concept map based formative assessment of structural knowledge in one of the author's taught study courses. Content requirements and their further implementation in the clip are specified in detail. An empirical study based on students' evaluation of easiness of perception, internal value, and sufficiency of the content presented in the clip is discussed as well.

Keywords: Concept mapping · Training strategy · Multimedia clip · Content requirements

1 Introduction

According to [1], structural knowledge, in the context of learning, is defined as the understanding of relationships between concepts within a knowledge domain taking into account that both concepts and relationships are stored in the human semantic memory and are acquired as a result of meaningful learning. The well-developed structural knowledge is essential for expert performance, problem solving, and knowledge transfer [2–4]. Therefore, there should be continuous development and assessment of students' structural knowledge in higher educational institutions through the implementation of activities of formative assessment as this type of assessment focuses on students' progress and improvement of ongoing learning [5].

There is a wide range of techniques that could be used for the elicitation, representation, and assessment of structural knowledge, for example, free and controlled word associations [6–8], concept sorting [4, 6, 7] and tree construction [7, 8], essay and concept rating [4], etc. However, concept mapping is an especially suitable tool for the mentioned purposes due to the following aspects:

© Springer International Publishing Switzerland 2016
A. Cañas et al. (Eds.): CMC 2016, CCIS 635, pp. 203–214, 2016.
DOI: 10.1007/978-3-319-45501-3_16

- It is based on the well-defined didactic theory rooted in the Ausubel's assimilation theory [9];
- Concept maps allow both acquiring of students' judgments on relationships between concepts and representation of these judgments in the form of knowledge structure. This is not always possible with other representations, for example, judgments about relationships between concepts are expressed in essays but the teacher should use additional tools to evoke structural characteristics of knowledge;
- After acquiring the structure of knowledge, it is not necessary to use complex statistical methods to analyse it and to make conclusions as it is in the case of concept rating, association or grouping by similarity [10].

Moreover, an exceptional suitability of concept maps for formative assessment of structural knowledge has been already justified in [11] taking into account possibilities of this tool to represent clearly differences between experts' and novices' structural knowledge, to support the main definitional aspects of formative assessment, and to minimize assessment costs.

However, before the implementation of concept map based formative assessment of structural knowledge, the teacher should decide on an approach that will allow preparing students for the regular assessment with the help of concept maps. This is a quite complicated issue as it is related to 3 general choices:

(1) Selection of a reasonable students' training strategy;
(2) Selection of a tool for the implementation of the chosen training strategy;
(3) Selection of the content to be taught to students and form(s) of its presentation.

Study courses in higher educational institutions usually have limited number of hours and large groups of students. Within the allocated time limits, the teacher should implement the full didactic cycle "theory-practice-assessment" in relation to the achievement of the defined learning outcomes of the study course and the study program. In this case, a time-consuming training strategy more likely would not be an appropriate solution. Large classes typically prevent the teacher from the usage of collaborative and peer-based training activities and demand excessive workload. In such circumstances (limited number of hours and large groups of students), students' self-learning seems to be the more reasonable training strategy.

Considering the selection of an implementation tool for the chosen training strategy, it is necessary to take into account that today students have strong dependence on technology and representation of information through different media. Therefore, one of the best choice for students' self-learning could be an online technology-based solution like a multimedia clip available in the university's e-learning environment.

However, the most significant choice is the selection of the content, which will be delivered to students, and its representational forms. It determines how well students will be prepared and motivated for the assessment process. The author believes that in case of the self-learning strategy, the content should be at least easily perceivable, internally valuable, sufficient for students, and promoting their involvement.

The paper describes the selection of the content and its representational forms for an educational multimedia clip that has been developed as a main tool for students' self-learning when performing the integration of the regular concept map based formative assessment of structural knowledge in one of the author's taught study courses. It also discusses an empirical study presenting students' opinion on easiness of perception, internal value, and sufficiency of the content delivered.

The paper is structured in the following way. Next two sections specify content requirements and features of the clip developed. After that, the empirical study is presented. Summary is given at the end of the paper.

2   Content Requirements

The main characteristics of the content to be presented to students were already mentioned in Introduction: easiness of perception, internal value, sufficiency, and promotion of students' involvement. They are understood in the following way in the paper:

- Easiness of perception is related to the correspondence of the content to perceptual styles of students, minimized cognitive overload, and familiar context that is used when giving explanations of concepts taught;
- Internal value of the content appears if the content presented corresponds to internal goals, tasks, and interests of students and it is based on knowledge structures already known to students and simultaneously supplements these structures (meaningful learning). The author believes that this could be achieved by presenting the concepts taught in the broader context of learning, knowledge acquisition and representation in the human memory (students' potential internal goal);
- Sufficiency of the content means that the content offered explains all the main concepts of the topic under consideration and their relationships, as well as demonstrates necessary skills needed for completion of future tasks;
- Students' involvement assumes promotion of students' active thinking (through activities to be completed by students) instead of passive watching or reading of the content delivered.

Taking into account the explanations given above, the following set of requirements is defined in relation to the content of the multimedia clip:

- Covering the broader context. The content of the clip should show clearly relation-ships between three main concepts: knowledge acquisition and internal representation in the human memory, structural knowledge, and concept mapping.
- Incorporation of real-life context. Explanations of the concepts mentioned above should be built around a real-life context which is familiar to all students;
- Provision of concept examples. Explanations of the concepts should be accompanied by examples demonstrating their application or making meaningful associations with concepts and facts already known to students;
- Usage of different types of media. The content should be presented using different types of media to support a variety of perceptual styles of students which, according to VARK modalities [12], are the following: visual (preference is given to schematic depiction of information in forms of maps, graphs, diagrams, etc.), aural (those people prefer information that is heard or spoken), read/write (preference is

given to information displayed in words), and kinesthetic (those people prefer simulated or real experience and practice);

- Promotion of students' active thinking. Questions and tasks activating students' thinking in relation to the analysis of the content presented should be included in the clip;
- Provision of the detailed information on concept maps. For successful use of concept maps in the assessment process, students should be aware of purpose, main elements and rules of this tool, as well as they should have impression on how a completed concept map could look and be assessed by the teacher. Incorporation of worked examples of semantically and syntactically clear propositions should be made with the aim to minimize cognitive overload of students in future concept mapping tasks. According to [13], concept mapping is a cognitively demanding task which could lead to students' cognitive overload in case if inappropriate instructional approaches and activities are used. The authors studied the usage of worked examples in the training session on concept mapping as an instructional strategy for dealing with potential cognitive overload and avoiding creation of semantically unclear propositions by students. Moreover, development and restructuring of knowledge is also affected by students' emotional reactions [14]. Therefore, the more familiar students are with an assessment tool, the more positive attitude and emotions could be expected from them in the assessment process.

Table 1 demonstrates the correspondence of the defined content requirements to the previously defined content characteristics.

Table 1. Correspondence of the content requirements to the content characteristics

Characteristics / Requirements	Easiness of perception	Internal value of the content	Sufficiency of the content	Students' involvement
Covering the broader context		X		
Incorporation of real-life context	X	X		
Provision of concept examples	X			
Usage of different types of media	X			
Promotion of students' active thinking				X
Provision of the detailed information on concept maps			X	

3   Features of the Clip

Taking into account the requirements defined in the previous section, the content of the clip is structured in the following way:

- Knowledge acquisition and representation in the human long-term memory:
  - characteristics of the long-term memory;

- sub-systems of the long-term memory;
- the semantic memory as a storage of concepts;
- Structural knowledge:
  - definition;
  - significance of the well-developed structural knowledge;
  - development of structural knowledge by participating in the active process of knowledge construction;
- Concept maps:
  - definition and main elements (focus question, nodes, arcs, and linking phrases);
  - semantic and syntactic clarity of propositions;
  - example of a concept map;
  - assessment of concept maps.

The mentioned content presents a summary acquired after the deep analysis of literature on cognitive psychology [15–19], structural knowledge [2–4, 6–8, 20–22], and concept maps [23–28]. It is incorporated in the clip in the form of the author's developed textual explanations and graphical artefacts what can be seen from the figures given later in this section.

The content given above is presented in a real-life situation based on talking of two students (Fig. 1) and a professor (Fig. 2) in the university's premises. The underlying story is the following. One of the students (boy) – Edgar – has difficulties in learning. After listening to his complains, other student (girl) – Mara – concludes that the main cause of Edgar's difficulties is weak developed structural knowledge. As a result, she starts explaining him the concepts on knowledge representation and structural knowledge from time to time asking Edgar to summarize the main points. After proceeding to concept maps as a tool for development and assessment of structural knowledge, students go to a professor who uses concept maps in her instructional practice for the regular development of students' structural knowledge. The professor then explains elements of concept maps and gives examples of semantically and syntactically clear propositions. At the end of the clip, the professor engages both students in the creation of a concept map and gives an overview of assessment of students' concept maps. Therefore, the real-life context used in the clip includes a story based on a situation from students' life, university's premises as a place for development of a plot, whiteboard used to display textual explanations, and supplementation of taught concepts by examples and images from everyday life of each person (Fig. 3). Moreover, when the professor demonstrates an example of a concept map, she uses a commonly known concepts on a right triangle taught in school time.

The clip contains a lot of examples. Literally each concept is accompanied by an example demonstrating its application, providing additional explanations or making associations with already known facts. The semantic and syntactic clarity of propositions is emphasized through the usage of worked examples by adopting this practice from [13].

Different media are used to present the concepts taught: videos show dialogues between students (Fig. 1) and between students and the professor (Fig. 2), text provides explanations of the main concepts, audio records duplicate text, animations and a lot of images supplement textual and audio explanations.

Fig. 1. Dialogue between students

Fig. 2. Students talking to the professor

Students' active thinking is promoted by offering questions and tasks at the end of a theoretical block (Fig. 4). The right answer always is delayed and it is shown after a pre-defined time.

In addition to the theory on concept maps defined at the beginning of this section, some explanations in the multimedia clip are already given in a simplified concept map before concept mapping is introduced to students (Fig. 5) in order to accustom students to such a way of knowledge representation.

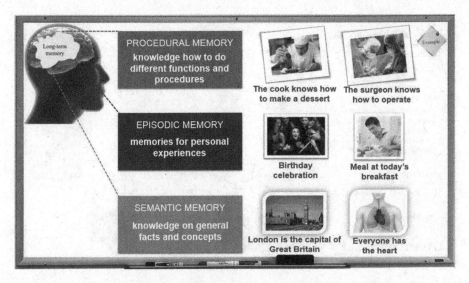

Fig. 3. Real-life examples accompanying the taught concepts

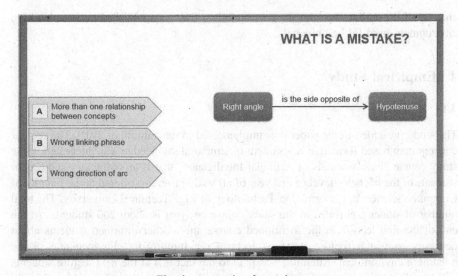

Fig. 4. A question for students

Videos were recorded using Sony video camera. Windows OS standard software "Sound Recorder" was used for audio records duplicating text on the screen. Animations together with textual explanations were created in MS Office PowerPoint 2013 and, after adding of audio records, were saved as MPEG4 files. The final multimedia clip entitled "Structural knowledge: their significance for learning and assessment through the usage of concept maps" was assembled in Sony Vegas Pro 12 software. The overall length of the clip is 27:04 min. The clip initially was uploaded to YouTube

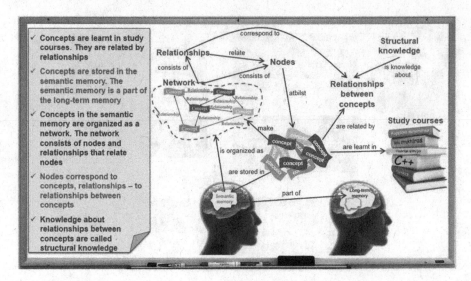

Fig. 5. Explanations given in the form of a simplified concept map

channel of the author and later the corresponding link was published in the e-learning environment used in the university.

4   Empirical Study

4.1   Procedure

The study presented in the paper was implemented in the autumn of 2015. The regular concept map based formative assessment of structural knowledge was integrated in the study course "Fundamentals of Artificial Intelligence" that is an obligatory subject for students of the bachelor level of 3rd year of all study programs offered at the Faculty of Computer Science and Information Technology of Riga Technical University. The total number of students enrolled in the study course per year is about 200 students. At the end of the first lecture in the mentioned course, the teacher informed students about necessity to watch (before the next lecture) the multimedia clip available in the e-learning environment. Attention was paid to the fact that at the next lecture students will be offered to create their first concept map. The reminder about watching the clip was sent electronically to each students 2 days before the next lecture. The next lecture started with the evaluation of the multimedia clip and then students proceeded to concept mapping.

4.2   Participants and Research Instrument

Eighty-six students evaluated the developed multimedia clip using 9 Likert-type statements (Fig. 6): 1 statement about easiness of perception of the content presented in the clip, 4 statements related to internal value, and 4 statements about sufficiency of the content provided. Five evaluation options were available to students: 1 – Strongly disagree, 2 – Disagree, 3 – Neutral, 4 – Agree, 5 – Strongly agree.

Evaluate your level of agreement with each of the statements given below
(put X in the corresponding column)

Statement ID	Statement	Strongly disagree	Disagree	Neutral	Agree	Strongly agree
A	It was easy for me to perceive content given in the educational multimedia clip					
Internal value of the content: For me, it was important to learn...						
IV1	...how knowledge is stored in human mind					
IV2	...what is structural knowledge					
IV3	...why structural knowledge is significant					
IV4	...how knowledge is acquired					
Sufficiency of the content: By my opinion, the content of the educational multimedia clip was sufficient in order I understood...						
S1	...what is structural knowledge					
S2	...why it is important to develop structural knowledge in the study process					
S3	...how to create a concept map					
S4	...how concept maps could help me in development of structural knowledge					

Fig. 6. Likert-type statements used in the evaluation of the clip developed

4.3   Data Analysis

The students' answers were processed by calculating frequency distribution, mode, median, range, and interquartile range (IQR) (Table 2). The data acquired allow making conclusions that there is a certain consensus among students because IQR is not greater than 1 for all statements. In general, most students indicated agreement that it was easy for them to perceive the content presented in the educational multimedia

Table 2. Descriptive statistics

Indicators	Statement ID								
	A	IV1	IV2	IV3	IV4	S1	S2	S3	S4
Frequency	Total number of answers - %								
Strongly disagree	0	0	0	0	0	1–1 %	1–1 %	2–2 %	1–1 %
Disagree	2–2 %	3–3 %	3–3 %	2–2 %	2–2 %	3–3 %	3–3 %	3–3 %	5–6 %
Neutral	20–23 %	29–34 %	17–20 %	28–33 %	26–30 %	19–22 %	26–30 %	22–26 %	27–31 %
Agree	49–57 %	46–53 %	55–64 %	44–51 %	51–59 %	49–57 %	48–56 %	38–44 %	42–49 %
Strongly agree	15–17 %	8–9 %	11–13 %	12–14 %	7–8 %	14–16 %	8–9 %	21–24 %	11–13 %
Mode	4	4	4	4	4	4	4	4	4
Median	4	4	4	4	4	4	4	4	4
Range	3	3	3	3	3	4	4	4	4
IQR	1	1	0	1	1	1	1	1	1

clip and the content was internally valuable and sufficient for them. In total, 74 % of students found the content to be easy perceivable. More than 73 % of students recognized that knowledge on what is structural knowledge was simultaneously internally valuable and sufficient. The content on knowledge acquisition and representation in the human memory, significance of structural knowledge, creation and usage of concept maps was valuable and sufficient for more than 62 % of students.

5 Summary

The integration of the regular concept map based formative assessment of structural knowledge in the study process should be preceded by the selection of an appropriate training strategy preparing students for the use of a specific assessment tool (concept mapping) and supporting positive attitude and emotions in the assessment process. In the light of the facts that modern students are strongly dependent on technology but study courses in higher educational institutions usually have the limited number of allocated hours and large groups of students, students' self-learning using an online technology-based solution like a multimedia clip seems to be a reasonable training strategy. However, in this case the teacher should decide carefully on the content to be delivered to students. It should be at least easily perceivable, internally valuable, sufficient for students, and promoting their involvement. The study presented in the paper has shown that the content, which takes the broader perspective, incorporates real-life context, provides concept examples, is represented in different types of media, promotes students' active thinking, and delivers detailed information on the assessment tool, could satisfy the mentioned characteristics. The students participated in the study agreed that it was easy for them to perceive the information presented in the developed multimedia clip and this could be related to usage of different media for the presentation of content as this supports different perceptual styles of students. Internal value of the content could come from showing interrelationships between the storage of knowledge in the long-term memory, structural knowledge, and concept mapping that more likely is a new information for students directly related to their potential internal goal - learning. Sufficiency of the content could be explained by the provision of detailed information on concept maps with the corresponding examples of syntactically and semantically clear propositions and demonstration of the process of the creation of a concept map for a pre-defined topic.

Acknowledgements. The author thanks her colleague Mara Pudane and her friend Edgars Valinieks for helping in the development of the educational multimedia clip by playing roles of the students.

References

1. Anohina-Naumeca, A.: The conceptual model of formative assessment of structural knowledge. In: Spector, M.J., Lockee, B.B., Childress, M.D. (eds.) Learning, Design, and Technology: An International Compendium of Theory, Research, Practice, and Policy. Springer International Publishing, Switzerland (2016)
2. Beissner, K.L., Jonassen, D.H., Grabowski, B.L.: Using and selecting graphic techniques to acquire structural knowledge. Perform. Improv. Q. **7**(4), 20–38 (1994)
3. Shavelson, R.J.: Methods for examining representations of a subject-matter structure in a student's memory. J. Res. Sci. Teach. **11**(3), 231–249 (1974)
4. Trumpower, D.L., Sarwar, G.S.: Effectiveness of structural feedback provided by pathfinder networks. J. Educ. Comput. Res. **43**(1), 7–24 (2010)
5. Black, P., Harrison, C., Lee, C., Marshall, B., Wiliam, D.: Assessment for Learning: Putting It into Practice. Open University Press, Berkshire (2003)
6. Clariana, R.B.: Multi-decision approaches for eliciting knowledge structure. In: Ifenthaler, D., Pirnay-Dummer, P., Seel, N.M. (eds.) Computer-Based Diagnostics and Systematic Analysis of Knowledge, pp. 41–60. Springer, London (2010)
7. Curtis, M.B., Davis, M.A.: Assessing knowledge structure in accounting education: an application of pathfinder associative networks. J. Account. Educ. **21**(3), 185–195 (2003)
8. Tsai, C.-C., Huang, C.-M.: Exploring students' cognitive structures in learning science: a review of relevant methods. J. Biol. Educ. **36**(4), 163–169 (2002)
9. Ausubel, D.P.: The Acquisition and Retention of Knowledge: A Cognitive View. Kluwer, Boston (2000)
10. Shavelson, R.J., Ruiz-Primo, M.A., Wiley, E.W.: Windows into the mind. High. Educ. **49**, 413–430 (2005)
11. Anohina-Naumeca, A.: Justifying the usage of concept mapping as a tool for the formative assessment of the structural knowledge of engineering students. Knowl. Manag. E-Learn. Int. J. **7**(1), 56–72 (2015)
12. The VARK modalities. http://vark-learn.com/introduction-to-vark/the-vark-modalities/
13. Rocha, R.L., Pereira, A.O., de Aguiar, J.G., Correia, P.R.M.: How to teach the concept of propositions? A worked-example approach to highlight the need of propositional semantic meaning in concept maps. In: Correia, P.R.M., Malachias, M.E.I., Cañas, A.J., Novak, J.D. (eds.) Concept Mapping to Learn and Innovate, Proceedings of the 6th International Conference on Concept Mapping, pp. 277–282. Escola de Artes, Ciências e Humanidades, São Paulo (2014)
14. Novak, J.D.: Meaningful learning: the essential factor for conceptual change in limited or inappropriate propositional hierarchies leading to empowerment of learners. Sci. Educ. **86**(4), 548–571 (2002)
15. Goldstein, E.B.: Cognitive Psychology: Connecting Mind, Research, and Everyday Experience. Wadsworth, Belmont (2008)
16. Quinlan, P., Dyson, B.: Cognitive Psychology. Pearson Education Limited, Harlow (2008)
17. Rutherford, A.: Long-term memory: encoding to retrieval. In: Braisby, N., Gellatly, A. (eds.) Cognitive Psychology, pp. 269–306. Oxford University Press, Oxford (2005)
18. Eysenck, M.W., Keane, M.T.: Cognitive Psychology: A Student's Handbook. Psychology Press, Hove (2000)
19. Lieberman, D.A.: Human Learning and Memory. Cambridge University Press, New York (2012)
20. Davis, M., Curtis, M.B., Tschetter, J.D.: Evaluating cognitive training outcomes: validity and utility of structural knowledge assessment. J. Bus. Psychol. **18**(2), 191–206 (2003)

21. Diekhoff, G.M.: Testing through relationship judgments. J. Educ. Psychol. **75**(2), 227–233 (1983)
22. Jonassen, D.H., Beissner, K., Yacci, M.: Structural Knowledge: Techniques for Representing, Conveying, and Acquiring Structural Knowledge. Lawrence Erlbaum Associates, Hillsdale (1993)
23. Novak, J.D.: Meaningful learning: the essential factor for conceptual change in limited or inappropriate propositional hierarchies leading to empowerment of learners. Sci. Educ. **86**, 548–571 (2002)
24. Novak, J.D., Gowin, D.B.: Learning How to Learn. Cambridge University Press, Cambridge (1984)
25. Cañas, A.J., Novak, J.D.: Re-examining the foundations for effective use of concept maps. In: Cañas, A.J., Novak, J.D. (eds.) Proceedings of the 2nd International Conference on Concept Mapping, pp. 494–502. Universidad de Costa Rica, San José (2006)
26. Cañas, A.J., Novak, J.D.: Freedom vs. restriction of content and structure during concept mapping – possibilities and limitations for construction and assessment. In: Cañas, A.J., Novak, J.D., Vanhear, J. (eds.) Concept Maps: Theory, Methodology, Technology, Proceedings of the 5th International Conference on Concept Mapping, pp. 247–257. University of Malta, Valletta (2012)
27. Cañas, A.J., Novak, J.D.: Concept mapping using CmapTools to enhance meaningful learning. In: Okada, A., Shum, S.J.B., Sherborne, T. (eds.) Knowledge Cartography: Software Tools and Mapping Techniques, pp. 23–45. Springer, London (2014)
28. Cañas, A.J., Novak, J.D., Reiska, P.: How good is my concept map? Am I a good Cmapper? Knowl. Manag. E-Learn. **7**(1), 6–19 (2015)

The Function of Concept Mapping in Hypermedia-Based Tutoring

Manuel F. Aguilar-Tamayo[1]([✉]), Antonio Padilla-Arroyo[1],
Edgar Vázquez-Contreras[2], and Santiago R. Acuña[3]

[1] Universidad Autónoma del Estado de Morelos, Morelos, Mexico
mafat@uaem.mx, antonin_19@yahoo.com.mx
[2] Universidad Autónoma Metropolitana, México, DF, Mexico
evazquez@correo.cua.uam.mx
[3] Universidad Autónoma de San Luis Potosí, San Luís Potosí, Mexico
santiagoacul@gmail.com

Abstract. This paper analyzes the function of the concept mapping (CM) in face-to-face tutoring. Through the study of 63 tutoring sessions developed during 36 months with 6 postgraduate students and the audio-writing recording of 200 pages of tutor's notes, the topics on which the CM is used are analyzed, its functions on the conversational processes between tutor and student, and other elements used in visual-conceptual representation. This analysis enables to recognize the CM as a flexible tool that allows organizing the tutoring sessions and that integrates with wider narrative structures; the CM is preserved into the hypermedia; as both a graphic organizer and as interface to access to the information, and as mediator of the interthinking processes between tutor and student. This research contributes to document and develop new instructional approaches for universitary tutoring within CM. It is also suggested ideas for a new function for CmapTools.

Keywords: Concept map · Tutoring · Hypermedia · Higher education · Instruction

1 Introduction

This paper describes and systematizes the use of the concept map as a mediator in the thinking, writing and conversation process in the tutoring to support graduate students' research in the master and Ph.D. programs in Education. The Hypermedia-based tutoring is a result of a techno-methodological approach; it integrates symbolic processes, organized as conversational methods and visual-conceptual representation systems, with a digital pen that is an artifact that allows to record the audio and writing synchronously. The description and systematization of concept map functions and its uses in this context let it to contribute to tutoring methodologies, the hypermedia production to support learning, and to a wider comprehension of educational possibilities of the concept map (CM).

The hypermedia-based tutoring (HBT) is a tutoring intervention method that is been systematized from the tutorship of a team of academic professors that began using the

© Springer International Publishing Switzerland 2016
A. Cañas et al. (Eds.): CMC 2016, CCIS 635, pp. 215–228, 2016.
DOI: 10.1007/978-3-319-45501-3_17

audio-writing recording pen (with brand name Livescribe) to register individual tutoring sessions and during the student's presentation of research progress in their graduate program. The audio-writing recording, that at first was considered to be registered with follow-up tutoring notes, became into a reference and support source to develop learning and research activities for the students. In this article is analyzed a part of the one-to-one tutoring sessions that aims to help the student's learning process and research development.

The recording of the tutoring session which has graphics, texts, drawings, signs, concept maps and diagrams, among other representational systems, can be transferred to a PDF file which makes it possible to distribute the recording to the students. Previous research [1] has shown that this file is repeatedly consulted by the students and used as a learning support resource. The possibilities of reading the hypermedia-based tutoring makes it a hypermedia resource because it enables the hypertextual reading and integrates audio-verbal and written-verbal information, graphics, schemas and dynamic images [2].

Figure 1 show a hypermedia-based tutoring (HBT) concept map and the relationships between the main psycho-pedagogical and technological elements that are part of this intervention proposal.

2 The Visual-Conceptual Representations and Its Function in the Educational Hypermedia

There are a large number and variety of representation techniques; these include concept maps, Vee diagrams, semantic networks, synoptic tables, tables, tree structures, flow charts and so on. The consideration of the representations distinguishes the external and internal nature. The external representation has a public attribute, that is accessible to others, captured through a support mechanism (i.e. paper, stone, cloth, software, PC) and uses culturally developed and socially accepted conventions (e.g. a graphic element like an arrow can be used as an indication, to show/point out something, even time, among other possibilities).

The internal representation has a private attribute, is a mental representation that is reachable only to those who conceive that representation [3, 4]. The language, concepts and images, can be elements of the internal representations. The thinking processes (e.g. during troubleshooting or social interaction of communication) include internal and external elements, the speech to others is an action that uses words, that can be considered an external representation, and meanings articulated in language that are internal (in this case). Thinking and speaking are different processes but interrelated by distinct representational ways [5].

In education, Novak [6] has argued that one of the biggest challenges faced by the professor is to share meanings; large part of teacher's labor in the classroom is to build up strategies with this purpose. The concept map is a tool that has been shown to be effective in helping the sharing meaning process and the learning of modifying and broaden meanings in the subjects. Communication and learning of concepts can be facilitated by the use of the concept map in different settings [7].

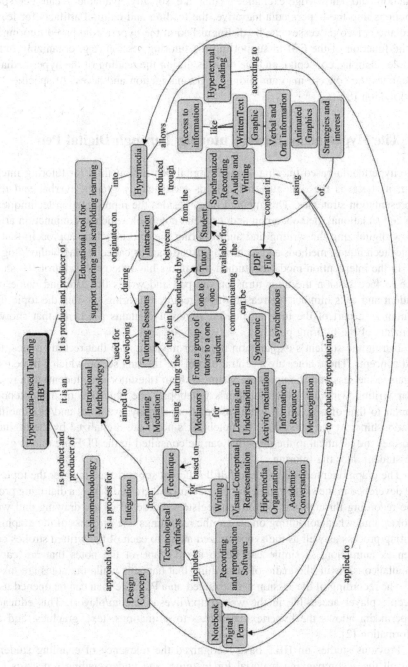

Fig. 1. The hypermedia-based tutoring (HBT) through digital pen

The usage of the concept map as a part of the representation techniques for construction and knowledge-exchange - that are socially available - can get specific functions into the hypermedia narrative, the reading and cultural artifacts for learning mediation. Two processes can be distinguished in the hypermedia-based tutoring. One is the function of the CM in supporting the tutoring session (e.g. organizing, making visible relations, concepts), and the other is during the reading of the hypermedia- that integrates the concept map and aiding in the navigation and access of specific information [8].

3   The Hypermedia-Based Tutoring Through Digital Pen

The hypermedia-based tutoring through digital pen is a method for tutoring intervention; its basis is the dialogue that unfolds mediated by graphic, verbal and textual representation strategies. This method uses, besides the representation techniques and the conversational method, a pen and a special notebook which in conjunction artifacts allow digitalizing the writing and audio during the tutoring. This approach, that integrates techniques, methods and technological artifacts is called technomethodology [2].

In the intervention modality studied, the tutors have the pen's control. To start the face to face session the tutor turns on the pen and writes the date and name of the student and asks him/her the reason of the required tutoring session, the topic is also written as a part of the tutoring header. Figure 1 contains a scheme that shows the elements of the tutoring pages.

During the student's explanation the tutor makes a note that records issues, topics and concepts. These notes are a central part of the tutoring script, which will be used to organize the session. The notes are visible to both (the tutor and student) as a result of their writing with ink over the tutor's notebook. The objective of the notebook is similar to that of a board to write information, display examples and/or establishing relationships. At the same time the notebook's notes are digitalized by the digital pen and they are identical to the ones that can be consulted in the PDF file that is given to the student after the tutoring.

The graphic representations can fulfill different support functions for the topics that are developed in the session; they are builded-up and created during a dialoging process. The recording through the digital pen registers the detail of the drawing and writing strokes, thus when consulting on screen the recordings, the progress of the graphic and writing process as well as the synchronized audio to each of the written strokes can be seen as animation. A simile can be to a videotape of the notes that are captured simultaneously with the audio of everything that happens while the notes are taken.

The recording of the session is distributed on a PDF file than can be opened using a specific player accessible in the web (http://livescribe.com/player). This educational hypermedia allows the hypertextual access to animations, text, graphics, and audio information [2].

Previous studies on HBT have recognized the relevance of enabling students to consult the accompanying material for learning, and understanding processes [1, 8]. The hypermedia-based tutoring can be one possibility to innovate the tutoring methods, moreover, to enlarge the benefits and effectiveness of the face-to-face tutorship interventions, such as tutoring.

Other analyzes of the graphic representation functions, and of its function in the organization of the hypermedia narrative in tutoring have been made on the page's structure, as a result it was possible to identify general narrative patterns/models that integrate a variety of graphics and narrative resources [1]. Figure 2 shows the pages' organization. Each of the models was built from the analysis of the experiences of using the pen during tutoring sessions that served to help learning and comprehension of the research process in an education graduate program. Other forms of organization could be found in other tutoring experiences with a different purpose.

As seen on Fig. 3, on details 3, 4 and 5, the concept map, represented by a symbol, accomplishes functions inside wider narrative strategies (e.g. the purpose of tutoring can be to discuss the analytical strategies for the literature review, and so the session - which is described in the following section - is organized to do so). In this tutoring session the concept map can be used to display approaches, to set out theory's elements, or to show the interconnections of a concept, and to specify approaches and trends, among other possibilities. The concept map construction is interrelated to the dialoguing conversation between tutor and student, the concept map it's producer and product of interthinking process.

In this paper the focus is on the concept map, which plays an important role into the general narrative, and sometimes can be the basic structure of this narrative.

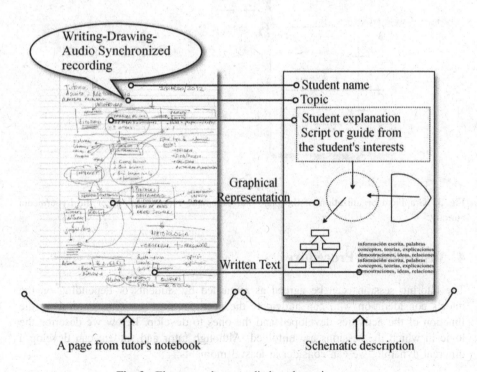

Fig. 2. Elements a hypermedia-based tutoring page

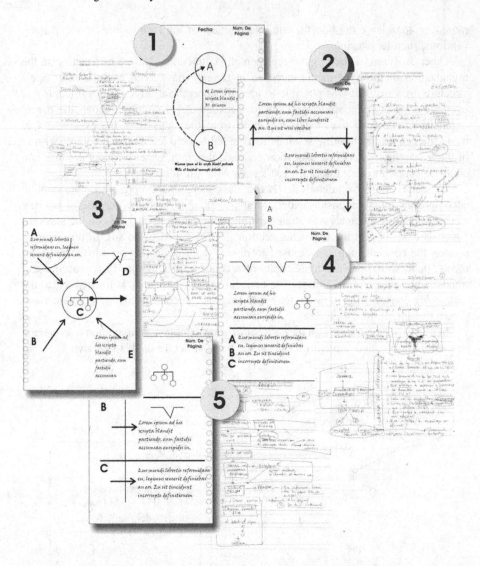

Fig. 3. Graphical organization of the page and schematic representations of the hypermedia narrative

4 Instructional Procedure

The tutoring sessions can be agreed as requested by students or depending on the tutor's consideration who can anticipate the need for intervention according to the function of the activities developed and the ones to develop. Below we describe the logic in which the sessions are unfolded. Although tutor and student can develop a different dynamic, we can consider at least 3 moments:

4.1   Beginning of the Session

The tutor asks the student to expose the reasons for the tutoring; these can be expressed through questions and problem statements. The first stage is helpful for the student to make more complex questions than the ones that originated the session. This elaboration process lets the professor recognize and evaluate part of the student's knowledge about the issue dealt with.

At this moment the tutor's role is to understand the problem or question from the student's perspective, and to do so he/she intervenes by asking questions or by asking the student to elaborate ideas on a topic, which will give the tutor some elements to decide whether to include new concepts to answer and to guide the student's activities [9]. Sometimes it is possible that the student uses the digital pen to make the notes, graphics or scrawls, which can help to express relationships, problems and/or to help the development of the idea [10].

During this process the instructor takes notes of what was said by the student which serves for two purposes. First, to make a script to develop the tutoring, as well to recognize topics, concepts and difficulties that must be attended during the session. Second, to prioritize and conceptualize the problems and student's questions.

The notes taken at the beginning of the session can fulfill functions as advance organizers during the posterior PDF's reading; those schemes, that are not necessarily graphics (e.g. subtitles) anticipate and set up concepts and hierarchy that guide the learning or the content reading [11]. It must be considered that, on the later PDF's reading and listening done by the student, this will not be just a recording; it will be an organized hypermedia with learning content and resource of information [2].

4.2   Development of the Tutoring

The main driver on the tutoring session is to carry on an academic conversation [12], which has different ways and technical resources, some of them could be a part of an academic and scientific culture of which the instructor is part of, while other techniques may imply a more specific training or development in the educational field [13].

Introducing a scientific language goes beyond just the words and the terms, it involves practices and knowledge of the scientific communities [14]. This is one of the more outstanding tasks in the learning of scientific concepts [6]. In the case of tutoring, conversation in its dialog form is, in addition to a way to mediate the relation between the tutor and the student, a method to think together about the problems and questions [15]. The rhythm of the conversation is not the same than that in a group class or a conference since the session is regulated in accordance with the dialogue.

The conversation in tutoring can change the strategy as long the understanding between tutor and student evolves. At some point the tutor will seek to persuade the student about some decision/consideration, to draw an argument, to explain or even to provide support or confidence to modify his/her attitude to engage in thinking that unfolds during tutoring.

In addition to the words, other resources come into play; notes, graphics and schemes accompany and complement the oral speech. The graphic expression of this narrative can be observed in the ways that the resources are organized and the instructor's instructional sequence in the notebook pages (see Fig. 2).

Other aspect that exists on the elaboration of the oral discourse and the graphic discourse, and the set that results from these (the hypermedia-based tutoring), is the use of metaphors. Metaphors are important elements for the construction of the scientific text [16], are psycopedagogical elements for the instruction [15], communication facilitators [6] and for the creative thinking [17], they're a resources to help the comprehension of relations, causes, consequences, diversity and complexity.

4.3   Closing of the Tutoring Session

Once topics have been addressed and discussed during the tutoring, the closing includes the tasks and commitments for the next session. This allows setting a goal for the student's learning process and it also sets elements for learning self-assessment and future tasks to do. Specific duties can be agreed, such as concluding procedures or activities and products, which allow the student to determine the need for additional tutoring, so he/she develop gradual independence on learning. The closing of the session is a moment to recapitulate the unfolded discussion and at the same time can give ideas for consulting or reading the hypermedia-based tutoring.

5   The Representation Techniques as a Part of Instructional Strategies

Different disciplines and knowledge fields have generated complementary representations to textual representation. In some cases, the visual representations are a result of a scientific methodology and consequently they are part of a disciplinary knowledge. Geographical maps, metabolic cycle diagrams, flow charts, knowledge models based on concept maps, are products of knowledge methods, they are knowledge in themselves, and they're not a simplified representation [3].

Other techniques serve other purposes, e.g., to represent process, relations, sequences, groupings, concepts and theories. Many of the cases are alternate representational means, but not necessarily simplifications. The representational techniques help developing an instructional procedure and they show which results more relevant or important according to the functions of the questions/problems raised in tutoring.

The hypermedia-based tutoring requires that the tutor have a basic domain of some representation techniques, some related to the fields or disciplines of study and others, like the re-representation of knowledge, which is a significant process for teachers and students on learning complex concepts and ideas, which requires constant representational redescriptions that let the conceptual change and the construction of a new complex knowledge. This semiotic artifact's role, and some others such as writing, are essential for learning and cognitive development [18, 19].

Two techniques have direct involvement in organizing knowledge and on being aware of the process that produced it: the concept map and the Vee diagram [6, 10, 20]. These techniques, in addition to their particular qualities, support conceptual learning as well as propositional logical thinking. They also open other creative possibilities for tutors and students, and they can work in different levels in consonance with the metacognitive strategies developed by the tutors and the students [21].

6 Methodology

The study of the student tutoring lasted of 36 months, during which some students finished their master's degree and continue on their PhD, while others only concluded the master's. Chart 1 shows the general data of the tutoring study. The names used are pseudonyms. 63 sessions were collected out of a total of 6 students, whose audio-writing recording gives a total of 3,485 recorded minutes and 200 note pages, out of which 29 pages with audio in which concept maps were used as a part of the instructional and conversational strategies during tutoring, were analyzed.

The tutoring sessions were concentrated in an electronic notebook per student and were checked through a PDF reader, the playback of the files includes the synchronized audio and writing.

The analysis involved first: (a) Identifying the use of the concept map in the tutoring sessions to select the pages to analyze, and determining the topic and subject of the tutoring. The sessions can include pages on which concept maps were not used; (b) Determining the function of the concept map with respect to the tutoring topic (e.g. if it was used to address issues of the conceptual frame, data interpretation, writing data, among other functions that will be described later); (c) Analyzing the development/writing of the concept map, its visual-conceptual characteristics and the relations of the graphic representation, the text, the oral information and the sequence as well as the synchrony among those data types.

Tables of notes were prepared for each page, and the graphic resources, narrative techniques and map concept functions were compared (Table 2).

Table 1. Participants and data selection for the analysis

Student	Level	Tutoring months	Minutes of accumulated tutoring	Tutoring sessions' total	Pages recorded in tutoring	Analyzed pages
Felipe	M*	23	308	8	20	5
Eric	M/D	36	432	6	29	7
Berenice	M	29	802	15	45	4
Alma	M	35	562	9	23	3
María	M/D	36	661	11	48	4
Rosa	D**	36	720	14	35	6
Total	–	–	3485	63	200	29

*M = Master's degree students. **D: PhD students.

7 Results and Discussion

The functions fulfilled by the concept map (CM), within the tutoring topics, can be seen on Table 2. The far left-hand column displays the research stages and processes, and the next column the tutoring topic/subject. As can be seen the CM backs up a variety of topics. Its constant use to establish relations between concepts, theories, methods and questions give it an integrative purpose of the process and elements of the research process. The CM's flexibility to represent details, sequences, procedures and concept relations, in addition to represent more general relations is what concedes this integrative function.

In all the analyzed cases, the concept maps are not graphically developed at all; they have a schematic form in which the more important concepts are only written, the relation lines and the linking phrases are rarely written. However, this doesn't imply that propositions are not developed, because these are orally enunciated. Although only drawn/written as a concept, the parallel verbal/oral information can include other more specific relations and concepts, and various helpful propositional links, that can also serve as an example and explanation of the schematized relations. In these cases, it is necessary that tutor and student know the technique, so that the CM can be completed as a propositional structure. What makes "evident" a Concept Map on the page or in the spoken speech is the common reference of both speakers that can share a meaning and a sense of the graphical representations as a result of a common knowledge context, in the same way how occurs during conversations that in some situations happen on its shortened expressions, references and words [5, 22].

The process of CM elaboration is linked to the tutor's narrative strategies, which are expressed on the expository order but also on the dialogue processes and in the questions done by the tutor and student. In none of the cases the CMs are made from the starting to the end without interruptions. A CM can be gradually completed as discussions, doubts or expositions about troubles/concepts last, this is seen on the way that CMs are integrated to the page logic (see Fig. 2), what means that the CM and other resources are complementary and related to the page through graphic resources such as frames, subtitles, connecting lines, arrows and propositions. The relations are established by the speech too, since the majority of the graphic emphasis is joined with a verbal explanation.

As a part of an audio-writing synchronization strategy, the tutor needs to draw and write one or two seconds before starting to speak, this allows that during the consulting and reading of the recording, when clicking on the graphic, concept or word, that information immediately makes sense regarding to the created graphic. In this respect the graphic strategies, and specially the concept map, are part of the script or argument to develop, the tutor's ability on representing through those techniques is important to solve fluidly the dialogue and to develop graphic examples.

Using numbers can help in the writing closing process to propose a reading strategy, because the expository order does not always match the order, sequence, hierarchy, logic methods, procedures and concepts. In some cases, the direct explanation is not possible and side explanations should be done, subsidiaries, clarifications or even relations depending on the learning needs. The numbers also give the chance to

Table 2. Results about the concept map functions in tutoring for research in postgraduate students

Research process or stage	Tutoring topic	Analyzed sessions	Analyzed pages	Concept map function with regards to the tutoring topic
Research project	Research problem	3	5	CM is used within the Vee diagram to establish relations between concepts and to develop the research problem related to determined theories
	Interpretative framework and theoretical foundations	3	4	The CM is used along with other graphic forms and representation techniques, which include charts, graphics and other concept maps
	Data collection methods	2	1	The CM is sometimes used along with the Vee diagram to show the relationship between the research question, theory and the chosen methods. The CM is also used to develop interview scripts
	Protocol and study design	2	2	
Data analysis	Data analysis and data interpretation	3	4	The CM is used to establish relations with the conceptual framework in order to do the development of categories in the data interpretation. Some concepts can be broadening to help code development (on qualitative research)
Thesis draft	What is the thesis and how is it written?	3	3	The CM is used to help the methodology writing process showing relations between methods, procedures and the theory. Sometimes the elaboration process is through dialogue among the tutor-student
	Draft revision	3	4	The CM serves to discuss concepts and statements of the written document. It enables to establish relations with other concepts and theories to give a more general/complex picture
Preparation for evaluations	Exam preparation and research	3	6	The CM is used to report in a synthesized way the more relevant features in presenting

(Continued)

Table 2. (*Continued*)

Research process or stage	Tutoring topic	Analyzed sessions	Analyzed pages	Concept map function with regards to the tutoring topic
	reports presentation			progress and/or exam application. The topics can vary depending on the evaluation moment
Grand Total		22	29	

visually reorder the possible disintegration of graphics and speech. They also work as navigation interfaces because they can represent units of information and with it the access to a certain block of information.

We note the importance in the use of visual metaphors in the integration of the representation techniques (CM, Vee diagram, lists, text box, underlined) and its graphic resources (lines, circling, squares, arrows) and also in the representation of complexity; to show simultaneous inter-relations, contexts, concepts and theories that are part of the knowledge problems and methods. These metaphors are expressed through the pages' organization that is shown on Fig. 2.

8 Conclusions

The CM can be used as a narrative organization resource in the tutoring session and fulfils different functions during the sessions. It can work as a diagnostic tool of the student's needs thus becoming into a script to develop tutoring. The CM is a visual-ization tool, moreover, an analytic resource; the construction of the CM during tutoring is not an end in itself, but a process that allows asking questions, discussing, visual-ization of relations, contradictions and contexts. The CM is product and producer of a conversation oriented to the co-construction of shared meanings.

The audio-writing recording thought the pen complements the concept map con-struction method. For this reason, the incomplete graphic elaboration (i.e. when it doesn't have all the concepts or propositions in a graphic-written way) doesn't imply an incomplete CM, because the propositional structure is complemented with the speech. The CM works, in this case, as a scheme and advance organizer, that in the reading process is completed by accessing to the verbal-oral speech, what allows emphasizing the construction process, and as a result the registering of the analysis process, the construction of questions, relations establishment in which tutor and student participates.

The possibility of registering and playing the construction and writing of the CM like a video implies designing instructional strategies and specific representation techniques that let to display the map in sync with time and the verbal processes. Some of these techniques and strategies have been described in this research.

The HBT is a new method in producing hypermedia material to support learning. The CM can be widely used in this process. More specific ways can be developed by means of other tools, like CmapTools' features to record the CM's elaboration process, such as the recording of synchronized audio. The uses of the audio synchronized with concept mapping process will help not just in the co-construction process, but in peer discussion, conversation among tutors and students, where arguments, changes and suggestions can be registered directly in the CM within CmapTools. This function in particular will be useful in the concept learning research and during interviews with the participants.

Acknowledgements. Fondo Mixto CONACYT y Gobierno del Estado de Morelos, México, FOMIX MOR-2014-C01-225102.

References

1. Aguilar-Tamayo, M.F.: Tutoría Universitaria con Soporte del Bolígrafo Digital: Análisis de una Experiencia. Rev. Electrón. Investig. Educ. **17**(1), 130–145 (2015)
2. Aguilar-Tamayo, M.F., Montero-Hernández, V., Acuña, S.T.: Hypermedia-based tutoring. In: IEEE Global Engineering Education Conference (EDUCON), Abu Dhabi, pp. 214–218. IEEE (2016)
3. Aguilar Tamayo, M.F.: Mapa Conceptual, Hipertexto, Hipermedia y otros Artefactos Culturales para la Construcción y Comunicación del Conocimiento. Bonilla Artigas Editores. Universidad Autónoma del Estado de Morelos, México (2015)
4. Olson, D.R.: El Mundo sobre el Papel. El Impacto de la Escritura y la Lectura en la Estructura del Conocimiento. Gedisa, Barcelona (1999)
5. Vigotski, L.S.: Pensamiento y Habla. Colihue, Buenos Aires (2007)
6. Novak, J.D.: Learning, Creating, and Using Knowledge. Concept Maps as Facilitative Tools in Schools and Corporations, 2nd edn. Routledge, New York (2010)
7. Novak, J.D., Cañas, A.J.: The universality and ubiquitousness of concept maps. In: Sánchez, J., Cañas, A.J., Novak, J.D. (eds.) Concept Maps: Making Learning Meaningful. Proceedings of Fourth International Conference on Concept Mapping, vol. 1, pp. 1–13. Universidad de Chile, Chile (2010)
8. Aguilar Tamayo, M.F.: Nuevas Tecnologías en la Formación: Asesoría Hipermedia con Plumas Digitales como Apoyo para la Elaboración de Trabajos de Investigación. In: Acuña, S.R., Gabino Campos, M., Martínez Lozano, C.P. (eds.) Multiculturalidad, Imagen y Nuevas ecnologías, pp. 263–291. Editorial Fragua, Madrid (2014)
9. Pozo Municio, J.I.: Aprendices y Maestros. La Psicología Cognitiva del Aprendizaje. Alianza, Madrid (2008)
10. John-Steiner, V.: Notebooks of the Mind. Oxford University Press, Oxford (1997)
11. Ausubel, D.P.: Adquisición y Retención del Conocimiento. Una Perspectiva Cognitiva. Paidós, Barcelona (2002)
12. Zwiers, J., Crawford, M.: Academic Conversation. Classroom Talk Foster Critical Thinking and Content Understanding. Stenhouse Publisher, Portland (2011)
13. Lemke, J.L.: Aprender a Hablar Ciencia. Lenguaje, Aprendizaje y Valores. Paidós, Barcelona (1997)

14. Pozo, J.I., Monereo, C.: Introducción: La Nueva Cultura del Aprendizaje Universitario o por qué Cambiar Nuestras formas de Enseñar y Aprender. In: Pozo, I., Monereo, C. (eds.) Psicología del Aprendizaje Universitario: La formación en competencias, pp. 9–28. Morata, Madrid (2009)
15. Mercer, N.: Palabras y Mentes. Cómo Usamos el Lenguaje para Pensar Juntos. Paidós, Barcelona (2001)
16. Locke, D.: Voices of science. Am. Sch. 3(67), 103–104 (1998)
17. Bohm, D., Peat, D.: Ciencia, Orden y Creatividad. Las Raices Creativas de la Ciencia y la Vida. Kairós, Barcelona (1988)
18. Pozo Municio, J.I.: Humana Mente. El mundo la Conciencia y la Carnes. Morata, Madrid (2001)
19. Pozo Municio, J.I.: Adquisición de Conocimiento. Morata, Madrid (2003)
20. Gowin, B.D., Alvarez, M.C.: The Art of Educating with V Diagrams. Cambridge University Press, New York (2005)
21. Aguilar Tamayo, M.F.: Didáctica del Mapa Conceptual en la Educación Superior. Experiencias y Aplicaciones para Ayudar al Aprendizaje de Conceptos. Juan Pablos Editor. UAEM, México (2012)
22. Littleton, K., Mercer, N.: Interthinking. Putting Talk to Work. Routledge, London (2013)

The Mapping of Pedagogic Frailty: A Concept in Which Connectedness is Everything

Ian M. Kinchin[✉]

Department of Higher Education, University of Surrey, Guildford, UK
i.kinchin@surrey.ac.uk

Abstract. When attempting to support the enhancement of university teaching, there is a tendency for institutions to focus on individual attributes of the learning environment. Such an itemized analysis of teaching practice neglects the integrated nature and complexity of the system. In addition, the ways in which university teachers interact with the academic environment are personal and idiosyncratic. In an attempt to support the simultaneous focus on key dimensions of the teaching environment, the concept of pedagogic frailty is introduced. The content and structure of academics' personal interpretations of these dimensions will either facilitate or hinder the development of connections between the elements of the model at the personal and/or inter-personal level. Where the formation of connections is hindered, the system is in a state of pedagogic frailty which results in a loss of adaptability and the conservation of traditional systems, even when they are seen as unfit for purpose. The mapping of pedagogic frailty provides an ideal frame for the development of personal narratives about teaching and an arena to support meaningful dialogue about the values that underpin teaching at university.

1 Introduction

Pedagogic frailty has been proposed as a concept that can help to bring a number of key ideas into simultaneous focus with the aim of enhancing teaching in the university context [1]. There are concepts from other disciplines that can sometimes be helpful in making useful analogies in educational research and pedagogic frailty has been derived from an analogy with clinical frailty. Within the clinical literature, 'frailty' is considered to develop as a consequence of a decline in a range of factors which collectively results in an increased vulnerability to sudden adverse actions triggered by relatively minor events [2]. Various indicators of frailty have been identified and include the inability to integrate responses to change in the face of stress [3]; the loss of adaptive capacity due to a loss of complexity [4]; the wear and tear that results over time by repeated efforts to adapt to change [5]; the sense of fatigue when change is implemented without consultation [6]. Drawing on this clinical analogy, these issues would appear to offer considerable resonance with the pressures felt by academics teaching at university. In the context of higher education teaching, one might observe pedagogic frailty, where the stresses of academia result in increased vulnerability to minor events.

Pedagogic frailty is not considered an internal capacity of an individual academic and such a personal characterization would be unhelpful in promoting openness to

A. Cañas et al. (Eds.): CMC 2016, CCIS 635, pp. 229–240, 2016.
DOI: 10.1007/978-3-319-45501-3_18

support academic faculty development. Rather frailty is seen as resulting from the quality and degree of interaction with and between key elements of the professional environment. Pedagogic frailty is independent from teacher agency - an individual who exhibits agency may also exhibit a profile that contributes to frailty within the institution.

Most concept maps are representations of subject content, a component of the instructional discourse [7] that could be assessed for its correctness. As the maps within a pedagogic frailty profile represent the values and beliefs of the mappers, related to Bernstein's regulative discourse, it would be inappropriate to attempt to allocate scores or grades to them. What is interesting is how these relate to and connect with the maps of their colleagues in constructing the profile of the institution. It is the presence and absence of connections that would be indicative of frailty [8]:

> *"The dynamics of complex systems are first and foremost relational: it is a relation or an inter-action that serves as a unit of analysis. Moreover, the interactions constituting the system's dynamics act in a non-linear manner"*

The morphology of each map is likely to influence the possible degree of connect-edness with other maps, with 'efficient', linear chain structures offering the least possi-bility of additional connections being made. Novakian concept mapping is the ideal tool for use in the visualization of pedagogic frailty (Fig. 1). Indeed, it was through the application of concept mapping that the model first emerged from discussions with university teachers. Guidance, through map-mediated interviews [9], helps to ensure the concept maps of the dimensions of pedagogic frailty exhibit the characteristics of excel-lence offered by Cañas et al. [10]. As such, the concept maps provide the ideal frame for the development of a personal narrative about teaching.

2   Concept Mapping as a Frame for Reflection

Engaging in self-reflection does not come naturally to many academics, and the prospect of writing about oneself can generate anxiety among colleagues. The process of concept mapping can help to provide a focus and a frame for self-reflection that can help in targeting key issues. As explained by Wilson et al. [11]:

> *Concept mapping is a medium through which people come to understand more about an event and about themselves. This change of self, re-shapes the meaning of the phenomenon that is being studied, and offers the participants an opportunity to "re-see" the significance the expe-rience and the mapping process offer them. Through this process of "re-seeing," participants develop an artistic expression of self-discovery (the concept map) and their voice resonates on both an individual and a social level.*

A model has been suggested by Quillin and Thomas [12] to summarize the complex interactions between the processes of learning and drawing (Fig. 2). It is important to realize here that the act of drawing may contribute to the development of mental models, and so concept maps produced by academics about their values underpinning teaching may not be a representation of what *has been* learned, but rather what is *currently being* learned. A concept map is therefore often to be considered as a 'work in progress'.

Buckley and Waring [14] concluded that the amalgamation of text and drawings can act as a powerful tool for the dissemination of complex ideas to critical audiences and

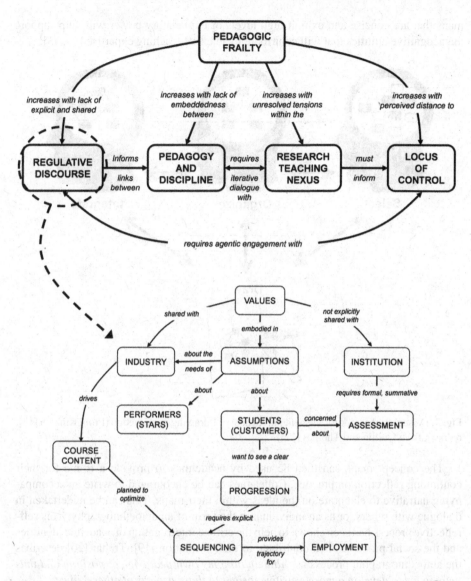

Fig. 1. Dimensions of pedagogic frailty with (inset below) one academic's view of the elements within the regulative discourse dimension (After Kinchin et al. [9])

that the use of diagrams for the development of theory still seems to be under-explored. The 'elaboration' of maps is not the same as simply adding more concepts and more links. As colleagues are guided through their reflections it may result in maps becoming smaller and more refined as the academic employs more inclusive concepts (rather than lots of specific examples), and more explanatory linking phrases. It has been noted in the literature that increased size of maps does not necessarily indicate more expert understanding [10, 15, 16]. Guiding colleagues in the development of excellent concept maps that are concise and exhibit high levels of explanatory power will help support metacognitive abilities that will contribute to adaptive teaching expertise [17, 18].

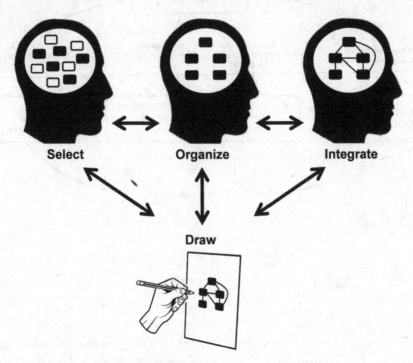

Fig. 2. Visual framework for the generative theory of drawing construction (From Kinchin [13], redrawn from Quillin and Thomas [12])

The concept maps can then be used by academics to provide a frame for their continuing reflection on practice. Colleagues can be encouraged to write an accompanying narrative to elaborate on the ideas within their maps. This can be undertaken in dialogue with others, or as an individual in the form of an autoethnography. This self-reflective process has been shown to help the critical interrogation of academic identities and the social processes that contribute to their formation [19]. Trahar [20] describes the autoethnographic process as, '*illuminating my own pedagogical position and thus helping me to develop a more sensitive insight to those aspects of others' lives*'.

3   The Dimensions Within the Pedagogic Frailty Model

The overarching concept of pedagogic frailty often displays considerable overlap between individuals. The same concepts often appear within the concept maps that are constructed by academics from different disciplines. The concepts of 'stress', 'change' and 'environment' typically dominate the maps [9], though they are arranged and linked in various ways. So whilst the frailty outcome exhibits considerable external consistency, the structure of the elements that contribute to its construction exhibit considerable heterogeneity. The four dimensions (regulative discourse, pedagogy & discipline, research-teaching nexus and locus of control) are interpreted in various discipline-sensitive ways, suggesting that whilst the appearance of pedagogic frailty might appear quite similar in different cases, the underlying structures that contribute to it can be quite diverse. This suggests that finding a 'universal quick fix' to the problem is unlikely.

Concept map-mediated interviews (as described by Kandiko and Kinchin [21]), were used to elicit teachers' personal perspectives of the dimensions of pedagogic frailty. To initiate dialogue a number of 'seeding concept labels' were used. These are summarized in Table 1. Interviewees were told that they could use as many or as few of the prompting concepts as they wished, and that they could include any additional concept labels that they thought were helpful or appropriate in explaining their viewpoint. Whilst helpful in initiating dialogue, it was important that the prompts did not stop the interviewee from making any personal inferences or conceptual leaps that might reveal some insight to their context and situated practice. It was stressed to the interviewees that what was important was the ways in which the concepts were linked to each other. A particular concept may be included within a map and linked to another concept in ways that can have different even contradictory meanings. So a particular concept label may be used to say 'xxxx is crucial to ......' or 'xxxx is irrelevant to' as appropriate to their context. In addition, interviewees were asked to consider whether a particular concept was central to the ideas they wanted to convey, or of it was a peripheral idea, and to position it in the map accordingly. Finally, interviewees were asked to really interrogate the meanings of the linking phrases that they offered in order to maximize the explanatory power of their maps. So where interviewees initially offered links such as 'including' or 'relates to' they were invited to offer something that might help the reader of the map to see details of what the relationship was. Through this dialogue, ideas emerged during the interview that had not been articulated previously, and in some instances, triggered an emotional response from the interviewee.

Table 1. Prompting concept labels for map-mediated interviews.

Pedagogic frailty	Regulative vs. instructional discourse	Pedagogy and discipline	Research-teaching nexus	Locus of control
Ability/Inability	Assessment	Activities	Motivation	Autonomy
Adapt	Assumptions	Authentic	Recognition	Best practice
Change	Course content	Disciplinary	Research	Decisions
Complexity	Sequencing	Practice	Rewards	Guidance
Environment	Theories	Professional	Status	Quality assurance
Integrate	Values	Strategies	Teaching	Regulation
Stress				
Sustainable				

4   The Emergence of 'Resilience' Within Frailty Profiles

A number of important concepts have emerged from the mapping of pedagogic frailty, undertaken with academics from a range of disciplines [9]. Here I focus on one that may be of wide-reaching importance – teacher resilience [22]. This has emerged from map-mediated interviews with academics recognizing the link between pedagogic frailty and resilience, often regarded with a focus on the individual [23].

Based on the historical psychological perspective of the literature on resilience, Garcia-Dia et al. [24] developed a concept map of resilience to consider the traits and experiences that accumulate to cause 'resilience' to surface. As a 'generic' map of the concept, it may have limited utility in supporting reflection among academics as it lacks analysis of the personal context in which resilient traits and behaviours would be required. A reworking of the map produced by Garcia-Dia et al. is given in Fig. 3. It can be seen that many of the concept labels (such as 'academic community' and 'coping strategies') need further elaboration and contextualisation for them to have personal meaning. However, this generic map may provide a starting point for discussion of resilience-building among academics by highlighting dynamic relationships between ideas. The development of personal, context-specific concept maps within the overall framework provided by pedagogic frailty may offer a positive contribution to the building of resilience by helping to frame personal narratives. Accessing personal narratives has been found to be of value in developing supportive relationships within an academic community [25] that are a pre-requisite for building resilience.

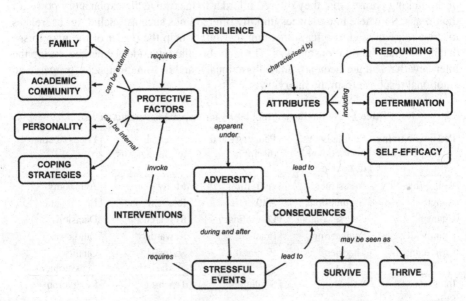

Fig. 3. A generic concept map of 'resilience' (Simplified and redrawn from Garcia-Dia et al. [24])

Resilience is often considered at the level of the individual and resilience refers to those teachers who withstand the ebbs and flows of the educational sector and who keep on teaching despite all the negative factors [26]. However, it can also be considered at the levels of the department or the institution in terms of ecological resilience, with Mumby et al. [27] stating:

> Ecosystem management is fundamentally charged with maintaining desirable levels of ecosystem function in a cost effective and socially responsible manner. The ability of an ecosystem to function depends on its state and the processes that support it.

It can be seen that if we substitute 'classroom management' into this text to replace 'ecosystem', the paragraph would make perfect sense. It is therefore important not to consider academic resilience of isolated teachers, but of the functional unit (e.g. the academic department) as a whole in which ecological resilience may depend on aspects of system resilience such as adequate functional redundancy of expertise [28].

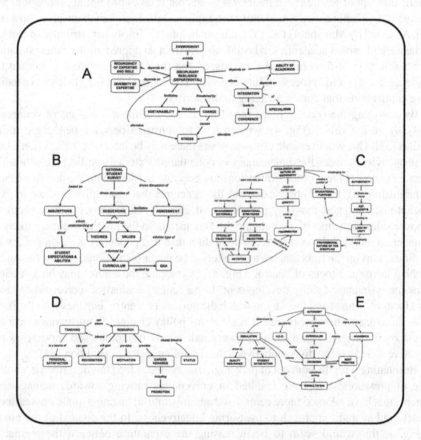

Fig. 4. A complete profile of an individual academic with maps for the overarching concept of pedagogic frailty (A), and for each of the contributing dimensions: Regulative Discourse (B), Pedagogy and Discipline (C), Research-teaching nexus (D) and Locus of control (E). (After Kinchin and Francis [29])

5   Implications for Faculty Development

Academic/faculty development that addresses pedagogic frailty will consider mechanisms to promote resilient behaviours among teaching staff that may evolve from a 'shared values literacy' that would result in a 'shared direction for resilient behaviour' [30]. To facilitate this, academics need to be encouraged to make their understanding of personal values that underpin teaching explicit so they can be the focus of discussion. The ability to articulate concepts related to teaching, such as resilience, is particularly important for senior academics who may be charged with mentoring and supporting junior colleagues through their early years of teaching. This may be helped by guided reflections with the context of pedagogic frailty as, 'teachers can express a generalized, generic concept of resilience in their own words but it takes prompting, reflection, and deconstruction before they can identify the explicit skills that they themselves possess' [31]. As stated by Mansfield et al. [32], it is not helpful to simply list attributes of teacher resilience and expect academics to be able to construct an appreciation of their situation from a selection of disconnected elements, as "on their own, they do not account for resilience as a dynamic process of interactions." The concept mapping helps to visualize those connections that confer meaning to the attributes.

By analyzing the concept maps produced for each of the dimensions of pedagogic frailty by an individual (Fig. 4), we can start to construct personal pedagogic frailty profiles [33]. This would enable us to see where there may be internal conflicts (i.e. a lack of connectivity between the dimensions), or potential for external conflicts (i.e. where the structure and/or content of the dimensions my generate tensions with the dominant view of the institution). Initial observations of the structures that academics produce in their concept maps, suggest that they have the most difficulty in relating the dimensions on opposite sides of the model, i.e. relating the dimensions on the left that are more likely to be under an individual's control (regulative discourse and pedagogy & discipline), with the dimensions on the right that are more likely to be under institutional control (research-teaching nexus and locus of control) (Fig. 5). Developing these links may be a sensible focus for systematic faculty development. In particular, academics' perceived distance from locus of control and the way in which the university 'centre' engages with the regulative discourse of the disciplines. It is clear that policy changes in universities over the years have impacted on the dynamic between individuals, disciplines and universities and may have increased the division between the discipline and the institution [34].

Resonating with the concept of pedagogic frailty, Jones [35] has described a 'confluence of pressures' that have resulted in universities moving towards management systems that have adopted more centralized administration; business quality assessment models and an audit approach to measuring effectiveness. In the context of the model in Fig. 1, this would seem to be increasing the separation between the regulative discourse of the disciplines and the locus of control (Fig. 5). A more distributed model of leadership would appear to be a way of redressing the balance and engaging with the diversity of expertise that would be found across a university. By considering the relationship between the locus of control and the regulative discourse, through the lens of pedagogic frailty, the development of more overtly values-based management systems may be a way of linking both these elements with reference to the overarching desired outcome of improving the student learning experience.

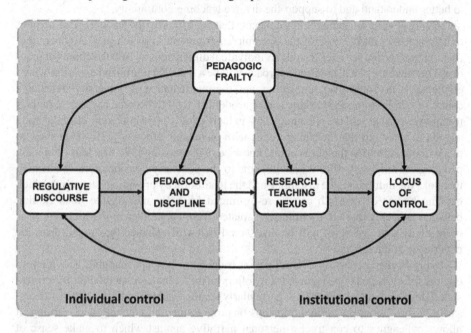

Fig. 5. Separation of dimensions within the model of pedagogic frailty (Redrawn from Kinchin et al. [9])

By allowing academics to focus on their own disciplines for their professional development as a university teacher, it should provide a more comfortable starting point (than for example workshops on general educational theory) that allows them to base their learning in the 'known'. However, it is evident from the work that has already been undertaken [9] that colleagues have rarely considered their own subjects from a structural perspective. Few are able to articulate integrative concepts for their subject, but when they can it makes the mapping process much easier and allows them to think more clearly about the links between dimensions. The re-purposing of disciplinary knowledge to generate active links with the pedagogic frailty model offers a route into the professional development of university teachers.

6 Summary

Observations from interviews undertaken with academics to visualize their pedagogic frailty profiles [9] resonate strongly with some of the findings gained by Stevenson, et al. [36], and show that to avoid a superficial dialogue that generates a surface learning approach to teaching [37], we need to investigate the deeper issues of pedagogy. Higher education institutions need to undertake genuine engagement and constructive dialogue with teaching staff as a way of developing institutional policy that aligns with their pedagogical values and practices without always assuming the necessity for homogenization. Institutions need to take seriously the implications of pedagogic frailty in order to better understand and to support the diverse teaching community.

Listing generic attributes of key concepts that contribute to the teaching does nothing to help teachers make sense of the dynamic environment in which they are operating. Lists encourage universities to address individual dimensions as isolated chains of practice. The outcome of a lists-based approach will be a focus on routinized expertise where efficiency is favoured over innovation, and the maintenance of university status as a centre of non-learning [38]. Many senior academics tend to become routinized in their teaching expertise, and are encouraged by an increasingly consumerist higher education agenda to carry out their teaching duties with increasing efficiency. However they do this without enriching their conceptual knowledge of teaching [39]. The lens offered by pedagogic frailty may offer a new impetus to the scholarly consideration of teaching that links the individual, the discipline and the institution by providing a lens with which existing bodies of research can be re-examined [40]. By making the links explicit between concepts that are traditionally isolated from each other in the literature, it is more likely that synergies will be discovered that will enhance the student learning experience at university.

Using framed reflection (i.e. reflection framed by concept mapping activities) to explore the elements of pedagogic frailty offers an individualized method for the professional development of academics, particularly senior teaching staff who do not necessarily wish to attend generic workshops or programmes on teaching and learning. It allows colleagues to construct a personal narrative against which to make sense of selected elements of the pedagogic research literature and the evolving university teaching environment. In this way, professional development may be seen as an individualized activity to support personal growth in directions that are pertinent to the individual rather than as a collective activity through generic courses. The learner-centred, discipline-sensitive focus of this type of professional development ensures a tight fit with disciplinary terminology and confers ownership of the process on the individual academic. This process increases the likelihood of the outcomes being shared with other members of the participant's community of practice and contributing to a scholarly conversation about teaching in higher education.

References

1. Kinchin, I.M.: Pedagogic frailty: an initial consideration of aetiology and prognosis. Paper presented at the Annual Conference of the Society for Research into Higher Education (SRHE), Celtic Manor, Wales, 9th–11th December 2015
2. Clegg, A., Young, J.: The frailty syndrome. Clin. Med. **11**(1), 72–75 (2011)
3. Rockwood, K., Fox, R.A., Stolee, P., Robertson, D., Beattie, B.L.: Frailty in elderly people: an evolving concept. Can. Med. Assoc. J. **150**(4), 489–495 (1994)
4. Lipsitz, L.A.: Dynamics of stability: the physiologic basis of functional health and frailty. J. Gerontol. **57A**(3), B115–B125 (2002)
5. Seeman, T.E., Singer, B.H., Ryff, C.D., Love, G.D., Levy-Storms, L.: Social relationships, gender and allostatic load across two age cohorts. Psychosom. Med. **64**(3), G95–406 (2002)

6. MacIntosh, R., Beech, N., McQueen, J., Reid, I.: Overcoming change fatigue; lessons from Glasgow's NHS. J. Bus. Strategy **28**(6), 18–24 (2010)

7. Bernstein, B.: Pedagogy, Symbolic Control and Identity. Rowman & Littlefield, Lanham (2000)

8. Semetsky, I.: Re-reading dewey through the lens of complexity science, or: on the creative logic of education. In: Mason, M. (ed.) Complexity Theory and the Philosophy of Education, pp. 79–90. Wiley, Oxford (2008)

9. Kinchin, I.M., Alpay, E., Curtis, K., Franklin, J., Rivers, C., Winstone, N.E.: Charting the elements of pedagogic frailty. Educ. Res. **58**(1), 1–23 (2016)

10. Caňas, A.J., Novak, J.D., Reiska, P.: How good is my concept map? Am i a good cmapper? Knowl. Manag. E-Learn. Int. J. (KM&EL) **7**(1), 6–19 (2015)

11. Wilson, J., Mandich, A., Magalhães, L.: Concept mapping: a dynamic, individualized and qualitative method for eliciting meaning. Qual. Health Res. **26**(8), 1151–1161 (2016). doi: 10.1177/1049732315616623

12. Quillin, K., Thomas, S.: Drawing-to-learn: a framework for using drawings to promote model-based reasoning in biology. CBE – Life Sci. Educ. **14**, 1–16 (2015)

13. Kinchin, I.M.: Visualising Powerful Knowledge to Develop the Expert Student: A Knowledge Structures Perspective on Teaching and Learning at University. Sense Publishers, Rotterdam (2016)

14. Buckley, C.A., Waring, M.J.: Using diagrams to support the research process: examples from grounded theory. Qual. Res. **13**(2), 148–172 (2016)

15. Kinchin, I.M.: Concept mapping as a learning tool in higher education: a critical analysis of recent reviews. J. Contin. High. Educ. **62**(1), 39–49 (2014)

16. Dowd, J.E., Duncan, T., Reynolds, J.A.: Concept maps for improved science reasoning and writing: complexity isn't everything. CBE – Life Sci. Educ. **14**, 1–6 (2015)

17. Carbonell, K.B., Stalmeijer, R.E., Könings, K.D., Segers, M., van Merriënboer, J.J.G.: How experts deal with novel situations: a review of adaptive expertise. Educ. Res. Rev. **12**, 14–29 (2014)

18. Salmon, D., Kelly, M.: Using Concept Mapping to Foster Adaptive Expertise: Enhancing Teacher Metacognitive Learning to Improve Student Academic Performance. Peter Lang, New York (2015)

19. Austin, J., Hickey, A.: Autoethnography and teacher development. Int. J. Interdisc. Soc. Sci. **2**, 1–9 (2007). http://eprints.usq.edu.au/3287/

20. Trahar, S.: Autoethnographic journeys in learning and teaching in higher education. Eur. Educ. Res. J. **12**(3), 367–375 (2013)

21. Kandiko Howson, C.B., Kinchin, I.M.: Mapping the doctorate: a longitudinal study of PhD students and their supervisors. In: Shedletsky, L., Beaudry, J.S. (eds.) Cases on Teaching Critical Thinking through Visual Representation Strategies, pp. 445–464. IGI Global, Hershey (2014)

22. Beltman, S., Mansfield, C.F., Price, A.: Thriving not just surviving: a review of research on teacher resilience. Educ. Res. Rev. **6**(3), 185–207 (2011)

23. Rees, C.S., Breen, L.J., Cusack, L., Hegney, D.: Understanding individual resilience in the workplace: the international collaboration of workforce resilience model. Front. Psychol. **6**, 1–7 (2015). Article 73

24. Garcia-Dia, M.J., DiNapoli, J.M., Garcia-Ona, L., Jakubowski, R., O'Flaherty, D.: Concept analysis: resilience. Arch. Psychiatr. Nurs. **27**, 264–270 (2013)

25. McDermid, F., Peters, K., Daly, J., Jackson, D.: Developing resilience: stories from novice nurse academics. Nurse Educ. Today (2016). doi:10.1016/j.nedt.2016.01.002

26. Ebersőhn, L.: Teacher resilience; theorizing resilience and poverty. Teach. Teach. Theor. Pract. **20**(5), 568–594 (2014)

27. Mumby, P.J., Chollett, I., Bozec, Y.-M., Wolff, N.H.: Ecological resilience, robustness and vulnerability: how do these concepts benefit ecosystem management? Curr. Opin. Environ. Sustain. **7**, 22–27 (2014)

28. Rosenfeld, J.S.: Functional redundancy in ecology and conservation. Oikos **98**(1), 156–162 (2002)

29. Kinchin, I.M., Francis, R.A.: Mapping pedagogic frailty in geography education: a framed autoethnographic case study. J. Geogr. High. Educ. (2016, in press)

30. Barnes, J.M.: Interdisciplinary, Praxis-focused auto-ethnography: using autobiography and the values discussion to build capacity in teachers. Adv. Soc. Sci. Res. J. **1**(5), 160–182 (2014)

31. Vance, A., Pendergast, D., Garvis, S.: Teaching resilience: a narrative inquiry into the importance of teacher resilience. Pastor. Care Educ. (2015). doi:10.108/02643944.2015.1074265

32. Mansfield, C.F., Beltman, S., Price, A., McConney, A.: "Don't Sweat the Small Stuff": understanding teacher resilience at the chalkface. Teach. Teach. Educ. **28**, 357–367 (2012)

33. Kinchin, I.M.: Visualising pedagogic frailty for academic faculty development. In: Watts, M., Pedrosa, H. (eds.) Academic Growth in Higher Education: questions and answers. Sense Publishers, Rotterdam (2016)

34. Henkel, M.: Academic identity and autonomy in a changing policy environment. High. Educ. **49**, 155–176 (2005)

35. Jones, S.: Distributed leadership: a critical analysis. Leadership **10**(2), 129–141 (2014)

36. Stevenson, J., Burke, P.-J., Whelan, P.: Pedagogic Stratification and the Shifting Landscape of Higher Education. York, The Higher Education Academy (2014). https://www.heacademy.ac.uk/sites/default/files/resources/PedStrat_Finalreport.pdf

37. Rowland, S.: Surface learning about teaching in higher education: the need for more critical conversations. Int. J. Acad. Dev. **6**(2), 162–167 (2001)

38. Kinchin, I.M., Lygo-Baker, S., Hay, D.B.: Universities as centres of non-learning. Stud. High. Educ. **33**(1), 89–103 (2008)

39. Crawford, V.M., Schlager, M., Toyama, Y., Riel, M., Vahey, P.: Characterizing adaptive expertise in science teaching. In: Annual Meeting of the American Educational Research Association, Montreal, Quebec, Canada (2005). https://www.scpa.sri.com/sites/default/files/publications/imports/MAESTRoAdEx.pdf

40. Kinchin, I.M., Winstone, N.E. (eds.): Pedagogic Frailty and Resilience in the University. Sense Publishers, Rotterdam (2017)

The Teachers' Voice:
Using Photovoice and Concept Mapping to Evaluate an Innovative Prekindergarten Robotics Program

Deborah L. Carlson[✉], Stephanie Wehry, and Bronwyn McLemore

University of North Florida, Jacksonville, USA
{d.carlson, swehry, bmclemor}@unf.edu

Abstract. The purpose of this paper is to describe the results of a photovoice evaluation of a robotics and programming project for prekindergarten (RAPP). RAPP researchers developed and implemented the program at three urban childcare centers in six teacher's classrooms. All of the teachers of prekindergarteners and rising prekindergarteners had opportunities to use the robot, KIBO, during implementation. Photovoice, using ten RAPP teachers, provided visual images as evidence and promoted sharing knowledge and experiences. Teachers submitted photographs of their children engaging with KIBO and participated in two discussions with their researcher concerning the pictures. At both times, the discussions were audio recorded and summarized. Researchers concept mapped the interviews to identify and communicate common themes. In order of importance to the teachers, the children when using KIBO were engaged, worked independently of the teachers and cooperatively with classmates, were persistent, learned academic knowledge and skills, and developed problem solving skills.

Keywords: Robotics · Programming · Engineering · Photovoice · Early childhood · Concept mapping · Prekindergarten

1 Introduction

The purpose of this paper is to describe a photovoice evaluation of the Robotics and Programming for Prekindergarten (RAPP) pilot project, a series of lessons designed to introduce 4- to 5-year-old children to robotics and programming. By using photovoice, the team directly gained knowledge of the teachers' perspectives of the project without undue influence of the researchers' perspectives. Over the period of the project, each teacher submitted to the research team two photographs per week of her class using the robot over 12 selected weeks. We used concept mapping to organize and then summarize the information we gained from each teacher's discussions of the importance of their submitted pictures. The remainder of this paper presents a brief review of early childhood robotics and programming, descriptions of RAPP, the participants, photovoice, concept mapping, results, and discussion.

© Springer International Publishing Switzerland 2016
A. Cañas et al. (Eds.): CMC 2016, CCIS 635, pp. 241–254, 2016.
DOI: 10.1007/978-3-319-45501-3_19

1.1   The Robotics and Programming Project in Early Childhood

The purpose of RAPP was to develop and implement innovative STEM lessons for children in prekindergarten classrooms. Promoting science in prekindergarten prepares children for later science learning and is a developmentally appropriate endeavor that capitalizes on young children's natural curiosity [1]. However, children's natural curiosity and intuitive sense of technology and engineering are rarely nurtured in typical prekindergarten classrooms. While understanding the natural world, the more common science focus, is important, developing children's knowledge of the sur-rounding man-made world is also critical [2].

The introduction of engineering and programming coupled with the use of robots helps children learn about abstract mathematics and science concepts in concrete ways and assists in the development of children's technological fluency [3]. Children as young as 4-years old can understand programming rules and create commands for robots to follow. Moreover, programming directly relates to foundational concepts including patterns, sequencing, modularity, and cause-and-effect.

1.2   Robotic and Programming Lessons

The research team selected KIBO, a robot developed at DevTech, Tufts University (Boston, Massachusetts, USA) and commercially available at KinderLab. KIBO is an interactive robot, designed specifically for 4- to 7-year olds, that uses programming blocks that describe their functions – icons for pre-readers and words for readers. KIBO has an embedded bar code scanner that requires no screen interface.

The RAPP project included lessons about engineers and problem solving. Children also learned about KIBO and how to scan the programming blocks that tell KIBO what to do. Children further worked to accurately complete teacher-directed challenges and then completed child-created challenges that included the use of the art plat-forms. During a typical week, RAPP researchers implemented two lessons in each class during the morning instructional block concurrently as the prekindergarten teachers were conducting lessons addressing the standards for state-funded prekindergarten. Most teachers also used KIBO and programming during the week without the researchers and in the afternoons with the children who remained at the childcare center after lunch. During the 3-month pilot project, RAPP researchers implemented 12 robotics and programming lessons and one concept-map-assisted review of the lessons in the participating classrooms. (See [4] for more complete RAPP details and results from other evaluations.)

2   Participants and Research Design

This section presents a description of the participants including the children, teachers, and childcare centers; information about the photovoice methodology including example pictures; and the use of concept mapping to map knowledge.

2.1   Participants

The RAPP pilot project involved developing, iteratively refining, and evaluating RAPP using a partnership between a university research team and six experienced prekindergarten teachers from three childcare centers located in an American urban area. However, at the three childcare centers, the RAPP team invited all prekindergarten teachers and teachers of children who are eligible to attend state-funded prekindergarten in fall 2016 to use KIBO in their classes with or without having the researchers work directly with their children. During February 2016, the teachers attended a 3-h professional development workshop designed to teach about KIBO and programming. Each attending teacher received a KIBO kit to use in her classroom. At that time, 11 teachers participated in the photovoice evaluation: nine prekindergarten teachers and two teachers of children who will be prekindergarteners in the fall. One of prekindergarten teachers was a teacher of children with special needs, two of whom were mainstreamed during morning activities in a class served by a RAPP researcher. During the RAPP implementation, this teacher accepted another position. Thus, ten teachers, all female, participated in our photovoice evaluation. In two of the three childcare centers, all of the teachers were Black. In one of these two childcare centers, all children were also Black. In the other, the children were of diverse ethnicities. In the third childcare center, two of the four teachers were White, one was Asian, and the other was Black. The children at this center were also of diverse ethnicities. All three childcare centers enrolled children from low-income families. In this area, the typical non-public-school-based childcare center teacher has no more than an Associate's Degree.

2.2   Methodology

Photovoice (photo voicing our individual and collective experience) is a highly flexible research methodology with roots in health education and community advocacy. The use of photovoice provides visual images as evidence and promotes participation as a means of sharing knowledge and experiences [5, 6]. Additionally, the photovoice process gathers copious amounts of complex data that can be difficult to summarize. As adapted for RAPP, photovoice is a process by which childcare center teachers with access to KIBO can identify, represent, and enhance their experiences through photographs of children learning by interacting with KIBO. Our purpose in using photovoice was threefold:

1. Record and reflect from the childcare center teachers' perspectives on the strengths and weaknesses of RAPP,
2. Promote knowledge sharing of critical issues through photographs and discussions, and
3. Document the needs and assets important to early childhood education stakeholders to encourage action by researchers and policy makers. Photographs provide tangible and immediate evidence of benefits and are an exceptionally powerful means of motivation.

As part of the photovoice evaluation, the RAPP research team asked teachers with KIBO to email two photographs per week (during 12 selected weeks) that they thought were most representative of KIBO use in their classrooms. Early pictures mostly depicted cute children exploring with a charming robot with details of their interactions. At first, we encouraged the teachers to be more specific about the importance depicted in the pictures, and we eventually decided to have a discussion with each teacher during second full week in April, after the children participated in six lessons. At this time, the research team had a complete set of pictures for the first four weeks of the project. During the third week of May, after the children completed a RAPP concept-map-assisted review of all lessons, the researchers conducted a second discussion with each teacher using the pictures from the remaining submissions. The first step in the process, at both discussion times, involved asking the teacher to narrow the field by selecting the three most important pictures and then to discuss with her researcher why the selected pictures were the most important. Nine of the ten teachers agreed to audio recordings of their discussions. The remaining teacher agreed to participate in the discussion without using audio recording. The pictures in Fig. 1 are representative of the teacher-selected photographs.

For the photovoice process, verbatim transcriptions of the teachers' discussions were not necessary because it is the essence or big picture of the teachers' explanation that is important. In fact, a good summary is sufficient. However, for the longer, more detailed discussions we used literal note-taking [7], a process used to provide evidence when making claims and judgements about observations. One of the RAPP researchers, highly trained in the literal note-taking, provided the non-verbatim transcriptions. The researcher who designed the RAPP project evaluation summarized the remaining audio recordings.

2.3   Using Concept Mapping to Organize and Present Knowledge

Authors at the Institute of Human and Machine Cognition [8] suggested that knowledge mapping, one purpose for using concept maps, is useful in recording both explicit and implicit knowledge. The implicit knowledge is knowledge that is held internally and, thus, not easily communicated. In using photovoice, researchers used photographs to elicit both types of knowledge from participants and concept mapping to organize their collective thinking. Concept mapping is an efficient and effective way to organize and present knowledge. In fact, visual presentation of knowledge is often more concise and easily understood than text [9].

3   Results

The results section includes three examples of the research team's use of photovoice and concept mapping. The first example, shows all steps in the process: the summary of the researcher/teacher discussion, the concept map formed from the summary, and a table of the concept map's propositions. The second example does not include the table of propositions, and the third example includes only the concept map. The researcher

Fig. 1. Sample of the important pictures selected by the teachers.

who summarized the discussions concept mapped all ten transcripts in an effort to synchronize the teachers' language across transcripts. For consistency, the first level of all concept maps was *Children* and the second level was *KIBO & Parts*. The listing of propositions function in the CmapTools [10] helped identify similar language. For example, most of the teachers indicated that the children were very excited or happy when a scanned program worked. In all maps, this became will try until they succeed. The last part of this section provides information about the final concept map summarizing what the teachers indicated was most important to them about KIBO.

3.1   First Example of Photovoice and Concept Mapping

The first example involves a prekindergarten teacher who worked with a researcher.

First Discussion with Teacher 9 – Length 2 min, 32 s

I chose the first picture because the children were sitting on the carpet looking and listening with KIBO sitting beside them. They learned that if you don't touch and program KIBO with the blocks then he does nothing. So he is sitting there being still just like them on the carpet. The second picture shows two boys and the garage they built. Because KIBO moves when he is programed, the boys thought that he was a lot like a car and their mothers park their cars in a garage. So at block time, they decided to build KIBO a garage – a house for KIBO. The last picture shows two girls racing each other to push KIBO's start button. They made a program for KIBO and knew that before he will move, you have to push the start button. Both girls wanted to push the button – raced to see which would be first.

(Researcher) Is there anything else you want to tell me about the impact of KIBO on you and your class?

The children learned to discuss and come up with one idea. KIBO has helped them learn to problem solve and to always come up with a plan. Now, whatever we do in the classroom, they want to talk about problem solving. They sing the PLAN song, and it is part of the music program.

Second Discussion with Teacher 9 – Length 1 min, 39 s

The first picture shows the entire class with Ms. B doing a whole group activity involving all of the children while starting circle time. Ms. B captures the attention of the whole class and involves each and every one of the children. Nice way to start circle time. The second picture shows a boy and a girl problem solving as they discuss the lesson, what they are going to do, and who is going to go first. The girl is holding KIBO. The third picture shows a boy and a girl using the map that Ms. B brought (a KIBO challenge) and showing off their scanning skills.

(Researcher) Is there anything else you want to tell me about the impact of KIBO on you and your class?

Kids discuss things by using problem solving, and they also frequently mention that like engineers they solve problems. They keep 'being like engineers' in their minds. Talk about engineers a lot.

Figure 2 presents the final concept map of the discussions with Teacher 9. This teacher mentioned that problem solving skills were transferring to other activities early on. She also mentioned programming and the children's persistence in the first discussion.

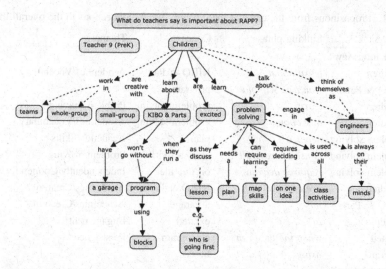

Fig. 2. The final concept map for Teacher 9. The solid lines represent the first discussion and the dotted lines are concepts added at the second discussion.

A team member used the concept maps and the CmapTools function that lists the propositions to code themes and to identify the most frequently used themes. Table 1 shows the propositions used in the Teacher 9 concept map and their relationship to the frequent themes.

3.2   Second Example of Photovoice and Concept Mapping

The second example is from Teacher 2, one of the two teachers who taught the younger children who will be prekindergarteners in the fall. Teacher 2 did not work with RAPP researchers. The following is summary of the two discussions with her. The concept map shown in Fig. 3 presents the concept map of the summaries.

First Discussion with Teacher 2 – Length 2 min

I chose this one of H scanning. I selected it because he was very excited that he could scan KIBO with no problem. The next one is when we first got KIBO, and I was introducing KIBO to them to show them how to hold KIBO like a sandwich. And they really enjoyed that, and everyone got a chance to hold KIBO like a sandwich. And the last one is V&A putting KIBO together. We had to learn how to put KIBO together in order to use him.

(Researcher) Is there anything else you want to tell me about the impact of KIBO on you and your class?

The impact, they really enjoyed it. They just wanted to keep on playing with KIBO. They wanted to keep on putting KIBO together. They help each other. They really enjoy using KIBO. Every day they ask, is KIBO coming out today? Is KIBO coming out today? I try to use him about 3 times a week.

Table 1. Propositions from the concept map in Fig. 2 with connections to the overall themes

Concept	Linking phrase	Concept	Theme
First interview			
Children	*learn about*	KIBO & Parts	Academics/Vocabulary
KIBO & Parts	*won't go without*	program	
Children	*learn*	problem solving	Problem Solving
Children	*talk about*	problem solving	Academics/Vocabulary
Problem solving	*needs a*	plan	Academic/Skills
Problem solving	*is used across all*	class activities	Problem Solving
Problem solving	*requires deciding*	on one idea	Independently/Cooperatively
Children	*are creative with*	KIBO & Parts	Academics/Creativity
KIBO & Parts	*has*	a garage	Academics/Creativity
Children	*are*	excited	Engagement
Excited	*when the they run*	a program	Persistence
Program	*using*	blocks	
Second interview			
Children	*work in*	teams	Independently/Cooperatively
Children	*work in*	small-groups	Independently/Cooperatively
Children	*work in*	whole-groups	
Children	*talk about*	engineers	Academics/Vocabulary
Children	*think of themselves as*	engineers	Creativity/Roleplaying
Engineers	*engage in*	problem solving	Academics/Vocabulary
Children	*talk about*	problem solving	Academics/Vocabulary
Problem solving	*is on their*	minds	Problem Solving
Problem solving	*as they*	discuss a lesson	Problem Solving
Lesson	*e.g.*	who goes first	Independently/Cooperatively
Problem solving	*can require*	map skills	Academics/Skills

Second Discussion with Teacher 2 – Length 2 min, 41 s

The first picture shows B. He missed a lot of KIBO time and needed help, so I taught him how to hold KIBO to scan. Once he figured it out, he really enjoyed KIBO. The second picture shows when I gave them all of the big cards (easier for them to scan than the blocks). The children picked out what they wanted KIBO to do and scanned the cards. The third picture shows K scanning. She knew to use the beginning and end blocks.

(Researcher) Is there anything else you want to tell me about the impact of KIBO on you and your class?

It was awesome to have KIBO in the room, and I hope that the kids will have the opportunity again in the next school year. They enjoyed working with KIBO and learned that engineers solve problems. The children use what they learned by using KIBO in other parts of the day, for example, when they are not sharing on the playground, she reminds them that they are engineers and they solve their problems.

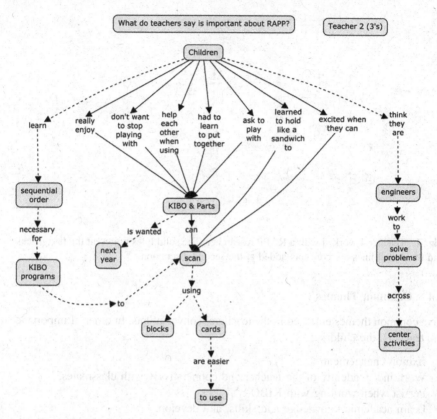

Fig. 3. Concept map of the discussion with Teacher 2. The solid lines represent the first discussion and the dotted lines are concepts added at the second discussion.

The emphasis of this teacher's discussion was the children's engagement and the transfer of problem solving skills to other activities. Academically, the children could successfully scan a program, especially when using the cards rather than the blocks, and were able to understand the sequential requirements of programming.

3.3   Third Example of Photovoice and Concept Mapping

The concept map in Fig. 4 is from another prekindergarten teacher, Teacher 4, who worked with one of the RAPP researchers. Her discussion summaries were too long to include in this paper and were transcribed using literal note-taking. Teacher 4 was the most academically focused of the teachers. She included all of the themes in her discussions with the exception of engagement in the first discussion. However, her children could only learn all that she included in her discussions with the researcher if they were engaged!

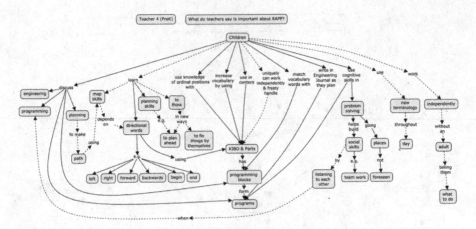

Fig. 4. Teacher 4 worked with a RAPP researcher. The solid lines represent the first discussion and the dotted lines are concepts added at the second discussion.

3.4 Common Themes

Five common themes emerged in the teachers' conversations. In order of importance to the teachers, the children:

- Exhibit engagement,
- Work independently of the teacher and cooperatively with classmates,
- Persist when working with KIBO,
- Learn academic knowledge and skills, and develop,
- Problem solving skills.

Figure 5 shows the final concept map of the teachers' voice. The most frequently mentioned important aspect of using KIBO was that children were engaged when given opportunities to work with KIBO. Picture 1 in Fig. 1 shows children with their hands up wanting to have the next turn to work with KIBO showing children's engagement. The second most frequently mentioned important aspect of using KIBO was that children work independently of the teachers and cooperatively with their classmates. Picture 4 in Fig. 1 shows two friends working together to build and scan a program for KIBO. The girls are fast friends and 'high five' each other's successes. Picture 5 in Fig. 1 shows a boy modeling for a classmate how to program KIBO. The third most frequently mentioned important aspect of using KIBO was that children are persistent and will keep trying until they are successful. In Fig. 1, pictures 3, 4, and 5 are show children successfully developing or scanning a program for KIBO. Picture 3 shows one of the younger children making a program to scan using the cards rather than the blocks. The fourth most frequently mentioned important aspect of using KIBO was that children learn academic knowledge and skills. Picture 2 in Fig. 1 shows a boy writing a programming plan for KIBO in his engineering journal.

The last most frequently mentioned important aspect of using KIBO was that children are transferring their problem solving knowledge to non-RAPP classroom

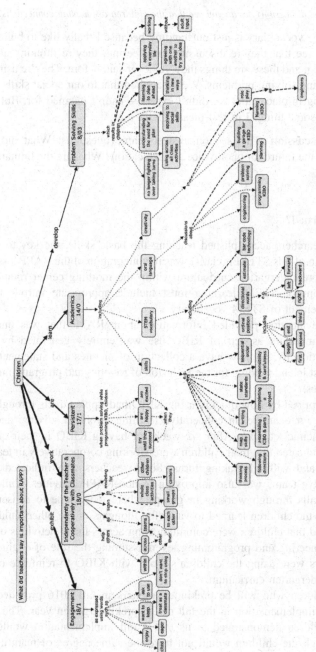

Fig. 5. Concept map detailing what teachers most frequently indicated was most important to them in using KIBO. The concept most frequently mentioned, engagement, is on the left side of the map with the heaviest line. The first number under the concept indicates the number of teachers who explicitly mentioned the concept during both discussions, and the second number represents the number of teachers who implicitly acknowledged the concept during either discussion. Words that the teachers used during the first discussions are connected using a dotted line, and those mentioned only in the second discussion are connected using a bolded, dashed line.

activities. No pictures explicitly show problem solving, but this transcript section of teacher's discussion is an example of what teacher's said.

(Researcher at the first discussion) So, do you see that the children are making connections?

Absolutely, and the vocabulary is just outstanding because I really like to build on vocabulary. You can see that they're discussing engineering, they're thinking about programs, and planning, and these are things they've never said before. They're using it in other centers now and solving problems. We've applied that to our social skills and overall, KIBO is going in places that we didn't expect – hadn't planned for. But it's awesome, it's an awesome thing. I'm real pleased with it.

Conclusions and Discussion. This section answers three questions: What did we learn? What might be the future for photovoice and education? What are the limitations of our study?

3.5   What We Learned?

While the RAPP researchers accomplished teaching the basic skills, the key to successful implementation of this STEM initiative was the integration of the RAPP lessons into the established prekindergarten curriculum within the morning center rotations. Building a foundation for STEM learning must include appropriate introduction, practice, and reinforcement of STEM vocabulary.

The photovoice evaluation provided information about RAPP that was unique because the list of important aspects of KIBO use was entirely generated by the teachers' voice. Additionally, we now have a collection of pictures and statements to use to generate interest in and funding for the inclusion of robotics and programming in prekindergarten classes.

The team was surprised by how quickly using KIBO had ripple effects throughout non-RAPP activities, for example, in cooperative learning, problem solving, and in support of other academic learning. After six weeks of having KIBO in their classrooms, the teachers indicated that their children were working co-operatively in teams, helping each other, and willingly taking turns. Some teachers also indicated that behavior in cooperative teams was also improving in non-RAPP activities. Children learned leadership skills through working in groups where they came to consensus about one idea, thus, the children learned to value the thoughts of the other children. The teachers indicated that children were communicating across many activities using the language of engineering and programming, even assuming the role of engineers. Early on, the teachers were using the children's work with KIBO to reinforce other aspects of the prekindergarten curriculum.

The younger children who will be prekindergarteners in fall 2016 provided an example of a KIBO implementation in the fall of the prekindergarten year. The two classes of young children demonstrated to us that a fall implementation would be successful even though the children would not have the same degree of maturity or academic knowledge as the end-of-year prekindergarteners in present study.

After hearing the teachers' voice, we also know that these important aspects of using KIBO would not happen unless robotics lessons were implemented by the children's teacher in the classroom. It is tempting to implement RAPP using a teacher or team of teachers who specifically teach robotics either by using a rolling cart to house the necessary equipment or by taking the children to a resource room for robotics lessons because it reduces the cost of materials and professional development. We believe that to obtain the results voiced by these teachers, multiple KIBO kits need to be available in all prekindergarten classrooms and used by the teacher as she works with the children across the curriculum and at centers where the children independently explore robotics.

Roberts-Holmes [11] encouraged researchers conducting research with young children to ask themselves, "In what ways does your research project allow children to surprise and astound you with their abilities and social competence?" (p. 44). Using photovoice provided the RAPP research team many opportunities to be both surprised and astounded by the children! Our initial thinking about the pictures mostly depicting cute children exploring with a charming robot turned out to be the truth – plus a whole lot more.

3.6   What Might the Future Hold for Photovoice and Education?

We used photovoice as an open-ended forum for teachers to discuss their thoughts on KIBO's impact on their children and classrooms. Another possible use for photovoice is using prompts that target specific areas of learning that the study purports to address. These would include, but not be limited to math skills (e.g. estimating, ordinal numbers, and sequence); problem solving skills (e.g. identifying a problem and using the steps in the Solve It 4! to problem solve); and transfer of knowledge to other settings (e.g. solve problems on the play-ground, sequence story events in reading, and use of new vocabulary in non-KIBO activities).

We have promising evidence that supports the notion that in just a 12-week period of time, with two lessons a week, 4- and 5-year-old children can learn to design simple programs, internalize and apply a problem-solving process, and complete simple challenges independent of adults. As RAPP researchers continue to design lessons for a 6- to 9-month implementation of robotics and programming, a challenge will be to balance the content and processes of the curriculum to maintain the motivation and learning curve demonstrated in the first 12 weeks.

3.7   What Are the Limitations to the Study?

The small sample size and the qualitative methodology limit the ability to generalize results of the study. Additionally, it would have been ideal to have gathered the participating teachers to collectively discuss and agree with our determination of the most important facets of the RAPP implementation. However, the ideal format requires that the teachers come together which is never easy when working with privately-funded childcare centers in contrast to teachers in the public school system. As the participants worked in three different childcare centers spread across the city, meeting at one facility was not realistic. Most of the teachers worked a full day and were not interested in attending meetings after the workday or on weekends. To meet during the day requires an additional person at the childcare center to cover the teachers' responsibilities. Overcoming this problem provides more validity to the findings.

A second limitation is the level of teacher's interest in this evaluation was not equal. Some teachers sent 10 pictures at each collection, while others sent none. Some teachers provided full-throated discussions while others just minimally mentioned their three pictures. In part, this is due to a lack of understanding of anticipated results of their participation. Photovoice was new to the research team and no doubt also to the teachers. Should we use this methodology again, which is very likely, we now have an example to show participants the use for their pictures and discussions.

Acknowledgement. The Crawford Early Childhood Research and Education Distinguished Professor Fund made possible the RAPP project through a generous gift to the University of North Florida Foundation and the Florida Institute of Education by Toni and Andy Crawford.

References

1. Duschl, R.A., Schweingruber, H.A., Shouse, A.W.: Taking Science to School: Learning and Teaching Science in Grades K-8. The National Academies Press, Washington (2007). Board on Science Education, Division of Behavioral and Social Sciences and Education
2. Bers, M.: Blocks to Robots: Learning with Technology in the Early Childhood Classroom. Teacher's College Press, New York (2008)
3. Rogers, C., Portsmore, M.: Bringing engineering to elementary school. J. STEM Educ. Innov. Res. **5**(3), 17 (2004)
4. McLemore, B., Wehry, S.: Robotics and programming in prekindergarten (RAPP): an innovative approach to introducing 4- and 5-year olds to robotics. In: Proceeding of Global Learn 2016, pp. 149–155. Association for the Advancement of Computing in Education (2016)
5. Evans-Agnew, R.A., Rosemberg, M.S.: Questioning photovoice research: whose voice? Qual. Health Res. **26**(1), 1–12 (2016)
6. Wang, C., Burris, M.A.: Photovoice: concept, methodology, and use for participatory needs assessment. Health Educ. Behav. **3**(3), 369–387 (1997)
7. Ribas, W.R.: Teacher Evaluations That Work!!, 2nd edn. Ribas Publications, Westwood (2005)
8. Cañas, A.J., Coffey, J.W, Carnot, M.J., Feltovich, P., Hoffman, R.R., Feltovich, J., Novak, J. D.: A summary of literature pertaining to the use of concept mapping techniques and technologies for education and performance support, IHMC report (2003)
9. Coffey, J.W.: Concept mapping and knowledge modeling: a multi-disciplinary educational, informational, and communication technology. Syst. Cybern. Inform. **13**(6), 122–128 (2015)
10. Cañas, A.J., Hill, G., Carff, R., Suri, N., Lott, J., Gómez, G., Eskridge, T., Arroyo, M., Carvajal, R.: CmapToos: a knowledge modeling and sharing environment. In: Concept Maps: Theory, Methodology, Technology, Proceedings of the First International Conference on Concept Mapping, Pamplona, Editorial Universidad Pública de Navarra (2004)
11. Roberts-Holmes, G.: Doing Your Early Years Research Project. Sage, London (2014)

The Use of Concept Maps
in Environmental Study

Jessica Algrain[✉]

Université Catholique de Louvain, Louvain-la-Neuve, Belgium
algrainj@gmail.com

Abstract. In the we tried to understand in which way the concept maps' teaching can have a positive effect on the acquisition of metaknowledges and on overall understanding in the class of environmental study. Moreover, we tried to find if the teaching method of concept maps, expositive on one hand, or accompanied by a pedagogical dialogue on the other hand, can amplify these effects. Through a serial of workshops of concept maps' teaching and tests, we have determined that concept maps teaching, regardless of the method employed, can have an impact on overall understanding in environmental study, which is a real benefit to our reflection on professional practices. Moreover, through a series of qualitative interviews, it appears that the teaching of concept maps by the expositive method may have a positive effect on the overall understanding of environmental study.

1 Introduction

In a search of refinement of teaching practices, our job is to show how the training of the concept map can improve training. So, we hope to open an additional way for the teacher who wants to equip himself with innovative pedagogic tools, in French-speaking Belgian education system. In this spirit, we want to bring the truth about the possible effects of the use of concept maps on one hand, when they are taught with an expositive pedagogic method and on the other hand, when they are used as support in a metacognitive reflection.

2 Theoretical Frame

2.1 Metacognition

Metacognition studies the consciousness of a person about its own mental gestures, as well as the control which he has of it. It is therefore about a human capacity to regulate knowledge voluntarily. It is a conscious operation of catch of detachment in comparison with trainings [1]. It can allow a learning to become more autonomous, because the student can then consider the object of training and its taking over to be subjects in reflection (Grangeat, 1997, named by Romainville [2]).

Metaknowledges. To exercise a metacognitive reflection requires the student that he already has some knowledge of himself, of the task he was asked, and the conditions

© Springer International Publishing Switzerland 2016
A. Cañas et al. (Eds.): CMC 2016, CCIS 635, pp. 255–264, 2016.
DOI: 10.1007/978-3-319-45501-3_20

of this one. It is what Moshman and Schraw, in the poursuit of research of Flavell and Brown, call metaknowledges (1995, named by Escorcia [3, p. 48]). Moreover, metacognitive reflection of student can scoop out from this metaknowledges to plan, to choose, to control and to assess the way he learns. It is what the authors name the regulation of cognition (1995, quote by Escorcia [3, p. 48]).

Pedagogic Stakes and Operationalization. The student who knows what he knows have more chance to improve his performances. «Quantity and variety of knowledge which a student has in a specific field, in a certain way, the effectiveness of his methodological competences in this field» [4, p. 7]. However, this finding should be nuanced because metacognition is not the only factor to consider in learning [4].

Besides, as underlines it Romainville, «*to have a metacognitive knowledge is a thing, to use it in training situation is another one*» [4, p. 4]. It is therefore necessary to take some precautions, such as checking the validity of metacognitive knowledge in the learner, check that the learner mobilizes indeed metacognitive knowledge (not that it performs a task by habit or because we asked him), and finally check that the metacognitive speech prepared by the student is not just adjusted to what we want him to say.

Metacognition is built gradually, meaning it can be good to make "meta breaks" that focus on what the student has thought to do right away, rather than his knowledge of metacognition after a resolution of a problem. Foster the "socio-meta-cognitive" conflict can change the preconceptions of learners by confronting them with those of others. Finally, using the teacher's or peer's mediation for a gradual internalization of metacognition can help the student to put words to his mental functioning.

2.2   Pedagogical Dialogue in the Service of Metacognition

To lead an activity of metacognition, the teacher can use the pedagogical dialogue such as imagined by La Garanderie [5, 6]. It is a form of possible mediation of the teacher that allows to emerge these mental gestures.

Evocative Habits. The evocative habits are personal methods to study new knowledge, which represent "true mental habits, since they are internal forms of operation to consciousness and acquired" [6, p. 81]. We talk about habits in the sense that they do not change or little during the life of an individual, but it is nevertheless possible to learn new ones.

Depending on whether these are more often pictures of objects, pictures of words, of sketch, projections of decors, of faces, then we speak of evocative visual habits; or if they are mostly auditory memories, remembered conversations, logical sequences of sentences, or an interior monologue, an invented story, then we say that evocative habit is auditory.

Learn by Pedagogical Dialogue. These evocative habits can, depending on whether they are rather visual or auditory, to lead the student to perceive, to understand and to learn in a different way. For the teacher who wants to teach his students more evocative habits, pedagogical dialogue can be an interesting way.

According to La Garanderie [6, p. 667], teacher using a pedagogical dialogue follow three principle: «*the pedagogic specificity*» of the dialogue is to inform the student about his ways of learning; «*the teacher resources recognition in students*» where he then becomes aware of his possibilities and «*the right of the student to the educational responsibility*» that give the student a major role.

Pedagogical dialogue can apparently allow to the student to become aware of his steps of training and to learn from it. For the teacher, it is about an opportunity to work the metacognition with his class. Moreover, he can favor a kind of «socio-meta-cognitive conflict» in the sense that it is social interaction for the acquisition of metacognitive skills. In this case, it seems that a communication medium might help clarify the purpose of the discussion. So, we propose to approach the concept maps to begin pedagogical dialogue in class.

2.3 The Concept Maps

Concept maps, such as imagined by Novak, are a spatial representation of concepts and of the relations which join these concepts some with others, in an organized and hierarchized way.

The building of the concept map [7] and its interpretation are governed by rules. It is made up of 4 important elements which we will not develop in this article: central question, concept, link and proposal. When the link is connecting two concepts of two different levels, the term "cross-link" is used. This usually shows a good mastery of knowledge [8, p. 114].

Also, to let student organize and choose his concepts allows him to represent his own cognitive structure. He can then easily describe and explain in a clever way his own map to others [7].

2.4 Problems and Research Question

We have wanted to know if learning concept maps can have an impact by itself on metaknowledges and on the overall understanding or if it should be accompanied by an pedagogical dialogue aimed metacognitive reflection, especially in environmental study's class. "EDM" is used in this article for abbreviation of "étude du milieu", that means environmental study, in French.

3 Methodology

3.1 Research Variables

- Metaknowledges assessed through a metacognitive test inspired by Dennison and Schräw [9];
- Overall understanding in EDM as capacity to establish sense links between the notions of lesson;

- Groups: two groups used for noticing the effects of the training of the concept maps on metaknowledges and overall understanding, by two different methods for each groups and a third one (the control group);
- Learning method: in the E group, expositive method (interactions of the students between them and with the teacher are avoided), and in the MC group, the method was accompanied by a pedagogical dialogue, to lead to more metacognitive reflection (inspired by the conditions of the pedagogical dialogue of La Garanderie [6]). Finally, the control group don't participate to workshops but do participate nevertheless in the same tests as two others and at the same time.

3.2   Research Procedure

To begin, it's important to note that all students continued to follow school program for the duration experience.

First, we compared the control group with the two other samples to check if the results which we get in overall understanding tests would not be only due to a possible training bias.

Then, we compared the sample E group with the sample MC group, to check if the impact of the concept maps training on overall understanding and on metaknowledges depends on whether the teacher accompanies it or not with a pedagogical dialogue.

We assessed three samples at two instants of research: a first time before the workshops of concept map and once after these, to notice a possible increase of performances both tests. We draw attention however to the fact that the metacognitive test, inspired by Dennison and Schraw [9], is not envisaged to be performed twice to the same population. He is therefore performed only once, at the end of workshops.

Between this two times of evaluation, three workshops of concept map are given in the E and the MC groups. Starting point of each of these workshops is identical in both classes, but the conduct varies, because of the variation of the method in a group and in other one (Table 1).

Table 1. Research Plan

	16/10/2014	23/10/2014	06/11/2014	20/11/2014	27/11/2014
E group	ECG/EDM	Workshop 1	Workshop 2	Workshop 3	ECG/EDM
	Time 1	50 min	50 min	50 in	Time 2 + MT
MC group	ECG/EDM	Workshop 1	Workshop 2	Workshop 3	ECG/EDM
	Time 1	50 min	50 min	50 min	Time 2 + MT
Control group	ECG/EDM	/	/	/	ECG/EDM
	Time 1				Time 2 + MT

3.3   Subjects and Equipment of Experience

Among all students of the secondary first one of French-speaking Belgium, the public chosen for this research lives in Mons' city. The school brings together a total of 11 classes of first year and nine classes that wished to participate.

The independent variable "Group" was used for the selection of research samples, namely three statistically comparable among the nine groups, based on the performances of the overall comprehension test (time 1). We noted ECG/EDM the overall comprehension test, which means "épreuve de comprehension globale en EDM", in French.

We did a one-factor anova, on base of results in ECG/EDM (time 1) what allowed us to see that there is not statistically significant difference between nine groups as for the results of ECG/EDM (time 1) both for variance and mean (Tables 2 and 3).

Table 2.   Variances homogeneity test (Levene test)

Levene statistic	ddl1	ddl2	Signification
,404	8	206	,917

Table 3.   ANOVA (1 factor)

	Sum of squares	Df	Mean square	F	Signification
Between-groups	117,315	8	14,664	1,036	,410
Within-groups	2915,585	206	14,153		
Total	3032,900	214			

Among these nine groups, we chose three groups for whom it was possible to set up workshops of concept maps.

The sample carries following names:

- E group: sample with training of concept maps by an expositive method;
- MC group: sample with the same training (as for the E), but by a method accompanied with a metacognitive processing (via a pedagogical dialogue);
- control group: sample which does not participate to the workshops.

The first two samples, E and MC groups, participated each in three sessions of 50 min on the concept maps. We name these sessions «workshops of concept maps». During these workshops, we put in the disposition of the student a basic equipment for the realization of maps (blank sheets A3, color pencils, post-it, etc.) and we used a PowerPoint projection.

The pedagogical objective, in both groups (except the control one), was to learn how to use concept maps in environmental study and in other courses. And moreover to use them to think about their own way of learning. The first workshop of concept maps intended to make discover this tool to students by a first experience of creating concept maps.

For the evaluation of three samples, we name «test of overall understanding in EDM» (noted ECG/EDM) two quizzes intended to assess the level of performance of subjects in overall understanding in environmental study, and more specifically capacity to establish logical links between different notions of the environmental study's lessons.

For the research needs, there two quizzes have therefore been written with the collaboration of three teachers on the basis of knowledge and skills of the educational program related to comprehension. To be more specific, the environmental study's program refers to overall understanding as the ability of students to make logical connections or links of meaning between the different concepts of this course.

Both quizzes account for a total of five types of questions and the evaluation result is noted as quoted on 39 points, divided according to questions. A corrective was made to ensure that ratings are equivalent. All items of both questionnaires were created and considered to reflect the overall understanding and to pursuing the research objectives. Quizzes do not evaluate all student skills, but their ability to select information and make links between different information the construction of meaning.

The first test was passed, the same day for all the students of the establishment, before the beginning of the workshops of concept maps. Results in this first test served, between others, for choosing 3 groups of experience, thanks to a statistical comparison of scores. The second test was also passed, the same day, to the students of three chosen groups, after the last workshop of concept maps.

On the one hand, comparison time 1 - time 2 (noted ECG/EDM1 & ECG/EDM2) serves primarily to rule on a possible effect of workshops on overall understanding through their performances, not so much to see appear better performances (which are not a goal in itself but an indicator of the evolution).

On the other hand, an intergroup comparison between the results of two tests ECG/EDM in the three groups (including the control one) allows to determinate an effect of the workshops on the overall understanding' student.

To asses a possible difference in the acquisition of metaknowledges, we used a metacognitive test, inspired by Dennison and Schraw [9] with the metaknowledges according to Moshman and Schraw (1995, named by Escorcia [3]). We name it «metacognitive test» (noted TM).

4   Analysis of Data

By performing an Anova, we try first of all to notice a difference between groups in comparison with the results of three tests.

In our analysis, results α in three tests are above the threshold of significance ($\alpha > .05$). As a result, we do not notice statistically significant difference between three groups for both times.

By performing Student's t test (for matched samples), we tried to notice a difference, for every group, between the results of the test of overall understanding in EDM in time 2 in comparison with time 1. In other words, we wanted to see if a progress has been made by students.

The table shows a statistically significant difference between the results ECG/EDM to two times of trial, and that, in E and MC groups. However, there was no statistically significant difference for the control group, although we can still draw our attention to the result of $\alpha = 0.06$ for the control group, which is relatively close to significance (0.05).

Considering the anova (Table 4) having shown that there is no statistically significant difference between groups (based on the results the three tests) we performed a Student's t test to compare the groups based on the same data.

Table 4. ANOVA (1 factor)

		Sum of squares	Df	Mean square	F	Signification
ECG/EDM1	Between-groups	7,447	2	3,723	0,22	0,803
	Within-groups	1034,143	61	16,953		
	Total	1041,59	63			
ECG/EDM2	Between-groups	53,656	2	26,828	1,146	0,325
	Within-groups	1428,496	61	23,418		
	Total	1482,152	63			
Metacognitive test (MT)	Between-groups	797,704	2	398,852	1,702	0,191
	Within-groups	14297,906	61	234,392		
	Total	15095,609	63			

First, the comparison of scores (Student t) obtained at three events in « E group versus MC group » shows that there is no statistically significant difference between the scores of the two groups ($\alpha > 0.05$) on ECG/EDM1, ECG/EDM2 and metacognitive test.

Secondly, the comparison of scores on three tests in « E group versus control group » shows that there is no statistically significant difference between the scores of the two groups ($\alpha > 0.05$) concerning ECG/EDM1 and ECG/EDM2 tests. But there is indeed a statistically significant difference between the scores on metacognitive test ($\alpha = 0.028$).

Third, the comparison of scores on three tests in "MC group versus control group" shows that there is no statistically significant difference between the scores of the two groups ($\alpha > 0.05$) concerning ECG/EDM1, ECG/EDM2 and metacognitive test.

Finally, we calculated a correlation (Bravais Pearson r) to observe whether a relationship existed between the results for the overall understanding test in EDM and score the metacognitive test. This table shows the one hand, that there is a significant relationship between the results for the overall understanding test in EDM at time 1 and the results of the same test time 2. Furthermore, this table indicates that there is no significant relationship between the results to overall understanding of events in EDM (with 2 times) and results in metacognitive test.

Table 5. Correlations

Groups		Paired differences		T	Df	Sig. (2-tailed)
		Mean	Std. deviation			
E	EDM1-EDM2	−3,4211	4,9617	-3,005	18	0,008
MC	EDM1-EDM2	−2,2381	4,5045	−2,277	20	0,034
Control	EDM1-EDM2	−1,8333	4,5532	−1,973	23	0,061

Our interpretations further to these results are the following:

In a general way, all groups advanced in overall understanding in EDM. Progress in overall understanding in both groups which participated in the workshops of concept maps is not due to chance. We are assuming that it is just the participation in these workshops (to which the group controls did not participate) who could explain these results.

The existence of a significant difference between the scores of the E group and of the control group in the metacognitive test could be explained by the fact that, in the E group, who had already met the teacher, the students want to pass the quiz to satisfy this one. It would be then possible to speak about desirability.

On the contrary, it is possible that three workshops would not have be enough for allowing measuring significant difference between three groups; and other biases are to take into account as beliefs of the teacher and of the students concerning what was expected from them, or else a possible class effect in the groups of experience.

The existence of a relation between the results of time 1 and of time 2 of ECG/EDM lets us assume that the results of the first time of ECG/EDM would be a good predictor of the results of the second time of test. On the contrary, the absence of relation between results in tests of overall understanding in EDM and results in the metacognitive test could be explained by the fact that the level of metaknowledges is perhaps simply not a good predictor of the level of overall understanding in EDM.

Table 6. Student's t test (for paired samples)

		ECG/EDM1	ECG/EDM2	Meta Test
ECG/EDM1	Pearson correlation	1	,471[a]	,149
	Sig. (2-tailed)		,000	,240
	N	64	64	64
ECG/EDM2	Pearson correlation	,471[a]	1	,087
	Sig. (2-tailed)	,000		,496
	N	64	64	64
Meta test	Pearson correlation	,149	,087	1
	Sig. (2-tailed)	,240	,496	
	N	64	64	64

[a]Correlation is significant (2-tailed) at level 0.01.

Note: we've made further statistical analysis but we've chose the relevant ones for this article.

Nevertheless, we wanted to deepen our analysis and we were able to highlight a few elements.

5 Discussion

We can announce first of all that our device did not allow to establish an obvious relation between the training of the concept maps, the metaknowledges of the students and their overall understanding in EDM.

The presence of difference between E group vs control group for the scores in metacognitive test (and not for the MC group) leads us to question the possibility that students in E group having received an expositive method and therefore being delivered to themselves in decisions they make to achieve their map, have anyway a reflection on how they plan the task, on the meanings of workshops, etc. In other words, we wonder if the fact of being less accompanied by a metacognitive reflection does not have them at the same time, pushed to think about themselves.

Having said that, to try to explore our results, we performed a series of qualitative discussions to the teacher of workshops and it emerges from it that the role of teacher, as well as the role of the students are decisive in the way workshops took place. Indeed, a class effect seems to have been present for at least to one of the groups, and some desirability is to envisage concerning the will of the teacher to bring this group to a deeper reflection than another group.

6 Conclusion

First of all, we assume that the training of concept maps leads nevertheless to a better overall understanding in EDM, since the evolution of the control group results were significantly worse than the other two groups (Tables 5 and 6). This is a real benefit to this research, as it allows considering new perspectives for our professional practice.

On the contrary, we are not really able to determinate if the training of concept maps leads to better metaknowledges. Nevertheless, by deepening analyses, we can think that expositive method could have had an impact on metacognitive scores. Indeed, we wonder about the possibility that the students who had an expositive method, being delivered to themselves, made a reflection on the way they plan to perform the task, on the meaning of workshops, etc.

Also, being a teacher is not just a question of transmitting knowledge, he grants a big place to the person of the young student and therefore all that is likely to represent an additional chance to help him grow. For the teaching in environmental study we wanted to investigate a tool which could help the teacher to make understand and to master his discipline.

Moreover, the teacher-student relationship in the exercise of metacognition has been a surprising lever. Indeed, the contribution of this research lead us to believe that if the teacher feels particularly concerned by the progress in metacognition in students, and if, moreover, he knows quite well the public to identify the mental habits of each one, he would be able more easily to engage in metacognitive dialogue with them. In a way, we wonder if the teacher's empathy for the student would not be as a gateway to mental functioning of the student and therefore, a facilitator for pedagogical dialogue.

Finally, we formulate a last remark regarding the metacognition, which the training of the concept maps is not very present in Belgian French-speaking education, its learning is a truly pioneering practice in our schools.

References

1. Ouellet, G., Portelance, L.: Vers l'énoncé d'Interventions Susceptibles de Favoriser l'émergence de la Métacognition chez l'Enfant du Préscolaire, vol. 35, no. 2, pp. 67–99. Paper of Moncton University (2004). http://www.erudit.org/revue/rum/2004/v35/n2/010644ar.html?vue=resume
2. Romainville, M.: Savoir Comment Apprendre Suffit-il à Mieux Apprendre? Métacognition et Amélioration des Performances. In: Pallascio, R., Lafortune, L. (eds.) Pour une Pensée Réflexive en Éducation, pp. 71–86. Quebec University Press, Quebec (2000). http://www.educacom.info/pedagogie-recherche/article-master/40-savoir-comment-apprendre.pdf
3. Escorcia, D.: Composantes Métacognitives et Performance à l'écrit: une Approche Sociocognitive du travail Étudiant. Ph.D. thesis in Educational Sciences unpublished, University Paris X, Nanterre (2007). http://halshs.archives-ouvertes.fr/tel-00170924/
4. Romainville, M.: Conscience, Métacognition, Apprentissage: le cas des Compétences Méthodologiques. In: Doudin, P.-A., Pons, F. (eds.) La Conscience chez l'Enfant et chez l'Élève, pp. 108–130. Quebec University Press, Quebec (2007). http://educacom.info/pedagogie-recherche/article-master/30-conscience-metacognition.pdf
5. de La Garanderie, A.: Le Dialogue Pédagogique avec l'Élève. In: de La Garanderie, A. (ed.) Réussir, ça s'Apprend, pp. 581–694. Bayard Edition, Montrouge (1984)
6. de La Garanderie, A.: Réussir, ça s'Apprend. Bayard Edition, Montrouge (2013)
7. Novak, J.D.: Concept mapping: a useful tool for science education. J. Res. Sci. Teach. **10**(27), 937–949 (1990)
8. Salamanca-Avila, M.E.: Exploration de l'Évolution des Représentations Scientifiques de l'Écologie chez les étudiants de Deuxième Baccalauréat en Biologie. Ph.D. thesis in Sciences unpublished, UCL, Louvain-la-Neuve (2013). http://dial.academielouvain.be/handle/boreal:135863
9. Dennison, R.S., Schraw, G.: Assessing Metacognitive Awareness. Departement of Educational Psychology, University of Nebraska, Lincoln (1994). http://wiki.biologyscholars.org/@api/deki/files/99/=Schraw1994.pdf

Transforming Science Pedagogy: Using Concept Mapping to Design an Interdisciplinary Approach to Teaching Middle School Science

Sumitra Himangshu-Pennybacker[✉]

Middle Georgia State University, Macon, GA, USA
sumitra.himangshu@mga.edu

Abstract. The purpose of this study was to apply concept mapping to the design of an interdisciplinary approach for teaching middle school science. The study was centered around the question: *What does it mean for pre-service teacher candidates to plan an integrated instructional unit using content from different science disciplines taught in middle school grades?* The study required pre-service teachers to (through their own understanding of science, math, and literacy content) be able to identify with an authentic real-world scenario and apply core elements to the design of an interdisciplinary approach to lesson planning, classroom instruction, and student assessment. Designing the unit involved the use of concept maps to visualize and communicate essential pedagogical elements and their relationships to each other. Analysis of pre-service teacher candidate concept maps provided a fluid basis for peer-learning, facilitated co-planning, and created a context for next level content understanding.

Keywords: Pre-service teacher · Middle school teaching · Interdisciplinary science · Unit planning · Co-teaching

1 Introduction

The purpose of this study was to develop an interdisciplinary model for enabling pre-service teachers (preparing to teach science in the middle school) to transform science pedagogy by establishing an innovative process for science instruction by identifying core concepts, enhancing content understanding, minimizing student misconceptions, and increasing science efficacy for their students. The impact of using concept maps to develop a process for authentic content instruction was supported by the question: What does it mean to integrate science content across all three middle school grades? The research was based on the hypothesis that given a real-world scenario, pre-service teachers would (through their own understanding of science, math, and literacy content) be able to identify and apply core elements to an interdisciplinary design approach to lesson planning, classroom instruction, and student assessment. In the current world of science education, where different scientific content is taught in silos (i.e. separated by grade level, during the middle school years) an integrated approach is critical for enabling students to understand the interdependent nature of science.

© Springer International Publishing Switzerland 2016
A. Cañas et al. (Eds.): CMC 2016, CCIS 635, pp. 265–274, 2016.
DOI: 10.1007/978-3-319-45501-3_21

Teacher candidates enrolled in a Capstone Course in the Middle Grades Education program at a University in South Eastern USA were involved in an eight-week-long thematic learning unit using the Flint, MI Water Crisis as a foundational case study to design a collaborative interdisciplinary unit for the middle school science classroom. In order to develop a process for engaging in authentic content understanding, the teacher candidates used concept maps to communicate, plan, and collaborate on research and design of the thematic unit. Class discussion and interactive simulations provided supplemental instruction for content standards. Throughout the developmental process for the thematic unit, each teacher candidate was required to create individual maps, which were then used to generate the group concept map.

Communicating abstract scientific concepts in the absence of a real-world context leaves teachers and students with a superficial understanding of the relevance of science in everyday life. Middle school students (6th–8th grade) are better engaged when knowledge and conceptual understanding is based in concrete experiences. Beyond mere hands-on science activities, active learning methods help middle school students deconstruct ideas and challenge their current understandings. This provides a platform for meaningful learning to occur by allowing an appreciation for the relationship between evidence and explanation. The initial foundation about the nature of science, how science works, and how science is a human and community endeavor, is built during the elementary school years. Using a case study approach, middle school students explore authentic situations that compel them to work on real-world problems developing skills of scientific investigation and an understanding of the nature and process of science. Irrespective of the discipline, conceptual understanding is greatly enhanced when students are allowed to gather relevant data, test their ideas, look for patterns in their data, communicate their findings, and listening/questioning the explanations proposed by their peers. Science instruction for middle school science teachers typically involves helping them develop scientific reasoning through problem solving, and using methods of science inquiry in order to engage the middle school student in active learning. Being able to apply conceptual understanding to authentic experiences, and communicate their understanding becomes a collaborative act, thus helping pre-service teacher candidates visualize their own learning about fundamental science principles primed towards novel teaching possibilities.

As part of a capstone course, four pre-service teacher candidates were given the task of designing a thematic unit that incorporated science content across all three middle school grades (6th–8th grade). In keeping with the next generation science curriculum, the teacher candidates were additionally required to align this integrated science content with literacy and mathematics standards. The Flint, MI water crisis case study was used to nucleate the design of an interdisciplinary thematic unit. Constructing individual and group collaborative concept maps, and incorporating strategies from teaching case studies, the teacher candidates were able to use peer-learning to enhance and improve their own learning, and to apply this learning process to visualize possible ways in which their middle school students learn, understand and comprehend science content. The design, implementation, and findings from this project are presented in the following sections of this paper.

2   Theoretical Framework

Application of the case study method during classroom instruction involves two elements: (i) presenting the elements of the case itself followed by (ii) the discussion of that case. A case study used for teaching purposes provides background information, but neither analysis nor conclusions. The analytical work of explaining the relationships among events in the case, identifying options, evaluating decision choices, and predicting the effects of actions, is the work done by students during the classroom discussion. By engaging in the case study, students "do" the work of the discipline by identifying the concepts, techniques and methods of the discipline and improve their ability to apply them. Discussions bring energy and excitement to the classroom, providing middle school students with an opportunity to work with a range of evidence, thus improving their ability to apply disciplinary vocabulary, theory, and methods. Additionally, the use of real-world case studies, such as the Flint Water Crisis, can help middle school students understand the collaborative and diverse nature of the scientific community. Real-world case studies in science allow middle school students to understand that science is a human endeavor reliant upon openness to new ideas. A cultural-gap is also bridged when middle school students observe scientists from different ethnic backgrounds engage in activities, which the scientists communicate to others by presenting evidence, and providing explanations.

Research suggests that pre-service teacher candidates have difficulty making content connections when planning sequential lessons that both use interconnected concepts, and span several days of instruction [1]. Concept maps visually communicate the thinking, planning and meaning-making process. According to Deniz and Akerson [2], the following four criterions are necessary to the meaning-making process: (i) the learner must focus on the information to be learned; (ii) the learner must try to create an understanding of the content by identifying relationships amongst related topics; (iii) the learner needs to relate new ideas to their prior knowledge about these ideas; and (iv) learners need to be able to identify their limits and constraints in order to maximize their depth of understanding. This makes concept mapping especially well suited for teacher preparation, especially for science education. The flexibility of the concept mapping process allows use both for planning and instruction, and for assessment [3, 4]. Instead of merely memorizing scientific facts, teachers can apply concept mapping attuned to the learning environment, and their own understanding of the topic [5, 6].

An increasing number of studies highlight the use of the pedagogical application of concept mapping to promote cooperative learning and enhance student understanding of a particular topic [7–10]. During group concept mapping, students work in small groups and discuss their understanding of a topic, then collaborate together to produce a group concept map. This approach is purposefully designed to engage students in discourse about particular concepts and allows students to articulate their thoughts about the concepts [11]. Since a group of students work on the same map, it helps in peer-learning, strengthens cooperation, and helps in the negotiation of meaning between the collaborating students [9].

The use of sequential concept maps provides a visual timeline depicting the development of group understanding and can be used as a framework to evaluate and guide content understanding through small group or whole class discussion. The sequential concept mapping process can be used to generate ideas through the process of brain-storming, either in class or by using electronic discussion boards. The ideas generated by individuals can be easily synthesized and organized by the participants sorting them as a group, then rating them based on variables of interest (such as relative importance, accuracy of relationship) [7]. Since concept mappers are actively involved in the interpretation of the resulting maps, it allows-through comparisons - to identify the level of content understanding and/or inaccuracies and misconceptions. Such comparisons allow individuals to identify the connections between their existing conceptions, and the true nature of the content. Concept maps used to monitor understanding provide a meaningful representation of information in a concise manner [12].

3   Methods

Pre-service teachers' design of an interdisciplinary thematic unit was determined by a set of four sequential concept maps. Four pre-service teachers enrolled in 1 section of a capstone middle grades science course, in Spring 2016, participated in the study. They were each required to construct individual, and group maps at four different times during a 8-week period of instruction. The individual map analysis consisted of a total of 16 concept maps, which were subsequently used to construct 4 group maps. For the purpose of analysis, the group concept maps were created in stages, at different points during the semester, and sequentially labeled as Initial Draft, Developmental Draft, Improved Draft, and Final Draft (Table 1). Group maps were also compared at each stage to the individual maps at that stage.

Table 1. Rubric designed by pre-service teacher researchers to monitor their understanding during the design progress.

Exemplary	Target	Developing	Superficial
Links are precisely labeled	Links are labeled	Links are not labeled	No links
Simple and complex relationships between content standards are mapped effectively	Relationships are mapped and aligned to content standards	Some ideas, concepts are linked but not distinctive	Difficult to follow relationships
Includes cross-links between inter-disciplinary concepts that are extremely suitable for the topic and that show original or creative understanding	Most or all concepts are suitable for the topic – not all are interdisciplinary – few cross-links observed	Most concepts satisfy basic requirements but do not directly relate to interdisciplinary content – no cross-links observed	Many concepts are inappropriate for the topic

The individual concept maps constructed by the pre-service teachers were required to demonstrate an alignment and relationship between the following six elements, which are essential in the instructional unit design process: Design Rationale, Content Standards and Alignment, Theoretical Framework, Scope and Sequence, Instructional Technology, and Assessments. In order to maintain a robust degree of reliability in the unit design process, the pre-service teacher candidates began mapping with this constrained set of essential elements [3]. Comparison of individual and group concept maps at each stage indicated that the individual maps were appreciable when compared to group concept maps at each stage of the sequential process. According to Safdar et al. [13], "If teachers learn how to construct concept maps and use them for planning and assessing lessons, they will be able to teach students better how to make concept maps to organize their thoughts and ideas". The construction of group concept maps (and subsequent discussion/interaction involved in reaching a consensus) allows pre-service teacher candidates to collaborate in the meaning-making process. At the beginning of the project, the four pre-service teacher candidates collaboratively designed a rubric to assess both their individual maps and their group maps (Table 1).

In order to meet the diverse needs of learners across the middle school environment, and in keeping with the interdisciplinary nature of the thematic unit, the pre-service teacher candidates participated in an experiential learning opportunity while using the following criteria to explore instructional practices:

  (i) Foster middle school students' scientific habits of mind and increased use of scientific vocabulary.
 (ii) Advance the ability to create rich environments for active learning to enhance teaching and learning.
(iii) Provide evidence of ability to transfer knowledge between literacy and science education content.
 (iv) Provide evidence of teacher candidates' confidence in science and literacy by providing strategies for collaborative integration of interdisciplinary content.
  (v) Provide evidence of teacher candidates' ability to decode and deconstruct complex concepts in order to recognize fundamental patterns of learning across multiple disciplines.

The participating pre-service teacher candidates were required to share their individual maps with their peers using an interactive Smart Board. They were allowed to use feedback from class discussions, comparisons, and analysis of their maps to inform their content understandings as they developed their group map for each stage of the design process, and build out to the next set of individual and group maps (Fig. 1). The rubric in Table 1 was developed by the four pre-service teacher researchers to analyze their individual and group maps. Individual pre-service teacher concept maps were analyzed according to content, and the structural parameters of the pre-service teacher maps based on accuracy of propositions were compared to the collaborative group map. During the eight-week project, pre-service teacher candidates were also exposed to hands-on activities related to the unit design process. For example, readings from *Silent Spring* and current science news were used as primary source material. Pre-service teacher candidates' comprehension of relationship between inter-disciplinary concepts was measured by whether they could accurately translate their understanding directly to the creation of unique assessments for different sections of the thematic unit.

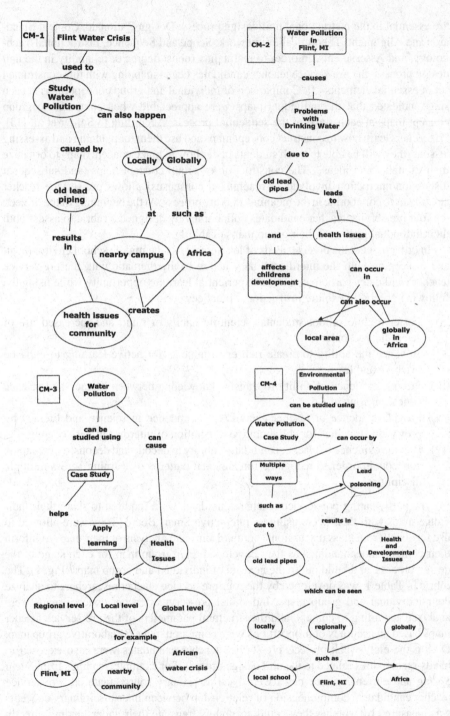

Fig. 1. Overlaps (denoted by text within Ovals) of propositions from the Final Draft concept maps constructed by each pre-service teacher candidate.

The instructor scored the group maps based on the following criteria: (i) presence of interdisciplinary cross-links; (ii) accuracy of interdisciplinary relationships; (iii) alignment to relevant standards; and (iv) proposition organization/hierarchy of concepts (Fig. 1). The final group map was scored on the completeness of the unit design and the inclusion of all elements identified as essential for the interdisciplinary unit.

4 Results

In the initial maps (individual + group), pre-service teacher candidates found it challenging to articulate the relationship between relevant interdisciplinary science content demonstrating merely rudimentary knowledge of content understanding, and an absence of accurate propositions. The initial maps showed scant hierarchy of content, limited/constrained relationship between interdisciplinary content, and naive understanding of assessment (Table 2). After initial group map presentations, there was a class discussion including immediate feedback gathered from the pre-service teacher candidates. A second set of concept maps (individual + group), was then constructed.

Table 2. Concept map analysis: individual and group cmaps (applying rubric in Table 1).

Stage of unit design	Individual Cmaps	Group Cmap
Initial draft	2 Developing/2 Superficial	Developing
Developing draft	3 Developing/1 Superficial	Developing
Improved draft	1 Exemplary/2 Target/ 1 Developing	Target - Exemplary
Final draft	1 Exemplary/3 Target	Exemplary

The second set of concept maps (individual + group), contained descriptors that showed a developing understanding of relationships between the elements of unit design. Pre-service teacher candidates were now able to see if a gap in understanding, inadequate understanding, and/or a misconception was present (Table 2). After further exposure to additional science content through research presentations on water pollution, lab activities, and online discussions, the third set of concept maps (individual + group), was created. Data shown in Table 2 indicates an interesting shift in one pre-service teacher candidate's comprehension of the interdisciplinary concepts, which moved the group concept map to a level in-between Target and Exemplary. This pre-service teacher candidate had implemented a section of her instructional planning in her seventh grade classroom. In her interaction with the middle school students, she had been able to visualize conceptual gaps in her instructional planning, which she needed to bridge in order for students to have an accurate understanding of concepts. Having the meta-tools to refine her own understanding made it possible for her to align them to students' viewpoints. She serendipitously transformed her peers' comprehension of the process, thus moving each of their concept maps to the Target level (Table 2). Analysis of the final set of concept maps (individual + group), showed that all four pre-service teacher candidates were able to articulate an advanced understanding of the unit design. The final group map provided evidence that structural development of concepts is evidently triggered by the ability to visualize misconceptions/superficial knowledge and gaps in content understanding (Fig. 1).

The comparison of propositional knowledge between the different types of concept maps (individual and group) for each set of maps indicates that there was not only a highly significant increase in content understanding for each stage of the group maps, but also that this knowledge was consolidated. The analysis of pre-service teacher candidate application of inter-disciplinary concepts used for both types of concept maps (i.e. individual and group) was specific to related design elements of the interdisciplinary unit. Such specificity allows for a valid comparison of the accuracy of propositional knowledge presented in the pre-service teacher group concept maps. Accurate relationships between elements/concepts demonstrate the degree to which the group understood how to incorporate inter-disciplinary concepts in classroom instruction. The consolidation of this knowledge largely depended on whether the pre-service teachers were able to accurately articulate their individual understanding and reach a consensus through group negotiation (Fig. 1).

End-of-term course evaluations suggest that 100 % of pre-service teachers (n = 4) reported that they benefitted from using the concept maps to monitor their own learning during the design of the inter-disciplinary unit. 50 % of the pre-service teachers (n = 2) indicated that they found concept mapping challenging because the inter-disciplinary nature of the project was challenging. All four pre-service teacher candidates reported that engaging in group discussions, and constructing sequential concept maps, helped them both figure out gaps/misconceptions in their understanding, and enhanced their self-efficacy for transforming middle school science instruction.

5   Conclusions and Implications

The findings from this study confirm concept mapping's positive impact on knowledge visualization for pre-service teacher candidate training at the undergraduate level. The capacity demonstrated by the pre-service students for distinguishing the relationship between the different science content and inter-disciplinary content areas is of critical importance. Pre-service teachers, especially those training to teach in middle school classrooms, are key in reinforcing and laying the foundation for science engagement. Therefore, more attention should be paid to the development of meta-conceptual awareness in teacher preparatory programs, so that the relationship and interdependence between content/concepts can be re-examined and ultimately reinforced. In an era of ever-increasing emphasis on accountability measures for teacher preparation, providing pre-service teachers with innovative pedagogical tools to empower classroom instruction engages students in a way that promotes meaningful learning. However, superficial pedagogical content preparation necessitates a large amount of time for re-learning and implementation, creating unique challenges and high stakes scenarios for middle school environments.

The sequential concept mapping process enabled identification of concepts with respect to an inter-disciplinary lens, which is aligned to content standards, and is fundamental to more than one discipline. The collaborative process of mapping provided a safe space for the pre-service teacher candidates to explore their own understanding, and incorporate a variety of instructional strategies in the planning process. In addition, they were able to refine the scope and sequence, task and time allocation, and selection of appropriate instructional materials. During this collaborative mapping process, the pre-service teacher candidates used peer-feedback and peer-learning to agree on why a particular concept was worth understanding and how it connected to the central concept of water pollution (both within the various disciplines of science and extending to the disciplines of literacy, math, and social studies). The final draft of the group concept map provided evidence that the pre-service teacher candidates were able to take the case study approach and extrapolate their understanding of the Flint, MI scenario to both a local (Central Georgia region,), and a global context (i.e. clean water crisis in Africa). This study suggests that concept mapping can serve as a useful tool in transforming science education by allowing pre-service teachers to promote student engagement through the design and implementation of an inter-disciplinary unit in middle school. Pre-service teacher candidates reacted positively to the use of sequential concept maps noting that it provides several benefits to their own learning, (ex. identification of gaps in/superficial understanding, promotion of collaborative learning, allowing for formative assessment) and for positively advancing their future teaching career. The findings from this study show the advantage of using sequential group concept maps in teacher preparation courses. By having the opportunity to deconstruct the limits of their content understanding, pre-service teacher candidates are empowered to engage both themselves, and their students in the learning process.

References

1. Lim, S.E., Cheng, P.W.C., Lam, M.S., Ngan, S.F.: Developing reflective and thinking skills by means of semantic mapping strategies in kindergarten teacher education. Early Child Dev. Care **173**(1), 55–72 (2003)
2. Deniz, H., Akerson, V.: Examining the impact of a professional development program on elementary teachers' views of nature of science and nature of scientific inquiry, and science teaching efficacy beliefs. Electron. J. Sci. Educ. **17**(3), 1–19 (2013)
3. Schau, C., Mattern, N., Zeilik, M., Teague, K., Weber, R.: Select-and-fill-in concept map scores as measure of students' connected understanding of science. Educ. Psychol. Measur. **61**(1), 136–158 (2001)
4. Stoddart, T., Abrams, R., Gasper, E., Canaday, D.: Concept maps as assessment in science inquiry learning- a report of methodology. Int. J. Sci. Educ. **22**(12), 1221–1246 (2000)
5. Dorough, D.K., Rye, J.A.: Mapping for understanding-using concept maps as windows to students minds. Sci. Teach. **64**(1), 36–41 (1997)
6. Reitano, P., Green, N.: Mapping expertise in social science teaching: the professional development of a beginning teacher. Crit. Reflect. Pract. Educ. **3**, 4–13 (2012)
7. Koc, M.: Pedagogical knowledge representation through concept mapping as a study and collaboration tool in teacher education. Australas. J. Educ. Technol. **28**(4), 656–670 (2012)
8. Luykx, A., Lee, O.: Measuring instructional congruence in elementary science classrooms: pedagogical and methodological components of a theoretical framework. J. Res. Sci. Teach. **44**(4), 424–447 (2007)

9. Mun, K., Kim, J., Kim, S.-W., Krajcik, J.: Exploration of high school students' concepts about climate change through the use of an issue concept map (IC-Map). In: International Conference on Science Education 2012 Proceedings, pp. 209–222 (2007)

10. Yin, Y., Vanides, J., Ruiz-Primo, M.A., Ayala, C.C., Shavelson, R.J.: Comparison of two concept-mapping techniques: implications for scoring, interpretation, and use. J. Res. Sci. Teach. **42**(2), 166–184 (2005)

11. van Boxtel, C., van der Linden, J., Roelofs, E., Erkens, G.: Collaborative concept mapping: provoking and supporting meaningful discourse. Theor. Pract., Winter (2002)

12. Gul, R., Boman, J.: Concept mapping: a strategy for teaching and evaluation in nursing education. Nurse Educ. Pract. **6**(4), 199–206 (2006)

13. Safdar, M., Hussain, A., Shah, I., Rifat, Q.: Concept maps: an instructional tool to facilitate meaningful learning. Eur. J. Educ. Res. **1**(1), 55–64 (2012)

Understanding Attitude Towards Concept Map Usage: An Exploratory Study in China

Jin-Xing Hao[1] and Yan Yu[2(✉)]

[1] BeiHang University, Beijing, China
hao@buaa.edu.cn
[2] Renmin University of China, Beijing, China
yanyu@ruc.edu.cn

Abstract. Although prior research has reported positive effects of concept mapping on teaching and learning in various education contexts, in China many students are still reluctant to accept concept mapping technologies. Therefore, education researchers require a better understanding of why learners resist or accept concept maps. In this study, we are particularly interested in proposing and evaluating a model of learner's attitude towards concept map usage in the context of undergraduate discrete mathematics education based on Technology Acceptance Model. The proposed model is evaluated by a field study with 23 undergraduate students in a famous university in China. Data analysis results using Partial Least Squares generally support our model. Perceived usefulness, perceived enjoyment and perceived ease of use are identified as key predictors of students' attitude towards concept map usage. Perceived ease of use regarding concept maps performs relatively poorer than perceived usefulness and perceived enjoyment in our field study. The dual utilitarian and hedonic characteristics of concept maps have been emphasized to improve future concept map research and practice.

Keywords: Concept map · Attitude towards usage · Technology acceptance model

1 Introduction

Concept mapping has gained increasing attention of educators in China [1]. Although prior research has reported positive effects of concept mapping on teaching and learning in various education contexts, in China many students are still reluctant to accept concept maps [2]. Therefore, education researchers require a better understanding of why learners resist or accept concept maps in general, undergraduate discrete mathematics education in particular. According to Ausubel's Assimilation Theory [3], learners' attitude takes a critical role in teaching and learning. Without learners' active participation, it would be impossible to generate meaningful learning [4]. Although investigators have widely studied the effects of concept maps, seldom study has focused on the antecedents of attitude towards concept map usage.

Attitude has been long studied by social psychology literature. It has been defined as an individual's positive or negative feelings (evaluative affect) about performing a

© Springer International Publishing Switzerland 2016
A. Cañas et al. (Eds.): CMC 2016, CCIS 635, pp. 275–286, 2016.
DOI: 10.1007/978-3-319-45501-3_22

target behavior [e.g., 5]. A person's attitude towards a behavior is determined by his or her salient beliefs about performing the target behavior [6]. Technology acceptance model (TAM) specifies the causal links between these key beliefs and user's attitude [7, 8], and it turns out to one of the most powerful theory to model new technology acceptance [9].

Discrete mathematics (DM) is a fundamental course for undergraduates majored in Information Systems. There are hundreds of abstract concepts scattered in topics of logic and proof, set theory and graph theory [10]. Students always feel difficult to understand, connect and apply these concepts. Concept map can effectively and efficiently represent domain knowledge using hierarchical structure, progressive differentiation and integrative reconciliation [11]. Therefore, we believe concept maps can provide good solutions to the above learning problems and DM education can be a desirable context to examine learners' attitude towards concept map usage.

Taken all together, in this study, we are particularly interested in proposing and evaluating a model of attitude towards concept map usage in the context of undergraduate discrete mathematics education based on TAM. Specifically, we work on the following research questions:

- What are the antecedents of attitude towards concept map usage in the context of undergraduate discrete mathematics education?
- How these factors are related together to influence learners' concept map attitude?
- What are implications to concept map research and practice?

The remaining sections of this paper are organized as follows: Section 2 reviews literature and provides our research model and hypotheses. Section 3 elaborates the employed research method. Section 4 provides results and discussions. And finally, Sect. 5 concludes the paper with limitations, implications and future work.

2   Theoretical Background and Hypotheses

In this section, we first review related theories guiding concept map practice. Based on these theories, we propose our model of concept map attitude and justify our hypotheses.

The constructivist perspective of learning highlights the active role of students during the teaching and learning process. More importantly, as the psychological foundation of concept maps, Ausubel made clear distinction between rote learning and meaningful learning, and purported three conditions of meaningful learning [3, 11]: (1) The learning material must be clearly conceptualized and presented related to the learner's prior knowledge; (2) The learner must actively process relevant prior knowledge; and (3) The learner must choose to learn meaningfully. Both conditions 2 and 3 are beyond the direct control of instructors and the motivation or attitude of students take a crucial role. This notion also aligns with Homans' [12] argument that the three elements of social behaviors – attitude, action, interaction – are interdependent: attitude leads to operations (activities) and interactions, which in turn modify attitude. Therefore, we need to clearly understand the attitude of students towards a particular learning tool, such as concept maps.

Attitude has been long studied by psychology and personality study. In prior research, it was sometimes used as a synonym for sentiment and attachment. These studies have resulted in an array of disorganized variables and incoherent themes [13]. Among these studies, the social exchange theory, the theory of reasoned action and the technology acceptance model are widely cited as the most popular theoretical foundations.

The social exchange theory (SET) was firstly brought up by George C. Homans [14, 15]. It states that all decisions about human relationships are arrived at after a subjective course of cost-reward analysis, and that social behavior is in essence a reciprocation process that involves the exchange of both tangible (such as material goods) and intangible (such as prestige) resources. In the context of learning, students are inclined to accept a learning tool when their perceived benefits brought by the tool outweigh the perceived costs incurred.

Fishbein and Ajzen's [5] theory of reasoned action (TRA) is a well-researched intention model that has proven successful in predicting and explaining behavior across a wide variety of domains including teaching and learning. According to TRA, a person's performance of a specified behavior is determined by his or her behavioral intention to perform the behavior, and behavioral intention is jointly determined by the person's attitude and subjective norm concerning the behavior in question. A person's attitude toward a behavior is determined by his or her salient beliefs about consequences of performing the behavior multiplied by the evaluation of those consequences.

TRA is very general and Davis [7] introduced an adaptation of TRA, the technology acceptance model (TAM), which is specifically meant to explain technology usage behavior. TAM uses TRA as a theoretical basis for specifying the causal linkages between three key beliefs: perceived usefulness, perceived ease of use and perceived enjoyment, and users' attitudes, intentions and actual technology adoption behavior [7, 8]. TAM is considerably less general than TRA, designed to apply only to technology usage behavior, but because it incorporates findings accumulated from decades of Information Systems research, it is especially well-suited for modeling concept map attitude.

Therefore, in this study, we define attitude towards concept map usage as an individual's positive or negative feelings (evaluative affect) about performing concept mapping in learning process. We propose the following attitude model depicted in Fig. 1.

We further provide the following hypotheses to elaborate the model in the context of undergraduate discrete mathematics education. Perceived usefulness, in this study, is defined as a learner's expectation that using concept map will result in an improved learning performance. Perceived usefulness is one of the most important key predictors of attitude in TAM. For discrete mathematics, it is not easy for students to master hundreds of abstract concept dispersed in different chapters using traditional learning tools. So it is not surprising that if students feel that concept maps will help them to achieve such a purpose, they will tend to accept such a learning tool in their current and future study. Therefore, we hypothesize that:

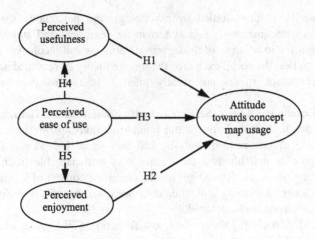

Fig. 1. Research model

H1: Perceived usefulness (PU) is positively related to attitude towards concept map usage (A).

Learners may engage in a particular behavior if it yields fun and enjoyment. In contrast with the utilitarian purpose of usefulness, perceived enjoyment refers to the extent to which the activity of using concept map is perceived to be enjoyable in it's own right, apart from any performance consequence that may be anticipated [8, 9]. Davis et al. [8] found that perceived enjoyment has significant effects on a word processing tool usage attitude. Similarly, Triandis [16] proposed that affects (i.e., the feeling of joy, elation, pleasure, disgust, displeasure) may influence behavior. For most students, discrete mathematics is generally not exciting and full of obscure and complicated proofs and calculations. In such a context, if a tool can allow them to "play" and "enjoy", they will tend to like and support to use the tool in their study. Therefore, we postulate the following hypothesis:

H2: Perceived enjoyment (PJ) is positively related to attitude towards concept map usage (A).

When learners carry out discrete mathematics tasks using concept maps, perceived ease of use can be inferred. Perceived ease of use refers to the degree to which a learner believes that using a particular tool would be free of effort. The importance of perceived ease of use is supported by Bandura's [17] self-efficacy theory. Self-efficacy theory distinguishes self-efficacy judgments from outcome judgments, the latter being similar to perceived usefulness. In the context of undergraduate discrete mathematics, if a learning tool is easy to use, it requires less effort on the part of learners, thereby, increasing the likelihood of its positive attitude toward its usage. Accordingly, we propose the following hypothesis:

H3: Perceived ease of use (PE) is positively related to attitude towards concept map usage (A).

Regarding usefulness, the easier the concept map is to use, the less effort required to carry out a given learning task. Since effort is a finite resource, the less effort that goes towards the use of a tool, the more that can be allocated to other learning tasks, which should benefit overall learning performance. However, the premise is that concept maps are assumed relevant to students' learning tasks. If students do not think a tool is useful for their study, no matter how easy the tool is, their attitude towards the tool will not likely to be positive. Similarly, we hypothesize that the perceived ease of use will also have a positive effect on enjoyment. Therefore, we have the following two hypotheses:

H4: Perceived usefulness (PU) is positively mediated the effect of perceived ease of use (PE) and attitude towards concept map usage (A).
H5: Perceived enjoyment (PJ) is positively mediated the effect of perceived ease of use (PE) and attitude towards concept map usage (A).

3   Research Method

3.1   Study Design

We have conducted a field study to test the above research model. The course was discrete mathematics taught for the information systems major in a famous university in China. The design and conduct of this field study followed principles of methodological triangulation [18]. We employed a teaching evaluation survey with Partial Least Squares (PLS) to verify the proposed model. We also used field observation and focus group analyses to solicit students' perspective regarding to concept map usage and to explain the reasons underlying the research model. The discrete mathematics course comprised of three major sections: logic and proof, set theory, and graph theory. After each section, the instructor conducted a review with a short quiz. At the same time, students were required to draw concept maps with provided concepts in this section.

In this study, we aimed to elicit the primitive attitude toward concept map usage. Therefore, the study design tried to minimize the influences of the instructor's promotion efforts. In this study, we only asked the instructor to use about 30 min to teach students how to draw a concept map with CmapTools following the guideline of Novak and Cañas [19] when the students were introduced to CmapTools for the first time. Figure 2 shows an example of a concept map drawn by a student regarding the topic of logic.

The subjects of this field study comprised second-year undergraduate students with similar backgrounds, learning and concept mapping experiences, as the vast majority of undergraduates in China had graduated directly from high schools. There were 23 students enrolled in this study. Table 1 summarizes their demographic information.

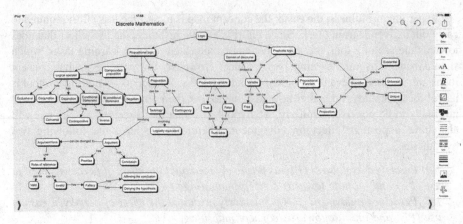

Fig. 2. A student's concept map drawn using CmapTools for iPad

Table 1. Demographic information

Age	18–20 years old with average age of 19
Gender	8 males and 15 female
Prior usage of concept maps	Majority had some experiences of concept maps, but no experience with CmapTools
Prior learning experience	Similar academic backgrounds, directly graduated from high schools
Course information	Title: Discrete Mathematics Category: Compulsory course for all Information Systems major students Duration: One semester (16 weeks)

3.2 Measures

A major source of data was a teaching evaluation survey, which guaranteed confidentiality and stated the purpose as to "evaluate the concept map usage in discrete mathematics course with no influences to the course score". Students who attended the last lecture of the semester provided anonymous feedback. Perceived usefulness, perceived ease of use and attitude were measured on a 7-point Likert scale. Perceived enjoyment was measured using 7-point semantic differential scales. The constructs with measurement items, reliability and convergent validity assessments are listed in Table 2. Perceived usefulness, perceived ease of use and attitude were measured with 3 items adapted from Davis [7]. Perceived enjoyment was measured with 3 items adapted from past enjoyment researches as Qiu and Benbasat [20] and Davis et al. [8].

Table 2. Constructs with measurement items and assessments

Constructs and measures	Loadings	AVE	CR	Alpha
Perceived Usefulness (PU)		0.709	0.880	0.800
PU1: Concept maps are helpful for me to evaluate my understanding level on the teaching materials of this class.	0.886			
PU2: Concept maps help me familiar with the teaching materials of this course.	0.789			
PU3: Concept maps are helpful for me to understand the teaching materials of this class.	0.849			
Perceived Enjoyment (PJ)		0.824	0.915	0.861
How would you best describe your mood of using concept maps?				
PJ1: Very bored … Very efficient	0.858			
PJ2: Very unpleasant … Very enjoyed	0.861			
PJ3: Very depressed … Very happy	0.932			
Perceived Ease of Use (PE)		0.782	0.933	0.900
PE1: Using concept maps is easy and simple.	0.916			
PE2: Using concept maps does not require a lot of my mental effort.	0.854			
PE3: Using concept maps is easy for me.	0.916			
Attitude towards concept maps usage (A)		0.852	0.945	0.913
A1: I like the idea of using concept maps in class.	0.895			
A2: I have a generally favorable attitude toward using concept maps in class.	0.942			
A3: I believe it is a good idea to use concept maps in class.	0.930			

Notes: All measures and statistics are significant at $p < 0.001$. AVE: Average Variance Extracted; CR: Composite Reliability; Alpha: Cronbach's Alpha.

4   Results and Discussion

4.1   Data Analysis

Survey data were analyzed in a holistic manner using the Partial Least Squares (PLS) with the bootstrap re-sampling procedure. PLS is appropriate for the investigation of research questions related to relationships among latent variables and to test the fit of a theoretical model to sample data. Specifically, PLS is able to model latent variables under conditions of non-normality, as well as being advantageous for small to medium sample size [21]. In general, the PLS has two parts: the measurement model and the structural model. The measurement model evaluates the psychometric properties of the scales used to measure latent variables, and the structural model estimates the strength of the measurement item loadings on their posited latent variables.

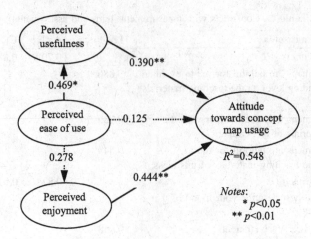

Fig. 3. The structural model

Table 3. Results of discriminant validity of constructs

Constructs	PU	PJ	PE	A
PU	**0.842**			
PJ	0.311	**0.884**		
PE	0.469	0.278	**0.908**	
A	0.586	0.600	0.432	**0.923**

Notes: Diagonal elements are the square
roots of the AVE values

Therefore, we tested structural relationships after assessing the measurement model, following the recommended two-stage analytical procedure [22]. The overall results of the PLS for this study are presented in Fig. 3. The descriptive statistics and the correlations of the latent variables are listed in Table 3.

4.2   Measurement Model Assessment

In this section, we assessed the measurement model by examining reliability, convergent validity and discriminant validity. The results are summarized in Table 2. Reliability measures the degree to which items are free from random error and generate consistent results. Cronbach's alpha is the most widely used measure for assessing reliability [23]. Cronbach's alpha ranged from 0.83 to 0.92 for all constructs, indicating high internal consistency.

Convergent validity assesses the consistency across multiple operationalizations of constructs. The convergent validity was assessed by examining composite reliability and Average Variance Extracted (AVE) from the measures. As shown in Table 2, the composite reliability of all constructs exceeds the threshold of 0.70, indicating that these measures are reliable. The AVE values range from 0.709 to 0.852, exceeding the recommended cut-off of 0.50. In addition, the path loadings of all items to constructs are above 0.70, providing further evidence for the convergent validity of measures.

Discriminant validity was tested by comparing the square roots of AVE value of each construct to the correlation of the respective construct and other constructs. Table 3 presents the discriminant validity statistics. The square roots of the AVE scores are much higher than the correlations among the constructs, demonstrating good discriminant validity.

4.3   Structural Model Assessment

Figure 3 presents the overall results of the PLS analysis of the proposed model. The overall explanatory power (R^2) is 0.548, indicating the model explains 54.8 % of the variance in attitude towards concept map usage with most path coefficients being significant, thus providing support for the research model.

The path coefficient in the structural model represents the impact of one variable on another. Specifically, the estimate coefficient of the path between perceived usefulness (PU) and attitude (A) is 0.390, which means one unit increase of perceived usefulness of concept maps will significantly increase 0.390 unit change of attitude towards concept map usage ($\beta = 0.390$, $t = 2.606$, $p < 0.01$). Therefore, it supports H1. Similarly, the path coefficient between perceived enjoyment (PJ) and attitude (A) ($\beta = 0.444$, $t = 2.612$, $p < 0.01$) supports H2, which means the more perceived enjoyment held by leaners, the better attitude towards concept map usage. However, the non-significant coefficient between perceived ease of use (PE) and attitude cannot support H3.

H4 purporting the mediation effect of PU between PE and A is supported by examining the path coefficient between PE and PU ($\beta = 0.469$, $t = 2.015$, $p < 0.05$), but H5 hypothesizing the medication effect of PJ between PE and A is not supported by this field study. The standardized coefficients, standard errors and t statistics of all path coefficients are illustrated in Table 4.

Table 4. Path coefficient with standard error and t statistic

Path	Standardized estimate	Standard error	t
H1: PU → A	0.390	0.155	2.606**
H2: PJ → A	0.444	0.177	2.612**
H3: PE → A	0.125	0.154	0.811
H4: PE → PU	0.469	0.233	2.015*
H5: PE → PJ	0.278	0.254	1.097

Notes: * $p < 0.05$; ** $p < 0.01$

4.4   Discussions

The purpose of the study was to investigate the influencing factors of concept map usage in discrete mathematics education for Chinese undergraduate students based on

Technology Acceptance Model. As hypothesized, our field study confirmed the significant direct effects of perceived usefulness ($\beta = 0.390$, $t = 2.606$, $p < 0.01$) and perceived enjoyment ($\beta = 0.444$, $t = 2.612$, $p < 0.01$) on attitude towards concept map usage. Such conclusions are consistent with prior research on general technology acceptance. These findings are also supported by a focus group conducted at the end of the semester. Nearly all participants mentioned that concept maps were very useful for them to review what they had learned and to establish connections among hundreds of abstract mathematics concepts. One participant emphasized that "Concept maps turn out to be very useful only when you draw them by yourself." In addition, most of participants enjoyed the drawing process with CmapTools, especially the iPad version. They also expressed they would continue to use them in their future study and other courses.

However, it worth noting the difference of path coefficients between perceived usefulness and perceived enjoyment on attitude. Prior research following the TAM by and large confirms the perceived usefulness is the strongest predictor of usage attitude, and the effect of perceived enjoyment is consistently weaker than the effects of perceived usefulness [9]. However, in this field study, we find that the path coefficient of perceived usefulness is actually weaker than that of perceived enjoyment in Table 4 ($\beta = 0.390$ vs. 0.444). It may be explained by the customer behavior literature, which distinguishes between utilitarian and hedonic technologies [24]. In contrast to utilitarian technologies, which serve to provide instrumental value to users and to improve the task performance, hedonic technologies aim to provide self-fulfilling value to users and to seek a pleasurable experience. Based on our findings, concept maps might have both characteristics of utilitarian and hedonic technologies. Taking the course of discrete mathematics for example, on one hand, students would like to use concept maps to understand and integrate the knowledge of predicate logic with set theory; on the other hand, students expected a pleasurable instrument to play with during such an abstract symbolic study process.

Another interesting finding is that we cannot find the significant direct effect of perceived ease of use on attitude. This leads to a full mediation effect of perceived usefulness on the relation between perceived ease of use and attitude towards concept map usage. Prior literature identifies the significant effect of perceived ease of use appearing in general technologies, such as email, mobile payment, etc. However, such insignificant direct effect in concept map usage may reflect the relative difficulty of use of concept maps. We utilized PLS to estimate the scores of latent variables and to compute the means and standard deviations of PU (Mean = 7.00, S.D. = 0.78), PJ (Mean = 6.13, S.D. = 1.45) and PE (Mean = 5.33, S.D. = 1.79). We find that students' PE regarding concept maps is significant lower than PU ($t = 5.08$, $p < 0.01$) and PJ ($t = 2.13$, $p < 0.05$) by t-test. This may be caused by two reasons. First, compared with other learning tools, concept maps may involve more cognitive effort, which makes student feel not easy. Second, the concept map software systems, such as CmapTools, are not so user friendly. Participants of the focus group challenged the Chinese interface of CmapTools. The iPad-verson of CmapTools was better but it still could not meet the increasing demands of students in terms of ease of use.

5   Conclusions and Implications

In this study, we explored the influencing factors of learners' attitude towards concept map usage and their relations in the context of undergraduate discrete mathematics course. Based on the technology acceptance model, we proposed a model of attitude toward concept map usage. The model is evaluated by a field study with 23 undergraduate students in a famous university in China. Data analysis results using PLS generally support our model.

There are several limitations of this study. Firstly, due to class size, the sample size is relatively small, which may limit the generalizations of the conclusions. In the future, we will extend our research by involving more samples. Secondly, we will consider more influencing factors such as individual psychological characteristics of participants and perceived difficulty of learning materials to get a more integrative model of attitude towards concept map usage. Lastly, the cross-sectional survey used in this study limits the exploration of the dynamics of concept mapping usage. A longitudinal study and a field experiment with a control group can be designed to examine this issue and to strengthen our research results.

Notwithstanding, our study has important theoretical and practical implications. Our study refined technology acceptance model in the context of concept map-based study. Although the general conclusions are consistent with prior research, our study has revealed several interesting findings, which extend the study of concept mapping. Firstly, perceived usefulness, perceived enjoyment and perceived ease of use are identified as key predictors of attitude towards concept map usage. These predictors are deserved intensive study to improve concept map research. Secondly, we conjecture concept maps have both utilitarian and hedonic characteristics. Most current study on concept maps can be categorized on the utilitarian perspective, such as the cognitive foundations and curriculum design of concept-map based education. However, in the future, it is suggested to put more attentions on hedonic perspective of concept maps, such as playfulness and pleasure involved during the concept mapping process. Thirdly, although perceived of ease of use is not a significant direct predictor influencing attitude in this field study, it is still an important, however, poor-performed factor to encumber the acceptance of concept map by Chinese students. More work should be carried out to improve the ease of use of concept map software.

Acknowledgements. This Research Project is partially supported by National Science Foundation of China (Nos. 71101005, 71471011, 71571184), Beijing Natural Science Foundation (No. 9142011), Beijing Social Science Foundation (No. 13JGC092), Fundamental Research Funds for the Central Universities of BeiHang University, and Teaching Development Grant of BeiHang University.

References

1. Hao, J.-X., Tang, R., Yu, Y.: Eye movement patterns of concept map novices: an exploratory study on Chinese tertiary students. In: Proceedings of the 6th International Conference on Concept Mapping (CMC 2014), Santos, Brazil (2014)

2. Zhao, G.: Concept map and mind map in teaching and learning in China. e-Educ. Res. **2012** (5), 78–84. doi:10.13811/j.cnki.eer.2012.05.014

3. Ausubel, D.P.: Educational Psychology: A Cognitive View. Holt, Rinehart and Winston, New York (1968)

4. Novak, J.D.: Meaningful learning: the essential factor for conceptual change in limited or inappropriate propositional hierarchies leading to empowerment of learners. Sci. Educ. **86**, 548–571 (2002)

5. Fishbein, M., Ajzen, I.: Belief, Attitude, Intention and Behavior: An Introduction to Theory and Research. Addison-Wesley, Reading (1975)

6. Ajzen, I.: Fishbein, M: Understanding Attitudes and Predicting Social Behavior. Prentice-Hall, Englewood Cliffs (1980)

7. Davis, F.D.: Perceived usefulness, perceived ease of use, and user acceptance of information technology. MIS Q. **13**(3), 319–340 (1989)

8. Davis, F.D., Bagozzi, R.P., Warshaw, P.R.: Extrinsic and intrinsic motivation to use computers in the workplace. J. Appl. Soc. Psychol. **22**(14), 1111–1132 (1992)

9. Van der Heijden, H.: User acceptance of hedonic information systems. MIS Q. **28**(4), 695–704 (2004)

10. Rosen, K.H.: Discrete Mathematics and Its Applications, 7th edn. McGraw-Hill, Singapore (2012)

11. Novak, J.D., Gowin, B.: Learning How to Learn. Cambridge University Press, London (1984)

12. Homans, G.C.: A conceptual scheme for the study of social organization. Am. Sociol. Rev. **12**(1), 13–26 (1947)

13. Davis, F.D., Bagozzi, R.P., Warshaw, P.R.: User acceptance of computer technology: a comparison of two theoretical models. Manag. Sci. **35**(8), 982–1003 (1989)

14. Cropanzano, R., Mitchell, M.S.: Social exchange theory: an interdisciplinary review. J. Manag. **31**(6), 874–900 (2005)

15. Homans, G.C.: Social behavior as exchange. Am. J. Sociol. **63**, 597–606 (1958)

16. Triandis, H.C.: Attitude and Attitude Change. Wiley, New York (1971)

17. Bandura, A.: Self-effcacy mechanism in human agency. Am. Psychol. **37**, 122–147 (1982)

18. Lee, A.S.: Integrating positivist and interpretive approaches to organizational research. Organ. Sci. **2**(4), 342–365 (1992)

19. Novak, J.D., Cañas, A.J.: The theory underlying concept maps and how to construct and use them. Technical report IHMC CmapTools 2006-01, Institute for Human and Machine Cognition (IHMC) (2006)

20. Qiu, L.Y., Benbasat, I.: A study of demographic embodiments of product recommendation agents in electronic commerce. Int. J. Hum.–Comput. Stud. **68**, 669–688 (2010)

21. Chin, W.W.: The partial least squares approach for structural equation modelling. In: Marcoulides, G.A. (ed.) Modern Methods for Business Research, pp. 295–336. Lawrence Erlbaum Associates, Mahwah (1998)

22. Anderson, J.C., Gerbing, D.W.: Structural equation modelling in practice: a review and recommended two-step approach. Psychol. Bull. **103**(3), 411–423 (1988)

23. Cronbach, L.: Coefficient alpha and internal structure of tests. Psychometrika **1951**(16), 297–334 (1951)

24. Hirschman, E.C., Holbrook, M.B.: Hedonic consumption: emerging concepts, methods and propositions. J. Mark. **46**(3), 92–101 (1982)

Using Concept Mapping to Assess 4- and 5-Year Old Children's Knowledge in the Robotics and Programming for Prekindergarten Project

Bronwyn McLemore[✉], Stephanie Wehry, Deborah Carlson, Heather Monroe-Ossi, Cheryl Fountain, and Madelaine Cosgrove

University of North Florida, Jacksonville, USA
{bmclemor, swehry, d.carlson, h.monroe-ossi, cheryl.fountain, mcosgrov}@unf.edu

Abstract. The purpose of this paper is to report on the concept map evaluation of an innovative STEM project for 4- and 5-year-old children. An American university research team developed and implemented a 3-month pilot program using engineering and robotics as the platform for teaching programming and problem solving. The engineering-focused lessons used a developmentally, age appropriate robot (KIBO) to teach simple programming skills while practicing a problem solving process designed to transfer to other settings. Researchers delivered the twice weekly lessons, integrated into the adopted prekindergarten curriculum, and implemented as part of the established center rotations. Researchers used child interviews and concept mapping as a measure of children's knowledge of robotics and problem solving to estimate growth in their knowledge over time. Results indicated that the children exhibited increased knowledge of robotics, 93 %, and problem solving, 42 %, mostly resulting from the increased use of propositions and cross-links.

Keywords: Concept mapping · Robotics · Programming · Engineering · Early childhood · Problem solving · Prekindergarten

1 Introduction

The purpose of this paper is to report on the concept map evaluation of the Robotics and Programming for Prekindergarten (RAPP) project. Because many jobs currently require proficiency in science, technology, engineering and mathematics (STEM) skills, the National Science Board advised President Obama in 2009 to make STEM education a priority in early childhood education [1]. The RAPP project, designed to prepare children for success in our increasingly complex world, teaches the skills, knowledge, and expertise needed to function in the 21st century. To work towards this goal, an American research center developed and implemented a 3-month pilot project focused on providing 4- and 5-year-old prekindergarten children opportunities to learn about robotics, programming, and problem solving. The research team used concept

© Springer International Publishing Switzerland 2016
A. Cañas et al. (Eds.): CMC 2016, CCIS 635, pp. 287–302, 2016.
DOI: 10.1007/978-3-319-45501-3_23

mapping to assess students' knowledge near the beginning and the end of the RAPP project when the team interviewed the children about the lesson objectives.

1.1 Robotics and Programming in Early Childhood

Most prekindergarten classrooms offer few opportunities for children to engage in activities involving real-world science [2, 3]. Young children's natural curiosity and intuitive sense of technology and engineering are even more rarely nurtured in typical prekindergarten classrooms. The common science focus in early childhood is under-standing the natural world. Though this is an important area of science for young learners to understand, it is also crucial that we develop their knowledge of the sur-rounding man-made world [4]. Knowledge of the man-made world is the domain of technology and engineering, which focuses on the development and application of tools, machines, and processes that solve human problems.

There is a substantial body of research documenting the benefits of integrating robotic technologies into the early childhood classroom in developmentally appropriate ways [4–7]. Over the past decade, research on developmentally appropriate practices with technology indicates that 4-year olds can understand the basic concepts of com-puter programming and can build and program simple robotic projects [4] and [8]. As a tool, robotics helps make abstract ideas more concrete, which is an important condition of learning for 4-year olds in Piaget's pre-operational stage model. Robotic manipu-latives help children learn about abstract mathematical and science concepts in a concrete way and assist in the development of technological fluency through the introduction of engineering and programming [6]. Research shows that programming can help young children improve visual memory, basic number sense, problem-solving techniques, and language skills [9]. Programming also directly relates to foundational concepts including patterns, sequencing, modularity, and cause-and-effect.

1.2 Robotics and Programming Project

The purpose of the RAPP project was to develop, implement, and embed innovative engineering lessons in the classrooms of 4- and 5-year-old children. But first, researchers had to select a robot for the project. For a robot to be developmentally appropriate for this project, the RAPP research team wanted it to be interactive, require no screen time, use lights and sounds to engage children, and provide opportunities for creative building or transformation. Several robotic kits designed for children at least 8-years old met most of the selected criteria (e.g. LEGO Mindstorms, Microbic Edison, and Wonder Workshop Dash and Dot). Three robotic kits, designed for children as young as 4-years old, met most of the criteria: Bee-Bot, Electronic Blocks, and KIBO. The RAPP team selected KIBO, developed by DevTech at Tufts University, because it met most of the project's requirements. KIBO, designed for 4- to 7-year olds, is interactive, has an embedded bar code scanner so that no screen time is required, and uses tangible programming blocks with functions described using icons for pre-readers and words for readers [10]. Figure 1 shows a picture of KIBO and a program made of tangible blocks.

Fig. 1. KIBO with wheels, a motor for the rotating art platform, the light, and an eye light sensor; the tangible programming blocks; and a complete KIBO program ready to be scanned.

The RAPP research team developed a set of engineering and robotics lessons for teachers to use in their prekindergarten classrooms. The lessons focused on what engineers do and how they solve problems, provided an introduction to programming, and engaged children in creating programs to solve problems using a robot. During the project, children had opportunities to use problem solving in a programming context. RAPP researchers implemented the lessons using a 4-step problem solving process titled Solve It 4 [11]. Figure 2 presents an overview of the RAPP project.

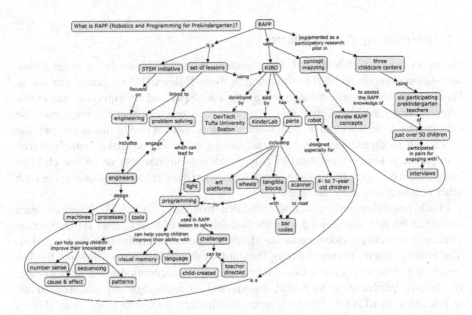

Fig. 2. An overview of the robotics and programming project.

2 Research Design

The following sections describe the childcare centers, teachers, and children who partnered with the research team in the pilot implementation of RAPP; the data; and the research methodology. Data collected for this paper include child interviews, their transcriptions, and the scored concept maps.

2.1 Participants and Data

The effort to develop, iteratively refine, and evaluate RAPP involved a partnership between a university research team, experienced working with young children, and six prekindergarten teachers from three local, urban childcare centers. The six teachers working with the researchers taught prekindergarten classes. All teachers implemented KIBO lessons in the mornings and two also used KIBO in the afternoons. All of the teachers were female, and five were Black and the other Asian. At one of the childcare centers, all of the participating children were Black, and, at the other two childcare centers, the children were ethnically diverse. Classes at one of the childcare centers included several children with special needs. The number of children in each classroom ranged from a low of 10 to a high of 18. The teachers participated in a 3-h professional development workshop designed to teach about programming KIBO and debugging programs. Researchers implemented lessons twice weekly in each classroom from the beginning of March through the end of May, 2016. Data reported in this paper include results from both sets of child interviews.

2.2 Interviewing Young Children

Interviewing young children and the subsequent transcriptions of the interviews form one measure used in the RAPP evaluation. Roberts-Holmes [12] suggested that young children can feel uncomfortable in one-to-one interviews and are especially vulnerable when strangers ask them questions. Therefore, it is essential that the interviewer be very familiar to the children. In fact, when strangers conduct one-to-one interviews, the results can be disempowering, and, thus, unethical. A way to make young children comfortable is to interview them in groups. Roberts-Holmes also stated that children enjoy the social aspect of the focus-group setting, are more relaxed, and encourage each other in articulating their thoughts.

Each researcher interviewed the children that they taught. The research team scheduled the first interviews during the first full week of March, after the completion of three lessons, to provide time for the children to become familiar with the researcher. The final interviews occurred during the third week of May, 2016 following the last lesson. We chose to interview two children at a time to accommodate the large number of children participating in RAPP lessons and to encourage shy children. When interacting with KIBO during the lessons, the children worked in pairs. Thus, pairing them for the interviews was an efficient and logical choice.

The classroom teachers selected pairs of children for each researcher to interview. Two focal questions shaped the interviews: What do you know about KIBO? What do you know about problem solving? Visual aids used during the interviews included the KIBO vocabulary card (Fig. 3) for the first question and the Solve It 4 poster for the second question (Fig. 4). The picture, Fig. 5, shows a girl working with the vocabulary cards.

Fig. 3. KIBO vocabulary card (with a QR code in the place of the word KIBO). A short video about the KIBO robot is available by scanning the code.

Fig. 4. Solve It 4 Poster

The researchers used the visual aids as they asked the focal questions to make the children more comfortable (seeing something familiar) and to maintain the children's focus on the topics. The interview process and the interviewed pairs were the same at both interview times.

2.3   Literal Note-Taking

One method to transcribe interviews is literal note-taking [13], a process used to collect data that serves as evidence when making claims, interpretations, and judgements about observations. The purpose of collecting interview data was to establish a measure of the children's knowledge necessary to investigate growth over time. Of great importance, due to the age of the children and specificity of the content, was the need for the literal note-taker to be familiar with the concepts and implementation of the project.

Fig. 5. A girl matching the vocabulary cards to the programming blocks.

The RAPP research team selected literal note-taking [13] as the means of transferring audio recordings of children's interviews to written word ready for concept mapping. One of the RAPP researchers, highly trained in literal note-taking, provided the non-verbatim transcriptions necessary for creating the concept maps. This researcher listened to each interview three times: the first to take literal notes and the other times to adjust the notes as necessary. Another team member read the transcripts while listening to the recordings to verify the completeness and accuracy of the literal notes, thus, validating the process.

2.4   Concept Maps and Scoring

Concept mapping is documented as a strategy for examining children's understanding of relationships among concepts [14]. Researchers at the Institute of Human and Machine Cognition summarized the uses of concept mapping in educational settings to include support for learning, assessment of learning, and for the organization and presentation of knowledge. Assessment applications of concept mapping included formative and summative assessments, and, as such, the documentation of changes in children's conceptual knowledge [15]. Many researchers have used concept maps to assess young children's knowledge [16–20].

The scoring system used in the present study [21], is an adaptation of a system developed by Novak and Gowin [14]. The scores for propositions are similar to that proposed by several researchers [22–24]. Three components of the concept map receive scores: propositions, cross-links, and hierarchy. The total concept map score is the sum of the component scores. Propositions receive no points if incorrect or not relevant, one point if only somewhat relevant, two points if they provide a quality link to the concept, and three points if the link is a causation. Propositions receiving two or three points are quality propositions. A cross-link scores five points when it connects two quality propositions, but is does not receive proposition points. The focal concept on the concept map is the first level and receives no points. A second level occurs when three or more quality propositions connect to the focal concept and results in five points. Each consecutive level containing three or more quality propositions results in five points. A generalizability study of the scoring system [19] indicated that the interrater reliability was .96, .86, .83, and .95 for the propositions, cross-links, levels, and total score, respectively.

A team member with the most concept mapping experience mapped the transcripts created using literal note-taking. Three researchers, all with concept mapping experience, scored the 71 concept maps from the first interview (36 KIBO and 35 problem solving concept maps) and the 51 concept maps from the second interview (27 KIBO and 27 problem solving concept maps). Figure 6 shows concept maps typical of those from the first child interviews. The figure also shows the scoring of the concept maps.

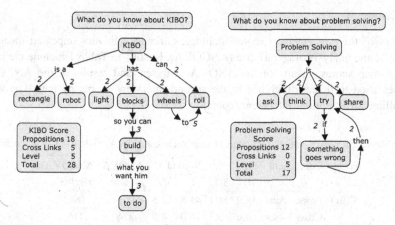

Fig. 6. Concept maps derived from an interview that reflects the typical first interview. The concept maps also show the scoring of each map.

3   Results

The following section reports on data collection including participants and attrition. The analyses section reports the results of a repeated measures analysis of variance (ANOVA) used to detect potential differences between the concept map scores from the first and second child interviews. Finally, the section reports results of the analyses of covariance (ANCOVA) used to detect potential differences in concept map scores from the second set of interviews controlling for the first interview scores and by the type of the children's interview pairings.

3.1   Data

Final data included 27 concepts maps for each question from 51 children which represents 28 % attrition. The first interview data included 16 boy-girl pairs, nine all-boy pairs, eight all-girl pairs, and three single-child girl interviews. The second interview data included 15 boy-girl pairs, four all-boy pairs, five all-girl pairs, and three single-child girl interviews. Thus, attrition resulted in losing interviews from nine pairs of children. To determine whether the attrition was systematic or occurred at random, we used ANOVA to detect any differences in the first interview total concept map scores of the pairs remaining in the study and of those pairs lost to the study. Results indicated that the first interview mean scores of the children lost to the study were not statistically different from the mean scores of the children who were not lost, $p = .237$ and $p = .303$ for the KIBO and problem solving concept map totals, respectively. However, the point estimates of the mean scores of the children lost to the study were lower, and, in a study with more power, these differences may have been statistically lower.

3.2   Analyses

Analyses of the concept map scores included summary statistics, repeated measures ANOVA, and analysis of covariance (ANCOVA). Results in Table 1 include the mean concept map scores, results of the ANOVA analyses, and results of the ANCOVA analyses used to detect difference in the second interview scores by pair type when controlling for the initial interview scores.

Table 1. Summary statistics of concept map scores, ANOVA, and ANCOVA results

Focus	Component	First		Second		ANOVA	ANCOVA
		M	SD	M	SD	p-value	p-value
KIBO	Propositions	18.9	11.1	41.8	12.5	<.001***	.096§
	Cross-Links	4.6	5.3	6.0	4.5	.326	.416
	Levels	6.9	3.2	10.8	4.3	.023**	.109
	Total	30.4	15.4	58.6	18.0	<.001***	.116
PS	Propositions	11.7	7.2	17.7	3.8	<.001***	.586
	Cross-Links	1.5	3.8	1.4	2.3	.935	<.001§
	Levels	6.2	3.9	8.4	2.5	.007***	.555
	Total	19.4	13.2	27.5	7.1	.002***	.056§

Note. *** indicates a statistically significant result at $p < .01$, ** indicates a statistically significant result at $p < .05$, and *indicates a statistically significant result at $p < .10$. § indicates a statistically significant interaction between the pair types and the time. PS is problem solving.

As can be seen, on average, the total concept map scores increased for both the KIBO and problem solving concepts, $p < .001$ and $p = .002$, respectively. The KIBO concept map scores increased from the first to second interview by 93 %, and the problem solving scores increased by 42 %. The KIBO propositions and level component scores also increased, $p < .001$ and $p = .023$, respectively. The KIBO propositions and level scores increased from the first to second interviews by 120 % and 57 %, respectively. The problem solving propositions and level component scores also increased, $p < .001$ and $p = .007$, respectively. The problem solving propositions and level scores increased from the first to second interviews by 51 % and 34 %, respectively. The cross-link component scores in both concept maps, on average, did not decrease from the first to the second interview.

The ANCOVA results indicated that, on average, there were no differences in the results by the four pairing groups on all but three of the analyses. On the KIBO propositions score, the analysis indicated an interaction between the time of the interview and the pairing groups, $p = .096$. On two of the problem solving scores, cross-links and total map scores, the analyses of the interaction between time and pairing groups was statistically significant, $p = < .001$ and $p = .056$, respectively. The three interactions resulted from the highest scores in the first round interviews being lower than in the second round of interviews.

The concept maps shown in Fig. 6 are from the first interviews. The typical KIBO concept map received 30.4 total points and component scores of 18.9, 4.6, and 6.9 points for the propositions, cross-links, and levels, respectively. The typical problem solving concept map received 19.4 total points and component scores of 11.7, 1.5, and 6.2 points for the propositions, cross-links, and levels, respectively.

The concept maps shown in Figs. 7 and 8 are from the second interviews. The concept map shown in Fig. 7 represents the typical KIBO concept map scores. The typical KIBO concept map received 58.6 total points and component scores of 41.8, 6.0, and 10.8 points for the propositions, cross links, and levels, respectively.

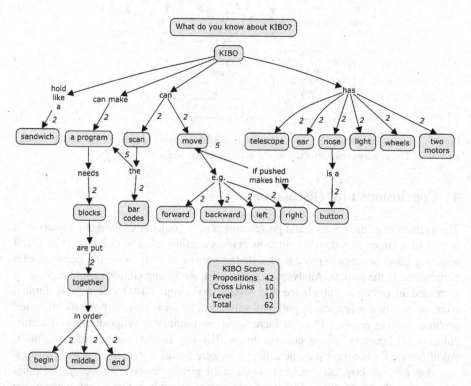

Fig. 7. Concept map that reflects the typical KIBO concept map at the second interviews. The concept map also shows the scoring of the map.

The concept map shown in Fig. 8 represents the typical second interview problem solving concept map scores. The typical concept map received 27.5 total points and component scores of 17.7, 1.4, and 8.4 points for the propositions, cross-links, and levels, respectively.

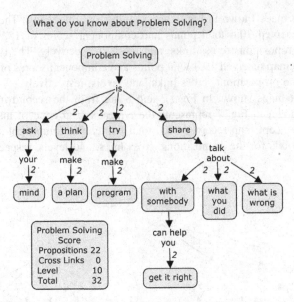

Fig. 8. Concept map that reflects the typical problem solving concept map at the second interview. The concept map also shows the scoring of the map.

4   Conclusions and Discussions

The evaluation of the robotics and programming pilot project that used child interviews is part of a larger mosaic of evaluation evidence collected. The child interviews and resulting concept maps represent knowledge gained directly from the children who participated in the project. Analyses suggested that the young children could express an increased hierarchical knowledge and vocabulary about KIBO and a more limited increase in knowledge about problem solving. The increases in both robotics and problem solving resulted from an increase in the number of propositions and hierarchical levels present in the concept maps, but not in the number of cross-links. Additionally, for the most part, no differences were found among the types of pairings, boy and girl, all boy, all girl, and single-child girl interviews. However, the point estimates of the mean scores indicated that across all eight analyses, on average, the single-child girl concept maps were the lowest scoring maps.

4.1   Use of Data

Throughout the implementation of RAPP, researchers used the information learned from the first set of concept maps to guide the remaining instruction. Researchers engaged children in frequent conversations about problem solving to strengthen their vocabulary and thinking about concepts. The RAPP team made vocabulary-word review a part of each lesson. Researchers also sang the RAPP songs more frequently because singing engaged the children and kept them focused.

Results indicated that the children learned more about KIBO after three lessons than anticipated. The RAPP implementation structure calls for the researcher to lead the RAPP lessons independently of the classroom teachers. In some cases, the childcare teacher was present and observed the lesson, and in other cases, she was not. However, early project assessments indicated that the six partnering teachers used KIBO in their classrooms independently of the RAPP researcher and developed unique opportunities for the children's learning. The RAPP researchers saw evidence of children implementing activities with KIBO that had not yet been taught in the RAPP lessons. The research team believes that having the teacher work with the children using the robot was key to how quickly the children learned the lesson concepts.

4.2 Child Interviews

The child interview process involved three facets: the actual interview, transcription of the interview, and mapping the transcriptions. We discuss all three facets in the following sections.

Interviews. RAPP researchers conducted 24 of the interviews using pairs of children with the pairings selected by the children's classroom teacher. Researchers working with the vast majority of the children thought that the pairings worked well and that the children's interviews support the view of Roberts-Holmes [12] that children enjoyed the social aspect of the group settings, were more relaxed, and encouraged each other in articulating their thoughts. Data suggested that higher concept maps scores were from pairs of children, however, results of analyses are inconclusive. Continued use of the practice would necessitate training interviewers to use similar techniques when prompting the children's responses. Prompts can range from tightly scripted phrases to an open-ended interview that is similar to a conversation. The effectiveness of the interview depends upon the skill of the interviewer, however, consistency is important to the validity of the process. The team also needs to streamline the interview process to address overly enthusiastic and talkative children, thus, providing more opportunities for shy children to speak up.

Transcriptions. The RAPP team selected literal note-taking [13] to transfer the sound recordings from the interview to transcript. We believe that using our team member with expertise in literal note-taking reduced the amount of time necessary to obtain transcripts by at least 50 % with no measurable loss in accuracy. A second member of the RAPP team checked each non-verbatim transcript against the audio recordings and found three mistakes in the 36 first interview transcripts. One error was trivial and the other two would result in a 2-point error in the concept maps. However, using this process on a larger scale would require the training of multiple team members in the literal note-taking process. Interrater reliability would need to be established at the rate of at least 80 %. This would take planning, resources, and a committed effort to this process. An alternative approach would be to hire persons trained in verbatim transcription.

Concept Mapping. One member of the research team mapped all of the transcripts. At the time of the first interviews, a different member checked the concept maps against the transcripts and found very few omissions. However, the second interviews were much more complicated, particularly about the robot because of the children's increased knowledge and programming skills. For the most part, the children spoke in a stream of consciousness style resulting in the interview representing thoughts as they passed through their minds without a mental framework for their thinking. Thus, for many of the interviews, the mapper added the framework using knowledge of the lessons and the concepts; however, the concept maps frequently reflect the order of the concepts in the transcript. Therefore, the mapping researcher's mental structures were also represented in the concept maps. For example, one child said, "The black stripes cause KIBO to move." The mapper's initial thinking was that the child referred to the bar codes on the programming blocks, but after discussing this with the interviewer, the mapper realized that the child was speaking of the black stripe on the wheels. The mapper knew that the stripes were not decoration, but rather a rubber insert to produce the friction that indeed caused KIBO to move. Because the mapper has more than a basic knowledge of force and motion, the resulting concept map scored higher than it might have if one of the other researchers were mapping. The complexity shown in the second interview concept maps suggests that inter-mapper reliability needs further investigation.

4.3   KIBO and Problem Solving Concept Map Difference

RAPP lessons embraced the engineering design process, focusing on how engineers solve problems which is the focus of the first lessons. Thus, the research team felt that problem solving even though an abstract concept, was fundamental to the RAPP experience. As such, the implementers used the Solve It 4, a simplified engineering cycle (ask, think, try, and share) presented in Fig. 4, throughout the lessons and as a visual aid in the interviews. However, the Solve It 4 poster represents a cycle rather than a hierarchy and requires dynamic thinking. Derbentseva et al. [25] suggested that concept maps can be static representing a hierarchy or dynamic representing concepts that change or cycle. At the very least, dynamic thinking requires a different kind of focus question than hierarchical thinking, and, thus, we should not be surprised that we got static, semi-hierarchical concept maps using our static focus question about problem solving. In several instances, the children attempted to describe problem solving as a cycle. For example, in Fig. 6, the map shows an if-then statement with a cycle involving try. Other examples of dynamic thinking are presented in the list of statements made by the children in the first interviews that represent dynamic thinking and include examples of problem solving.

- If you didn't have a wall, then the whole house would break apart.
- Problem solving is when someone is like hungry and then we can go to the store and get some groceries for the food for them to eat.
- When you need something that you cannot get, you can just ask (pause) then you can just borrow some money.

- If you didn't have a toilet, then you couldn't go potty.
- If you have a problem cleaning up your toys and you have to call the engineer to have him bring you a box so the toys don't get lost.
- If you don't have something you really need, an engineer can build it.
- If you don't have any friends and you need one, an engineer will make you one.
- You have to problem solve if you are an engineer.

The second interviews of some of the children, in accordance with Derbentseva et al. [25], resulted in cross-links to indicate dynamic thinking. The KIBO concept map presented in Fig. 9 shows the use of the programming blocks to solve a KIBO problem.

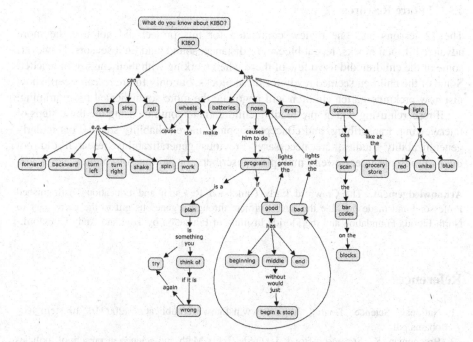

Fig. 9. Concept map showing the children's hierarchical thinking and incorporating the problem solving knowledge relevant to programming KIBO.

4.4   Limitations of the Study

The size of the study limits the potential power of the analyses. The design is actually a Hierarchal Linear Model (HLM) because the children were nested pairs (27) nested in classes (6) which were nested in researcher/childcare centers (3), thus, the analyses potentially involves three levels with the context of the childcare center confounded with the style of the particular researcher working with the children at the center. Further limitations result from the imbalance of the study at the researcher level: one researcher worked with three classes, one with two classes, and one with one class.

Another limitation of the study is the level of attrition, 28 %. Analyses indicated that the attrition did not result from the loss of the children with lower scoring first interview concept maps, but that does not necessarily mean it occurred at random. Most of the attrition was caused by the inability to interview one member of a pair. The project concluded at the end of the school year which is the time for prekindergarteners' graduation. Most of the children will matriculate from a privately owned childcare center to public school kindergarten classes in neighborhood schools. As such, much pomp and circumstance surrounds the end of the year which involves lots of practice time. This results in less time for the research agenda.

4.5   Future Research

The 12 lessons and one review conducted for this project did not use the more advanced if-then blocks; repeat blocks; or distance, sound, and light sensors. However, some of the children did use a few of these when working with their classroom teacher. Some of the children seemed ready for these blocks, but only future research will show just how prekindergarten children will negotiate the more sophisticated programming.

If research using young, pre-reading children is to continue using the three steps of interviewing, transcribing, and concept mapping, more reliability studies, particularly generalizability studies, are necessary. Previous generalizability research did not involve multiple interviewers, multiple transcribers, or pairings of children.

Acknowledgement. The Crawford Early Childhood Research and Education Distinguished Professor Fund made possible the RAPP project through a generous gift to the University of North Florida Foundation and the Florida Institute of Education by Toni and Andy Crawford.

References

1. National Science Board. https://www.nsf.gov/nsb/publications/2009/01_10_stem_rec_obama.pdf
2. Brenneman, K., Stevenson-Boyd, J., Frede, E.C.: Math and science in preschool: policies and practice. Presch. Policy Brief **19**, 1–12 (2009)
3. Greenfield, D., Jirout, J., Dominguez, X., Greenberg, A., Maier, M., Fuccillo, J.: Science in the preschool classroom: a programmatic research agenda to improve science readiness. Early Educ. Dev. **20**, 238–264 (2009)
4. Bers, M.: Blocks to Robots: Learning with Technology in the Early Childhood Classroom. Teacher's College Press, New York (2008)
5. Bers, M.U., Ponte, I., Juelich, K., Viera, A., Schenker, J.: Teachers as designers: integrating robotics into early childhood education. Inf. Technol. Child. Educ. **1**, 123–145 (2002)
6. Rogers, C., Portsmore, M.: Bringing engineering to elementary school. J. STEM Educ.: Innov. Res. **5**(3), 17 (2004)
7. Weyth, P.: How young children learn to program with sensor, action, and logic blocks. J. Learn. Sci. **17**, 517–550 (2008)

8. Cejka, E., Rogers, C., Portsmore, M.: Kindergarten robotics: using robotics to motivate math, science, and engineering literacy in elementary school. Int. J. Eng. Educ. **22**, 711–722 (2006)
9. Clements, D.H.: The future of educational computing research: the case of computer programming. Inf. Technol. Child. Educ. Annu. **1**, 147–179 (1999)
10. Sullivan, A., Bers, M.U.: Robotics in the early childhood classroom: learning outcomes from an 8-week robotics curriculum in pre-kindergarten through second grade. Int. J. Technol. Des. Educ. **26**, 3–20 (2016)
11. Center on the Social and Emotional Foundations of Early Learning. http://csefel.vanderbilt. edu/resources/training_preschool.html#mod2
12. Roberts-Holmes, G.: Doing Your Early Years Research Project. Sage Publications Ltd., London (2014)
13. Ribas, W.R.: Teacher Evaluations that Work!!, 2nd edn. Ribas Publications, Westwood (2005)
14. Novak, J.D., Gowin, D.B.: Learning How to Learn. Cambridge University Press, New York (1984)
15. Cañas, A.J., Coffey, J.W., Carnot, M.J., Feltovich, P., Hoffman, R.R., Feltovich, J., Novak, J.D.: A summary of literature pertaining to the use of concept mapping techniques and technologies for education and performance support, IHMC report (2003)
16. Cassata-Widera, A.E.: Concept mapping and early literacy: a promising crossroads. In: Cañas, A.J., Reiske, P., Åhlberg, M., Novak, J.D. (eds.) Proceedings of the Third International Conference on Concept Mapping, Tallinn, Estonia, and Helsinki, Finland, pp. 189–196 (2008)
17. Figueiredo, M., Lopes, A.S., Firmina, R., deSouse, S.: Things we know about the cow: concept mapping in a preschool setting. In: Cañas, A.J., Novak, J.D., González, F.M. (eds.) Proceeding of the First International Conference on Concept Mapping, Pamplona, Spain, vol. 2, pp. 163–166 (2004)
18. Hunter, J., Monroe-Ossi, H., Fountain, C.: Young florida naturalists: concept mapping and science learning of preschool children. In: Cañas, A.J., Reiske, P., Åhlberg, M., Novak, J.D. (eds.) Proceedings of the Third International Conference on Concept Mapping, Tallinn, Estonia, and Helsinki, Finland, pp. 756–763 (2008)
19. Monroe-Ossi, H., Wehry, S., Algina, J., Hunter, J.: Healthy habits through literacy: a concept mapping and health curriculum for preschool and prekindergarten children. In: Cañas, A.J., Reiske, P., Åhlberg, M., Novak, J.D. (eds.) Proceedings of the Third International Conference on Concept Mapping, Tallinn, Estonia, and Helsinki, Finland, pp. 422–429 (2008)
20. Novak, J.D., Cañas, A.J.: The theory underlying concept maps and how to construct and use them. Technical report IHMC CmapTools 2006-01, Institute for Human and Machine Cognition (IHMC) (2006). http://cmap.ihmc.us/docs/theory-of-concept-maps
21. Wehry, S., Algina, J., Hunter, J., Monroe-Ossi, H.: Using concept maps transcribed from interviews to quantify the structure of preschool children's knowledge about plants. In: Cañas, A.J., Reiske, P., Åhlberg, M., Novak, D. (eds.) Proceedings of the Third International Conference on Concept Mapping, Tallinn, Estonia, and Helsinki, Finland, pp. 732–739 (2008)
22. Kinchin, I.M.: Using concept maps to reveal understanding: a two tier analysis. Sch. Sci. Rev. **81**, 41–46 (2000)
23. McClure, J.R., Bell, P.E.: Effects of an environmental education-related STS approach instruction on cognitive structures of preservice science teachers. ERIC Document Reproduction Service No. ED 341 582 (1990)

24. Yin, Y., Vanides, J., Ruiz-Primo, M.A., Ayala, C.C., Shavelson, R.J.: Comparison of two concept mapping techniques: implications for scoring, interpretations, and use. J. Res. Sci. Teach. **42**, 166–184 (2005)
25. Derbentseva, N., Safayeni, F., Cañas, A.J.: Concept maps: experiments on dynamic thinking. J. Res. Sci. Teach. **44**, 448–465 (2007)

Using Concept Maps to Develop a Didactic Explanation of a Dress with Ambigous Colours

Francisco Luis Naranjo[1(✉)], Guadalupe Martínez[1], Ángel Luis Pérez[1],
Pedro J. Pardo[1], María Isabel Suero[1], and Manuel Melgosa[2]

[1] University of Extremadura, Badajoz, Spain
{naranjo,mmarbor,aluis,pjpardo,suero}@unex.es
[2] University of Granada, Granada, Spain
mmelgosa@ugr.es

Abstract. We report on an experience carried out to show the didactic use of concept maps as tools for the development of a progressive explanation of the colour perception of a dress with ambiguous colours. Concept maps are used to promote a conceptual change in our students trying to answer the question: Why some people perceive the dress as blue & black and others as white & gold? We must first answer another preliminary question: On what depends the colour we perceive in a given object? We have used observations of the original dress in our colour laboratory by more than 300 people. The concept maps developed are based on a test for the detection of preconceptions about colour that can be taken online. In addition, we use different concept maps in successive levels of elaboration about the different factors that determine the colour a certain object is perceived.

Keywords: Concept maps · Colour perception · #thedress

1 Introduction

Concept maps, since its inception in the sixties by Novak [1] have become a powerful educational resource with various applications. Numerous investigations indicate that concept maps are an excellent teaching tool to represent organized knowledge. As it is well known, the theoretical foundations of concept maps focus on Ausubel's Assimilation Theory [2, 3] and Novak's Theory of Learning [4]. Specifically, from the perspective of the meaningful learning theory, concept maps allow us to visually represent relationships between concepts of a particular subject in a graphically hierarchical fashion. This is useful to optimize the processes of teaching and learning, and to determine the degree of meaningful learning achieved by our students during the explanation of content. In this regard, several studies have used concept maps at all educational levels in order to help students to get a better assimilation of the concepts studied, by developing new proposals that are naturally integrated in the cognitive structure of the student [5–10]. In line with these works, previous research of our team revealed the effectiveness of concept maps in teaching and learning physics [11] and their usefulness for the achievement of conceptual changes in students [12]. Likewise, concept maps can be

© Springer International Publishing Switzerland 2016
A. Cañas et al. (Eds.): CMC 2016, CCIS 635, pp. 303–314, 2016.
DOI: 10.1007/978-3-319-45501-3_24

used to establish a teaching sequence designed from the most general to the most specific, alternately carrying out processes of analysis and synthesis [3]. Thus, we can deepen into the meaning of the content developed, using a hierarchy of concepts in the explanation or teaching sequence showing a process of progressive differentiation and integrative reconciliation [2].

In the present work we will use concept maps to facilitate the process of conceptual change in students from the analysis of their preconceptions on a particular topic, namely the perception of colour of the famous dress with ambiguous colours. Concept maps were key tools to carry out a process of assimilation, in which previous ideas about colour perception are modified to acquire new meanings, producing a progressive differentiation through a new hierarchy of propositions. This is a dynamic process necessary to carry out a meaningful learning about the concept of colour. To develop the didactic explanation of the phenomenon with concept maps we also used Reigeluth and Stein's Elaboration Theory [13], using a sequence of contents through different levels of elaboration which constitute the backbone in the teaching sequence developed for learning colour perception, starting from the simpler and general ideas to the more complex and specific concepts.

The topic selected for this experience has been the ambiguous dress colours which went viral on internet. Figure 1 shows several photographs of the dress, which we have used to carry out the current study or some previous ones [15].

Fig. 1. Photographs of the dress with ambiguous colours: original viral photograph, retailer's photograph, and photograph taken in our laboratory (Color figure online) (left, source: swiked.tumblr.com), (centre, source: Roman Originals) (right, source: the authors)

This phenomenon began on late February 2015, when a user of the social networking service Tumblr published a photo of a dress and asked people about what colour was the dress [14]. Surprisingly, the answers to this simple question were divided into two very different categories, and a high percentage of people answered that blue and black while another large number of people responded that white and gold.

2   Methodology

2.1   Objective and Approach

The overall objective of this study was to develop an educational and informative explanation using concept maps to promote conceptual change on colour perception responding to why the dress is perceived in different colours by different people. To achieve this goal, we took into account the two main lines of research of our group: Optics and Teaching of Physics. Thus, from each of these two perspectives, we have attempted to obtain data to answer the question raised by this paper: Why some people perceive the famous dress that became viral on the Internet as having some colours and others as having completely different colours? To answer this question, we must first answer another preliminary question: On what depends the colour we perceive in a certain object?

2.2   Design of the Experience

First, in order to answer the questions raised in the previous section, a model of the dress was acquired from the original manufacturer. An experimental design was developed in our colour laboratory to obtain data on the perception of the colour of such dress. Specifically, we used a sample of more than 300 people of different ages and educational backgrounds. They had to complete a questionnaire with independent variables related to gender, age, education, etc., and they also identified the perceived colours of the dress under different light sources. The results obtained in this initial phase of data collection will complement technical aspects on the subject already published [15, 16].

Secondly, and based on previous results of our research in optics, it has been developed an educational and informative explanation using concept maps from the perspective of the teaching of physics. The purpose is to make the subject understandable to the general public, even those who are not familiar with optics and colour. For this key phase of our work, it has been followed a methodology which is based on constructivist theories of learning [2]. Following the provisions of this theory of meaningful learning, as a starting point for the construction of knowledge, we have looked into the ideas people have about the possible factors that influence how the colour of the objects is perceived. Also, it has been necessary to identify any misconceptions on this issue. For the analyses of misconceptions about colour, we used a previously developed test [17], which was subsequently implemented online [18] and is available at http://grupoorion.unex.es/test. This test allowed us to detect the misconceptions regarding the factors on which colour perception depends. Overall, the results showed that only 15.7 % of the over 20,000 respondents answered correctly, and the vast majority (78.2 %) of incorrect response patterns matched just four sequences, corresponding to four types of misconceptions. This high percentage of wrong answers revealed the need to develop educational tools to achieve progressive conceptual changes, allowing us to combat the misconceptions found around the perception of colour, and help our students to improve their understanding on what factors perceived colour depends. In this regard, from the Theory of Elaboration of Reigeluth and Stein [13], it is appropriate to establish different levels of elaboration to understand the colour perception of a particular object, in our case the viral dress. In Subsect. 2.3 we will show the teaching sequence with the different elaboration levels developed.

2.3 Didactic Explanation with Concept Maps

First Elaboration Level: What Colour do you See this Object? It is advisable to take first the online test available at http://grupoorion.unex.es/test to detect colour misconceptions. One of the most widespread misconceptions is to consider colour as a property of the object [11, 19, 20]. The origin of this misconception is the extrapolation from usual observations in which the illumination is daylight to any other situation where the illumination does not contain a full range of colours. When using the verb "to be" to indicate the colour of an object, we are implicitly assuming that the object is being illuminated by daylight. Thus, the sentence "Lemons are yellow" really means "Lemons are yellow when illuminated by daylight", but the last part is generally ignored. To combat this misconception, it is useful to use concept maps allowing us to refine the meaning of the propositions within. Thus, the first conceptual change needed to explain the perceived colour of a given object is to clarify that it depends not only on its characteristics, but also on the incoming light, which is reflected by the object and travels from it to our eyes. As an example, Fig. 2 shows, on the left, the concept map of a subject with such a misconception and, on the right, the concept map of the subject who experienced this first conceptual change.

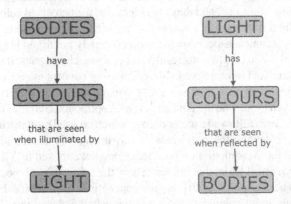

Fig. 2. Concept maps with concepts "Bodies", "Colours" and "Light", showing a misconception (left) and the correct relationship (right).

Second Elaboration Level: Influence of Surrounding Colours. Figure 3 shows images of a stick figure wearing a dress supposedly similar to the one under study [21]. Commonly, we will perceive the blue faced stick figure on the left dressed in "white and gold" and the yellow faced stick figure on the right dressed in "blue and black".

Fig. 3. Two stick figures wearing the same dress (Color figure online) (source: [21])

However, despite perceived differently, if we check the RGB colour coordinates we can note that both dresses have the same colour coordinates (Fig. 4). You may easily check it by yourself if you are viewing these images on a screen and you just isolate the small regions under comparison.

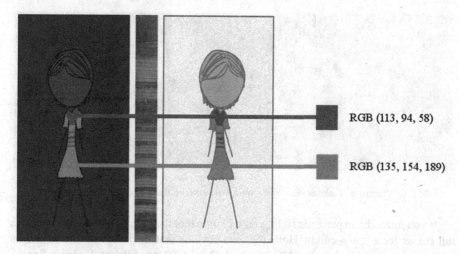

RGB (113, 94, 58)

RGB (135, 154, 189)

Fig. 4. RGB colour coordinates of two key regions in both dresses

The experience in Figs. 3 and 4 shows that the colour of the environment (background and surround) strongly influences the colour we perceive in an object. If we want to incorporate this content in a concept map, we must expand the proposition developed, which implies a second conceptual change. The colour an object is perceived depends on, both the colour of the light traveling from the object to our eyes and also the colours of the environment (background and surround). Figure 5 shows the sequence of the modified concept maps.

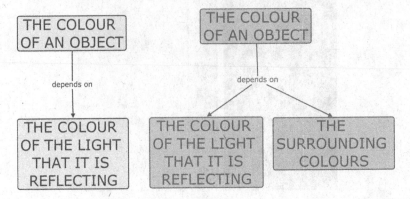

Fig. 5. Concept maps about the dependence of colour of an object: first level of elaboration (left) and second level of elaboration (right)

Third Elaboration Level: Chromatic Adaptation. In Fig. 6, we ask the reader to stare at the black dot in the centre of the left image for 30 s, and then change and stare at the same black dot in the centre of the right image.

Fig. 6. *Puerta de Palmas* (Badajoz, Spain) afterimage illusion (source: the authors)

If you make the experience right, you will note that the image on the right will look full colour for a few seconds. However, it is obvious that the image on the right is in fact a black and white photograph of *Puerta de Palmas* (Door of Palms, Badajoz, Spain). This is due to the phenomenon known as "chromatic adaptation", which leads us to add another progressive differentiation in our concept map. The perceived colour for a given object depends on the colour of the light traveling from the object to our eyes, the colours of the surrounding environment and also the colours visualized immediately before. Figure 7 shows the new concept maps developed.

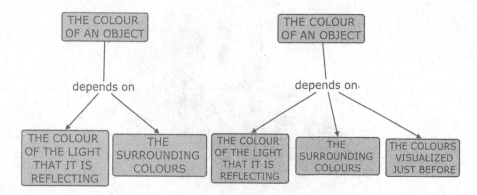

Fig. 7. Concept maps about the dependence of colour of an object: second level of elaboration (left) and third level of elaboration (right)

Fourth Elaboration Level: Subjective Factors. Figure 8 shows a checkerboard with a standing cylinder. Have the squares marked A and B the same colour?

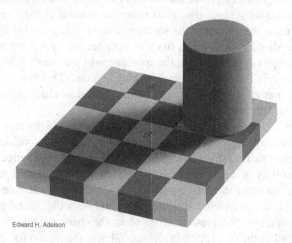

Edward H. Adelson

Fig. 8. Checker shadow illusion (source: [22])

Most probably, you will answer that the squares A and B have different colours. However, if we add two grey vertical strips trying to isolate these regions, as intended in Fig. 9, we can note that these two squares have exactly the same colour.

As the author of this illusion states [22], the perceived colour of the squares depends on the context. Our visual system needs to determine the colour of objects, and, as in this case, it uses several mechanisms to determine where the shadows are and how to compensate for them, in order to determine the "true colour" that belongs to the surface. Thus, our visual system takes into account first local contrast: a square that is lighter than its neighbouring squares is probably lighter than average, and vice versa. In Fig. 8, the light square B in the shadow is surrounded by darker squares. Thus, even though the square is physically dark, it is light when compared to its neighbours. The dark checks

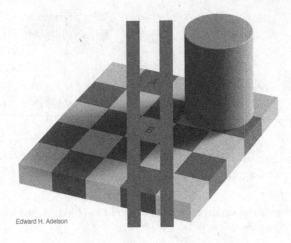

Fig. 9. Checker shadow proof (source: [22])

outside the shadow, conversely, are surrounded by lighter checks, so they look dark by comparison. The visual system also tends to ignore gradual changes in light level, so that it can determine the colour of the surfaces without being misled by shadows [23, 24]. In Fig. 8 the shadow looks like a shadow, both because it is fuzzy and because the shadow casting object is visible. Last, the appearance of the square is aided by the form of the cross-junctions formed by 4 neighbouring squares. This type of intersection is usually a signal that all the edges should be interpreted as changes in surface colour rather than in terms of shadows or lighting.

However, the factors that influence the perceived colour are not only of an objective nature, such as the wavelength of the light illuminating the object (physical), the composition of said object that makes it absorb certain wavelengths and reflect others (chemical), or the sensitivity of the receptors in the eye (physiological). The perceived colour may also depend on other subjective psychological factors, whose role is not yet fully understood. To further complete the concept map shown in Fig. 7, and gradually differentiate such factors, now the question arises about the characteristics of the psychological factors related to the perception of colour. What is the reason for its existence and what benefits does it brings to our visual system?

Previous works [25, 26] showed that Constructivism and Meaningful Learning Theory are not a pedagogical current trend, but facts with a physiological justification: that our brain works meaningfully, that is, searching for the meaning of the information that comes through the senses. Specifically, the authors established an analogy between the brain processes of visualization and conceptualization. In both processes, the relevant characteristics of the objects or events are abstracted, and it is built either a visual world [27] or a cognitive structure [28]. These authors pointed out, based on prior theoretical framework, that neurology establishes the need for symbolic representations to know and understand reality. Thus, Crick and Koch [29] stated that, although the main function of the visual system is to perceive objects and events in the world around us, the information available to our eyes alone is not enough to the brain to produce its unique interpretation of the visual world. The brain has to rely on previous experiences to interpret the information it receives through the eyes in a complete way. This explanation is closely related to Ausubel's Meaningful Learning Theory [2].

If we look for a physiological explanation of this fact, we could say that the fundamental objective of our visual system is to identify and recognize objects, and colour is one of the most useful tools for this goal. In the case of non-luminous objects, if we change the illuminant (e.g. daylight at midday or dusk, light from a bulb...), the light reflected by the objects will also change. Thus, we should perceive them with different colours, which might make us think them as different objects. Within certain limits, we have a tendency to perceive an object always with the same colour, regardless of the type of illumination. To avoid confusions, our visual system has evolved by developing what is known as colour constancy. Colour constancy [30] is a mechanism by which our visual system evaluates all colour information coming from the whole scene we are viewing. From this information, it can be assumed that our brain attempts to determine the approximate composition of the illuminating light, which is then discounted. This effect really proves the success, rather than the failure, of our visual system, which is not very good as a physical light meter, since that is not its purpose. The important task is to break the image information down into meaningful components, and thereby perceive the nature of the objects in view.

Figure 10 shows the concept map developed to include the proposition related to subjective factors that influence colour perception. The perceived colour of a given object depends on the colour of the light traveling from the object to our eyes, the colours of the environment, the colours visualized immediately before, and the perceptual mechanism called "discounting the illuminant" [31].

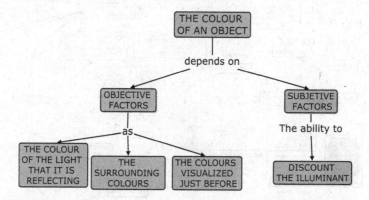

Fig. 10. Fourth level of elaboration concept map about the dependence of colour of an object

3   Results

The results obtained in our colour laboratory, where the dress has been shown to a set of more than 300 people, have revealed that the problem of disparities in colour perceptions is not attributable to the dress itself, because all the respondents have expressed that they saw such dress as blue and black. However, we obtained different answers if they were shown the viral photograph. Thus, we can ask the following questions: In what conditions was that picture taken? What kind of illumination was used? Which camera model and settings were used? In our colour laboratory we unsuccessfully tried to answer some of these questions trying to take a photograph of the real dress with the same characteristics of the famous viral photograph.

However, the most interesting question to us is: How can we explain that most people perceive the dress in the photograph with so different colours? The answer to this question, from an educational and informative point of view, is related to the different levels of elaboration shown in the concept maps that have guided the development of this work. As we have seen, our visual system is probably able to discount the illuminant in a different amount, or as a consequence of different unknown factors. That is, the colours that people perceive in the photograph of the dress depend not only on the colours of the light traveling from every area of this photo to their eyes, but also on the specific backgrounds and surrounds behind this dress, the subjects' specific ability to discount the illuminant, etc. Nevertheless, this mechanism of colour constancy is not triggered equally in all individuals, and some are abler than others to discount the illuminant.

Figure 11 shows the global concept map developed to give an educational and informative answer to the colour perception of the dress with ambiguous colours. As you can

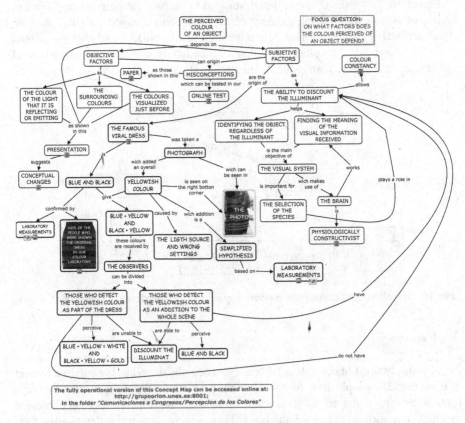

Fig. 11. Global concept map about the colour perception of the dress with ambiguous colours.

see, the bottom of our proposed concept map assumes that the so-called "discount of illuminant" is the most relevant factor to explain the differences between colours reported by different observers asked on the viral photography (not on the real dress). While currently this seems a reasonable hypothesis [32], it cannot at all be discarded that other factors like observers' pupil size [16], etc. may have also played an important role in the problem we have considered here.

Acknowledgements.   This Research was supported by the European Regional Development Fund (ERDF), the Ministry of Economy and Competitiveness of the Government of Spain, and the Regional Government of Extremadura, through grants FIS2013-40661-P and GR15102.

References

1. Novak, J.D.: Learning, Creating, and Using Knowledge: Concept Maps as Facilitative Tools in Schools and Corporations. Lawrence Erlbaum Associates, Mahweh (1998)
2. Ausubel, D.P.: Educational Psychology: A Cognitive View. Holt, Rinehart and Winston, New York (1968)
3. Ausubel, D.P., Novak, J.D., Hanesian, H.: Educational Psychology: A Cognitive View. Holt, Rinehart and Winston, New York (1978)
4. Novak, J.D., Gowin, D.B.: Learning How to Learn. Cambridge University Press, New York (1984)
5. Okebukola, P.A., Jegede, O.J.: Cognitive Preference and Learning Mode as Determinants of Meaningful Learning Through Concept Mapping. Sci. Educ. **72**(4), 489–500 (1988)
6. Roth, W.M., Roychoudhury, A.: Science discourse through collaborative concept mapping: new perspectives for the teacher. Int. J. Sci. Educ. **16**(4), 437–455 (1994)
7. Fraser, K., Edwards, J.: The effects of training in concept mapping on student achievement in traditional classroom tests. Res. Sci. Educ. **15**, 158–165 (1985)
8. Horton, P.B., McConney, A.A., Gallo, M., Woods, A.L., Senn, G.J., Hamelin, D.: An investigation of the effectiveness of concept mapping as an instructional tool. Sci. Educ. **77**, 95–111 (1993)
9. Martínez, G., Pérez, Á.L., Suero, M.I., Pardo, P.J., Naranjo, F.L.: Using concept maps to create reasoning models to teach thinking: an application for solving kinematics problems. Knowl. Manag. E-Learn. **7**(1), 162–178 (2015)
10. Cañas, A.J., Ford, K.M., Coffey, J., Reichherzer, T., Carff, R., Shamma, D., Breedy, M.: Tools to build and share knowledge models based on concept maps. Rev. Inform. Educ. **13**(2), 145–158 (2000). (in Spanish)
11. Martínez, G., Pérez, Á.L., Suero, M.I., Pardo, P.J.: The effectiveness of concept maps in teaching physics concepts applied to engineering education: experimental comparison of the amount of learning achieved with and without concept maps. J. Sci. Educ. Technol. **22**(2), 204–214 (2013)
12. Pérez, A.L., Suero, M.I., Montanero, M., Pardo, P.J., Montanero, M.: Concept maps and conceptual change in physics. In: de Câssia Veiga Marriott, R., Lupion Torres, P. (eds.) Handbook of Research on Collaborative Learning Using Concept Mapping. IGI Global, Hershey (2009)
13. Reigeluth, C.M., Stein, F.S.: The elaboration theory of instruction. In: Reigeluth, C.M. (ed.) Instructional Design Theories and Models: An Overview of their Current Status. L. Erlbaum, Hildsdale (1983)

14. BuzzFeed Life. What Colors are this Dress? http://www.buzzfeed.com/catesish/help-am-i-going-insane-its-definitely-blue
15. Melgosa, M., Gómez-Robledo, L., Suero, M.I., Fairchild, M.D.: What can we learn from a dress with ambiguous colours? Color Res. Appl. **40**(5), 525–529 (2015)
16. Vemuri, K., Bisla, K., Pulpuru, S., Varadharajan, S.: Do normal pupil diameter differences in the population underlie the color selection of #thedress? J. Opt. Soc. Am. A: **33**, A137–A142 (2016)
17. Martinez-Borreguero, G., Pérez-Rodríguez, Á.L., Suero-López, M.I., Pardo-Fernández, P.J.: Detection of misconceptions about colour and an experimentally tested proposal to combat them. Int. J. Sci. Educ. **35**(8), 1299–1324 (2013)
18. Naranjo, F.L., Martinez, G., Perez, A.L., Lopez, M.I., Pardo, P.J.: A new online tool to detect colour misconceptions. Color Res. Appl. **41**(3), 325–329 (2015)
19. Eaton, J.F., Anderson, C.W., Smith, E.L.: Students' misconceptions interfere with learning: case studies of fifth-grade students. Elem. Sch. J. **64**(4), 365–379 (1984)
20. Guesne, E.: Light. In: Driver, R., Guesne, E., Tiberghien, A. (eds.) Children's Ideas in Science. Open University Press, Philadelphia (1985)
21. Munroe, R.: XKCD - Dress Color. http://www.xkcd.com/1492/
22. Adelson, E.H.: Checker Shadow Illusion. http://web.mit.edu/persci/people/adelson/checkershadow_illusion.html
23. Adelson, E.H.: Perceptual organization and the judgment of brightness. Science **262**, 2042–2044 (1993)
24. Adelson, E.H.: Lightness perception and lightness illusions. In: Gazzaniga, M. (ed.) The New Cognitive Neurosciences. MIT Press, Cambridge (2000)
25. Martínez-Borreguero, G., Pérez-Rodríguez, Á.L., Naranjo-Correa, F.L., Suero-López, M.I., Pardo-Fernández, P.J.: Meaningful learning in physics education. is our brain physiologically constructivist? In: Gómez Chova, L., López Martínez, A., Candel Torres, I. (eds.) Proceedings of ICERI2012, pp. 5494–5503. IATED, Valencia (2012)
26. Martínez, G., Naranjo, F.L., Pérez, Á.L., Suero, M.I., Pardo, P.J.: Meaningful learning theory in science education: just another pedagogical trend? J. Sci. Educ (2016, in press)
27. Zeki, S.: The visual image in mind and brain. Sci. Am. **267**(3), 68–76 (1992)
28. Ausubel, D.P.: The Acquisition and Retention of Knowledge: A Cognitive View. Kluwer Academic Pubishers, Dordrecht (2000)
29. Crick, F., Koch, C.: The problem of consciousness. Sci. Am. **267**(3), 153–159 (1992)
30. Fairchild, M.D.: Color Appearance Models. Wiley, Hoboken (2013)
31. McCann, J.J.: Do Humans Discount the Illuminant? In: Proceedings of SPIE, vol. 5666, pp. 9–16 (2005)
32. RIT University News: RIT Color Scientists Explain the Dress that Went Viral. https://www.rit.edu/news/story.php?id=51266

Using Semantic Reference Set of Linking Words for Concept Mapping in Biology

Meena Kharatmal[⊠] and G. Nagarjuna

Homi Bhabha Centre for Science Education,
Tata Institute of Fundamental Research, Mumbai, India
{meena,nagarjuna}@hbcse.tifr.res.in

Abstract. Inspired by the semantic network studies we propose additional conventions for choosing linking words and arrive at a Reference Set of semantically well-defined linking words drawn from the Knowledge Representation area of research in the domain of biology. Each linking word in the set is assigned a dimension: part-whole, class-inclusion, spatial-inclusion, function and attribution. We study expert representations by content analysis of biology texts at three levels of increasing subject complexity. We compare the linking words used in these representations with the Reference Set and find an increasing degree of proximity to the latter. This indicates that experts tend to use more well-defined linking words. Regarding this proximity as a characteristic of expertise, we can encourage novices to re-represent their concept maps using the linking words from the Reference Set. We discuss the implications of the approach for science education.

1 Introduction

The Concept Map method was developed by Novak and his group [1], influenced by the Ausebelian perspective of meaningful learning which posits that new knowledge is constructed by connections to the prior knowledge in the domain [2]. It has since been used widely in eliciting knowledge in a variety of domains.

A Concept Map is a graphical representation in which nodes (concepts) and connecting lines (linking words) are arranged in a dendritic form at various hierarchical levels. A scoring rubric assigns a score to each concept map depending on the number of propositions, levels of hierarchy, cross links and examples. There are standard conventions for creating and scoring a Concept Map. In science education studies, the Concept Map has been used extensively as a learning tool, as a way to study conceptual change and assess student knowledge, and model expertise (See, for example, [3]). Some later studies modified the rubric and included the number of concepts and branches for scoring; see, for example, [4].

For over a decade now, several researchers have adopted semantic network principles to concept mapping. The basic aim in concept maps is to create meaningful propositions. This requires explicit and semantically valid relations between concepts. Syntactic clarity is achieved by the mere presence of a linking word or phrase, but semantic clarity critically depends on the kind of linking word or phrase used [5]. Semantic based scoring rubric has been developed that evaluates concept maps taking

A. Cañas et al. (Eds.): CMC 2016, CCIS 635, pp. 315–329, 2016.
DOI: 10.1007/978-3-319-45501-3_25

propositions as semantic units, among other criteria, which shows a high inter-rater reliability measure [6]. In another study, semantic flow and clarity was one of the three aspects examined for readability of concept maps based on the Gestaltian law of proximity and law of similarity [7].

The general semantic network approach has had a long history. Perhaps the best-known theory of semantic networks to model the structure and storage of human knowledge is due to Quillian [8]. These comprise nodes and ordered relationships or links connecting them; they are not necessarily hierarchical. The nodes are instances of concepts or propositions, and the links describe the relationship between them. Semantic networking programs are computer-based, visualizing tools for representing semantic networks.

In a semantic network, each relation between concepts is given an explicit relation name. Holley and Dansereau [9], in their study on using networking as a spatial learning strategy, identified six relations – *part of, type of, leads to, similar to, has characteristics, indicates/illustrates*. In addition, these six relations were classified into three types of representational structures – *hierarchies (type-part); chains (lines of reasoning, temporal orderings, causal sequences);* and *clusters (characteristics-definitions-analogies)*.

The act of naming relations is not necessarily a conscious activity unless it is required to be, and often the relation names are implicit in text and language. Therefore, analyzing relations and naming them so as to make them explicit is an important part of constructing a semantic network. Naming of relations is a challenging task, as it requires careful identification to capture and clarify the meaning, which otherwise could remain vague. The naming of relations enhances the depth of understanding and clarity of thought. These ideas were implemented in the knowledge construction tool called SemNet [10].

Faletti and Fisher [11], using SemNet in biology, reported 3 relations – *set/member, whole/part,* and *characteristic* – being used more frequently than other relations. In one of the studies on concept mapping, linking words such as – *is measure of, has property of, depends on, is a form of, is mass divided by, divided by volume, equals* were provided, and it was established that the scoring of maps in this case was straightforward, and hence could be applied for large scale assessment [12]. A form of concept map, called a knowledge integration map has been deployed in an online inquiry-based learning unit where it is suggested that students in a peer-review condition focused more on links and linking words [13].

Inspired by the semantic network studies, we adopt additional conventions for choosing linking words for obtaining a Reference Set of semantically well-defined linking words drawn from the Knowledge Representation area of research in the domain of biology, and propose the use of the Re-represented Concept Map (RCM) in biology education. In Sect. 2 we provide the motivation for our work and situate it in the framework of science education studies. In Sect. 3 we briefly describe the relational ontology in biomedical domain (Open Biomedical Ontologies (OBO)) developed by the KR community and the Reference Set of semantically well-defined linking words in cell biology. In Sect. 4, we describe the method of content analysis with reference to three internationally known biology texts of increasing expertise level in the topic of cell biology. We then carry out the re-representation of the propositions using the

Reference Set of linking words. A Re-represented Concept Map (RCM) is illustrated. Section 5 is devoted to data analysis and results. We end with some remarks on the implications of the study in science education.

2 Motivation and Rationale for RCM

The motivation and rationale for RCM in science education derives from a number of considerations:

1. The Standard Concept Map (SCM) method is intended to organize knowledge in terms of concepts and their relations to promote meaningful learning. However, the linking words reflecting the connections in a SCM are generally an unconstrained set drawn from natural language. Since natural language is tolerant of semantic ambiguity, the SCM is vulnerable to the same. Thus disambiguation of linking words seems essential in mapping of knowledge.
2. Student difficulties of comprehending scientific texts arise as much from the imprecise and inappropriate use of grammar as from the unfriendly technical terms [14]. Since grammar resides in the connections between words, the difficulties may be regarded as relating essentially to the kinds of linking words used. Again this means linking words in a text need to be well-defined and unambiguous.
3. Linking words along with their characteristics of *connectedness*, *link quality*, and *link variety*, have been considered to be indicators of expertise. Experts not only use appropriate linking words, but also use a diversity of linking words. On the contrary, the links used by novices are often inappropriate, and the same linking words are used for various kinds of links resulting in ambiguity, and lack of clarity and precision in expression [15].
4. Re-representation (Representational Re-description) of knowledge from implicit to explicit form is now thought to be the hallmark of cognitive development. The explicit knowledge undergoes the successive phases of conscious, and conscious and verbal knowledge in natural language [16]. In this important theoretical perspective, expert scientific knowledge may be viewed as yet another re-representation of novice knowledge. Representations of expert's knowledge emerge over a period as a function of repetitive refinements [17]. In the context of concept mapping, this would entail making the linking words increasingly more precise and explicit.

These theoretical insights and empirical studies all point in the same direction, namely that we must use semantically precise linking words in a concept map. As our general domain of interest is biology, we turn to a major international effort to formalize the content and structure of this domain—the development of Open Biomedical Ontology (OBO) as part of KR. The KR research community is basically involved in re-representation of existing scientific knowledge in formalized ontologies of concepts and relations in different domains. Our work appropriates this massive resource for re-representing the linking words for concept mapping. The re-represented concept map (RCM) results in disambiguation and explicitization of meaning and can facilitate meaningful learning with rigor.

3 Additional Conventions for RCM and Reference Set of Linking Words

3.1 Additional Conventions for RCM

Recently, the conventions and specific criteria for constructing good standard concept maps have been reviewed [18]. The criteria are: to mention an explicit focus question, to avoid redundancy (i.e. not repeat the same concept in a map), use one or a few words for a concept, to use one or a few words for a linking phrase, not to use concept words on linking lines, to have hierarchical organization of concepts, to link three-four sub-concepts below a concept (branching), and to add cross-links as interrelationships between two sub-domains at the end.

We follow all the above conventions, and in addition suggest some more conventions focusing on the nature of linking words to be used in the propositions (see Table 1). It is important to mention that our proposed conventions are suggested to be supplementary to the existing conventions and not alternative or competing. These are informed by the guidelines suggested by Jonassen [19] for the words and phrases used for links in a semantic network: preciseness, succinctness, parsimony and consistency.

Borrowing from Wittgenstein's [20] definition, *"a proposition is either true or false"*, we suggest that concept map should express only propositions that can be decided to be true or false (semantic criterion). If the linking words are *prepositions* (*of, with, from, on,* etc.) the resulting relations between ideas form at best an expression and would not be qualified as *propositions*.

Whenever we use *'has/have'* as linking words we seek to replace them by explicating the intended meaning explicitly by the relation that actually holds between them (e.g. *'consists of'*, *'enveloped by'*, etc.). This additional constraint as a convention provides an opportunity for reflection and critical thinking, and weeds out ambiguity. Further, disambiguation requires us to replace lone uses of *'is/are'* with appropriate linking phrases (e.g. *'is/are divided into'*, *'is/are located in'*, etc.).

In addition to disambiguation, parsimony is considered to be a hallmark of expert articulation of knowledge. Thus for a given intended meaning, the same linking word should be used throughout. Thus if part-whole relation is intended, the same linking word *'consists of'* should be used.

Hierarchical organization of knowledge is another distinguishing characteristic of expert knowledge. While talking about the need for hierarchy in concept maps, Novak refers to Ausubel's notion of *subsumption*. In a concept map, relations used in a hierarchy are not necessarily logically transitive. The additional conventions for RCM facilitate identifying hierarchical relations that are logically transitive by simply looking at the repetition of a linking word. Thus RCM affords a new scoring measure for counting hierarchy.

Table 1. The proposed list of additional conventions for using re-represented linking words (RLWs).

Principles of mapping	Conventions
Propositions as unit of analysis	Linkage between the two concept terms should yield a proposition that can be decided to be either true or false
Disambiguation	Replace lone use of *'has'*, *'is/are'*, etc. by the linking word that conveys the intended meaning explicitly
Parsimony	Use the same linking word for the same meaning in all parts of the map
Hierarchy	Count hierarchy levels only when the relations are transitive i.e. the same linking word is used

3.2   Reference Set

Although the semantic principles were laid down in 1960's [8], their wider use is being implemented in the growing interdisciplinary research area of Knowledge Representation (KR) which draws on computer science, linguistics and philosophy. KR in terms of vocabulary, glossaries, thesauri, taxonomy is thought to bear weaker semantics; while ontologies, databases, and formal languages involve stronger semantics.

An ontology defines terms referring to classes of objects, properties, events, processes and relations in every domain of reality. Domain experts define ontologies of a given domain that are logically well-formed and scientifically accurate. There is a collective of ontology developers that are committed to collaboration and adherence to the shared principles of KR. The integration of semantic web strategies into ontology development uses the formalized languages OWL/RDF [21]. A collection of ontologies related to anatomy, processes, events, for the domain of cell, gene, plant, mouse, fly, zebra fish, neuroscience, semantic science, etc. have been published at NCBO Bioportal [22]. An OBO Foundry (http://obofoundry.org/) hosts ontologies related to open biomedical ontologies.

To illustrate, definitions of two relations: *'part-of'* and *'located in'*, are given by Relations Ontology (RO) group as follows [23]:

part_of =def. For continuants: C part_of C' if and only if: given any c that instantiates C at a time t, there is some c' such that c' instantiates C' at time t, and c *part_of* c' at t.

located_in =def. C located_in C' if and only if: given any c that instantiates C at a time t, there is some c' such that: c' instantiates C' at time t and c *located_in* c'.

For arriving at a Reference set of linking words for our study, we referred one such site called 'Ontobee'. This page lists the detailed information of Gene Ontology, annotations, and terms. In the third section, the list of linking words related to Gene Ontology can be viewed from 'Object Properties'. The linking words listed therein are: *'ends during'*, *'happens during'*, *'has part'*, *'negatively regulates'*, *'occurs in'*, *'part of'*, *'positively regulates'*, *'regulates'*, *'starts during'*. Out of these, we extracted the linking words relevant to mapping the domain of *'Cell Structure and Function'* in our study. A partial list of the selected linking words and the sources is shown in Table 2.

Table 2. Partial list of RLWs from the reference set.

Dimension	Linking words	Found in ontology	URL
Part-whole	Consists of/part of	Cell line ontology	http://www.ontobee. org/ontology/GO? iri=http://purl. obolibrary.org/ obo/BFO_ 0000050
	Composed of	Relations ontology	http://www.ontobee. org/ontology/RO? iri=http://purl. obolibrary.org/ obo/RO_0002473
Class inclusion	Classified into/divides into	*Subclass relation*	*Logic*
	Includes		
	Kind of/type of		
Spatial-inclusion	Attached to	Relations ontology	http://www.ontobee. org/ontology/RO? iri=http://purl. obolibrary.org/ obo/RO_0002371
	Bound by/bound to	Foundational model of anatomy	http://www.ontobee. org/ontology/ FMA?iri=http:// purl.obolibrary. org/obo/fma% 23bounds
	Contained in	Cell line ontology	http://www.ontobee. org/ontology/ CLO?iri=http:// www.obofoundry. org/ro/ro.owl% 23contained_in
	Enclosed	Human phenotype ontology	http://www.ontobee. org/ontology/HP? iri=http://purl. obolibrary.org/ obo/UBERON_ 0012467
	Envelopes	Gene ontology	http://www.ontobee. org/ontology/GO? iri=http://purl. obolibrary.org/ obo/GO_0031975

(Continued)

Table 2. (*Continued*)

Dimension	Linking words	Found in ontology	URL
Function	Has function/helps/performs	Biological collections ontology	http://www.ontobee. org/ontology/ BCO?iri=http:// purl.obolibrary. org/obo/RO_ 0000085
	Has role/plays role	Biological collections ontology	http://www.ontobee. org/ontology/ BCO?iri=http:// purl.obolibrary. org/obo/BCO_ 0000058
Attribution	Has length	Phenotypic quality	http://www.ontobee. org/ontology/ PATO?iri=http:// purl.obolibrary. org/obo/PATO_ 0000122
	Has property/has characteristics/has nature	Physico-chemical methods and properties	http://www.ontobee. org/ontology/FIX? iri=http://purl. obolibrary.org/ obo/FIX_0000481
Others	Similar to	Semantic science integrated ontology	http://www.ontobee. org/ontology/SIO? iri=http:// semanticscience. org/resource/SIO_ 001156
	Proposed by	NIF gross anatomy	http://www.ontobee. org/ontology/ NIF_ GrossAnatomy? iri=http://www. w3.oorg/2004/02/ skos/core% 23related

The full Reference Set used in our study is available at: http://gnowledge. org/~meena/Ontology/reference-set.pdf. The dimension to each linking word in the Set is discussed in Sect. 4.

To summarize, the RCM is a re-representation of the standard concept map wherein the unconstrained set of linking words/phrases is replaced by a controlled vocabulary of a parsimonious set of unambiguous linking words drawn from the OBO of the KR community.

4   Research Question and Methodology

Having motivated the need for RCM, we pose the main research question of this study: Does the choice of linking words characterize expertise? To answer this question, we carry out a detailed qualitative content analysis of three biology texts at increasing levels of subject complexity. This involves the following steps:

1. *Content choice.* The study was based on the content of cell biology from three textbooks which are used in many countries for teaching biology at three different stages of college education: UG-1 [24], UG-2 [25], and UG-3 [26]. As the text books under consideration are very detailed, it would have been difficult to analyze the entire topic of cell biology. Therefore, for the analysis, we focused on just two topics: *'Mitochondria'* and *'Nucleus'*. Only text passages were extracted from the books, excluding activities, questions, exercises and pictures.
2. *Paraphrasing.* Each passage on a topic comprises a number of sentences, simple and complex/compound. The latter kind can be equivalently written as two or more simple sentences. Each simple sentence is paraphrased in the form of concept–linking word–concept (C-LW-C) proposition(s). A simple sentence can yield a number of propositions. Thus a given passage is converted into a large number of propositions. These propositions when represented graphically constitute the standard concept map (SCM). This method of paraphrasing is similar to that of translating online content into basic propositions, as, for example, adopted in creating Medical WordNet from WordNet database [27].
3. *Re-representing.* The verbatim set of linking words in the extracted propositions from the texts are replaced by the controlled vocabulary of linking words from the Reference Set discussed in Sect. 3. This process is not as mechanical as it might seem. It involves the following steps:

Informed by the classic work of Winston et al. [28] we assign to each linking word of the Reference Set a dimension from the following list: *part-whole, class inclusion, spatial inclusion, function and attribution.* See Table 2.

We next look at the role of the original linking word and see if it is a *structure-structure, class-subclass, structure-region, structure-process, and structure-property relation.* This requires some domain familiarity. We then identify the appropriate linking word of the relevant dimension from the Reference Set and replace the original linking word by it. In case the original proposition already uses the linking word from the Reference Set, it remains as it is. Note that the concept names and terms are not changed in re-representation. The re-represented propositions when displayed graphically constitute the RCM. Figure 1 schematically shows the procedure of paraphrasing and re-representing. Table 3 gives re-represented propositions of a sample text passage at UG-3 level. Figure 2 gives the corresponding SCM and RCM for the sample text.

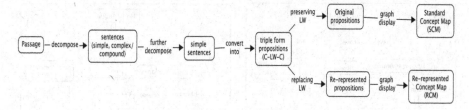

Fig. 1. The procedures involved in content analysis.

Table 3. Example of re-represented propositions of a sample text.

Verbatim sentences	Paraphrased propositions (SCM)	Re-represented propositions (RCM)
• Mitochondria has atleast two membranes separating the innermost space from the cytosol	• Mitochondria *have* two membranes • Two membranes *separate* the innermost space from cytosol	• Mitochondria *consists of* two membranes • Two membranes *have role in* separting the innermost space from cytosol
• Their membrane proteins are made not by ER, but by free ribosomes in the cytosol and by free ribosomes contained within the organelles themselves	• Membrane proteins *not made by* ER • Membrane proteins *made by* free ribosomes • Free ribosomes *in* cytosol • Ribosomes *contained in* organelles	• Membrane proteins *not synthesized by* ER • Membrane proteins *synthesized by* free ribosomes • Free ribosomes *located in* cytosol • Ribosomes *contained in* organelles
• These organelles have ribosomes, also contain a small amount of DNA	• Mitochondria *have* ribosomes • Mitochondria *contain* small amount of DNA	• Mitochondria *consists of* ribosomes • Mitochondria *contain* small amount of DNA
• Mitochondria are semi-autonomous organelles that grow and reproduce within the cell	• Mitochondria *are* semi-autonomous organelles • Semi-autonomous organelles *grow, reproduce* within cell	• Mitochondria *are kind of* semi-autonomous organelles • Semi-autonomous organelles *has property* to grow, reproduce within cell
• Some cells have a single large mitochondrion, but more often a cell has hundreds or thousands mitochondria	• Some cells *have* a single large mitochondrion • More often cell *has* hundreds or thousands mitochondria	• Some cells *consists of* single large mitochondrion • More often cell *consists of* hundreds or thousands mitochondria

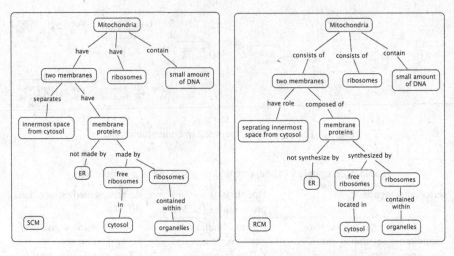

Fig. 2. An example of SCM and RCM on the topic of mitochondria.

5 Data Analysis and Results

We return to our research question on the connection between expertise and the choice of linking words. In the analysis of college textbooks, the topics on *'Mitochondria'* and *'Nucleus'* were considered as the units of analysis. Table 4 shows the linking words used and their frequencies of usage for the topics from all the three textbooks, and their classification on the basis of their semantic dimension. The frequency of each linking word indicates wider and greater use of a specific linking word in the text. For example, the linking words, *'consists of'*, *'made of'*, *'contains'*, *'enclosed by'*, *'has function'* are most widely and repeatedly used.

Table 4. List of linking words used by college textbooks at UG-1, UG-2, UG-3 levels for the topics of *'Mitochondria'* and *'Nucleus'*. The frequencies of each linking word is indicated in the parentheses.

Dimension	Linking words UG-1	Linking words UG-2	Linking words UG-3
Part-whole	Composed of (1), exists (1), in form of (1), may be present in (1), not consists of (1), perforated by (1)	Consists of (9), is perforated by (1), made of (5)	Composed of (1), consists of (5), is associated with (1), is interrupted by (1), present/seen in (3)
Class-inclusion	Includes (1), kind of (1), type of (2)	Divides into (1), includes (1), kind of (2), type of (1)	Divides into (1), includes (1), type of (1)

(Continued)

Table 4. (*Continued*)

Dimension	Linking words UG-1	Linking words UG-2	Linking words UG-3
Spatial-inclusion	Bound to (1), contains (11), covered with (1), is continuous with (1), located inside (1), occur near (1), packed in (1), surrounded by (2), wound around (1),	Are continuous (1), contain (6), enclosed by (5), exit through (1), extends through (1), is lined by (2), is organized (1), separated by (2), located (3), occurs in (1),	Aligned (1), attached to (4), contains (10), continuous (1), encloses (1), located between/are situated between (2), occupied (1), packed in (1), projects into (1), separated by (2), surrounded by (3), is traversed by (1)
Function	Are sites of (3), formed by (1), has function (6)	Are sites for (2), has function (11), play role (1), synthesized by (1),	Is site for (1)
Attribution	Has diameter (1), has form (1), has length (1), has property (1), has shape (1), has size (1)	Appears as (1), has form (3), has length (1), has nature (3), has number (2), has property (2), has size (1)	Has form (1), has nature (3), has shape (1), has size (1)
Others	Called (5), means (1)	Called (1)	Called (1)

An overall summary of results from the content analysis is provided in Table 5.

Table 5. Summary of results of content analysis of college textbooks.

	College textbooks		
	UG-1	UG-2	UG-3
Sentences	32	49	45
Propositions	60	72	53
Concepts	63	74	80
Linking Words (LW)	30	35	29
LWs match with reference set	25	30	26
Required re-representation	5	5	3
Re-represented Linking Words (RLW)	29	33	26
Proximity (%) with reference set	83	86	90

Figure 3 depicts part of the data in Table 5 concerning the number of concepts, linking words and re-represented linking words in the sample text at different levels.

Two noteworthy features emerge from the data:

(i) As the subject complexity increases from UG-1 to UG-2 to UG-3, the number of concepts increases, but there is no significant change in the number of linking words or the number of re-represented linking words. Thus the number of RLWs (which is only slightly less than the number of LWs) seems to show the property of *saturation*. This property was seen even more markedly in our earlier study of school level texts for the entire topic of cell biology [29].

(ii) The proximity index is calculated as the number of common linking words between the LWs and RLWs divided by the number of LWs for a topic. The *proximity* (or overlap) of the LWs in the college texts with the RLWs of the Reference Set increases with UG level 1 to 3. The increase is not dramatic since the UG-1 level text already has excellent proximity (83 %). This trend is more apparent when the same analysis is carried out for school texts where the proximity is found to be only about 50 %. The implication of this finding is clear: proximity of linking words used in a text with those of the Reference Set correlates with expertise.

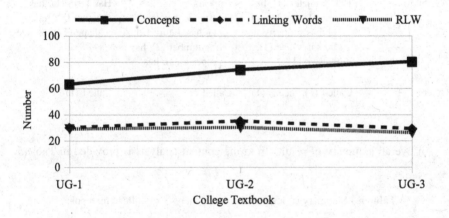

Fig. 3. Graph depicting the results, showing the proximty of linking words to Reference Set of linking words.

6   Concluding Remarks

In this work, we follow the semantic web principles and ontology based research to obtain a Reference Set of semantically well-defined linking words in the domain of biology. To enable us to choose the appropriate linking word from this set in a proposition, each linking word is assigned a semantic dimension: part-whole, class-inclusion, spatial inclusion, function and attribution. Using the Reference Set, we obtain the RCMs of the topics of *'Mitochondria'* and *'Nucleus'* appearing in three well-known college texts at UG-1, UG-2 and UG-3 levels. The qualitative data thus obtained show two clear features: saturation of the number of linking words used, and increasing proximity of linking words with those in the Reference Set as we go to higher levels of subject complexity.

Generating an RCM involves an iteration of representational re-descriptions: (i) sentences to C-LW-C propositions and (ii) C-LW-C to C-RLW-C propositions. Iterative representational re-descriptions of knowledge, according to Karmiloff-smith's [16] model referred to earlier, helps make implicit knowledge explicit and underlies the novice-expert transition. The proximity of RCM with expert knowledge suggests that the process of achieving expertise entails acquiring re-represented linking words, if only unknowingly, in the attempt to express clearly and economically. Turning the argument around, an explicit use of RCM can aid novice-expert transition. It is then plausible that the method of RCM which imitates the same process consciously may aid in cultivating expert-like thinking.

Some characteristics of expert knowledge are already well-known: hierarchically and tightly organized coherent structure of concepts and their relations. Meaning in the Ausebelian sense derives from this structure and this is what motivated the concept map technique. Higher level of expertise needs the additional notion of rigour for its characterization. Now we cannot have one model of meaning and another for rigour. Rigor may be best viewed as repetitive disambiguation of meaning and that is precisely the objective of RCM. In other words, the SCM gives meaning to knowledge and RCM adds rigour to it [30].

The implications of the work for science education are then clear. Concept maps have been widely used as an instructional strategy to facilitate novice-expert transition. The use of RCM for the purpose involves just one modification of the strategy. We provide the set of RLWs to students when generating concept maps. When the set is provided, the learners can carefully choose which linking word to use for depicting the dimension of the relation in question. The learner's focus is to choose the linking word that leads to a meaningful and unambiguous proposition, thus enhancing rigour of the representation.

Yin et al. [12] referred earlier have shown that providing linking words in concept mapping was effective in scoring concept maps with high inter-rater reliability. Providing RLWs during mapping can be similarly useful for reliable scoring on a large scale. Lastly, as we found in an earlier study [31], generating RCM is a perfectly feasible exercise even at the school level since the vocabulary for linking words, though controlled, consists of simple non-technical words of everyday natural language.

To conclude, the RCM method, motivated as it is by a convergence of several theoretical perspectives, is equally a practical modification of the existing SCM method for learning and assessment. Its effectiveness for achieving learning goals is, however, yet to be ascertained empirically on a large scale.

Acknowledgements. It is a pleasure to acknowledge invaluable inputs provided by Prof. Arvind Kumar in regard to the presentation of this work.

References

1. Novak, J.D., Gowin, D.B.: Learning How to Learn. Cambridge University Press, New York (1984)
2. Ausubel, D.P., Hanesian, H., Gowin, D.B.: Educational Psychology: A Cognitive View, 2nd edn. Holt McDougal, New York (1978)
3. Mintzes, J., Wandersee, J., Novak, J.D.: Teaching Science for Understanding: A Human Constructivist View. Academic Press, San Diego (1998)
4. Martin, B., Mintzes, J., Clavijo, I.: Restructuring knowledge in biology: cognitive processes and metacognitive reflections. Int. J. Sci. Educ. 22(3), 303–323 (2000)
5. Pereira, A., Rocha, R., de Aguiar, J., Correia, P.: Using worked example to teach the role of focus question: building conceptual understanding about concept mapping. In: Correia, P., Malachias, M., Cañas, A.J., Novak, J.D. (eds.) Concept Mapping to Learn and Innovate. Proceedings of the Sixth International Conference on Concept Mapping, Brazil (2014)
6. Miller, N., Cañas, A.J.: Effect of the nature of the focus question on the presence of dynamic propositions in a concept map. In: Cañas, A.J., Reiska, P., Ahlberg, M., Novak, J.D. (eds.) Concept Mapping: Connecting Educators. Proceedings of the Third International Conference on Concept Mapping, Tallinn, Estonia and Helsinki, Finland (2008)
7. Derbentseva, N., Kwantes, P.: Cmap readability: propositional parsimony, map layout and semantic clarity and flow. In: Correia, P., Malachias, M., Cañas, A.J., Novak, J.D. (eds.) Concept Mapping to Learn and Innovate. Proceedings of the Sixth International Conference on Concept Mapping, Brazil (2014)
8. Quillian, M.: Semantic Memory. In: Minsky, M. (ed.) Semantic Information Processing, pp. 227–270. MIT Press, Cambridge (1968)
9. Holley, C., Dansereau, D.: Networking: the technique and the empirical evidence. In: Holley, C.D., Dansereau, D.F. (eds.) Spatial Learning Strategies: Techniques, Applications, and Related Issues, pp. 81–108. Academic Press Inc., Orlando (1984)
10. Fisher, K.: Semantic networking: the new kid on the block. J. Res. Sci. Teach. 27(10), 1001–1018 (1990)
11. Faletti, J., Fisher, K.: The information in relations in biology, or the unexamined relation is not worth having. In: Fisher, K., Kibby, M. (eds.) Knowledge Acquisition, Organization, and Use in Biology, pp. 182–205. Springer, Berlin (1996)
12. Yin, Y., Vanides, J., Ruiz-Primo, M., Ayala, C., Shavelson, R.: Comparison of two concept-mapping techniques: implications for scoring, interpretation, and use. J. Res. Sci. Teach. 42(2), 166–184 (2005)
13. Schwendimann, B., Linn, M.: Comparing two forms of concept map critique activities to facilitate knowledge integration processes in evolution education. J. Res. Sci. Teach. 53(1), 70–94 (2015)
14. Halliday, M.A.K.: The Language of Science. Continuum, London (2006)
15. Kinchin, I.M.: Concept mapping in biology. J. Biol. Educ. 34(2), 61–68 (2000)
16. Karmiloff-Smith, A.: Beyond Modularity: A Developmental Perspective on Cognitive Science. MIT Press, Cambridge (1995)
17. Mack, R., Robinson, J.: When novices elicit knowledge: question asking in designing, evaluating, and learning to use software. In: Hoffman, R. (ed.) The Psychology of Expertise: Cognitive Research and Empirical AI. Lawrence Erlbaum Associates, New Jersey (1991)
18. Cañas, A.J., Novak, J.D., Reiska, P.: How good is my concept map? Am I a good Cmapper? Knowl. Manag. E-Learn. 7(1), 6–19 (2015)
19. Jonassen, D.: Semantic Networking Tools: Mapping the Mind. Prentice Hall, New Jersey (1991)

20. Wittgenstein, L.: Tractatus Logico-Philosophicus (Trans. Ogden, C.K.). Kegan Paul, London (1922). http://www.gutenberg.org/ebooks/5740

21. Eskridge, T., Hayes, P., Hoffman, R., Warren, M.: Formalizing the informal: a confluence of concept mapping and the semantic web. In: Cañas, A.J., Novak, J.D. (eds.) Concept Maps: Theory, Methodology, Technology. Proceedings of the Second International Conference on Concept Mapping, vol. 1. Unversidad de Costa Rica, Costa Rica (2006)

22. Whetzel, P., Noy, N., Shah, N., Alexander, P., Nyulas, C., Tudorache, T., Musen, M.: BioPortal: enhanced functionality via new web services from the national center for biomedical ontology to access and use ontologies in software applications. Nucleic Acids Res. **39**, W541–W545 (2011)

23. Smith, B., Ceusters, W., Klagges, B., Kohler, J., Kumar, A., Lomax, J., Mungall, C., Neuhaus, F., Rector, A., Rosse, C.: Relations in biomedical ontologies. Genome Biol. **6** (R46) (2005). http://genomebiology.com/2005/6/5/R46

24. Taylor, D.J., Green, N.P.O., Stout, G.W.: Biological Science, 3rd edn. Cambridge University Press, Cambridge (2003)

25. Campbell, N.A., Reece, J.B.: Biology, 7th edn. Pearson Benjamin Cummings, San Francisco (2005)

26. De Robertis, E.D.P., De Robertis Jr., E.M.F.: Cell and Molecular Biology. B. I. Waverly, New Delhi (1995)

27. Smith, B., Fellbaum, C.: Medical WordNet: a new methodology for the construction and validation of information resources for consumer health. In: Proceedings of the 20th International Conference on Computational Linguistics, p. 371. Association for Computational Linguistics (2004). http://www.aclweb.org/anthology/C04-1054

28. Winston, M.E., Chaffin, R., Herrmann, D.: A taxonomy of part-whole relations. Cogn. Sci. **11**(4), 417–444 (1987)

29. Kharatmal, M., Nagarjuna, G.: An analysis of growth of knowledge based on concepts and predicates—a preliminary study. In: Chunawala, S., Kharatmal, M. (eds.) Proceedings of epiSTEME 4 – International Conference to Review Research on Science, Technology and Mathematics Education, pp. 144–149. Macmillan, India (2011)

30. Kharatmal, M., Nagarjuna, G.: Exploring the roots of rigor: a proposal of a methodology for analyzing the conceptual change from a novice to an expert. In: Cañas, A.J., Reiska, P., Ahlberg, M., Novak, J.D. (eds.) Concept Mapping: Connecting Educators. Proceedings of the Third International Conference on Concept Mapping, Tallinn, Estonia and Helsinki, Finland (2008)

31. Kharatmal, M., Nagarjuna, G.: Refined concept maps for science education—a feasibility study. In: Subramaniam, K., Majumdar, A. (eds.) Proceedings of epiSTEME 3 – Third International Conference on Review of Science, Technology and Mathematics Education, Mumbai, India (2009)

Author Index

Printed in the United States
By Bookmasters

Printed in the United States
By Bookmasters